D1496127

The National Basketball League

A History, 1935–1949

MURRY R. NELSON

McFarland & Company, Inc., Publishers
Jefferson, North Carolina, and London

GV
885.515
.N37
N45
2009

Library of Congress Cataloguing-in-Publication Data

Nelson, Murry R. *cat*
    The National Basketball League : a history, 1935–1949 / Murry R.
Nelson.
        p.   cm.
    Includes bibliographical references and index.

    ISBN 978-0-7864-4006-1
    softcover : 50# alkaline paper ∞

    1. National Basketball League — History.   2. National
Basketball Association — History.   I. Title.
    GV885.515.N37N45   2009
    796.323'640973 — dc22   2009007138

British Library cataloguing data are available

Cover Image ©2009 Shutterstock

Manufactured in the United States of America

*McFarland & Company, Inc., Publishers
    Box 611, Jefferson, North Carolina 28640
    www.mcfarlandpub.com*

To Richard "Dick" Triptow and
the other players of the National Basketball League

Acknowledgments

Any book involving the research and archival searching that this volume required is a reflection of the cooperation of many people. More than anyone else, however, I need to recognize the contributions of Dick Triptow for so many things. Dick encouraged me from the beginning of the project, set up and participated in many of the interviews, shared his own personal resources with me and offered the insights that only a former NBL player with historical wisdom and insight could provide. His patience, support, friendship and enthusiasm were instrumental to any success that this book might have. All of the former NBL players who I interviewed were gracious and helpful and it is they who provide the human aspects of this book. These former NBL players include the late George Mikan, Dolph Schayes, Al Cervi, Stan "Whitey" Van Nieda, Arnie Risen, Carlton "Blackie" Towery, Fuzzy Levane, the late Stan Szukala and Erv Prasse. John Wooden graciously answered questions in handwritten letters, as did Ray Meyer. Former NBL and Fort Wayne executive and coach Carl Bennett was interviewed and followed up with written materials more than once. Former Sheboygan coach Frank Zummach provided supportive comments in an interview. John Isaacs, former New York Renaissance star, provided many insights on playing NBL teams through interviews and letters. The late Les Harrison, owner-coach of the Rochester Royals, gave a lengthy phone interview.

The archives and archivists of the James Naismith Basketball Hall of Fame offered me great freedom in examining files, copying papers and film. I also visited archives at the University of Akron, where the Firestone and Goodyear materials are housed, and was helped greatly by former archivist John Miller and current archivist Victor Fleischer of the University of Akron. The archives of Sheboygan County, Wisconsin (located in Sheboygan Falls), Oshkosh Public Library and the Public Museum of Oshkosh (Scott Cross, archivist) were also of great help, particularly the Gene Englund Collection.

Robert Luksta of Cicero, Illinois, shared his materials and insights on the Kolar brothers as well as Chicago basketball in the 1930s. Roger Meyer willingly shared his research on Bobby McDermott and I thank him for assistance and insights. Phil Deitrich of Akron and the *Akron Beacon Journal* also was helpful in a phone interview. Jack Rimer provided excellent photo reproductions of old photographs and Seymour Smith aided me by sharing his research. Jose Padilla provided lots of materials, asked me tough questions and suggested changes to the manuscript.

The Interlibrary Loan staff members at Pattee Library of Pennsylvania State University were fantastic in helping me track down and obtain newspaper microfilms and the microfilm librarians were always wonderful in assisting me. My staff assistant, Diane Paules, aided me in setting up phone interviews and transcribing those interviews, with transcription assistance from Christina Varner. Kara Kauffman and Jennifer Glasgow aided in compiling the final manuscript.

My colleague, Jacqueline Edmondson, associate dean of education at Pennsylvania State, was gracious enough to read and comment on the manuscript as did Jose Padilla and Dick Triptow. Colleagues at the North American Society for Sport History (NASSH) were supportive and critical of papers that I presented at annual NASSH meetings on the topic of the NBL. Finally, the support of my wife, Elizabeth, through these years, has always been steadfast and loving.

Table of Contents

Preface

This book tells the story of the National Basketball League, a league that is obscure or unknown to most basketball fans, despite the fact that it was the top professional league in the country from 1937 to 1949. The book traces the creation of the league from its forerunner, the Midwest Conference, that operated from 1935 to 1937, through the life of the association. During that time franchises came and went, but there was a stable core, which dropped to three during World War II when most of the top players were absent at some point.

After the war, the league blossomed with more teams and the best players in the country. Also, after the war, a rival loop was organized, the Basketball Association of America. The glory years of the NBL were tarnished by the fighting for primacy among the two leagues. The NBL had the top players, but its strength was in the Midwest, often in smaller cities with similar sized arenas. The BAA was a league of large venues with an inferior product. Nevertheless, both suffered financially and the leagues finally merged in 1949 to form the National Basketball Association.

Illustrating the NBL's superiority, no former BAA team won a title for eight years as three NBL teams took the championship over that time. All-league teams were also dominated by the former NBL squads. In the first two years of the NBA, 16 of the 20 players named all-league were former NBL players. Surprisingly, the NBA has chosen to largely ignore the NBL, tracing its roots only through the BAA and dating the beginning of the NBA to 1946 when the BAA started, rather than 1937 when the NBL was formed.

Thus, this is a story that should be told and misinformation corrected and it was this misinformation that was the initial impetus for the book. In 1996 and 1997, the NBA was touting its 50th anniversary and this perplexed and disturbed me enough to write a letter of protest to a national sports magazine. A former NBL player, Dick Triptow, saw my letter and contacted me

1

and his encouragement and inspiration pushed me to research and write this book. During the research, Dick also arranged telephone interviews of former NBL players, a vital addition to this story.

In addition to interviews and voluminous reading of microfilm newspapers from most NBL cities, I also visited the archival collections of the James Naismith Basketball Hall of Fame, the University of Dayton archives, the archives of the Sheboygan County Historical Society and the archives of the Kenosha Museum. I also read and researched all of the books on the NBL, though there are none devoted solely to the NBL story. Robert Peterson's *Cages to Jumps Shots*, with a chapter on the NBL, and Todd Gould's *Pioneers of the Hardwood* and *The Encyclopedia of Pro Basketball* were three of the best sources. There were also smaller volumes on specific teams. These are all listed in the bibliography.

The best, most detailed sources were the newspapers of the NBL cities, particularly the *Oshkosh Daily Northwestern*, *The Fort Wayne Sentinel*, the *Akron Beacon Journal* and the *Rochester Democrat and Chronicle*, but also the *Sheboygan Press*, *Minneapolis Star* and the *Denver Post*, among others. I also had access to Dick Triptow's vast collection of personal memorabilia that included programs, yearbooks, photographs and newspaper clippings.

I hope that this book will fulfill a debt that all lovers of professional basketball have to these great NBL players whose exploits have been ignored or forgotten for much too long.

Introduction

Professional basketball came about not long after the invention of the game itself in 1891. Proponents of the game were generally lower or working class and the game was quite rough with a minimal number of rules governing behavior. This made the game both dynamic and unpredictable in the way basketball evolved. The professionalism of the game was largely limited to a small number of men who became adroit at the sport and used that ability to augment their working class incomes. As the game became more accepted and tried at colleges in the early 1900s, there was a definite split between those who played the game for money and those who played it for sporting recreation.

In the 1910s a number of professional leagues began (and soon ended), but some did last five or even 10 years. These leagues were built around geography and civic pride and though initially populated largely by local players, they moved more toward the hiring of full-time professionals in the latter part of this period. Many of the leagues were forced to fold during World War I as the armories that were used for many of the games were unavailable and the railroads, which served to make these professional players itinerant independent contractors, were nationalized and the access to their lines somewhat restricted.

After World War I ended, leagues and players proliferated. Jobs were available and the economy grew rapidly. A leisure class became more pronounced and even those of the working and lower classes began to have small amounts of money which could be spent on leisure activities. Professional basketball was just one of those activities and, in contrast to the other sports, was largely viewed by these working class members. Teams often became the source of local community pride and were sponsored, to a degree, by local businesses or communities themselves. The support was minimal. Teams were often composed of local tradesmen with team names reflecting that trade. These might include the Glassblowers, the Shoe Pegs, the Miners, Potters or Electrics, for example. Some of those players might have worked within that local trade, but it was not required. What was originally common was that the players were local boys who could represent their community, and trade, well. The seeping of regular professional players into these teams altered this equation in the 1920s.

Some teams also represented various ethnic groups within a community, mostly in bigger cities where there would be teams of Irish, Jews, African Americans or Poles, to name just a few instances. These teams might have played for a mythical city or town championship.[1]

The prosperous 1920s gave way to the economic uncertainties of the Great Depression and this affected all sectors of the economy adversely. Professional basketball, which was not on steady ground before, now became impossible to sustain in any organized manner. The American Basketball League, which had begun in 1925 and had been relatively stable for its first few years, succumbed in 1931, although it did return as a limited regional league in 1933. Other leagues came and went in the early 1930s, but most followed a similar pattern. They limited their geographic area in order to save on travel and lodging bills. Most, if not all, of the players held other full-time jobs and used their basketball play as a supplement to their incomes. The team owners sought community links by signing players who either had played locally at some level or who were now living in the area. Many of the owners hoped that their teams would provide free publicity for their businesses.

A number of successful teams were considered amateurs, although there was some stretching of the term. Such teams were begun and supported by a particular company. Often the company had built recreational facilities for their employees and had large athletic programs and leagues within the company. Two of the best examples of this were the Goodyear Tire and Rubber Company and the Firestone Tire and Rubber Company, both headquartered in Akron, Ohio. Both programs began in the 1910s and shortly after their beginnings, the companies established elite teams which played visiting barnstorming teams and their rival tire company in Akron. Generally these company teams did not travel because their employees were expected to be at work in various areas of the company each day. An exception was the annual AAU basketball tournament, held in Kansas City and, later, Denver each year.[2]

The consistently best professional basketball in the 1930s was played by barnstorming teams, most of which traveled almost endlessly, playing as many as eight times a week, with different venues each night. The best of these were the New York Renaissance, the New York Celtics, the South Philadelphia Hebrew Association (SPHAs) and the Harlem Globetrotters. The Renaissance team ostensibly played at the Renaissance Casino, but there were seasons in which they never played there and were strictly a road squad. The Celtics, a resurrected version of the original New York Celtics, occasionally played in the regional ABL as did the SPHAs for many years, but the league played only about 20 games a season and the teams would go on tours, often adding 40 to 50 games to their record. The Globetrotters were actually headquartered in Chicago but played there infrequently. The players on these teams were usually of the working and lower class, just as the professional basketball players of the 1920s had been. Most were high school graduates, at best, but there were notable exceptions.

In 1935 Frank Kautsky, the owner of a grocery store in Indianapolis, and Paul Sheeks, the athletic and recreation director of Firestone Tire and Rubber, decided to try to resurrect a Midwestern Professional Basketball league, reminiscent of one that they'd been part of in 1932-33. That league had lasted one year and, of the nine teams, only five remained in the league from start to finish. The two didn't have a real plan for their new league, eventually called the Midwest Conference, except that they wanted to have a basketball league with good competition. Over the two years of its life, the Midwest Conference had as many as 12 teams in any year, and as few as nine, and 16 teams comprised the total number of squads that played in the league during those years. Almost all of the teams would have been considered amateur or semi-professional with nearly every player holding down some sort of job, usually in the company sponsoring the team or in that local community. It was this community link that became the bedrock foundation when the league grew into becoming the National Basketball League in 1935. Initially the league existed to not lose money, but, over time, some of the owners sought to make and, indeed, made, small profits from their teams.

There were some significant differences from the teams and leagues of the 1920s. First, as noted, was the strong community identification. This was reinforced by the players having local ties, and actually living in the communities in which they played. They were neighbors, fellow employees, and friends and their ties to the community made the teams sources of local pride. Another difference was the educational background of the players. Whereas in the 1920s, most players had not even attended college, let alone graduated, the NBL's players were largely college graduates. The Depression and the team members' desire to continue to play basketball were the major factors in playing pro basketball. The composition of the players also altered the appeal of the fan base. No longer just a roughhouse sport played by working and lower class players, the NBL players attracted a decidedly middle class clientele as well as the working class members of the communities.

This was a new kind of business plan, one that evolved for the league, rather than one that had been laid out in advance. It was a plan that worked surprisingly well and brought relative stability and success to this professional enterprise in the years before World War II. The war, however, altered the league, its plans and its players. First, many of the players were either drafted or enlisted and by 1942 the NBL was down to four teams. No business model was of use here as the league struggled to just exist. Fred Zollner, the owner of the Fort Wayne Zollner Pistons team, essentially bankrolled the other three teams as needed in the 1942-43 and 1943-44 seasons. Two of the teams that continued to exist during this time were teams that had either community ownership (the Oshkosh All Stars) or broad-based community involvement (the Sheboygan Redskins).

After surviving the worst of the shortages of World War II, the NBL grew to six teams in 1944-45 and was at nine teams in 1945-46. The success of any NBL team was directly tied to its strong community ties and the appeal to local pride. Many of these medium sized American cities' leaders and citizens saw that having a top professional team in the top professional league made their town big league. The populace did not necessarily aspire to being bigger because they liked the home town nature of their cities and the league. They did, however, want to be recognized as being big in stature. Community leaders saw that this would also increase recognition and bring more industry to these cities. In that sense the league and the community operated in a mutualistic relationship, with success for one leading to success for the other.

By the 1946-47 season, the league had grown to 13 teams and the most successful squads, economically, were those that had strong ties to the community. Rochester's Royals, owned by Les Harrison, were embraced by their city and, despite Harrison and his brother being the sole owners, became the darling of their home town. Syracuse's Nationals were another example of this. The Tri-Cities Blackhawks, after moving to the cities of Rock Island, Illinois, Moline, Illinois, and Davenport, Iowa, were immediately embraced by their communities and fans, who filled the Wharton Field House in Moline. The Anderson (Indiana) Duffey Packers were owned by Ike Duffey, a prominent meatpacking owner in Anderson, and the team played at the Anderson High School and drew capacity crowds.

That same year, another professional league began, and this ultimately spelled doom for the NBL. The Basketball Association of America (BAA) was begun by National Hockey League owners who also owned or had exclusivity rights to the large arenas in major metropolitan areas of the Northeast. They sought to utilize their arenas on nights when their NHL team was on the road. Most had little or no interest in basketball except as a means to provide more income. After a very uneventful year in which all of the owners lost money, they needed to decide to either drop basketball altogether or to invest in it more heavily with the expectation of making a profit in the long run. These BAA owners developed a business plan that would accentuate entertainment and profit with little or no concern for their status as cities. There was no effort made to involve the communities where their teams were based, except for seeking ways in which the BAA owners could put more fans in the arenas for games.

The BAA product was inferior, and the owners knew it, so they decided to improve the product by offering selected NBL teams the opportunity to really be big league and get to play in New York, Philadelphia and Boston. For some of the new NBL owners and teams, such as those from the new Minneapolis franchise, the appeal was right in line with their community's objectives. Generally the largest NBL cities and owners made little effort to embrace the community and their goals were to become big league by being with the bigger cities.

Thus, in 1948, four NBL teams were admitted to the BAA, none of them realizing the precarious financial position that the BAA was in. Despite an inferior product, the BAA had the prestige of being in real big league cities and seemed to have deeper pockets. It was an illusion, however. Nevertheless, the BAA used this illusion to broker a merger between the leagues, both of which were losing money because of battling over players and having salaries go up as a result. This was great for the players but was to doom the sustainability of both leagues.

In 1949 the NBL merged with the upstart Basketball Association of America, which had begun play in 1946, to form the National Basketball Association. Although a number of histories of the NBA have been written and almost all contain the BAA's three years of existence, no comprehensive history of the NBL has ever been done. In fact, the NBA has seemed to do its best to not recognize the NBL and its contributions to the NBA and professional basketball. With that concern paramount, there was a clear need to provide a history of this league, a history that would examine the creation of the league and the major parties who had developed the league over its 14 years of life.

It became apparent early on that the re-creation of an NBL history would not be able to rely upon previous studies to any great degree. The two books that gave the most attention to the NBL were Robert Peterson's *Cages to Jump Shots* (Oxford University Press, 1991; University of Nebraska Press, 2002) and Todd Gould's *Pioneers of the Hardwood* (Indiana University Press, 1998). The latter focused only on Indiana professional basketball, which for the NBL meant examination of the teams in Fort Wayne, Indianapolis, Hammond-Whiting and Anderson. Peterson discussed the entire NBL but only as a chapter and part of another in his larger study of professional basketball from its inception until the early years of the NBA. Neither book provided footnotes and most of the data seemed to be from newspapers of the time and some interviews of former players. Neil Isaacs had used the oral history technique to provide player views of professional basketball from the inception of the

NBA in 1949, but since a few of the players had also played in the NBL, there was some attention to that league.

The best readily available source of raw statistical data on the league as well as limited commentary on each league year from 1937 to 1949 was the *Sports Encyclopedia: Professional Basketball* by Neft, Johnson, Cohen and Deutsch (1978) and revised in 1989 by Neft and Cohen. *Total Basketball* (2003, 2005) by Leonard Koppett with contributions from Ken Shouler and Bob Ryan, added great individual data on NBL players. There were a few autobiographies of NBL players and team histories available, but only one, Dick Triptow's *The Dynasty that Never Was*, held useful artifacts and information, rather than simply being an undocumented narrative. Though the book was not footnoted, Triptow included copies of contracts, programs, team guides and other artifacts that were contained in his own personal archives, collected over 50 years as a player, coach and fan.

Finding appropriate archives was not easy since the teams, for the most part, had vanished with little fanfare. The James Naismith Memorial Basketball Hall of Fame held a number of interesting items on the NBL but the gaps therein were also disappointing. Besides a number of programs and other team publications, mostly from the late 1940s, the hall also has the Lester Harrison Collection. Harrison had been the owner, general manager and coach at various times of the Rochester Royals from their inception and entrance into the NBL in 1945. All of his personal and league materials are in the Hall and provide some insights into the league's operation, but not to the degree hoped for.

As noted earlier, the keystones of the league were in Wisconsin, Akron and Fort Wayne, and travel there seemed necessary. Accompanied by Dick Triptow, a visit was made to both Sheboygan and Oshkosh, where the archives revealed great information on the Sheboygan Redskins, the Oshkosh All Stars and the NBL. Another trip to the University of Akron's archival collection allowed examination of the Goodyear and Firestone materials, most notably the weekly company newsletters which featured team information regularly. A most reliable and unusual source for Fort Wayne was Carl Bennett, the former general manager of the Fort Wayne Pistons, who was an employee of the Zollner Piston Company and confidant of Fred Zollner for more than 25 years. Mr. Bennett is the only NBL or BAA executive still living and his insights are invaluable. In addition, the Pistons' publicity director, Rodger Nelson, had written a book on the Zollner Pistons' softball and basketball teams that used company archival data, as well as his personal experiences, and this was also helpful.

From early on it became apparent that the professional teams held a unique spot in the history of the small cities which they represented. In fact, a history of the NBL is as much an examination of the small cities where the

NBL was successful as it is a history of the basketball played. The teams were integral parts of the community's identities and the owners were, more often than not, local business and civic leaders. The most successful teams were not necessarily in the biggest cities, but were often in the smaller cities where the teams could help to form an image of the city for the outside world. Since there were few aspects of life in Oshkosh, Anderson, Fort Wayne and Rochester, for example, that made them different from many other cities of similar size in the United States, the location of a National Basketball League franchise made the leaders and residents of these cities feel a greater sense of pride in themselves and their respective cities. This elevated status, due to the NBL, was not evident in larger NBL cities that came and went such as Chicago, Cleveland, Pittsburgh and Detroit. These cities had so many sources of community pride, among them major league baseball and football teams, that the addition of an NBL franchise was not such an important factor in each city's life.

In Fort Wayne, Fred Zollner, probably the wealthiest man in the city, saw the Pistons as a source of pride to him and his fellow citizens of that city. In the darkest economic days of World War II, Zollner single-handedly propped up the NBL financially. This resulted in financial losses for him, but continued respect and esteem in Fort Wayne and the rest of the professional basketball world. Similarly, Ike Duffey supported the weaker franchises of the NBL in its latter years because of his interest in basketball and, more importantly, for the greater good of Anderson, Indiana. Les Harrison was a civic leader of Rochester, New York, and he saw his franchise as a gift to Rochester, as did civic leaders of the community who crowded into the arena in Rochester, dressed in their finest clothes, to cheer their Royals. Similar stories are found in Moline, Denver and Oshkosh. In Sheboygan and Whiting and Hammond, Indiana, local leaders formed syndicates to own and operate their franchise. In Akron, the two giant rubber companies, Firestone and Goodyear, had started sports programs to provide for their workers' well being (and to keep them healthy so they would not lose work days). The company saw the NBL as a great way to advertise and remained in the league as long as they perceived that to be the case.

Because of this import to the local community, the local media in the smaller cities gave in-depth coverage to their NBL teams and usually assigned a regular sports writer to the team as his regular beat. Thus, coverage of the league was best in cities like Oshkosh, Rochester, Fort Wayne and Akron and the bylined articles take on primary source documentation rather than being secondary sources, since the stories are usually by first hand observers. The newspaper coverage also extended beyond the games to the operation of the franchise and its place in the community. In addition to newspaper coverage, many of the small cities found that coverage using the nascent medium of radio was cheap and had potential benefits by increasing demand for radios in order for people to follow their teams on the road.

As for the actual players, they, too, felt that they were a vital part of the community and usually ensconced themselves totally in that environment. Many stayed on in the communities after their playing careers ended, often opening small businesses or working as representatives of local businesses, interacting with communities that knew, trusted and respected them.

For 13 years the NBL was a fixture in the Midwest and the acknowledged top league in professional basketball. It had the best players in the world and, for a section of the country that revered basketball, the result was packed gymnasiums and basketball excitement. Problems began to arise after World War II when there was competition from a new league, and many of the NBL franchises were hampered by playing in small arenas, over which they had little control.

These problems worsened, leading to financial difficulties that could not be overcome, at least in the short run, without a radical solution and that was the merger with the Basketball Association of America in 1949. Although the NBL died, it initially seemed that the small franchise cities could continue; but within two years, all that had changed, and the big league status of these smaller cities ended. Thus, the end of the NBL really signaled the end of the elevated status of these smaller cities so the history of the league is a nostalgic view of some smaller American cities whose best days, economically and sociologically, are likely behind them. This, then, is a story of a league, its local environments and its members that include players, owners, media and local citizens.

Midwest Conference: 1935–1937

Basketball was invented in 1892 as a wintertime activity at the YMCA Training School in Springfield, Massachusetts (now Springfield College). The game spread quickly through YMCAs and settlement houses in the United States and Canada. Thus, the initial popularity of basketball was largely among the working classes, although there were some colleges that adopted the sport in the late 1890s. At about the same time the first professional basketball league was formed in 1898 in Philadelphia and there were several professional leagues that came and went over the next 35 years. Almost all of the initial players had not been college players and most professional teams evolved from town or local church or business related teams.[1]

College basketball in the United States began to grow in the early 1900s and by 1920 almost every major college or university had a team which competed against other colleges as well as local athletic clubs, YMCAs, even some high schools and, in the 1920s and 1930s, professional teams. College basketball grew in a different direction from professional basketball in terms of fan appeal. College basketball was much more the sport of middle and middle-upper class fans, those who had attended college or felt more affinity for these young men who played for the pure pleasure of sport and competition. In contrast the professional game appealed to lower and lower-middle class fans who were much more interested in the status that local teams brought to their towns or clubs. The professional game was much rougher and this too appealed more to the working class who saw the struggle in more socioeconomic terms.[2]

In the 1930s players who populated the professional leagues were more commonly former college players. Many of the players were among the first generation to really grow up with basketball, particularly in the industrial areas of the cities where play space was limited. The players often had used basketball to move from a working class to a middle class status. Many players were first generation Americans born of immigrant parents who had little understanding of the game or of sport, generally, particularly as a source of income. "Workers," according to French theorist Pierre Bourdieu, "who use their bodies all day in their manually-based economic practices, would have little use or understanding of such pretensions as jogging, health-fitness centers or much of sport, which are largely the preserve of the middle classes." And when sport is chosen, working class members usually choose muscular sports while middle classes choose more restrained individual sports.[3] American professional basketball afforded another cultural and economic path for the nation's proletariat. For many professional players, this path led to fame, economic successes and respect, all forms of "cultural capital" as described by Bourdieu.[4] Families were tolerant, if not encouraging of these sporting endeavors because they saw economic benefits, as Steven Reiss notes, "the addition of a well paid breadwinner to the family."[5]

Theorist John Hargreaves and, by extension, cultural critic Antonio Gramsci argue that the topic of sport makes little sense without a historical framework and this leads to the view of sport as a way to cement class solidarities. Hargreaves uses football and rugby players and audiences as example to suggest that attempts to codify popular sports can help to turn them into moral demonstrations where official actions differ depending on the audience.[6] In the case of professional basketball, the audience mirrored the players' backgrounds so the level of roughness of the game was appropriate to the daily life experiences endured by the working class. This contrasted with American high school and college basketball, where the games were far less physical. Historian Allen Guttmann noted that English football was frowned upon as a pastime for more genteel folk and that the upper classes often watched but seldom admired the spectacle.[7] In one sense, professional basketball, as contrasted with college basketball, illustrates historian Eric Hobsbawm's view of "labouring people to fashion their own lives" or in this case their own games, even if they were very serious about them.[8]

With little government help for workers in the Great Depression, working and middle class Americans did make efforts to shape ways to relieve the exigencies of that time. Sport was one of their remedies to hardship. The Depression had a debilitating effect on every aspect of American life and professional sports were no exception. In 1929 the National Football League had 12 teams; by 1932 the number was down to eight. For the remainder of the 1930s there were nine or ten teams each year. Football was generally played only on the weekends so players could have regular jobs with little interference in their football playing. Professional baseball did not lose large numbers of teams but salaries remained low for almost all players, who had to have off-season employment to meet economic demands. Baseball was, from its inception, distinctly middle class in spectator appeal.[9] Any profit in professional basketball at this time was problematic. The support from companies like Goodyear, General Electric and Firestone was motivated by a desire for both cheap advertising and as a morale booster for employees.

In the fall of 1935, with the Depression now in its sixth year, being a professional basketball player would have been less than an enriching economic endeavor. Still, there were players who had played in college and were not ready to give up the game that they loved. Basketball, in many cases, had been the vehicle that had allowed working class young men to attend college and move into the middle class. But professional basketball was not well paying and appealed mainly to working class sensibilities and economics. If the players could not make a living from it, they would compromise and continue to play on independent teams or play on industry-sponsored teams while they worked for the business in return. Basketball historian Robert Peterson notes that "with the onset of the Depression, it was hard for even a college graduate to find a job — any job — and professional basketball offered a good living in season and sometimes a job for the off-season."[10]

Professional basketball players were engaged in the sport because they enjoyed the physicality of the game. Basketball was embraced by the working class fans, because of both that physicality, and because the sport was a metaphor for Americanism and the possibilities that America, and Americans, had. The game was young (relatively speaking), it was rough and required teamwork. Success in the game could be achieved by anyone who worked at it, and limited abilities could be offset, to some degree, by some specialty like excelling on defense or ball handling. Scoring was not high because of limitations on equipment, rules and the flow of the game itself.

The notion that any American could rise to middle class success through hard work was one that Americans wanted to believe, even in the face of evidence to the contrary. The Depression only made that ascension harder, but it was a myth that was clung to, and professional basketballers seemed to be illustrative of that. This continued to contrast, so it seemed, with the strict European notion of class that came with birth and was nearly impossible to transcend. American opportunities made America a more exceptional, more equitable environment for human advancement. Whether it was true or not was immaterial; professional basketball seemed to reinforce it.

In the Midwest a number of teams operated at this time, some connected to a company, while others were independent or operated by an owner-businessman who was also infatuated with the game and would support the team and use it to advertise his store or product. There was a recent history of this in professional basketball; the American Basketball League (the first real geographically national league in basketball) had teams that reflected the ownership of George Preston Marshall — the Washington Palace Five — named for his Washington Palace Laundry; Max Rosenblum — the Cleveland Rosenblums after his department store of the same name; and the Toledo Redmen after their owners— Red Man Tobacco. Marshall was from an upper middle class background and was able to begin a string of laundromats in the Washington, D.C., area. He later purchased the Boston Redskins of the National Football League and moved them to Washington where they still play. Sports teams were less about advertising and more about engaging his interest in sportsmanship. Rosenblum, on the other hand, was a second generation Eastern European Jew who started as a small merchant and developed a large department store. He moved from the working class to the upper middle class and saw the team as a business investment in that it provided useful publicity for his business establishment if not huge revenues from spectators.[11]

The Midwest Conference Begins

Most teams in 1935 were independent, playing other local teams and travelling regionally within a couple of hundred miles, generally. A couple of short-lived attempts had been made (in 1929 and again in 1932) to create a league of Midwestern teams, but both failed within the year. The latter circuit was called the National Basketball League and featured teams from Ohio and Indiana, highlighted by the Akron Goodyears, the 1932 National Industrial League Champions.[12] In 1935 Paul Sheeks, the coach and manager of the Akron Firestone teams, and Frank Kautsky, coach and owner of the Indianapolis Kautskys, decided to try again. They recruited six other squads to form the Midwest Conference. Both Sheeks and Kautsky had been part of the 1932-33 effort, but rather than trying to reinvigorate that group of teams, they contacted other teams to form the league. In November the league began operations with Sheeks acting as executive officer.

Originally from Mitchell, South Dakota, and a 1913 graduate of the University of South Dakota who became coach there in 1915, Sheeks had been recruited from Wabash College in Crawfordsville, Indiana, where he had been both football and basketball coach. After coming to Akron about 1920, he also played professional football for the Akron Pros (one year he played behind the legendary Fritz Pollard) in addition to coaching basketball. Always a sport entrepreneur, he sponsored professional wrestling in the Akron Firestone's Clubhouse in the 1930s.[13]

There was no league schedule for the new basketball league; instead each team made its own scheduling arrangements with the only caveat being that each squad had to play at least 12 games against league opponents in order to qualify for the league title, which was to be decided in some type of playoff format at the end of the season.[14] Some time after the beginning of the

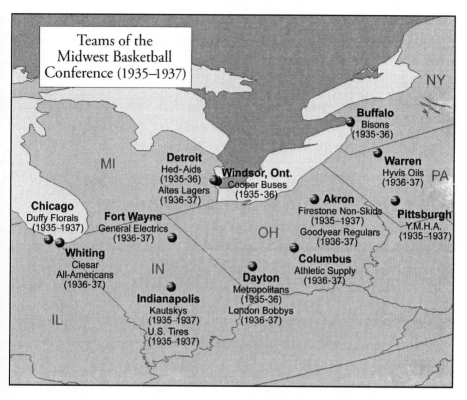

Teams of the
Midwest Basketball
Conference (1935–1937)

NY

Buffalo
Bisons
(1935-36)

MI

Detroit
Hed-Aids
(1935-36)
Altes Lagers
(1936-37)

Windsor, Ont.
Cooper Buses
(1935-36)

Warren
Hyvis Oils
(1936-37) PA

Chicago
Duffy Florals
(1935-1937)

Fort Wayne
General Electrics
(1936-37)

Akron
Firestone Non-Skids
(1935-1937)
Goodyear Regulars
(1936-37)

OH

Pittsburgh
Y.M.H.A.
(1935-1937)

Whiting
Ciesar
All-Americans
(1936-37)

IN

Columbus
Athletic Supply
(1936-37)

Dayton
Metropolitans
(1935-36)
London Bobbys
(1936-37)

IL

Indianapolis
Kautskys
(1935-1937)
U.S. Tires
(1935-1937)

Teams of the Midwest Conference, 1935–1937. The Midwest Conference was disbanded in 1937 and reorganized as the National Basketball League the next season. (Map designed by Steve Gardner)

season, a ninth team, the Chicago Duffy Florals, joined the league.[15] Despite this odd number of teams, the looseness of scheduling meant that there were no worries over an unbalanced schedule.

The teams comprising the league were the Akron Firestone Non-Skids (a great name for a tire, but not as attractive a name for basketball players), which had been Industrial League champs the prior year; the Indianapolis Kautskys, sponsored by a wholesale grocer, Frank Kautsky, and a team that had been playing regularly as a barnstorming squad since 1931; the Pittsburgh Young Men's Hebrew Association (YMHA) squad and the Buffalo (New York) Bisons. Kautsky loved basketball once he was exposed to it and started his team in order to be involved with high quality basketball.[16] The YMHA team was composed, almost entirely, of Jews from the Pittsburgh area and reflected the great interest that Jews had in basketball from the early days of the game's invention.[17] Other teams were the Dayton (Ohio) Metropolitans, the Detroit (Michigan) Hed-Aids (sponsored by a company offering a headache cure),

---

Renaissance Club Had 88 Straight Wins Last Season

The Renaissance Club, greatest colored basketball team in existence, lost only a few games last season, and after they got started won 88 games straight. Tonight the Regulars will try their best to beat this great team which ranks with the New York Celtics. Maybe the Regulars won't win, but if they don't it won't be for lack of trying. And when a team is giving everything it has, anything may happen.

The December 11, 1935, *Wingfoot Clan* newsletter hyped the upcoming contest with the New York Renaissance team with this photograph and caption. Left to right: Charles "Tarzan" Cooper, Jackie Bethards, Johnny Holt, Clarence "Fats" Jenkins, Bill Yancey, Eyre "Bruiser" Saitch, "Wee" Willie Smith. (Used by permission of the Goodyear Tire and Rubber Company and the University of Akron Archives.)

the Indianapolis (Indiana) U.S. Tires (another team sponsored by a tire company), the Windsor (Ontario) Cooper Buses (with obvious support from that company) and the aforementioned Chicago team sponsored by the floral concern.[18]

Anticipation was high in the two founding cities— Akron and Indianapolis. The coverage that those two teams received in the local media reflected strong local interest. The same cannot be said for every city. In Chicago and Pittsburgh, for example, the daily newspapers provided almost no coverage of the Midwest Conference generally, nor of the hometown teams specifically. In Akron the talk was of a stronger club, despite a change in personnel on the team.

Akron was a city of about 250,000 with three major rubber plants (Goodyear, Goodrich and Firestone) employing 70 percent (about 80,000) of the approximately 130,000 rubber workers in the United States.[19] The city's employment was thus dominated by the rubber companies and, beginning in the early part of the century, at least two of them (Goodyear and Firestone) had seen it as their obligation to provide more than simple employment to their workers. They offered a wide range of sports activities at various ability levels as well as other forms of entertainment for their employees. Having a top team in the AAU and then the Midwest League was seen as an integral part of that entertainment function.

The sports editor of the *Akron Beacon Journal*, James Schlemmer, observed, "Although the Firestone squad, which is entered in the newly organized basketball conference, has been riddled by shifting around of men in the Firestone organization, Sheeks has assembled another formidable array of talent that threatens to make Akron followers forget Non-Skid greats of yore."[20] The Firestone Company newsletter, the *Firestone Non-Skid*, hailed the creation of the new league and the Firestone team as a member. The newsletter advertised a $2 purchase price for all twelve league home games (general admission) and $3 for reserved seats for all Firestone employees. The regular prices were 30 cents and 40 cents per game.[21]

Akron seemed to be the favorite in the Eastern Division of the conference. In the Western Division, Indianapolis was favored. Indianapolis, with a population of about 375,000, was the largest city in Indiana, probably the most basketball-crazy state in the country. Many high school gymnasia seated many more than there were residents of a town, and the Indianapolis team in the Midwest Conference would be playing at Butler Fieldhouse, which seated more than 15,000. The Kautskys were a squad made up almost entirely of holdovers from the previous year's squad. These players included three former Purdue stars — Norman Cottom, who led the Big Ten in scoring in 1934; Ed Shaver; and John Wooden, who was captain of the 1931-1932 squad that won the national title in college basketball. Wooden parlayed his playing success into high school coaching success in South Bend, Indiana. He then coached at Indiana State University after World War II and his success there led to his hiring by the University of California at Los Angeles (UCLA) where he won a record 10 NCAA basketball championships.[22]

The Midwest Conference made a significant but little acknowledged change in basketball rules for the 1935 season. Up until that time a center jump followed each score by a team, making the game slower and giving the team with a dominating tipper a clear advantage. In 1935 the new league decided to accelerate play and did so by eliminating the center jump after foul shots were made. This did indeed speed up the game.[23] The next year there were predictions that the center jump after baskets would be eliminated. Jim Tobin, chairman of the International Rules Committee, noted that the rule had been removed in international rules and would be gone from American basketball within a year. His prediction was correct, as it turned out. He also noted, parenthetically, that another proposal (from Japan) that would limit players to 6'2½" in height had been rejected.[24]

Two years later, college basketball decided to do away with the center jump altogether after any score, clearly influenced by the Midwest Conference rules and results. The Midwest Conference then adopted a policy allowing the home team in the league to decide on whether a center jump would be held after baskets or not. What effect did the elimination of these center jumps ultimately have on the game, its growth and its progress? No less an authority than John Wooden calls this rule "the most significant rule change ever made."[25]

The Midwest Conference also adopted other new rules: making five rather than four fouls for disqualification from a game (though a player could re-enter the game after fouling out if his team was down to four players); the start of the dribble or traveling would not be called "too closely" unless a real advantage were gained; and fouls in the offensive end would be called only if the player was shooting or if advancing the ball was affected, unless the foul was deemed flagrant.[26]

The Start of Conference Play

After codifying these rules, the league looked for a swifter, more fan-friendly game. League play began in December and the Indianapolis Kautskys started off strongly in the league, posting a 6–2 record in mid–January and finishing the league season at the end of February with a 9–3 mark and first place in the West. The squad also played outstanding touring teams that came to Indiana, most notably the famous New York Renaissance team, an African American squad considered by many to be the finest professional team of the 1930s. In the 1932-33 season the Rens won 88 consecutive games, a record that still stands.

In a series of four games on consecutive weeknights in early January 1936, the two teams played at venues in central Indiana. The Kautskys edged the Rens 45–42 in Marion, but the Rens came back to win the next three games played in Anderson, Bedford, and Indianapolis, respectively. John Wooden, the Kautskys' leading scorer, was able to play in only the Marion and Indianapolis games since his duties teaching high school English and coaching basketball at Central High School in South Bend, seventy-five miles from Marion, precluded his playing in Anderson or Bedford. Despite being mid-week games, each of the contests drew large crowds (and concomitant large gates). In Bedford, a town of around ten thousand, four thousand attended the game. A similar number were in Butler Fieldhouse in Indianapolis for the Thursday night contest. Rabid interest in basketball by Indiana fans was not, apparently, limited to scholastic contests. The Rens played the Kautskys again a week later in Indianapolis, again winning by one point.[27]

In February the Rens made another swing through Indiana and played the Kautskys once again, defeating them 39–38. Wooden did play in this game (scoring 12 points) as did Leroy "Cowboy" Edwards, apparently loaned for the game from the U.S. Tires team.

Edwards was not a total stranger to the Kautsky squad, having played for them briefly the previous year in a series of games against the South Philadelphia Hebrew Association SPHA team.[28] But, Edwards was not enough as the Rens, led by "Tarzan" Cooper's 15 points, edged the Kautskys. An additional gate booster was the appearance for the Rens of Dave DeJernett, former Washington, Indiana, high school and Indiana Central College star.[29] DeJernett's high school team from Washington was the first integrated squad to win the Indiana high school basketball championship (in 1930).[30]

The existence of two Midwest Conference squads in Indianapolis created an instant rivalry, one that already had been fierce when both squads were independent. The two teams played in Indianapolis at either Butler Field-house or the Indianapolis Armory. In February the Kautskys defeated the U.S. Tires to take first place once again in the Midwest Conference.[31] And the next month the Kautskys won again in the closing game of the conference season 25–20.[32] Almost all of the players on both teams were either directly from or had a strong connection to Indiana, particularly central Indiana. The U.S. Tires starting five, for example, featured players from Butler University and from high schools in Indianapolis, Muncie and Washington.

This pattern was repeated throughout the league, an extension of the hometown team tradition, an effort to make for easier fan identification with players and more popularity for the game. The U.S. Tires team was "one of the tallest in the country" with five players at 6'3" or better.[33] The Akron team had players from Ohio University, a Columbus semi-pro team (the Olson Swedes) and the University of Akron. Dayton featured players largely from that area including Bill Hosket, whose son later starred in basketball at Ohio State. Buffalo had players from the University of Buffalo, Canisius College, and a former star for the Buffalo Colored Giants, Hank Williams. Williams was the first African American to play in an established professional league since the early 1900s when African Americans played in both the New York State League and the New England League.[34]

The Pittsburgh YMHA squad featured college stars from both Pitt and Duquesne. "Reiter, Moore, Feldman and Brennan played together for three years at Duquesne."[35] The Windsor squad was stocked with featured graduates of the University of Toronto and other Canadian schools in the lineup. Those schools included McMaster University, the Royal Military College, Pickering College and Ontario Agricultural College.[36] The inclusion of this Canadian team made the Midwest Conference the first international basketball league.

The Season of 1935-36

Scheduling the league games would prove to be a challenge, but the plan for the season was that most of the league games would be on the weekends, usually Sunday afternoons, so that other non-league games could be scheduled freely on other nights. As noted, this meant that great squads like the Rens were often playing league teams and usually beating them, but most of the league teams also played regional squads, many of which were quite good. There were other touring African American teams, such as the Chicago Crusaders, who played throughout the Midwest. The Indianapolis teams both played the Jasper Coca-Colas (sponsored by a local bottler) of Jasper, Indiana, a town in southern Indiana near Evansville. The Jaspers featured former Indiana college and high school players including Ray Eddy, a former Purdue star. The Akron Goodyears, an Industrial League team that had often opposed the Non-Skids, continued to play them and other Midwest Conference teams.[37]

For most of the Midwest Conference teams, the season began in late November or early December and continued with Sunday games against league opponents through the end of February, meaning that most league teams achieved the 12 game minimum against other league teams. Two teams fell short, the Dayton Metropolitans with ten games (they won four and lost six) and the Chicago Duffy Florals with five games (they won three and lost two). The Kautskys started early by defeating Windsor, Pittsburgh and Chicago, but losing to Akron before the end of 1935. During that same period, the U.S. Tires team defeated Buffalo and Dayton, while Akron defeated Dayton, Buffalo and Indianapolis, but lost to Pittsburgh. Few game highlights were reported in the newspapers but John Wooden was often high scorer when he was able to play. He ended up leading the league in scoring that first year. He also continued to teach and coach at South Bend Central High School, a position he retained until 1943. For Akron the leading scorers were usually Howard "Soup" Cable and "Beanie" Berens.[38]

The emphasis on Sunday games also was an indicator of the mostly working class appeal of the game of professional basketball. In most parts of the United States at this time, Sunday blue laws were in effect, limiting the availability of entertainment on Sundays. But most of the laws were not heavily enforced; instead it was the people themselves or their respective churches that prevented such entertainment offerings. Almost exclusively these people were middle or upper class individuals who worked five or five and one half days per week. For the working class, Saturday was just another workday and Sunday was the only day for play that they had.

Professional basketball, even for the top players, was not enough to provide a living wage, especially with a season that ran only four months. In Akron all of the players had jobs within the Firestone organization and, after the Midwest Conference season ended, the players played as captains on teams within the Firestone factory leagues.[39] For many of the players, basketball had been their ticket to college and a middle class life. The Depression interceded and basketball became the factor that helped them find jobs with Firestone or Goodyear that sponsored basketball teams. On at least one team, the Kautskys, most of the players were teachers and coaches. Bill Perigo taught and coached at Benton Harbor, Michigan, High School, thirty miles north of South Bend where Wooden taught and coached. Norm Cottom and Cy Proffit taught and coached in Terre Haute, Indiana; Ed Shaver in Frankfort, Indiana; Frank Baird in Indianapolis (at Broad Ripple High School) and Maurice Wooden (John's brother) in Versailles, Indiana.[40] The Wooden boys had come from a poor family in Martinsville, Indiana. Their father had been a farmer who lost his land and ended up having to live in town and work in various agricultural jobs in the region. Wooden's first house lacked electricity and plumbing. He used basketball to move from working class to the middle class. Frank Baird remembered that Bill Perigo coached at Markleville, Indiana, and Proffitt at Spencer, Indiana, and that George Chestnut worked for Delco Remy in Anderson, Indiana.[41] Wooden was paid fifty dollars a game plus travel money[42] which was probably a bit more than some of the players, but a few would have received about that sum. Baird said that he was paid $25 per game.

> I didn't get much more than $25 a game. Whether the other fellows were getting more, I have no idea. Probably Johnny Wooden got more because he was a great drawing card; he had been All-America at Purdue for three years.[43]

An owner's expenses would have been in the neighborhood of $500 per game for the players. With admissions at forty cents to a dollar per person, many games would have had minimal profits, but gates of three thousand or more would almost always mean a good payday for the owners. Frank Kautsky could be a bit generous in his enthusiasm. Wooden recalled that when he hit his hundredth consecutive free throw in competition, "Frank Kautsky stopped the game and came out and handed me a $100 bill. That was a lot back then.[44] Wooden "went on to make 34 more free throws in succession."[45]

As noted earlier, the Kautskys were 6–2 by mid–January, which tied them for the league lead with the Detroit Hed-Aids. At that point Wooden led the conference with 90 points (an 11.2 ppg average) and Leroy Edwards led Indianapolis with 51 points in 7 games (7.3 ppg). The Akron Firestone Non-Skids were 8–2 in league play, 11–4 overall. The last month of the season saw some fading by the Non-Skids, probably due to the schedule that saw them play six games in eight days in mid–February. Despite losing four of seven league games, the Akron squad managed to right themselves at the end of the month to claim the Eastern Division with a record of 11–7 to Pittsburgh's 10–7. Meanwhile in the west, the Kautskys won their last three league games to finish 9–3. Detroit finished second with a record of 9–7.[46]

After the Kautskys' season-ending triumph against U.S. Tires, the *Indi-anapolis Star* speculated about the playoffs. At that point it was intended that the two leaders in each of the divisions would participate in a round robin series for the league championship putting the Kautskys, Detroit, Akron and Pittsburgh in the playoffs. Chicago, it was noted, had a better winning percentage than Detroit but did not play enough games to qualify for the series. The announced beginning of the series was March 15 in the Indianapolis Armory.[47] The view from Akron on March 2 was that "a meeting will be held Tuesday (March 3) in Columbus to determine if two or four teams will take part in the playoffs."[48] Akron was still playing games after the league season ended, even as the meeting in Columbus went on regarding a playoff. The feeling was that "the playoff would get underway Sunday, March 15."[49] Two days later the playoff date seemed to have been shifted to March 8 and the combatants had changed a bit also. According to that day's newspaper, the Non-Skids would leave for Indianapolis to play the upcoming Sunday in Round 1 of the playoffs. Pittsburgh and Chicago would fill out the field. Chicago did not play the required 12 games but the conference managers declared them one of the best teams in the league and voted to substitute them in the place of the Detroit Hed-Aids.[50]

In their only meeting of the season Chicago had defeated Detroit decisively, it was noted, but this was surely not enough to completely alter league rules agreed to at the beginning of the year and maintained throughout that year. The likelihood was that this was all about money. At a time of economic instability money was almost always the determining factor in decisions in the league. Which venues were bigger and would attract larger gates and which teams were bigger draws were most likely the key determinants in any decision made. When interviewing Les Harrison, the founder and owner of the Rochester Royals, he sometimes grew irate at the author's naïveté, linking almost all decisions made in the early years of pro basketball to money, period.[51] Since there was probably some shakiness to the Detroit franchise it was felt that the Chicago squad's inclusion in the playoffs would be more likely to add to the coffers of the owners. The proposed playoff was to be a "'double knockout' system staged at Indianapolis Sunday (March 8), at Chicago March 15, at Pittsburgh March 21 and at Firestone March 22."[52]

Two days later the whole system was changed when the owners found that the venues that they sought were not all available. The likelihood was that the tournament would now be staged March 20–22.[53] Those plans were also modified and the tournament was changed to a one-day affair with all four teams meeting in Chicago.

The Kautskys will leave early tomorrow for Chicago to participate in the Midwest Conference playoff series. The locals will meet Pittsburgh YMHA in the first game and the Chicago Duffy Florals will meet Akron Firestones in the second tilt of the afternoon session. The winners will clash tomorrow night for the championship.[54]

The result was unexpected and disappointing, as least as far as the fans and media of the favorites, the Kautskys and the Non-Skids, were concerned. Akron was upset by Chicago 33–30 in the semifinal contest, but came back to finish third with a victory over Pittsburgh 33–29.[55] Chicago then defeated the Kautskys in the finals 39–35. The *Indianapolis Star* uncharacteristically included no box score, noting only that Bob Kessler, who had joined the Kautskys only after completing the 1935-36 season at Purdue as their team scoring leader, had 23 points to lead the team while Eddie Kolar of Chicago had 14.[56] Eddie Kolar and his brother, Otto, were the heart of the Duffy Florals squad. Both had attended Morton Township High School in the Chicago suburb of Morton Park, but both had left school before graduating in order to play professional basketball.[57]

The *Akron Beacon Journal* failed to mention the league championship match, instead covering the Non-Skids' opening loss to Chicago and their consolation win over Pittsburgh. The paper did claim extenuating circumstances for the opening loss.

> Weakened by a last minute injury to Beanie Berens who could not make the trip, (instead, the Non-Skids) took Ed "Stretch" Sadowski, former North (Akron) High School star along, but he was of little value, having never practiced with the team (and was only 18 years old).[58]

Thus, the Midwest Conference ended its first season. Was it a success? One would have to say yes in comparison to other leagues over the previous twenty years or so. First, the league showed great stability. All of the teams finished the season as league members, a triumph in itself. Second, there were good crowds in a number of cities and the best players from each region were playing on the teams from the respective regions. The players were not highly paid but this was their second job, their hobby, as it were. Almost all were playing for the love of the game, a phrase that has been so overused as to draw inner groans whenever one hears it. In this situation, it was true because the pay and travel conditions were so poor. Unlike a squad such as the Rens, which travelled together in their own bus, these teams travelled by car, often one of the players' cars. Frank Baird recalled playing games on weeknights, then "driving like wild to get back home" in order to be at work the next day. Sometimes, they "would get back to Indianapolis at 5 o'clock in the morning — if it was really icy, maybe 6 or 6:30 — and there were a few times I was late getting on the job Monday morning."[59]

Though basketball was revered in many of the Midwest regions, this reverence extended more often to high school or college teams. In Indiana the big stories in the basketball season were the play of these teams. The professional Kautskys and U.S. Tires squads got lesser but acceptable and regular coverage. That would change the next season.

The 1936-37 Midwest Conference Campaign

Most of the league members felt that the initial foray into an organized league had been successful and six of the nine teams decided to compete in the league the next year, although a couple of the sponsors of the teams changed. Twelve squads (three more than 1935-36) began the season as league members. The 1936-37 season started with considerable changes in the teams. First, the increased number of teams indicated that the product seemed to be a potential money-maker or had the potential for providing some advertising for some of the team sponsors. In the Eastern Division only the Non-Skids and the Pittsburgh YMHA teams returned as members. The Detroit Hed-Aids were replaced by another Detroit squad, the Altes Lagers, with most of the same players. Akron's other great industrial league team, the Goodyear Wingfoots, which had chosen to not join the league in 1935, now changed its mind and became members in 1936-37 as did another team that had played many of the Midwest Conference foes the previous year, Columbus Athletic Supply of Ohio. The last slot in the East was taken by the Warren Hyvis Oilers of Pennsylvania. In his book *Cages to Jumpshots*, Robert Peterson, a native of the area, noted that "the Warren, Pa., Hyvis Oils (were) operated by Gerry Archibald with financial support from an oil refinery."[60]

In the Western Division there were three returning teams, the defending champion Chicago Duffy Florals and the two squads from Indianapolis, the Kautskys and the U.S. Tires. The Dayton Metropolitans were replaced by the Dayton London Bobbys, again with many of the same players. The other two teams were the Fort Wayne, Indiana, General Electrics and the Whiting, Indiana, Ciesar All-Americans, a team sponsored by a car dealer named Eddie Ciesar.

The minimum number of games required in league play was reduced to eight from twelve for this season, which meant there would be more games against non-league teams. There was still a lack of confidence (justifiably, it would seem) that a league playing only against its own members would be successful. This pattern (of playing outside teams) was kept up into the 1960s by the NBA in its exhibition games.[61]

The 1936-37 season began in late November. The Kautskys started slowly with a number of new players and did not perform well. They failed to play the minimum number of games, going 2-5. The team still had John Wooden, Cy Proffitt, Frank Baird and George Chestnut, as well as Bob Kessler, whom they had added at the end of the previous season. They played well early in

In November of 1936, the *Firestone Non-Skid*, the weekly newsletter of the Firestone Company, showed the Non-Skids beginning their practice sessions. *Front row, left to right:* ____ Sketres, ____ Black, Talmadge "Wes" Bennett, Bill Reeves, and Paul Sheeks (Coach). *Back row, left to right:* Ward "Horse" Myers, ____ Seidel, Ed Garner, Ed "Stretch" Sadowski, Milos "Slim" Shoun, Howard "Soup" Cable. (Used by permission of Bridgestone Americas Holding, Inc., and the University of Akron Archives.)

the season, but faltered later. As in the prior year, most of the Kautsky players were coaching high school teams in Indiana, but unlike the previous year, they could not "get away from their jobs for anything other than Saturday night or Sunday games."[62]

This would have been less of a problem with the former industrial league teams since their employers were also their basketball sponsors. These would have included the teams from Dayton, Fort Wayne, Columbus, U.S. Rubber and both Akron squads. The Kautskys failed to maintain their edge as the year went on. Frank Kautsky failed to schedule enough league games, John Wooden was often absent at the mid-week games and there was something missing from their play. In an effort to improve their play, Kautsky added Leroy "Cowboy" Edwards to the squad in late January for a game against the South Philadelphia Hebrew Association SPHAs who, along with the Rens, were the best professional teams of the 1930s. Edwards had left U.S. Tires and had been playing for the Dayton London Bobbys.[63] Against the SPHAs, Edwards contributed 10 points to lead the Kautskys in scoring as they lost 37–27 to the touring Philadelphians.[64]

The U.S. Tires team had not just lost Edwards; they had a completely

new lineup with new additions from the Detroit Hed-Aids, two former Butler players, and one new member from the Olson Swedes, an independent
team. The implication (hope) from the media was that the team would be
better than the 5–9 squad which had competed in the league the year before.[65]
That preseason hope was soon dashed. The Tires did defeat the Akron Firestone Non-Skids in January 49–40 as well as Fort Wayne General Electrics
43–24 a month later, but the season ended with the Tires again out of the
playoffs and the team left the league after that year.[66]

Both the Tires and the Kautskys continued to book the best travelling
teams into Indianapolis and those contests drew consistently large crowds.
Besides the SPHAs team, the reconstituted travelling New York Celtics squad
with Davey Banks, Red Hickey, Paul Herlihy, Paul Birch and the young Bobby
McDermott played in Indiana. Two African American teams, the Rens and
the Chicago Crusaders, made more than one visit and drew large crowds. In
January the Kautskys and the Tires hosted the Rens and the Crusaders in a
Wednesday night doubleheader at the Butler Fieldhouse. These "black-white"
contests were very popular and made large profits. The U.S. Tires lost to the
Crusaders who now had Dave DeJernett (from Washington, Indiana, who had
played briefly the previous year for the Rens) and he led the Crusaders with
ten points as they defeated the Tires 38–31. In the second game the Rens
opened up a ten point halftime lead (27–17) and coasted to victory over the
Kautskys 47–32. Three Rens, led by "Fats" Jenkins' 13 points, scored in double figures. The Kautskys were led by Baird's 11 points and Wooden's 8 points,
but no other player scored more than 5 points. More than 6500 fans were in
attendance for the contests, more than double the average crowd at a Midwest Conference game.[67]

Three weeks later the Crusaders returned to play the Kautskys and the
Rens then played them in Terre Haute and Nappanee (near South Bend) the
next week. The Kautskys won in Nappanee 51–46 but lost the two other games.
Only the local game in Indianapolis was covered with a box score. The Kautskys romped 50–32 over the Crusaders as DeJernett was held without a field
goal, while Kessler and Wooden each scored 16 for the Kautskys. The last
Rens' visit was in March when they defeated the Tires 39–34 in a fight-marred
game. The Rens' center, "Wee" Willie Smith, "was banished by Referee Rich-
eson amid the boos of spectators, while (Bill Schrader) the Tires's center,
went to the showers near the close of the half minus two lower teeth and with
a cut lip."[68]

The strength of the league was clearly in Akron where the Non-Skids
went 13–5 but were only the second best team in the division as well as the
city. The Goodyear Wingfoots won sixteen of eighteen games to finish with
the best record in the league. The Firestone Non-Skids swept the Kautskys in
an early season doubleheader in Akron and then proceeded to play mostly

eastern teams. The Goodyear Wingfoots started off 4–0 and led the league from the start. The Non-Skids had added "Horse" Myers, a former Fort Wayne star in the old ABL, and Wes Bennett and Ed Sadowski, former high school stars in Akron at East and North High Schools, respectively. Bennett had also led the nation in scoring while playing for Westminster College in Pennsylvania.[69]

Goodyear started off the season out of the league, but after splitting two games with the University of Pittsburgh, the decision makers at Goodyear applied for entrance into the Midwest Conference. The application was accepted unanimously.[70] According to the Goodyear Company newsletter, the Wingfoots were to play a minimum of ten league games and the season would end February 16.[71] A week after joining the league, the long time Goodyear coach, Edgar "Smiley" Weltner, was promoted to assistant recreational director in the company and Clifton "Eagle Eye" Byers became the new coach. His appointment marked the first time that a former Firestone Non-Skid had become the coach of the Goodyear Wingfoots.[72] Byers had played college basketball at Kansas State, then quit to play AAU ball. He joined the Firestones, then returned to Kansas State to get his degree in science and engineering in 1933.[73] The hope was that by hiring Byers Goodyear would gain some polish and reserve strength and become a power in Midwest competition.[74]

This hope was met far beyond the greatest expectations of the team's followers. After joining the league, the Wings played a non-league game against the Cleveland Pennzoils, another African American touring team that included a number of former New York Renaissance players, according to the Akron writers, including Jim Sledge, Fletcher Reed and Ernie Seats.[75] Goodyear lost 44–40 to the Pennzoils, but began winning consistently after that, going 8–0 in the Midwest Conference Eastern Division. Meanwhile the Non-Skids started 6–0 in the division before losing to Fort Wayne on December 15. Just prior to that game the Non-Skids had played games in Pennsylvania and New York and, according to James Schlemmer, *Beacon Journal* sports editor, were tired from their trips, having just returned home on the afternoon of the Fort Wayne game.[76]

On December 29, the Non-Skids met the defending Midwest Conference champions, the Chicago Duffy Florals, in Akron. Chicago had started 1–2 in the league, losing in Columbus and to the Kautskys in Indianapolis in two overtimes. Their core players from the prior year — Willie Young, the Kolar brothers and Johnny Ivers — had been joined by Ray Adams, the leading scorer for DePaul University in 1935-36, and Harry Mead, a seven-footer who had played at Augustana College. The Non-Skids won 40–34, boosting their record to 7–1 and making them the favorites to win the conference title.[77]

Goodyear was undefeated in the league but had played fewer games and had lost non-league games to Pitt and to Wilmerding (Pennsylvania), the national YMCA champion. In early January, Goodyear also defeated Chicago in Akron before several hundred fans, including the president of Goodyear, Paul Litchfield.[78] Eddie Butler of the *Beacon Journal* noted that the Wingfoots played possession basketball, led by center Bob Cope and forward Russ Ochsenhirt. They were able to control the tip-off and the ball throughout the game, seldom passing wildly or taking ill-advised shots. This kind of praise was not given easily. It is clear that the Non-Skids were the fans' and the newspaper's favorites. Goodyear's management and play over the years had not been as admired or as consistent as that of the Non-Skids. Led by Cope, Ochsenhirt, Charley Shipp and Ray Morstadt from Marquette, the Wingfoots were beginning to draw a greater following as they played better basketball.[79]

In mid–January the Midwest Conference standings showed Goodyear tied with Firestone for first in the Eastern Division and Fort Wayne with a two game lead over Dayton. James Schlemmer, *Beacon Journal* sports editor, saw the season slipping away from the Non-Skids and indicated that the key would be the upcoming games with Goodyear, games that Firestone had traditionally dominated.[80]

The first of these was set for January 19. The Wingfoots-Non-Skids contests were the highlights of the year for Akron basketball fans and the atmosphere reflected that. The doors were to open at 7 P.M. and there would be table tennis and badminton exhibitions to occupy the early arrivals for the 8:30 tip-off. An element of mystery was added when it was announced that Goodyear had added a transfer from its Salt Lake City operations to the squad. He was 6' 4" and had been playing in Salt Lake City for three years and, it was suggested, might suit up for the Non-Skids contest. Today the idea of any mystery player existing is comical. The quaint notion of a mystery player is a pleasant reminder of a previous era's pace. (Ultimately it came out that the mystery player was named Ralph Crowton. He played in the game and did not score.) The game, itself, did not disappoint with Goodyear winning in a close contest 31–27. Charley Shipp, two years out of Cathedral Catholic High in Indianapolis and former U.S. Tires player, led the Wingfoots with 10 points. Firestones' star guard Howard "Soup" Cable missed the game with a severe ankle sprain but Non-Skids fans took heart from the fact that he would be able to play in the rematch on January 30.[81]

The anticipation for the next Firestone-Goodyear match was high and fans began ordering tickets the day after the first contest had been completed. This next game would be at Goodyear's gym which could "hold 3800 if the fire wardens permit."[82] At first, Firestone came out of their loss to Goodyear looking like they were regrouping in a positive way. On January 24, a Sunday, they won an unusual doubleheader, defeating Dayton 40–34 in the afternoon at Dayton, then defeating Columbus 48–45 at Columbus that evening.

"Horse" Myers and Jack Shaffer led the Non-Skids, who were confident as they prepared to face the touring AAU powerhouse Phillips 66 Oilers in a two-game set in Akron, January 26 and 27. The Oilers were the top team from the West and they played a much more fast-paced brand of basketball than the Midwest Conference teams usually played. The game was higher scoring than usual as well as very close, but the Non-Skids lost 57–55. The Oilers and Non-Skids followed with a slower paced contest the next night where Firestone again lost, this time 38–37. Meanwhile Goodyear continued to win and as the Non-Skid-Wingfoot contest neared; the teams records were Firestone 20–5 (12–3 in league play) and Goodyear 16–6 (12–1 in league). The next contest would surely decide the league champion.[83]

The day of the big game James Schlemmer predicted the way the game would be played.

> Few fouls will be called in the backcourt. Fouls which definitely interfere with scoring opportunities will be called. The game will be rough, but not dirty. Only he-men will engage in it. It will not have quite as much shoving and holding as did the first meeting of the teams.[84]

Schlemmer was describing the kind of rough contests that the working class fans wanted to see. There were 3760 seats with room for an additional 400 to 500 standing. This game, however, lacked the intensity of the first contest with Goodyear again winning, this time by a 37–25 margin. There was real disappointment expressed in the newspaper at the lack of enthusiasm on the part of Firestone.[85] This may have affected the Non-Skids in their next game as they trounced the U.S. Tires squad 58–30. U.S. Tires fell to 2–7, last in the Western Division of the league.[86]

The playoff format was announced on February 8 and the top two teams in each division were to meet in best of three game series. In the East, the two Akron teams once again collided. In the West, the Fort Wayne General Electrics would meet the Dayton London Bobbies. The two winners would then meet in a best of three championship round.[87] Before the playoffs, however, the Wings and Non-Skids were to meet once more, on February 9, in regularly scheduled league play. Firestone led most of the game, but Goodyear triumphed once again 32–30 on a steal and basket by Bob Cope at the end of the game. This latest Goodyear victory inspired James Schlemmer to devote his column to prior coach Edgar "Smiley" Weltner and his important role in building the team that was so successful that year. Schlemmer also noted the change in attitude and action on the part of the Goodyear administration.

> For years Goodyear high officials have suppressed basketball enthusiasm and interest. Weltner once was fired temporarily for having the Wings away from their jobs too long on one trip. Without previous warning Goodyear once was ordered to resign immediately from the Midwest Industrial league.

The Wings played basketball under wraps. Players who had been promised advancement in their jobs failed to get them and, in turn, played without spirit. But the change in coaching administration early this season was accompanied by a change in attitude of the Goodyear officials who have the most to say.[88]

This comment illustrates the peculiar situation the teams sponsored by industry could face. The company wanted high production from the employees and also wanted to have athletic outlets to keep those employees reasonably happy in terrible economic times. When the company, in this case Goodyear, decided to enter the Midwest Conference and to try to succeed in that venue, difficulties arose. Rather than emphasize basketball success, the company chose to win only if it didn't interfere with production. This led, however, to desultory play and unhappy company team supporters. It was then that the company management decided to loosen their tight emphasis on production at the loss of successful basketball.

The next week, stories appeared that built the playoff excitement. All seats were to be reserved at a cost of 60 and 40 cents each. A question of eligibility also arose. This was not a question of league eligibility, but rather one that had been established by the two Akron teams for their games against each other. It had been agreed for the previous 15 years that players had to be bona fide employees for 90 days prior to participation, but just before the game it was announced that the rule was voided by Goodyear's failure to agree to it for these playoffs. Just before game time, Goodyear officials changed their minds and announced that the old eligibility rules would be followed. It probably would have made little difference as Goodyear won 36–24, with Charley Shipp the leading scorer with 12. Four nights later, the series ended with Goodyear's 40–24 triumph, the first time that it had swept every game against Firestone in one year in the history of the series.[89]

Now, the Wingfoots waited to see who their opponent would be in the championship series. Dayton defeated Fort Wayne in the first game of their series 36–25. In the second contest Fort Wayne also won at home 31–28. The first game had been clouded by a dispute over distribution of gate receipts by Dayton. The second game saw Fort Wayne duplicate the practice, which cut the shares of the visiting players a great deal. The third game was scheduled for Fort Wayne, but Dayton failed to appear and the contest was awarded to Fort Wayne by forfeit. This embarrassment brought cries, demanding that Dayton be expelled from the league and forfeit its $500 league fee.[90] Despite the controversy, the stage was set for the final games of the year beginning in Akron on February 27.

Game one went to Akron 28–22 before 2200 spectators. The next night, the Wingfoots came from behind to win 27–24. Down 14–5 at the half, Goodyear closed to 21–15 at the end of three periods before outscoring the

Hoosiers 12–3 in the final quarter.[91] The second Akron Goodyear triumph ended the second Midwest Conference season and brought guarded anticipation for a third in 1937-38. There were some fears about the new champions staying together. "This could be the end of the Goodyear team as many are scheduled for advancements which will make it impossible for them to play basketball next season."[92] This, in a nutshell, summarizes the state of the Midwest Conference, a league that came together overly dependent on industry sponsored teams.

The peculiar circumstances of the Great Depression, combined with the players' love for the game, made the Midwest Conference an entity unique to the 1930s. The teams were not the best around; those were clearly the touring teams of professionals like the Rens and the SPHAs. Players could not make a yearly living wage as professional basketball players in a league. Owners could hope to break even or, at best, make a small profit. Fans chose to attend the games because of the cheap entertainment and the chance to support their local community heroes.

And the communities themselves made more efforts to provide leisure activities during the Depression, especially for youngsters, though some were also for adults. This pattern was the case with many Midwestern communities. In Akron much of this responsibility seemed to be undertaken by the Firestone and Goodyear companies, whose recreation programs were extensive. The U.S. Tire Company in Indianapolis also provided extensive recreational opportunities. In Pittsburgh the YMHA provided an outlet for recreational activities for more than just Jews in the community.

This league represented an opportunity for the pursuit of reasonably priced leisure entertainment at a time when money was very tight. These mostly Midwestern small cities were very much like the Middletown (in reality, Muncie, Indiana) described in Robert and Helen Lynd's studies.[93] In *Middletown in Transition*, published in 1937, the Lynds note that "Middletown clearly operates on the assumption that the roots of its living lie in the acquisition of money."[94] It also provided an opportunity for hometown (or workplace) pride. The owners were a mixture of corporate leaders, trying to serve both their employees and the community, and small business people with an interest in sport who wanted to be part of basketball and gain some publicity for their businesses. Until the post World War II period, when the economy boomed and a pool of great players was available, there would be little interest in spending on luxury goods such as professional basketball which would lead to significant economic improvement for the players and owners. The Midwest Conference laid the foundation for later prosperity by relying on community-oriented appeal to sell professional basketball. Much of the success of the sport in the post-war era was a result of the struggles of the Midwest Conference, a short-lived phenomenon in the mid–1930s.

The National Basketball
League Begins

The Midwest Conference completed its second season in March of 1937. There had been problems; the league was still playing an open schedule and the number of games within the league was not standardized for each league member. Play was still largely on weekends and the players were not able to have league games as their top priority if their industry sponsored teams had demands made from their employers. Economics was the major concern of Firestone, Goodyear, General Electric and the other companies that were involved as league members. Basketball was entertaining, but there was a limit to how much of a commitment of time and money certain companies would make. A number of the independent teams of 1936-37 could not continue to meet league demands and decided to cut back their schedules to more local play. The Depression still had the country in its grip and there were limiting economic factors that affected the fan base. Television was only experimental at the time and only a few clubs broadcast on radio so media coverage was often limited to newspapers. Endorsement contracts for players were rare, if they existed at all, though in the smaller cities of the league the players were clearly local heroes.

October of 1937 found the world edgy, with conflicts in Spain, China and parts of Africa and fears of Germany rising in Europe. The Spanish Civil War had raged for more than a year and Britain, fearing greater escalation of the war, warned Mussolini and Italy, which in December 1936 had begun sending troops and equipment to support the Nationalists, to stop their own troop advancement in Africa in support of Spain. British fears focused on Spain and Italy closing or disturbing the shipping lanes in the Mediterranean, thus cutting off British supplies to Egypt, a British colony.

Japan's armies continued to advance in China with some push back from the Chinese in the north of the country. Japan began bombing and strafing the international community in Shanghai in October and the British made stronger demands on the Japanese to vacate China. The United States was suspicious of continued Japanese advancement, but the U.S. sought to avoid war with Japan or any combatant on the world stage. By December, Japan had sent 50,000 additional troops to Canton and continued its advancement throughout China.

In the fall of 1937 Midwest Conference officials met to determine which teams would continue in the league. Some of the teams affiliated with industries — Goodyear, Firestone, General Electric, Columbus Athletic Supply — returned to play in the newly renamed National Basketball League. Other returning franchises were Warren (PA), the Indianapolis Kautskys and the Whiting (IN) Ciesars. Teams were from Pittsburgh and Dayton but they were not the same franchises that had been in the Midwest Conference the previous season. New to the league were Buffalo, Kankakee (IL), Richmond (IN) and Oshkosh. The beginning of the league season was in late November according to Neft, et al.[1] This is contradicted, at least to a degree, by the written account in the *Oshkosh Daily Northwestern*, the daily paper of Oshkosh, Wisconsin.[2] What may be true is that the league had been reconstituted before December, but Oshkosh joined that month and the new league's regulations were that each team would play 20 games, home and home games with teams in their division, and also play others in the other division. There were then 13 teams, seven in the Western Division, six in the Eastern. The league had changed names, according to Gerry Archibald, who was the owner and manager of the Warren team, in order to give the league more of a "national effect" and seem more than a regional league.[3]

Despite their problems with fairness in scheduling the prior two years, the new league still allowed teams to make their own bookings and the stated goal of 20 league games for each team was met by only one franchise, the Fort Wayne squad, which went 13–7 for the league season. Actual league games played varied from a low of nine to the high of 20. As in prior years of the Midwest Conference, most teams tried to recruit players with regional ties to their respective franchises. Peterson highlighted the Warren players whom Archibald signed. "Three of the Penns' players were semipro stars, from Erie, Pa., and Archibald recruited college men from Westminster, Duquesne, Edinboro State Teachers College, and other colleges in western Pennsylvania."[4]

The Oshkosh Franchise

Oshkosh entered the league in December 1937, but the team had been playing together since the 1929-30 season when Lon Darling, a seed distributor and salesman, organized the team at the suggestion of Art Heywood, sports

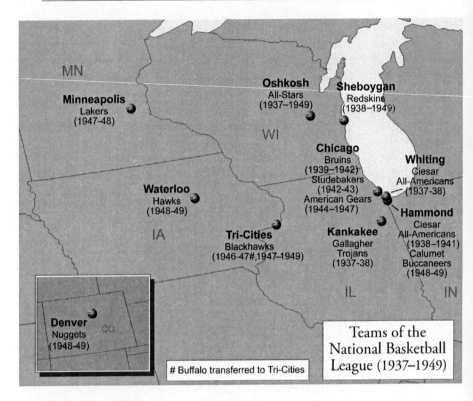

MN

Minneapolis
Lakers
(1947-48)

Oshkosh
All-Stars
(1937-1949)

Sheboygan
Redskins
(1938-1949)

WI

Chicago
Bruins
(1939-1942)
Studebakers
(1942-43)
American Gears
(1944-1947)

Whiting
Ciesar
All-Americans
(1937-38)

Waterloo
Hawks
(1948-49)

Hammond
Ciesar
All-Americans
(1938-1941)
Calumet
Buccaneers
(1948-49)

IA

Tri-Cities
Blackhawks
(1946-47#,1947-1949)

Kankakee
Gallagher
Trojans
(1937-38)

IL   IN

Denver
Nuggets
(1948-49)

CO

Buffalo transferred to Tri-Cities

Teams of the
National Basketball
League (1937-1949)

Above and opposite: The teams and locations of the National Basketball League, 1937–1949. (Maps designed by Steve Gardner.)

editor of the *Oshkosh Daily Northwestern*.[5] The first years the team played squads in Appleton, Beloit, Wisconsin Rapids, Fond du Lac, Manitowoc, Milwaukee, Neenah and Racine.[6] These towns would be revisited over the years, as Oshkosh would play some of their home games throughout Wisconsin. The enthusiasm for the team was almost immediate, fostered by Heywood's newspaper. Darling, who according to his sister, Beatrice, "never played a game of basketball in his life," took on the Oshkosh team as his life, according to his wife, Marge.[7] The city of 40,000 (it has since grown to almost 60,000) on the shores of Lake Winnebago about 75 miles northwest of Milwaukee took to the league as a prime attraction for the long, cold Wisconsin winter nights. The All Stars also became a regional team, playing home games throughout south central and southeastern Wisconsin. At that time, "any good sized city had a team."[8] In November 1937 the All Stars began their season with a game in Fond du Lac, Wisconsin, twenty miles south of Oshkosh at the southern tip of Lake Winnebago. They faced the Chicago Duffy Florals, the Midwest Conference champion in 1936 with a number of the players from that team

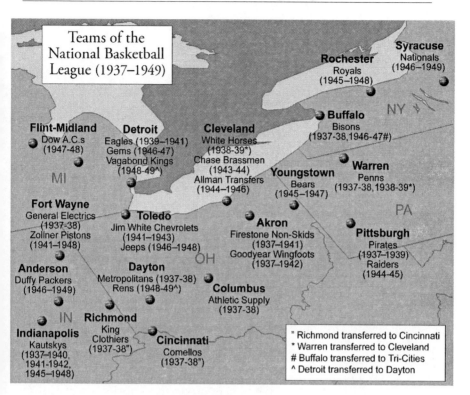

Teams of the National Basketball League (1937–1949)

Syracuse Nationals (1946–1949)

Rochester Royals (1945–1948)

Flint-Midland
Dow A.C.s (1947-48)

MI

Detroit
Eagles (1939–1941)
Gems (1946-47)
Vagabond Kings (1948-49^)

Cleveland
White Horses (1938-39*)
Chase Brassmen (1943-44)
Allman Transfers (1944–1946)

Buffalo
Bisons (1937-38,1946-47#)

Youngstown
Bears (1945–1947)

Warren
Penns (1937-38,1938-39*)

NY

Fort Wayne
General Electrics (1937-38)
Zollner Pistons (1941–1948)

Toledo
Jim White Chevrolets (1941–1943)
Jeeps (1946-1948)

Akron
Firestone Non-Skids (1937–1941)
Goodyear Wingfoots (1937–1942)

Pittsburgh
Pirates (1937–1939)
Raiders (1944-45)

PA

Anderson
Duffy Packers (1946–1949)

Dayton
Metropolitans (1937-38)
Rens (1948-49^)

OH

Columbus
Athletic Supply (1937-38)

IN

Richmond
King Clothiers (1937-38")

Indianapolis
Kautskys (1937-1940, 1941-1942, 1945-1948)

Cincinnati
Comellos (1937-38")

" Richmond transferred to Cincinnati
* Warren transferred to Cleveland
# Buffalo transferred to Tri-Cities
^ Detroit transferred to Dayton

still on the squad. These included the Kolar brothers, Ed and Otto; Bob Young, who had played at North Central College, just outside Chicago; and Ray Adams from De Paul University. Also on their squad was a former Oshkosh All Star, Bill Mangan, and Joe Reiff, an All America player from Northwestern.[9] The Oshkosh newspaper went on to lament the loss of a top player from the squad, illustrating the fragility of team rosters. "Gordon Fuller, captain last year of the University of Wisconsin team will be lost to the All-Star squad. Because of a job in Madison, he will be unable to take the time to make trips with the team and for that reason he has withdrawn from the roster."[10]

The All Stars managed to eke out a win over Chicago with Reiff leading all scorers with 15, while Leroy Edwards, the former star for both the Indianapolis Kautskys and the U.S. Tires in the Midwest Conference, had 11. Edwards had begun playing with the All Stars the previous year and was a fixture in that city's basketball picture for a many years. Two nights later, they played a home game against the House of David, then the next afternoon played the same opponent in Waupaca, 40 miles northwest of Oshkosh. The next night they played them again, this time in Ripon, 30 miles southwest of Oshkosh. The hype for the House of David game had to do with the fact that one of their players, "Tiny" Burnette, was 7'7" and weighed over

300 pounds. The All Stars won all these games before crowds of 600 to 1000 persons, then defeated the Chicago Elks and, on December 4 and 5, the Harlem Globetrotters in Oshkosh and Waupaca. The All Stars had won their first seven games and then defeated the Celtics of New York 36–23. This was seen as especially significant because the Celtics had defeated the New York Renaissance team the previous year in four of seven contests, causing the Celtics to claim the title of champions of professional basketball. At this point the All Stars joined the National Basketball League and, in announcing the entry, the *Daily Northwestern* provided a rationale for its occurrence. "While the fame of the Oshkosh All Stars has been spreading through victories over the best teams in the country, it is expected the local aggregation will become best known through membership in a league."[11]

The All Star lineup was set with Eddie Mullen, Leroy Edwards, Pete Pre-boski, Augie Vander Meulen and Herman Witasek. The only change was the addition of Ray Adams, formerly of the Duffy Florals, who had joined the Osh-kosh team as of December 8. The star of the team was young Leroy Edwards, referred to as "Lefty" by the *Daily Northwestern*, but often known since then as "Cowboy." Edwards had grown up in Indianapolis and graduated from Tech High School in 1933. He then enrolled at the University of Kentucky and led the freshmen team in scoring. The next year he averaged 20 points a game, an amazing total for that time, and the Wildcats went 19–2. Edwards was named college player of the year by some basketball observers but he left school the next year, apparently more interested in playing basketball for money than playing for the fiery, young coach, Adolph Rupp, who had come from Kansas in 1931 to become head of the basketball program. Edwards loved to shoot and he was a great scorer. He could hook with either hand, had great fakes and could lay the ball in from a variety of angles. His range was limited, but he was, at 6'5", a big, tough rebounder. Many of his baskets were follow-in shots after he or a teammate had missed. John Isaacs, who played for the New York Renaissance team for many years in the 1930s and 1940s, called Edwards a "light hearted guy." He knew all the little tricks to get an advantage on an opponent like holding the shirt, hooking his fingers in an opponent's arm or clothing, according to Isaacs. Though he was a big, burly player, he "never tried to hurt you."[12] George Mikan remembered a bigger, stronger and rougher Edwards when Mikan entered pro basketball in 1946. He recalled that Edwards had a strong temper as well as the ability to hold and grab.

> I was on Edwards and tried to hold him out — you could hear my gym shoes squeaking as I strained to hold my position. Cowboy threw a nice little elbow and hit me right in the midsection. He knocked me over and made another hook shot.... (T)he next time we played, he reminded me what I had learned, I got too close to him again, and he hit me with an elbow in the mouth that knocked out four teeth.[13]

Mikan's memory was of an older, wiser, hoarier Cowboy. In 1937 Edwards was just 22 years old and had not bulked up to the 280 pounds Mikan claimed he was in 1946. In 1937 Edwards was much "friskier" and loved to shoot.

Despite the announcement of the All Stars joining the NBL, they did not play a league game until January of 1938, nearly a month later. In the interim Oshkosh faced some stiff opposition. They played two games with the New York Rens, who were on their December Midwestern swing. Before 1500 in Oshkosh the All Stars won 34–30 and before 4000 in Madison Oshkosh won again 41–31. Then the team boarded the Milwaukee Road to head east for five games. The day that they left, the *Daily Northwestern* noted two significant changes in the National Basketball League. First was the announcement that the center jump after baskets would be optional with the decision for each game to be made at the home team's discretion. The jump after the made free throw had been eliminated in the Midwest Conference and this now pushed the center jump even more from the integral rhythm of the game. This would accelerate the pace of play and scoring, which seemed to be more to the liking of fans. The other announcement was that the Richmond, Indiana, NBL franchise was moving to Cincinnati after only three league games.[14] Richmond, with a population of less than 30,000, could not draw enough fans with all the competition from Indiana high school ball, so the franchise moved 35 miles south to draw on a larger fan base. It didn't help much. Though the Cincinnati Comellos finished the league season (2–5 plus the 1–2 of Richmond for a 3–7 league mark), they failed to generate great interest and left the league after the year ended. Cincinnati did not return to professional basketball until 1957 when the Rochester Royals moved there, remaining for 15 years until moving once again to Kansas City-Omaha as the Kings.

The All Stars went first to Allentown, Pennsylvania, where they beat an Allentown squad 29–25. They moved on to Brooklyn to play before five thousand fans and defeat the Jewels, who were a member of the American Basketball League (ABL) 22–14. The ABL had been formed in 1925 and was the first truly, geographically national professional basketball league with teams stretching from Boston to Chicago. When the Original Celtics joined the league in 1926, they became a dominant force and won the league championship in 1927 and 1928. After that, the league forced the Celtics to disband and be redistributed to provide for league parity, but the Depression drove the league out of business after the 1930-31 season. In 1933 the ABL returned as a regional league with teams only in the Philadelphia and New York City metroplexes. There were some excellent teams in the league, most notably the South Philadelphia Hebrew Association squad, which won league titles in 1934, 1936, 1937, 1940, 1941 and 1945 before the league succumbed once again in 1946. In 1937 the Jewels were a good squad which would win the second half title in the league. After this victory, the All Stars had won 15 games in a row.

The Oshkosh team returned home where they faced the Celtics who were making a Midwestern swing of their own. The All Stars won 40–36 as Pete Preboski led the team with nine points and Edwards was held to only four. The Celtics got 11 points from Paul Birch and six from both Rusty Saunders, an old ABL star since the 1920s, and Bobby McDermott, who was just starting his long career after becoming a professional right out of high school. He would later join the NBL and be one of its brightest stars for most of its existence.[15] In the next Celtics-All Star contest, the Celtics triumphed 44–39 as Nat Hickey dropped 25 points, including 11 of 12 free throws, on the Oshkosh team. Preboski again led Oshkosh with 8, followed by Edwards's 6.[16]

Finally, as 1938 began, the All Stars had their first NBL game. As they readied themselves for the game the NBL standings looked like this:

Western Division			Eastern Division		
Dayton Metropolitans	1	0	Akron Goodyears	3	0
Fort Wayne	3	1	Akron Firestones	4	1
Whiting Ciesars	4	3	Pittsburgh Pirates	3	2
Richmond King Clothiers	1	2	Buffalo Bisons	1	4
Indianapolis Kautskys	1	3	Warren Penns	1	2
Kankakee Gallaghers	0	2	Columbus Athletic Supply	0	0
Oshkosh All Stars	0	0			

In their first NBL game the All Stars defeated the Dayton Metros 44–43. Dayton was led by Lou Rutter from Otterbein College with 15; Bob Colburn, an All America from Ohio State, had 9 and Bill Hosket had 8.[17] Three nights later Oshkosh faced Kankakee on ladies night. Each lady was admitted free with her husband or boyfriend or two ladies could enter for the price of one. Borrowed from a baseball practice, which had been successful, the All Star management wanted to also send the message that professional basketball was a family sport. The Kankakee contest proved to be no contest at all. The Kankakee squad was a team of students who attended a local trade school — Gallagher — and were the only purely amateur team in the NBL. The score, 75–42, reflected that. Edwards led with 21, Augie Vander Meulen had 16 and Herman Witasek had 13. These were the biggest and strongest of the All Stars so they undoubtedly simply outmuscled the Gallaghers.[18]

In the same article, the newspaper also reported on the team's shooting percentages for the game. These kinds of data were not kept as league records since the league structure was so loose and finding such data is not easy. Viewing it, however, provides greater insight into the way the game was played and what was expected of professional players. The *Daily Northwestern* would keep such data and report them on a regular basis. For this game, the team went 31–84, a .369 percentage. This was viewed as solid. Edwards was 7–18 but Vander Meulen was 7–20. Since he did not often shoot that much, the implication would be that most of these were put-backs. In fact, with most of the shots inside, the percentage was amazingly low.

The next week opened with two All Stars victories in non-league contests against the Bendix Brakes of South Bend, Indiana. The first, at Oshkosh, was 48–34. The second, at Waupaca, was 49–33. The excitement over the All Stars and their success was clearly infectious, indicated by the note in the *Daily Northwestern* before the Whiting Ciesars game in Milwaukee. "Two special cars of the Chicago and Northwestern were to be added to the train leaving this city at 4:35 o'clock for the accommodation of Oshkosh fans."[19] The railroad added flexibility to a team's planning to accommodate its fan base. Evidence of a railroad's willingness to do this goes back at least to the Penn State League in the 1920s when teams in the Wyoming Valley were able to add cars for their fans at relatively short notice.[20] The All Stars lost their first league game to the Whiting Ciesars 29–26 on January 10 before a crowd of four thousand in Milwaukee. Leroy Edwards led both teams in scoring with 11, but seven of those came on free throws as he shot two of sixteen from the floor. Edwards' hapless shooting was due, in part, to the fact that the Ciesars' center, Vince McGowan, rode him until fouling out.[21] Edwards' shooting was not only matched by his teammates, but the Ciesars did not do much better. In a rare (but very much appreciated) instance, the *Daily Northwestern* carried shooting percentages for each player for the game and it was not pretty. The All Stars went seven for 78 from the floor, for 9 percent while the Ciesars burned the nets at a rate of 18½ percent with 10 for 54.[22] What was even more amazing was that not a word was mentioned in the article about the horrific shooting, leading one to speculate that it was not that unusual. If fans were coming to NBL contests for dazzling shooting, they were going to be disappointed, so rugged play may have been a substitute for that in terms of providing fans with excitement and enjoyment.

Following up on this performance the Oshkosh quintet dropped their next game to the Akron Firestones 42–37. They then entertained the Chicago Duffy Florals in Oshkosh and Wisconsin Rapids on two consecutive days and swept the Chicagoans by scores of 52–40 and 51–37.[23] The next game that the All Stars played did little to solidify the major league status of the NBL and its representatives. Though a non-league contest, the game against the Enzo Jels of Sheboygan was always a regional grudge match, and this was no different. The Enzo Jels won 46–43, but the modification of the rules was unique, if not embarrassing. First, the Enzo Jels did not have more than six players so the All Stars agreed to waive the foul limit in the game. Ray Adams ended up with seven fouls, as did Johnny Posewitz of Sheboygan. Then, the floor was extremely slippery and the officials "quite apparently had not 'worked' games of the caliber of professional contests." The result was clearly ugly. The All

Stars shot 16 of 65 for 23.8 percent while Sheboygan shot "32.7 per cent (17–52), which is generally winning basketball in any league."[24]

The All Stars returned to league play to end the month, defeating the Firestones in Menomonie and the Cincinnati Comellos, twice, in a double-header on January 29 in Oshkosh. Then on Sunday, in Antigo, Wisconsin, Oshkosh defeated the Duffy Florals 50–36. The game had been postponed because "neither team could get through the snowdrifts to Antigo,"[25] a town of about 7500 located 75 miles north and west of Oshkosh. In all of these games, "Lefty" Edwards was a double figure scorer with 11, 15, 13 and 15 points. His scoring pace was beginning to become noteworthy to the media and would be followed more closely as the year neared an end. At the Saturday doubleheader against Cincinnati, Lonnie Darling, the Oshkosh manager, received the award of Outstanding Young Man of Oshkosh for 1937 from the mayor of Oshkosh, who, it was noted, was formerly of Cincinnati.[26] Here was tangible evidence of how highly the All Stars and professional basketball were held by the city officials and businessmen of this city.

After defeating the Kankakee Gallaghers handily on February 2 to retain their lead in the Western Division of the NBL, the All Stars prepared for a big weekend game against the Sheboygan Enzo Jels. The Gallaghers game proved little to the All Stars but it did allow Leroy Edwards to set a new NBL scoring record with 28 points. The Enzo Jels, formerly the Art Imigs, were a rugged squad led by Rube Lautenschlager, a former standout at Oshkosh Teachers College who was now a teacher in Sheboygan. In addition they had the Posewitz brothers, Johnny and Joe ("Scoop"), at guards and rugged inside men — Carl Roth from Wisconsin, whose nickname was "Toughy"; Les Kuplic from Beloit; and "Slim" Lonsdorf, a 6'4" center-forward. The game was played with unlimited fouling once again. This led to players on Sheboygan having 7, 6 and 5 fouls, respectively and continuing to play in the contest. Frank Linskey played with five for Oshkosh. The unlimited fouling was not originally planned, but "the visitors were down to five so it was necessary to abrogate the five foul rule and from then on the fans saw ju-jitsu and Apache dancing mixed in with basketball."[27] Even in these early years, professional basketball saw that rules were made to be broken if it meant more fan appeal and higher revenue. With such a shoestring operation, these kinds of concessions were vital to keep the clubs' revenue streams flowing. The All Stars ran away with the contest 55–36, led by Edwards with 16 and Preboski with 11. Johnny Posewitz had 13 for the Enzo Jels. The next day the All Stars traveled to Hammond, Indiana, to play the Whiting Ciesars and lost 42–39 in a

Opposite: In November of 1937, the *Firestone Non-Skid* provided this "Who's Who" of the team. (Used by permission of Bridgestone Americas Holding, Inc., and the University of Akron Archives.)

WHO'S WHO
On Your Firestone Basketball Team

MILOS "SLIM" SHOUN—Graduate Carson-Newman College, Tennessee. 6 feet, 11 inches, weight 200 pounds. Has played with Firestone since 1930. Very valuable. For a big man, he is an all-around player. Center.

ED GARNER—Center and Forward. 6 feet, 6 inches, 195 pounds. Graduate University of Michigan in 1933. Third year with Firestone. Was Michigan's high scorer final year in college and chosen as All-Western Conference center by numerous sports writers.

BERNARD "BEANIE" BERENS—Center and Forward. 6 feet, 4½ inches, 180 pounds. A product of Lancaster, Ohio High School and a star from Ohio University. Chosen All-Buckeye Conference center in 1932-33-34. Second year with Firestone. One of leading scorers in Midwest Conference last year. Shoots equally well left or right handed.

"CLEO" JACK SCHAFFER—6 feet, 4 inches, 189 pounds. A product of the West and was graduated from Nebraska University where he was chosen All-Missouri Valley Conference forward. Second year at Firestone. One of the best shots in America and a high scorer in all games. Forward.

HOWARD "SOUP" CABLE—6 feet, 3½ inches, 173 pounds. A product of Akron West and independent ball. Fourth year at Firestone and probably the best all-round player on the team. Always a high scorer, a good shot, and fine team player. One of the leading scorers last year in the Midwest Conference. Forward.

WM. "BILL" REEVES—5 feet, 10 inches, 170 pounds. Smallest man on team and probably the best guard. Not a high scorer but strong defensively. Was graduated from Indiana State Normal and choice for All-Indiana guard. Fifth year at Firestone.

ED "STRETCH" SADOWSKI—6 feet, 6 inches, 199 pounds. Center. Was graduated from Akron North and two years ago All-State High School center. Played in Cleveland Class AA last year and was a star at the National A. A. U. Tournament in Denver, scoring over 60 points in the three games in which his team participated. Promises to develop into a star for Firestone. First year at Firestone.

TALMADGE "WES" BENNETT—6 feet, 3 inches, 175 pounds. Was graduated from Akron East where he was an All-State center. Westminster College, 1936. Final three years in college led all scorers in America each year, with a total of over 1,000 points. Center and guard. First year at Firestone.

WARD "HORSE" MYERS—6 feet, 190 pounds. Learned his basketball at Ft. Wayne, Indiana, where he was a star on General Electric and in independent circles. Wonderfully fast as a guard. Also a big scorer due to his fast cutting, and a keen eye which enables him to sink the long ones.

game that went to two overtimes. Both Edwards and Reboski got 13, but Johnny Wooden of Hammond took game scoring honors with 17, including 9–11 from the free throw line.

The All Stars were now playing almost every night and their contest against Kankakee, played in Plainfield, Wisconsin, forty miles west of Oshkosh, was a nice antidote to the previous day's defeat at Whiting. Again they coasted to victory, this time 56–40, and then won again in Oshkosh the next night 58–33. In the latter game Edwards again set a new NBL scoring record for a game, this time with 30, including 14 field goals.[28]

The All Stars played Fort Wayne twice, the Akron Goodyears twice, the Kautskys twice and Whiting twice over the next seventeen days to close their NBL season. In Fort Wayne on February 10, the All Stars managed to slip by the General Electrics by a 33–30 margin. Back in Oshkosh they defeated Akron the next day 39–29, and on February 12 and 13 they played Saturday and Sunday games against the Kautskys, led by former Purdue All America Bob Kessler. The first game was in Oshkosh and the All Stars triumphed 52–39 with Edwards leading the way with 18 points while Kessler had 15 for Indianapolis. The next day the two teams piled into autos and drove to Menasha, just over 20 miles away at the northern end of Lake Winnebago. There, before 900 fans in the local high school gym, the All Stars again won 48–46. Kessler had 15, once again, for the Kautskys and Edwards 14 to lead Oshkosh. The next weekend the All Stars, who were already assured of a playoff berth, clinched the first position in the West with a 54–38 win in Oshkosh over Fort Wayne. Edwards continued his double figure scoring with 13 and was joined by Preboski with 12 and Vander Meulen with 11.

Two days later Oshkosh opened the first round of the playoffs by defeating Whiting (which had finished 12–3 to the All Stars' 12–2) in Hammond 40–33 to avenge the earlier loss at that venue. Edwards had 16 on 6 of 22 field goals and John Wooden had 17 to pace the Ciesars' scoring. Four days later the All Stars ended the three game series with a 41–38 victory over Whiting with Edwards and Wooden again leading their teams in scoring with 15 and 16, respectively. Neither team shot very well; the All Stars were 11–64 (17.5 percent) and the Ciesars 11–55 (20 percent).[29] The championship round would open the next night against the Eastern champion Akron Goodyears.

The Goodyears and the Firestones

The Firestones had most of their team return for the 1937-38 season as well as four new players and looked to do well in the new National Basketball League's inaugural year. The new additions included Warren Whitlinger, captain of Ohio State's 1935-36 team; Malley Johnson from South Carolina

State; Jack Ozburne of Monmouth College and Robert Dowell from Marysville, Kansas. The latter two were both highlighted as former Amateur Athletic Union (AAU) stars and all were noted as being "part of Firestone's student sales class which will undergo a special period of additional training."[30] The Firestone team began the NBL season in November with wins over the Indianapolis Kautskys (who had combined with the U.S. Tire team) and the Buffalo Bisons in Buffalo. The latter game was quite low scoring (21–19) but Ozburn led the team in scoring with 6. A week later the Non-Skids suffered their first loss of the season in Akron to Whiting by a 40–34 score. Ken Gunning, a former Indiana star, had 12, and John Wooden and Vince McGovern got eight each for the Ciesars. Ozburn again led the Firestone squad with 12.

The other Akron team, Midwest Conference champion Goodyear, opened its season with the same basic lineup as the year before. In downing Buffalo 36–19, the team exhibited balanced scoring led by Ray Morstadt and Charley Shipp with 9 each. In the Buffalo lineup that evening was a 20-year-old named Al Cervi. He scored only two points but these would be only the beginning of an NBL-NBA playing career that would resume in 1945 with Rochester and last until 1953. A week after that, Goodyear defeated Kankakee for its fifteenth straight victory (nine from the prior year, six for 1937-38) while the Non-Skids dropped a league game to the Pittsburgh Pirates. The next night the Goodyear streak was snapped at Fort Wayne 29–25.[31]

As Firestone prepared to play the Columbus Athletic Supply team, the *Akron Beacon Journal* offered some insight into the opponent's composition noting that the Columbus roster was built around "the powerful 1936-37 Otterbein College quintet" (which had gone 11–5 the previous year). The team was led by Harold "Cookie" Cunningham from Ohio State, who had played in the National Football League in the late '20s and early '30s. Cunningham was the coach of the team but still averaged more than seven points per game at the age of 33, old at that time for a professional basketball player. The three Otterbein alums were Sam Loucks, Denny Elliot and Herb "Reindeer" Hutchinson. Columbus was 1–1 in the league, splitting games, home and home on the same day with Dayton. The buildup to the game was not justified as the Non-Skids rolled to a 52–33 win to go 5–2 in league play. Cable had 13, Whitlinger 11 and Ozburn eight to lead the scoring. For Columbus, Cunningham had 11 and Woody Pitzer seven.[32]

In early January the Non-Skids topped the Buffalo squad in a tight contest 38–37. The game was notable for a number of things. First, 20-year-old Al Cervi was beginning to show the scoring and leadership that would ultimately lead to his election to the Basketball Hall of Fame. After graduating from East High in Buffalo, Cervi played in a YMCA league where he led the league in scoring. He recalled that his Buffalo Bisons team was good, good enough to win one game against the Non-Skids later in the season.[33] He and Bello Snyder led the Bisons with 9 points each. Snyder's points, however, were a bit "tainted," as described in the Akron newspaper:

> Snyder, incidentally, established some kind of record when he committed eight personal fouls. National League rules call for ejection after the fifth foul, but the official scorekeeper became mixed up and Snyder kept fouling away to his heart's content.

It was incidents like this that added a colorful quality to the play of the NBL, but also made its performance seem less than professional. A week later the Non-Skids defeated Oshkosh, the Western division leader, 42–37, but the game did not count as a league game because of another quirk of the NBL's scheduling wherein Firestone had already scheduled its maximum of 20 NBL games before the Oshkosh contest was arranged. The game was won at the free throw line as the All Stars went 7–22 and the Non-Skids 12–15. The Non-Skids got 12 from Cable and the All Stars 19 from Edwards, whose brilliant all around play was lauded by Elliott of the *Beacon Journal*.[34]

The All Stars played Goodyear the next night, also another non-league battle for the same reason that the previous night's contest did not count in the league standings. In this game, won by the Wings 42–40, Ray Adams scored 26 points in defeat. As in the week before, this was also a bit tainted, but not from ignorance. Both Adams and Leroy Edwards committed five fouls but were allowed to keep playing. "Coach Lefty Byers of the Wings 'permitted' Adams and Edwards to continue to play on the condition that should either commit another foul, the shooter would be permitted to take twice as many free throws as awarded by the referee."[35]

Despite both Akron teams now being in the NBL, the annual battles between the two still were more important than any league games. Only the first two games would count in the league standings, but all would be hotly contested, especially in light of the thumping that Goodyear had laid on Firestone the previous year, after years of Firestone dominance. The first game was on January 15, 1938, and 2500 filled the arena to capacity. Ray Morstadt of Goodyear was injured and missed the game. Heading into the contest, the standings showed Goodyear atop the Eastern Division of the NBL with nine wins and one loss, while Firestone was second at seven and two. The Non-Skids took this contest 35–30 as Cable had 16 points. The unexpected hero, however, was Milos "Slim" Shoun, a 32-year-old 6'11" journeyman who had his greatest game as a Firestone player, according to the *Beacon Journal*. Though he scored only two points, he "controlled the tip off constantly..., played the pivot well ... he took balls off the backboard."[36]

Shoun's rejuvenation continued the next week as he tied for the scoring lead (with Malley Johnson as both got 7) in the Non-Skids' victory over Dayton. Dayton was led by Lou Rutter with 11 and Bob Colburn with 10, nearly the entire team total of 28.[37]

A few days later as the Non-Skids prepared to play the Phillips 66 Oilers, the defending AAU champions, *Beacon Journal* sports editor James Schlemmer discussed in his column the conundrum of AAU amateur standing. The NBL was a pro (or semi pro) league except when the league member teams played AAU teams. Before playing top AAU teams like the Oilers, players on NBL teams would register as AAU members and then the games would be games between two amateur squads. If that wasn't the case, Phillips couldn't and wouldn't play. To Schlemmer this was really playing "fast and loose" with the reality of things.

> Since they (the Oilers) are amateurs to the AAU, traveling advertising gas and oil. Some teams are pro, Whiting Oshkosh, Pittsburgh, e.g., but Kankakee is strictly amateur with its players being bona fide students at Gallagher Business College. Firestone, Goodyear, Fort Wayne are industrial amateurs, called that because some *were* pros, but now are paid only for working at these industrial plants with basketball only a sideline.

He went on to complain of the hypocrisy in this whole business and said that a national open tournament would end this (as well as the National AAU Tournament). To Schlemmer, amateur status was on sale at 25 cents a card.[38] And in the game, the Non-Skids topped the Oilers 47–41 as Jack Ozburn had 13, Soup Cable 12 and Milos Shoun 10 in a contest played under "strict collegiate rules."[39]

The Goodyear Regulars continued to march toward the playoffs, crushing Warren 42–17 on January 29 to go to 12–2 in the league. Two days later Firestone met and defeated Goodyear once again in a tremendous second half comeback. Both teams had great balance in their scoring in what was described as one of the greatest contests the two teams had ever waged.[40] That same day, James Schlemmer noted that the NBL could be rebuilt on "smaller lines" the following season with Cleveland in the league and some teams, like Pittsburgh, out. A problem in Pittsburgh had been the simultaneous lack of media coverage and the duping of local fans by the team, leading the fans to believe that Pittsburgh was in first place. The league was now sending out publicity sheets to local media to provide more accurate information. A week later Goodyear finally beat Firestone 23–21 (in a game that did not count in the league standings) after losing in Buffalo to the Bisons 33–29. In that game Al Cervi again led Buffalo with 13 points.

Just before the playoffs began, the New York Renaissance made a swing through the Midwest and the resulting Goodyear-Rens contest was significant only in that it ended in a forfeit with a 2–0 Goodyear victory. According to the *Beacon Journal*, "Wee" Willie Smith had floored Charley Shipp with a right to the jaw and many of the 2600 fans and the other Goodyear players rushed Smith. Titus Lobach, the referee, ejected Smith but the Rens wanted Shipp ejected too, claiming that he had sucker punched Smith. Goodyear coaches said that Smith could stay, but Lobach said no and the Rens left the floor in protest, leading to the forfeit. There was a history to this. Two years earlier, Shipp had tangled with the Rens when he had been on the U.S. Tires team and Lobach had ejected Smith from a game in Akron just the year before. The Rens, according to the newspaper, were now "personae non grata with Goodyear."[41]

It was not unusual for the Rens to be the perceived villains in many small, white communities where blacks were hardly ever seen, let alone resided. The Rens traveled in their own bus and always had the bus to use if they were refused a place to eat or sleep for the night. The Rens fondly called their bus "the Blue Moose."[42]

At this point both Goodyear and Firestone had clinched (or were about to clinch) the two Eastern Division playoff berths, but they had one more game to play against each other. Firestone won the game and the city series (3–1) with superior shooting from the field. The Non-Skids were 15–31 on field goals, while the Regulars were 14–40. Free throws were nearly even in percentage and those made. Jack Ozburn had 17 to lead all scorers and Chuck Bloedorn led Goodyear with 13. With the regular season at an end, the teams now prepared to meet again, this time in the playoffs. Before that, however, both teams traveled to Cleveland for a doubleheader where both lost. The Non-Skids lost to the Rens 39–34, then traveled to Rushville, Indiana, with them where they played once again. Before more than 3000 fans the Rens topped the Non-Skids 53–42 as Smith, "Fats" Jenkins and Al Johnson all scored in double figures while "Bruiser" Saitch and "Tarzan" Cooper had nine and eight, respectively. Ozburn had 17 and Cable 8 for Firestone.[43]

The battles of the NBL weren't quite as fierce as the wars in China and Europe. In February a British ship was sunk off Spain and there were daily war updates from Tokyo, Shanghai and Madrid as well as Berlin. The leaders of Hungary and Poland were meeting to discuss the Danube basin, but both expressed fear of Hitler's designs on Austria. The prediction was that the war in Spain would likely go on for two more years.

The end of the NBL season saw Firestone at 14–4 to Goodyear's 13–5 in the league. Oshkosh had gone 12–2 and Whiting 12–3 in the West. Overall standings were:

Eastern Division	W	L	Western Division	W	L
Akron Firestone	14	4	Oshkosh All Stars	12	2
Akron Goodyear	13	5	Whiting Ciesars	12	3
Pittsburgh Pirates	8	5	Fort Wayne	13	7
Buffalo	3	6	Indianapolis	4	8

Eastern Division	W	L	Western Division	W	L
Warren, PA	3	9	Cincinnati	3	7
Columbus	1	12	Kankakee	3	11
			Dayton	2	11

The scoring leader for the league was Leroy Edwards of Oshkosh with 182 points and a 14 points per game average. John Wooden was the only other player to average in double figures; he had a 10.7 average for Whiting. These figures don't precisely square with those in some other, later sources, but there is no question that Edwards and Wooden were the two top scorers.[44]

The Eastern Division playoffs began February 24 and the Wingfoots of Goodyear topped the Non-Skids 26–21. Poor shooting doomed the Firestone squad as they made only five of 34 attempts from the field (14.7 percent). The Wings weren't a whole lot better, going 9 for 32 (28 percent), but that was good enough to win. Cable led Firestone with 10 while Bloedorn had 11 for Goodyear. The game was played with no center jump, but that would be used again in game two.[45] In that game, Firestone built up a 20–14 lead at the half but faded in the second half and Goodyear won the game and the series 37–31.[46]

The Goodyear victory was a bitter pill for the Firestone squad to swallow since they had dominated Goodyear during the season, had a better overall record and Goodyear had lost one of their top players, Ray Morsadt, to an injury. The Non-Skids would be looking to 1938 to improve their club and go further in the playoffs. Meanwhile, Goodyear headed to Oshkosh to open the first finals series of the NBL. It would be a best of three series and it opened on February 28.

Game one found Goodyear surprising the All Stars at home where they had been nearly unbeatable 29–28. The coach of the Regulars, Lefty Byers, started his second unit in the games against the Non-Skids, the idea being that they would wear out the opposition's first team and then *their* first team would enter the contest and take control. It worked well against Firestone and against Oshkosh in the first game. The first team entered the game for Goodyear with three minutes left in the second quarter and the score Oshkosh 13, Goodyear 8. In those three minutes they made some slight progress against the lead, being down at the half by 15–12. After halftime the strategy of Byers kicked in as the Wingfoots outscored the All Stars 14 to 2 in the quarter on six of 12 shooting. With three minutes to go, the score was 28–22, but the All Stars, led by Edwards with four free throws in that span, cut the lead to 28–26 before Goodyear hit a free throw to make the last basket at the buzzer meaningless. The All Stars had outscored Goodyear 11–3 in the fourth quarter. It was the first home loss of the season for Oshkosh, which was led by Edwards with 13 points. Oshkosh shot eight for 60 from the field for 15 percent while

Goodyear was 11 for 40 for 27 percent. Bloedorn had nine and Ochsenhirt seven for the Wingfoots.[47]

Game two was in Akron on March 3 and was to be played after three high school games were contested and the gym cleared. To mollify the Goodyear fans, there would be entertainment in the Goodyear theater before the game, then the fans would be let directly into the gym. On the day of the game, Jim Schlemmer noted that Goodyear had overcome Morstadt's injury and triumphed through good team play, good coaching and, more importantly, good support from fans and the Goodyear executives. With a chance to win the title at home, Goodyear failed to capitalize and lost 39–31 to Oshkosh. Oshkosh led in every quarter, though Goodyear tied the game at 28 with six minutes to go. An All Stars spurt pushed the lead back to six and the final count of eight. Edwards had 16 and Preboski 12 to pace the scoring for Oshkosh while Ochsenhirt and Wes Bennett had eight and seven, respectively.[48]

Game three was back in Oshkosh and the All Stars suffered their second home defeat of the season as Goodyear claimed the first NBL title. The game was rugged with a second period fight between Wilson Fitts of Goodyear and Augie Vander Meulen of Oshkosh, leading to both being ejected. With the latter a starter and scorer for Oshkosh and the former only an occasional player, the loss was more for Oshkosh. Goodyear ran out to leads of 7–0 and 10–1 and led 24–13 at the half. Charlie Shipp's defense against Leroy Edwards held him to nine points and this was seen as a key to the victory. Shipp also led Goodyear with eight points in the 35–27 victory.[49] This ended the NBL season, but the All Stars had another series that began immediately after that, a five game series with the Rens to close the season.

Even as the *Daily Northwestern* reported the loss of the NBL crown, the games against the Rens were being touted as just as important to the Oshkosh team. "The fight for the championship in the National League meant a great deal to the All Stars and the series with the Rens is of almost as much importance."[50] Over the prior 16 games that these teams had played the record was eight victories for each with the All Stars winning the previous four. The series opened in Oshkosh on March 5 and then moved to Milwaukee for a game on March 6. The All Stars won both games 49–40 and 49–38. In the first game Preboski had 20 points while Edwards and Witasek had eight each. For the Rens, Johnny Isaacs had 15 points while Al Johnson and Wee Willie Smith contributed nine apiece. In the second game Edwards broke out for 19 with Augie Vander Meulen supporting that effort with nine points of his own. The Rens had three players with nine points— Isaacs, Johnson and Tarzan Cooper.

Three nights later the same teams met in West Green Bay, 125 miles north of Milwaukee. In this contest the Rens managed to eke out a victory in overtime by a 40–39 score. Edwards and Witasek had 15 and 8, respectively, but Vander Meulen missed the game because his Waupaca High School team was in the state district basketball tournament. For the Rens, Cooper had 15 and Bruiser Saitch picked up 11 points. From Green Bay the caravan rolled south to Fond du Lac, 50 miles south on the southern shore of Lake Winnebago for a game the next night. The All Stars returned to their winning ways, defeating the Rens 45–37. Edwards was unstoppable again with 21 while Preboski chipped in with 8. John Isaacs recalled that Tarzan Cooper used to tease Edwards when he went to the free throw line, betting him Cokes on whether Edwards would make the shot or not. It was just a little attempt to get Edwards thinking too much.[51] For the Rens, Smith had 11 and Johnson 10.[52]

The two teams played in Fond du Lac again two nights later in the close of the series and the Rens defeated Oshkosh handily 45–27. The game attracted 1600 fans, "the largest crowd for a little world series game," according to the Oshkosh paper. The Rens went with only five players and their scoring was very balanced. Cooper and Johnson had 11 each, Smith and Isaacs had eight each and Saitch had seven. Edwards had 13 for Oshkosh but the next highest scorer had only four. The *Daily Northwestern* printed the all time records for the Rens-All Stars games, showing the closeness of the contests over the three-year period. In 22 games Oshkosh averaged 43 points, the Rens 41. The loss made the All Stars record for the year 54–12, with a few contests still to go.[53]

The All Stars defeated a Stevens Point team, winning handily 60–27. Edwards got 27 points which gave him a total of 848 points in 66 games, a 13 points per game average. Three nights later Oshkosh defeated a team of College All Stars in Milwaukee by a score of 59–35 before 2500 fans. Jewell Young of Purdue, who would join the NBL the next year for Indianapolis, led the College players with nine. The next night the All Stars beat the collegians once again, this time by a 59–31 score. The 31 points scored by the collegians were matched by Edwards, as he also scored 31.

The league season was over, as was the Rens' series, but the new media interest centered around Edwards and his quest for 1000 points for the year. Against another collegian squad he got 25 points in a 67–38 victory in a contest played in Escanaba, Michigan, 150 miles north of Oshkosh. Rather than returning home, the All Stars were forced to spend the night in Green Bay because of tire trouble, a reminder of the travails that teams then faced.[54] Upon returning, the All Stars faced NBL foe Whiting, defeating them 63–54. Edwards had 24 on nine of 20 shooting with six of ten free throws. Wooden had 15, Kessler 11 for Whiting. The next night Oshkosh was in Marshfield, Wisconsin, 100 miles northwest, where they again met a collegian all-star team. In a 73–48 game, Edwards got 39 points on 16 field goals and seven free throws.[55] The next night in Eau Claire, Wisconsin, Edwards got 16 to pass the 1000 point mark for the season as the Oshkosh cagers won 45–32 over an Eau

Claire team. Two night later, the season finally ended for the All Stars with a 42–29 win over a team called the O'Brien Oilers. The victory gave Oshkosh a 62–12 record for the year and a three-year mark of 116 and 24, a percentage of .829. The year had been a fine one for the All Stars, Lefty Edwards and the NBL. The Oshkosh team was, truly, a state-wide representative as it played in no fewer than ten sites around the state. The only disappointment was not winning the NBL title, but that, too, would come in the future.

There was a strong feeling expressed in the newspaper and also in a commemorative magazine about the season, sold locally, that, despite the loss to Goodyear, the All Stars were the better team. Much was made of the dominance of the All Stars over the Rens for the previous two years and the fact that as the All Stars traveled around the country they were "billed as 'Western Professional Champions.'"[56]

This little magazine illustrated the place that the All Stars had in the life of the city of Oshkosh and their importance to the way the city viewed itself. "In New York City where many of the fans had not heard of the name of Oshkosh, they had read much about the All Stars."[57] The souvenir magazine had advertisements which were really just paeans to the All Stars and to Oshkosh. The banks of Oshkosh had a full page ad with a photograph of a skyscraper and a team photograph of the All Stars with text noting how Oshkosh had no "skyscrapers, roaring subways or seething millions." But it did have vitality and the basketball season, so they said, proved it.

> Oshkosh, the town, gratefully accepts the team as a publicity producing unit, one that has carried the city's name before thousands and thousands, the players animated and thrilling billboards advertising Oshkosh [sic]. A team that has emblazoned the city's name across millions of priceless headlines ... publicity that couldn't be bought at any price. A team that stimulates the city's drawing power, that bolsters its staying power ... that proves to the city's people all over again ... Oshkosh IS a city of opportunity.[58]

A column on page eight gave the same message and also claimed that the team "brought a substantial number of visitors into the city during the season.... These visitors spent money with local business men. Of greater importance commercially, it made them think of Oshkosh for entertainment."[59] The columnist (unnamed) also saw the All Stars making Oshkosh basketball-conscious, like Green Bay's Packers made that region football-conscious. Noting that it may be a coincidence, it was pointed out that in addition to the All Stars, the Oshkosh Teachers College won the southern division championship of the Teachers Conference, the Oshkosh High School tied for the Fox Valley High School title and the Oshkosh Vocational School won the state Vocational School title. Another column speculated on the future of the NBL and its members and finally there was a short piece advocating a new arena in the city. So for cities like Oshkosh, Akron and Whiting, the National Basketball League brought not only big league status, but many fringe benefits that served the entire community, things very much appreciated in a country entering nearly ten years of the Depression. How would that play out in the future? That, of course, remained to be seen.

The National Basketball League's Second Year: Movement Towards Stability

The new season for the NBL found an altered United States with concerns more international than national. To be sure, the Depression was still holding sway in the country, but there were indications that it had bottomed out, and there was slow but steady improvement in employment and production. Domestic in-fighting between the AFL and CIO centered around John L. Lewis, and suspected communists among his lieutenants. More prevalent in the media was the concern for a world heading into war, with various conflicts erupting all over the globe.

In September of 1938 the Munich Accords, brokered largely by British prime minister Neville Chamberlain, had allowed Adolf Hitler and the German army to occupy and annex the Sudetenland, a section of Czechoslovakia that bordered Germany. This concession was meant to ensure "peace in our time," according to Chamberlain, and there were reports of people along the French-German border celebrating that peace as the fear of war ended.

War continued in Spain as the Fascist forces battled the Loyalists. In December the Fascists allowed the deposed king, Alfonso XIII, to regain his citizenship, but this applied only in that area controlled by them and was seen as a ploy for outsiders to view the Fascists more moderately.

In the NBL, after the exciting and disappointing finish to the previous year, the Oshkosh All Stars and their coach, Lonnie Darling, were determined to take the last step in 1938-39, the step that would leave them alone as champions of the NBL. The prior year the All Stars had gone to the final game of the championship series before losing to the Akron Goodyears. Leroy Edwards, the league's scoring champion with more than 16 points per game, had been held to 9 in the deciding contest, and both Edwards and the All Stars wanted to erase this bad memory from their minds. In a similar manner, the Akron Firestones were also eager to reverse their fortunes from the previous year, especially in their own dealings with their crosstown rivals, the Akron Goodyear Wingfoots. The previous year, the Firestones had a better overall record and had beaten the Goodyears in the city series, but in the playoffs, the Goodyears had swept the stagnant Firestones in two straight contests. The season, then, would start with some deep grudges being held, ones that would be eased only by different outcomes at the end of the season.

The league, too, had issues, mostly financial, that had led to a contraction of the size of the circuit. The weakest squads the previous year had given up before the season ended, and they officially announced their intention not to return to the league shortly after that. These included Dayton, Columbus, Cincinnati, Buffalo, Fort Wayne and Kankakee. There was one addition to the league: the Sheboygan squad. Sheboygan was a city of 40,000 located on Lake Michigan, about 65 miles from Oshkosh, which was on the western shore of Lake Winnebago. The addition of Sheboygan set up a natural rivalry with Oshkosh because of both proximity and size of the two cities. The Sheboygan team had begun in 1933 as the Ballhorns, sponsored by a local florist and funeral parlor, and played under that banner for two years. The squad's sponsorship was then taken over by a local cleaners, owned and operated by Art Imig and the team was called, not coincidentally, the Art Imigs. For two years after that, the team competed as the Enzo Jels, sponsored by a local gelatin manufacturer, before finally incorporating as a team owned by a local syndicate of community members. During all this time the local team played touring squads like the New York Rens, the Original Celtics and the Terrible Swedes, offering them competitive games.

In October of 1938, Lonnie Darling of Oshkosh was elected president of the NBL and on December 31, the Sheboygan Redskins entered the league. The plan of the league was much more formal than it had ever been before. First there were to be two divisions (Eastern and Western). This was not new, but now each team had to play at least two games (a home and away game) against every team in the opposite division with at least that many against teams in the same division. The league would follow collegiate rules except that it would take five, rather than four, fouls to disqualify a player from a game. This was done to aid traveling teams with small squads. Most teams had 10–12 players available at home, but some took only seven or eight on the road to keep expenses down. In some non-league games the previous year, this had occurred a number of times and the foul rule was waived as players picked up six, seven or even eight fouls. The league also hired its own referees and they would be assigned to games by league commissioner Johnson.

The Season Opens

The league season opened on November 26. The All Stars had begun their play in mid–November against non-league squads, most notably the Globetrotters, who played a two game set in Wisconsin against Oshkosh. The Globetrotters were a top squad playing legitimate basketball with some free-lance clowning. They would not switch to an all scripted performance, with particular routines repeated each night, until the 1950s. The first contest was played in Oshkosh with the All Stars winning 44–30. Leroy Edwards had injured his knee in training camp and was to play little in the games. Nevertheless he scored 11 to lead the All Stars, backed by Pete Preboski's 7. High for the 'Trotters was Harry Rusan with 10, but his shooting was way off as he hit 4–24 from the field. In hyping the games, the *Oshkosh Daily Northwestern* noted that the Globetrotters had been 151–7 the previous year with two of those losses to the Oshkosh team.[1] In the first contest, played at Merrill Junior High (the home court of the All Stars with seating for 1200), the difference was free throws with the All Stars making sixteen of eighteen. The two teams met the next night in Waupaca, 50 miles northwest of Oshkosh, where the All Stars won in two overtimes 51–46. Edwards and Preboski had 18 and 16, respectively, while Rusan and Hood had 11. The high scorer for the 'Trotters, however, was Strong with 16 who also had six fouls. His six fouls were matched by Ford as the teams agreed to allow unlimited fouling. The games were such a success that a rematch was booked two weeks later in Cassville.

The next week the All Stars and Akron Firestones met in a four game exhibition series in four Wisconsin cities. In a series that foreshadowed the end of the season, the All Stars dropped three of the four to the Non-Skids. In Menasha, on the northern tip of Lake Winnebago, thirty miles north of Oshkosh, the Firestones eked out a 41–40 victory. Both Edwards and Ray Adams missed the game with knee problems but Preboski picked up the slack by pouring in 11 baskets and 24 points. Johnny Moir and Jerry Bush, two of the hot rookies that the Non-Skids had signed out of Notre Dame and St. Johns, respectively, led in scoring with 13 and nine. The next night the teams met in Antigo, 75 miles north of Menasha, and the Non-Skids again won 48–45, despite being down at the half 30–20. Ed Mullen, with a dislocated finger, joined Edwards on the sidelines. For the victorious Firestone squad, Jerry Bush and the third hot rookie, Paul Nowak (also from Notre Dame), each had eleven.

The next night the teams moved on to De Pere, near Green Bay, approximately 70 miles east and slightly south of Antigo. There, in the St. Norbert College gym, the All Stars finally won a game 37–19. Edwards returned and, according to the newspaper account, was "himself, although he still favors an injured knee"[2] as he led all scorers with 16 points. The last contest of the series was played in Fond du Lac, at the southern tip of Lake Winnebago, and the Firestones again triumphed 42–30 on the day after Thanksgiving. There were some comments that maybe the All Stars had overdone themselves at the dinner table the day before, leading to their off night. The team shot nine of 63 from the field (14 percent) with just three of 30 in the first half. Though sorry about the loss, the newspaper was pointing fans toward the game two nights later when the league season would open with the Pittsburgh Pirates visiting Oshkosh.[3] With five players from Duquesne, one from Pitt and one from Geneva College (near Pittsburgh), this was a squad with mostly local Pennsylvania talent, led by former Celtic Paul Birch.

The All Stars began the league season by humbling the Pirates 55–33 as Edwards had 20, Preboski 10 and Armstrong 9. Walt Miller had eleven and Paul Birch nine to lead Pittsburgh, but Birch's 4–29 shooting was certainly not an asset to his team. The rest of the week the All Stars played non-league teams, two of which were quite weak, comparatively, with the rematch against the Globetrotters ending the week. The All Stars played a local team in Montello, 40 miles southwest of Oshkosh, then a team from Menominee, Michigan (100 miles north), in Oshkosh, winning both easily, before meeting the Globetrotters again in Cassville, 150 miles southwest of Oshkosh on the Mississippi River. This was about equidistant for the Globetrotters to travel from their homes in Chicago. Before 600 fans, the 'Trotters won 37–31 with Harry Rusan leading with 14 and Edwards high for the All Stars with 9.

The Kautskys and the Goodyears

In Indianapolis the Kautskys opened against the defending champion Akron Goodyears. The Kautskys, like the Firestones, had added new players and were confident that they would be an improved team. Foremost among the additions was Jewell Young, All America performer from Purdue, and he was joined by his Purdue teammate Johnny Sines, an All Big Ten player. Jim Birr, a center from Indiana; Glynn Downey, another Purdue All America from 1935-36: Dave Williams, an All Indiana College player from Indiana Central; and Rex Rudicel, an All Indiana guard from Ball State, rounded out the newcomers. In the first league game, the Kautskys won 40–25 as Young had 15, Sines, 9 and Frank Baird, 10. The Goodyears, who altered their lineup little from the previous year, were led by center Wes Bennett and guard Wilson Fitts, with 7 each. Before 2500 fans, the *Indianapolis Star* sports editor noted only one "blemish" on the game and that was a tantrum thrown by Goodyear guard, Charlie Shipp after his fifth foul.

> [He] threw the ball at the unprotected head of the referee, the leather smashing directly into his face. What the rules are in this professional basketball

league we do not know, but we do know that in either baseball or football it would call for a heavy fine and suspension.[4]

Interestingly, the Akron account of the game failed to mention this incident and no punishment was noted either. Instead, the game was reported as one where the methodical Goodyear pace, which had been successful at keeping them in the game, was altered in the second half and "the Wings found themselves playing the Indianapolis 'race horse' offense and it was too bad."[5] Earlier the Goodyears had defeated Hammond 33–30 to open their season, but Johnny Wooden, "agile as ever, led the Indiana five with eight markers." This game also marked the league debut of Nat Messinger, a new referee, "imported from New York who proved sensational in his debut."[6] The losses continued to pile up for Hammond as they dropped 13 of their first 14 games and then traded Wooden back to Indianapolis (for Bob Kessler) where Wooden had begun his professional career. This was a factor, along with his knee problems and his family obligations, in hastening Wooden's retirement since he coached and taught at South Bend Central High School, only 50 miles from Hammond. The greater distance from Indianapolis (125 miles) caused Wooden to play less regularly (he played in just five league contests in the rest of the year) and he ended his playing career after the season.

December began for the Kautskys with the announcement of a new coach, Bob Nipper, former Butler star and a member of the Shortridge (Indianapolis) High School coaching staff. The Kautskys then headed to Akron for games against both Akron squads. The Goodyears defeated them 42–36 and the Firestones did the same 39–34 with the Non-Skids' spurt at the end sealing a victory after the game had been tied at 34.

The Kautskys returned home and played Warren five days later, winning 39–37 as Young had nine, and Sines and Baird eight each. The Penn Oilers were led by Bill Laughlin with 14, Walt Stankey with 10 and rookie Buddy Jeannette, from Washington & Jefferson College, with eight. The two squads played in Warren two nights later with the Penn Oilers winning 49–41. Oshkosh had trouble with Warren earlier in the week, losing 38–37 in overtime in a game where neither team shot well, but Warren shot better. The All Stars went 13–80 from the floor (16 percent) while the Penn Oilers went 15–51 (29 percent) to win the game. In addition the All Stars went five for 15 from the free throw line in the second half, highlighted by Leroy Edwards' five consecutive misses from the line.[7] The All Stars feasted on the House of David team right after that, winning 52–13 in La Crosse and 63–36 in Columbus, Wisconsin, and then met the Goodyears twice in Wisconsin.

The Goodyears were on a Wisconsin swing that brought them first to Sheboygan, where they defeated the Redskins 32–30. They then played the All Stars in Oshkosh on a Saturday and in Madison on Sunday. The first game counted as a league contest and the Goodyears won 30–26 before 1200 fans, "the biggest crowd to date." Then on Sunday, in a non-league game before 3500, the All Stars won 40–24. [8] The *Akron Beacon Journal* claimed 5000 were at the game. Earlier in the week the Goodyears had beaten Westinghouse Air Brakes (of Wilmerding, Pennsylvania) 29–16 in Akron as the Firestone Non-Skids defeated the South Bend Bendix squad (in Plymouth, Indiana) by a 49–45 score. Both teams played non-regulars a lot in these contests and Goodyear was led by rookie Floyd Ebaugh, while Firestone was paced by Paul Tobin and Glen Roberts. The Firestones went on to defeat Warren 45–32 on December 8 before defeating Pittsburgh 44–35 on December 14. In that game Birch had 17 for Pittsburgh while Moir led the Non-Skids with 14.

December also saw continued unrest worldwide. The Nazis, making good on their pledge to rid Austria of Jews by 1940, had allowed and encouraged one-quarter of the 300,000 Austrian Jews to flee the country. France sent troops to French Somaliland in an effort to curb Mussolini's efforts to gain control of this region of the world. At the same time Italy was involved with supporting the Fascists in the Spanish Civil War. In February the British tried political intervention in the Spanish conflict. The U.S. was fearful of impending war and the Congress allocated more than $400 million to increase American air strength to over 5500 warplanes. There was constant debate between the Congressional interventionists and the isolationists.

Mid-December saw the Firestones still undefeated in the league at 5–0 with Goodyear second in the division at four and two. In the west, Sheboygan had a four and two record while Indianapolis was two and two. The All Stars had played just two games in the league by December 13. The leading scorers for the league were Chuck Bloedorn of the Goodyears with 11.3 points per game, Walt Stankey of Warren with 11.2 and Bill Laughlin of Warren with 11.1. The defending scoring champion, Leroy Edwards, had a 10.3 average, fifth just behind Paul Birch's 10.5. [9] The New York Celtics came through Indiana that month, defeating the Kautskys in Kokomo, and the Ciesar All Americans in Hammond. The Kautskys played the Ciesars in between those contests, with Indianapolis winning in Hammond 44–33. Hammond was led by 11 points from Lou Boudreau (the Cleveland Indians' shortstop) and Vince McGowan's nine, while the Kautskys had Johnny Sines get 15 and Wooden 13. Indianapolis was virtually even with Sheboygan at this point in the Western Division, both with records just above .500. In the Eastern Division, Firestone had still not lost a league contest and Goodyear was nine and two, to remain close.

Indianapolis played Sheboygan in early January in a contest for the divisional lead. At Butler Fieldhouse, the Kautskys won 52–38 before 3500 fans. Jewell Young had 26 points and Wooden 13 while Babe Lautenschlager had 17 for Sheboygan. [10] The Redskins moved on to Hammond, where they defeated the home team 42–37, sending them to their fourteenth defeat in fifteen league contests. The Kautskys, meanwhile, played the Rens in Butler Fieldhouse and were soundly defeated by the traveling New Yorkers. "The visitors passed, shot and handled the ball with a varied attack which had the local professionals outclassed for a major portion of the time."[11]The visitors were led by "Pop" Gates, with 14, while Jewell Young had 10 to top Indianapolis.

Oshkosh had started the league season slowly and had played only three league games by mid–December. Nevertheless, the *Oshkosh Daily Northwestern*, which covered a number of league games, rather than just the All Stars' contests, expressed satisfaction at the league's success at that point. "(O)ne sixth of the 112-game schedule has been played and from the scores reported and the results, it has been shown that the National League took a wise step in strengthening the circuit and limiting each division to four teams."[12]

The All Stars were still playing more games against Wisconsin teams, as they had historically done, rather than league contests. They won at Superior and Phillips, Wisconsin, then, went to Oconto, Wisconsin, to defeat a team from Jordan College of Menomonie, Michigan. In late December the Rens came back to Wisconsin and played the All Stars in Oshkosh and New London, Wisconsin, on consecutive weekend days. *Oshkosh Daily Northwestern* hyped the game with features on the Rens and some cartoon depictions of the Rens' players. The games were always a good draw and this publicity only solidified that likelihood. On Saturday the two teams met in Oshkosh, where the All Stars played their best game of the season to date, crushing the Rens 59–37 behind 16 by Edwards and 15 from Scotty Armstrong. "Bruiser" Saitch had 16 and "Tarzan" Cooper 10 to top the Rens, who shot 14 of 76 from the floor. The All Stars had their best shooting night of the season with 24 of 70 (34 percent).[13]

The next day the teams met in New London, thirty miles to the north. Most likely both teams stayed in Oshkosh where the Rens could actually eat and find accommodations, unlike in many Wisconsin towns. In Oshkosh the Rens players felt almost welcome by the fans and citizens of the small city, according to Johnny Isaacs. The Sunday contest illustrated the resilience and stamina of the Rens, who were always on the road and were not discouraged by the blow out the previous night. Led by "Pop" Gates with 13, the Rens exhibited their trademark balance with Cooper again getting ten and Isaacs and Saitch eight each in the 43–38 victory. The All Stars were led by "Pete" Preboski's 16, but Leroy Edwards was held to five points. Often Edwards and Cooper would tangle in these games, but never in malice. Rather, they were both passionate, aggressive players who liked to win. It was not uncommon for Edwards to growl to Cooper, "Tarz, you're too rough," and for Cooper to respond, "Leroy, I got it all from you!"[14]

The All Stars were shaken a bit the next day when Augie Vander Meulen, one of the stalwarts of the team for seven years, announced his retirement. Vander Meulen was a coach and teacher at Beaver Dam High School, forty miles south of Oshkosh. He was 29 and the oldest player on the team. Despite the need for extra money to augment the Depression era teaching salary, playing for the All Stars had just gotten to be too difficult. Vander Meulen, a rugged 6'4", 190 pound former Chicagoan, had come to Wisconsin to attend Carroll College in Kenosha, then had coached in Waupaca while playing for the All Stars. He had begun skipping some away games, as some of the players would sometimes do, because of other employment demands, but now even home games were becoming a chore. Also announced that day were two new league rules, one to speed up the game even more and another to ensure the best teams, as advertised, would take the floor. The first rule was that the official would not handle the ball after a field goal. The second was that a fine would be imposed on teams which advertised big stars and then didn't have them when the team appeared for a game.[15]

The next day an article illustrated the hometown nature of many of the cities in the league and the closeness that the players felt to their adopted towns. The All Star team was entertained at the Knights of Columbus in Oshkosh at a Christmas party with gifts and lunch. The players were introduced and each gave a brief history of his career. The idea of this occurring in such a manner today is hard to fathom, what with appearance fees, agents and media demands, but at that time, the gesture was appreciated and very much welcomed by the players. The team returned to league action two nights later, defeating Pittsburgh 36–29, and sending the All Stars into first place in the division (a 2–2 record had them tied with Sheboygan at 5–5). Edwards led the team with 15, including nine of 13 free throws. Paul Birch missed the contest with the Pirates because of his high school coaching commitment.[16] The Pirates moved on to Sheboygan where the Redskins won on Christmas Day 43–38, led by Babe Lautenschlager's 15 and Paul Sokody's 11. Birch returned to the Pirate squad to tie Fortney for the team high in points at 11.

The All Stars closed out the calendar year with a loss to the Kautskys 51–46, a game in which John Wooden did not appear, despite being advertised to be there. It was not noted whether the Kautskys were, indeed, fined by the league for this transgression. Despite his absence, Indianapolis easily outshot the All Stars, who hit only 17–94 (18 percent) from the field. Jewell Young had 19 and Johnny Sines 9 for the visitors, while Edwards and Armstrong each netted 12. The year ended with Oshkosh at 2–3 in the league and still stalled. Indianapolis was at 4–4 and Sheboygan 7–5. In the East, the Firestones had still not lost a league game.

Picking up the Pace

The league season would accelerate much more as January began and the need to complete 28 league contests became more pronounced. In Akron the Firestones were beginning the year with eight games in the east, after ending the year with an easy victory over Hammond 60–34. The *Beacon Journal* was cautious in its expectations regarding the eastern swing since "officiating (in New York City) is distinctive, if not plain homerish," and also noted that the "holiday jaunt comes at a time when the players will miss a minimum of work. (Since) they will be away only four days."[17] The trip began with victories over two New York area squads, the Collegiate All Stars and the Yonkers Knights of Columbus. From there the Non-Skids went to Fall River, Massachusetts, where they defeated a local team 54–37. Two days later the win streak was ended by Kingston of the American Basketball League, reconstituted as a regional eastern league in 1933. Kingston would be the league champion that year as well as the next year. The Firestones returned to their winning ways in Rochester, defeating the Kodaks 42–25 as Cable had 10 and Moir 11. The Non-Skids closed their road swing with two league games, one in Sheboygan and one in Oshkosh with the latter being the closest win that Firestone had had in the league, edging the All Stars 46–44. In the easy Sheboygan victory (51–35) Cable (18) and Moir (13) again topped the scoring. In Oshkosh the trend continued with Cable picking up 16 and Moir 13, while Edwards had 18 to lead the All Stars.[18]

The Goodyears, meanwhile, opened the new year at home with a defeat of Buffalo, a former league member now playing as an independent. The Bisons were led by 21-year-old Al Cervi, former star at Buffalo East High School. Cervi did not disappoint with 14 points to take game scoring honors, but the Wings won 43–28.[19] The Wings then lost in Pittsburgh and won in Warren, setting the stage for the first Goodyear-Firestone clash of the year. As usual, this was a sellout, but the stakes were for more than just this game. Firestone had the monkey of last year's unexpected playoff loss on its back, so the victory was much more important to them. In addition they did not want Goodyear to be the team to break their league winning streak. In a tight game, Firestone edged Goodyear 43–41 as Cable (17) and Moir (10) again topped the scoring, followed by Charlie Shipp (10) and Chuck Bloedorn (9) of Goodyear.[20]

In the Western Division, Indianapolis began 1939 on January 2 with a resounding defeat of Sheboygan before 3500 spectators in Butler Fieldhouse. Jewell Young was spectacular with 26 points and fellow Purdue alum John Wooden followed with 13. Babe Lautenschlager had 17 for the Redskins. Two nights, later, however, the Kautskys lost in Pittsburgh on a Wednesday night, when they were without Wooden, Sines, Baird and top reserve, Dave Williams. They then returned to Indianapolis and prepared to meet the touring Rens on January 9, a Monday night. The game drew seven thousand fans, but the contest was never close as the Rens ran to a 47–33 victory. "The visitors passed hot, and handled the ball with a varied attack which had the local professionals outclassed for a major portion of the time."[21] Young had 10 and Sines 9 for the home team while Pop Gates led the balanced Ren attack with 14. On the 23rd of the month Oshkosh, on a two-game win streak, came to Indianapolis, where the Kautsky defense held the All Stars to 24 points in eking out a 25–24 victory. Leroy Edwards was held to two points as Preboski led the All Stars with seven. For Indianapolis, Johnny Sines had nine while Young was held scoreless. The victory seemed to bring the Kautsky squad back to life and they reeled off wins against Hammond and Pittsburgh. In the Pittsburgh game, Paul Birch was absent when he was unable to make flight connections in Columbus, Ohio.

The Kautskys traveled to Oshkosh, where they were routed by the All Stars 57–45. The South Philadelphia Hebrew Association squad (with a 17–4 record in the American Basketball League) was on a Midwest swing and slated to meet the Kautskys on February 6. The week before that game the Sphas defeated the Rens in Detroit and the Hebrews arrived in Indianapolis ready to play. This they did, as they stopped the Kautskys 43–34 before 2500 fans. Neither Young (1) nor Sines (4) did much damage as Jim Birr topped the Kautsky team with 12. For the Sphas, Lautman had 13 and Mike Bloom, former Temple star, had 11. The Kautskys were up next against Oshkosh, once again, this time in Butler Fieldhouse, with the winner becoming the leader in the division. Oshkosh had lost twice to Indianapolis before defeating the Kautskys the week before. The contest was heavily publicized in the Indianapolis papers and the game was highly anticipated to be a close contest. It was not. The All Stars were finally playing the type of basketball that they had the year before, and they defeated the Kautskys soundly 47–25. Leroy Edwards had 19 to lead all scorers, despite hitting only one of six free throws. He was backed by Armstrong's 14 and Preboski's 10. Jim Birr had 9 for Indianapolis.[22]

The Kautskys then met the two Akron squads, splitting the contests. In the first, played in Rushville, Indiana, 30 miles east of Indianapolis, the Kautskys topped the Goodyear Wingfoots 52–48 before 2800 fans. The game was doubly devastating for the Goodyear team because Chuck Bloedorn, their top scorer, left the game with a broken blood vessel in his left ankle, was hospitalized and lost for the season. In the game Jewell Young had 17 and was aided by Jim Birr's 12. For the Wings, Charlie Shipp had 12.[23] The Kautskys then were soundly defeated at home 64–40 by the Firestones, who had clinched the Eastern Division title the night before in Hammond. Al Bonniwell had 16 for Akron with Jack Ozburn netting 14. For Indianapolis, Johnny Sines had 14. Indianapolis, with a record of 11–12, was now 4 1/2 games behind Oshkosh at 12–8. With only the top team in each division playing in the playoffs, the Western title seemed settled. At this time, news of the first Professional World Tournament, to be played in Chicago March 26–28, appeared. The Celtics, Sphas, Rens and Globetrotters had agreed to play, along with the Jersey City

Reds of the ABL and five NBL squads—Oshkosh, Indianapolis, Hammond, Sheboygan and the Firestones of Akron. Two teams from the west were expected to round out the field.[24]

Indianapolis played out their league season with their final games being largely ignored in the local papers as the Celtics and Rens came through Indiana together, playing a series of games as they toured. In Anderson the Rens won 51–45. In Indianapolis the Celtics reversed the result, winning 36–33. Nat Hickey was out with a bad back, so Jewell Young of the Kautskys stepped into a Celtics uniform for the game. He ended up being the leading scorer with 13, which tied Bobby McDermott for game honors. McDermott, 25, had begun with the Celtics in 1936 and played with them until 1942 with a number of stop outs to play other places closer to home more regularly. The Rens had all eight players score but none had double figures in the loss.[25]

Oshkosh had put on a fine finish to their league season over the previous four weeks. After losing four league games in a row and falling to 7–8 on January 30, they reeled off five league victories in a row defeating Goodyear and Indianapolis in Oshkosh, the latter squad in Indianapolis, Sheboygan and Hammond. In addition the All Stars defeated the Newark (New York) Elks, a squad from Crystal Falls, Michigan, another from Whitehall, Wisconsin, and the Green Bay Packers in Oshkosh. The latter game was decided by a 60–36 margin.[26] At the beginning of the winning streak, Augie Vander Meulen returned to the team at the urging of Coach and General Manager Lonnie Darling. In the Hammond game on February 19, Vander Meulen scored in double figures with 10 to trail teammate Edwards and Lou Boudreau of the Ciesars who both totaled 13.

The last two league victories in the All Stars run were over Sheboygan. The first game in Fond du Lac was officially not a league contest, but a charity bout, and many players on both teams came down with the "flu" "from which they are expected to recover by next game."[27] Vander Meulen had 14 in the game while Babe Lautenschlager and Ed Dancker led the Redskins with nine each. In the next contest the All Stars won by 13, with Edwards picking up 16, Preboski 14 and Paul Sokody 13 for the Redskins. Fighting marred the game, but the officials, Jim Enright of Chicago and Jack Norris of Dayton, managed to finally get the game under control after the police were called in to clear the floor of spectators.[28]

The All Stars then went on the road and dropped contests to Hammond, the Akron Firestones and Cleveland before righting themselves with victories over the Goodyears, the Firestones and Sheboygan, twice, to finish 17–11 in the league. The defeat of the Firestones, before a record crowd of 2200 in Oshkosh, was only the second Non-Skids loss in league play and foreshadowed a rugged playoff series which would pit the Firestones against the Western Division champions, the All Stars. Pete Preboski led Oshkosh with 19 and shot nine of 16 from the floor. Jack Ozburn had 16 for the Non-Skids with eight of 13 shots converted. (The *Beacon Journal* credited Preboski with 17 and Ozburn with 14.[29]) Distressing to Akron was the shooting of Al Bonniwell (zero for nine) and Jerry Bush (zero for ten).[30] The All Stars closed the regular season with two games against Sheboygan in Stevens Point, 50 miles to the northwest of Oshkosh, and in Antigo, forty miles farther north, the next night. In the latter game the All Stars inserted George Svenden, the athletic director at Antigo High School and a former All Star player, into the lineup and he responded with eight points from his center position. Leroy Edwards had 11 to lead the team while Paul Sokody and "Moose" Graf, in his only game of the year for the Redskins, each had eight.[31]

The Firestone Non-Skids, after beginning the season with 17 consecutive wins, coasted to the Eastern Division title with a 24 win and three loss record, 10 1/2 games better than the Goodyears and the Cleveland White Horses (who had moved from Warren in February), both of which fashioned records of 14 wins and 14 defeats. Along the way, the Firestones became "the greatest drawing card outside of collegiate basketball," a very telling remark, indeed. This statement was made shortly before a game in Cleveland, where 11,000 viewed the Firestone victory, with seven thousand of those tickets being purchased by White Motors (the Cleveland owner-sponsors) and various Firestone plants.[32]

The only pleasure in a disappointing Goodyear season (the poorest Goodyear record in the last decade[33]) was when they were the team to end the Firestone win streak at 17, with a 40–37 victory in mid–February. The loss made the Non-Skids 17–1 in the league and 34–3 for the year.[34] Before meeting the All Stars in the League Championship, the Non-Skids played three games against the New York Renaissance. The first, played in Fort Wayne, Indiana, resulted in a 49–43 Firestone win, noted as only the fifth defeat for the Rens in 100 games that season. Willie Smith led the Rens with 11 while Johnny Isaacs followed closely with 10. For the Non-Skids, Al Bonniwell had 17.[35] In the next contest, played in Indianapolis, the Rens won 28–26 with Bonniwell and Isaacs tying for scoring honors with eight each.[36] The final contest was played in Akron and the Non-Skids added Chuck Chuckovitz from the University of Toledo to their roster for the game as the regulars got a bit of rest. Chuckovitz ended up leading the Non-Skids in scoring as they lost to the Rens 39–27. Cooper, Bell and Saitch all had nine for the Renaissance.[37]

The NBL Championship Series opened on March 14 in Akron. The Non-Skids had finished the year with a record of 44–4 (24–3 in the league) and the All Stars had finished 31–15 (17–11 in the NBL) but had played much better in the second half of the season. The games in Akron were played in Goodyear's gym, which had a capacity of 4000, rather than the Firestone floor, which accommodated only 1700. Tickets were 40 cents for general admission,

60 cents for reserved seating. Thus, the house take would have been no more than $2000 if the game were a sellout.

Championship Series

Game one of the series was unexpectedly easy for the Non-Skids, especially since the All Stars had beaten Firestone in their last encounter. The *Beacon Journal* noted,

> The All Stars failed so miserably in offensive work that many times their shots didn't even hit the backboard. They played as though under impression there was a rule prohibiting follow up shots.[38]

Considering that the series had been hyped as pitting two of the biggest teams in basketball with "Oshkosh averaging slightly more than six feet four inches, while Firestone's average is only half an inch less," this was pretty embarrassing for Oshkosh, and particularly "Lefty" Edwards, who still led the team with 12. For Akron, Johnny Moir had 15. The next contest was also played in Akron, but the All Stars came out a much tougher team and scored an upset victory 38 to 36. The *Beacon Journal* saw the loss as largely due to biased reffing on the part of referee Nate Messinger. Referring to Leroy Edwards as "Messinger's boy," James Schlemmer cried that "when Edwards apparently was driving his elbows deepest into the men guarding him, Messinger called fouls on the latter, for preventing Edwards from going entirely through them, and when the Non-Skids so much as made contact with Edwards he called fouls on them for holding."[39] Edwards, not surprisingly, was the leading scorer with 17. Bush had 10 and both Moir and Ozburn nine for Akron. Shooting percentages favored Akron as they went 13 for 51 (26 percent) and Oshkosh 14 for 76 (18 percent), but the extra bucket was the difference as both teams had two free throws.

The series shifted to Oshkosh two nights later and the Non-Skids regained the edge with a 40–29 victory. Shooting was even worse in this contest as Oshkosh was eight for 77 (10.4 percent) while the Non-Skids were 16 for 62 (25.8 percent). Edwards had seven and Armstrong six to lead the All Star scoring while Jack Ozburn and Soup Cable topped Firestone with 15 and 11, respectively. The Non-Skids were a win away from keeping the title in Akron (though in a different clubhouse) and the All Stars were a loss away from continuing the frustration of barely losing out on a title. The next night, March 18, the All Stars tied the series with a 49–37 win. The Akron writers saw the referee as the factor, as in game two of the series.

> There were charges made by parties accompanying the Akron team that referee Nat Messinger again served as Edwards' guardian. His tactics allowed Edwards almost unhampered freedom.[40]

With the help of Messinger, Edwards went for 25 points, more than half the All Stars' total. Moir and Ozburn had nine each for the Non-Skids. The All Stars shot better (though it would be hard to call it well) as they went 18 for 73 (24.7 percent) and the Non-Skids shot much more poorly (12 for 73, 16.4 percent). The last game was played on March 20, meaning that the Firestone team had been in Oshkosh for at least three nights and probably four, unless they were able to catch a late train to Milwaukee and on to Chicago and Cleveland. The Firestone team was eager to get home and wanted to leave on a win, which they did 37 to 30. Before 3000 fans (capacity was 2800) Firestone succeeded in shutting down Leroy Edwards for the second year in a row in the deciding game. Edwards was held to nine by Jerry Bush and a series of double teams. He was two for 14 from the floor.[41] The rest of the team shot a similar percentage (10 for 73 which is 13.7 percent), while the Non-Skids were twice as accurate with 13 of 44 from the floor (29.5 percent). Cable had 11, Ozburn 10 for Firestone and Herm Witasek 11 for Oshkosh.

Akron players hurried home and back to work in the plants. The All Stars prolonged their season, first with three games with Sheboygan. This was another tour designed to take the game to parts of Wisconsin and the region. The first was played in Crystal Falls, Michigan, 150 miles north of Oshkosh, followed by a contest in Ashland, Wisconsin, 100 miles farther to the north and west on Lake Superior. The last exhibition was back in Sheboygan after which both squads headed to Chicago for the first World Professional Basketball Tournament played at the 132nd Infantry Armory with the semi finals and finals in the Coliseum. The tournament's commissioner was George Halas with Nat Holman as the honorary referee.[42]

World Professional Tournament

Eleven squads were entered in the invitation-only tournament, with only the Wisconsin teams representing the NBL. The Sphas were to be in the tournament, but cancelled because of injuries, and their spot was taken by the Illini Grads. In the first round, both NBL teams won — Sheboygan 47–29 over the Illinois Grads of Champaign and Oshkosh 40–33 over the Clarksburg (West Virginia) Oilers. According to the Oshkosh paper, "the All Stars were inspired by four former members rooting for them on the bench — Branch McCracken, now Indiana University coach; Bud Foster, coach of the University of Wisconsin; "Feed" Murphy and Bill Mangan. Also Coach Ruck (sic) was there watching."[43] Adolph Rupp, of course, had been Leroy Edwards' coach for his year at Kentucky and Leroy scored 18 to lead his team. Other teams entered included the Globetrotters, the Fort Wayne Harvesters, the New York Yankees, the House of David (Benton Harbor, MI). Three teams received first round byes— the Chicago Harmons, led by Bob Neu (De Paul's captain for the recently completed season), Vince McGowan of the Hammond Ciesars and Willie Phillips; the New York Celtics and the New York Rens. Before a crowd of 8,000, Sheboygan defeated the Celtics in the second round 36–29, with the Rens and Trotters also winning. Oshkosh received a second round bye. In the semi-finals, played in the Chicago Coliseum before 8,000 fans, the Rens defeated the Globetrotters 27–23 and the All Stars beat their old friends from Sheboygan 40 to 23. Frank Linskey had 12 to lead Oshkosh and Paul Sokody 10 for the Redskins.

The victories by the Rens and the All Stars set up a final for two teams with a long and involved history of playing each other. In 1935-36, the Rens had won the season series three games to two. In 1936-37 the All Stars had taken four of seven games and the next year six of eight. For 1938-39, the teams had split two games, so this was the real rubber match. In the game for third place, the Globetrotters defeated Sheboygan 36–33. In the final, the Rens tri-umphed 34–25 for their 110th win of the year (against seven losses). The game was played before 3,000 fans and the winners took home $1000 — total, not per man. The box score is below

New York Rens	FG	FT	PF	PTS
Gates	4	4	2	12
Cooper	1	3	5	5
Smith	2	2	5	6
Bell	1	2	0	4
Saitch	1	0	4	2
Clayton	0	0	0	0
Isaacs	2	1	1	5
	11	12	17	34

Oshkosh All Stars	FG	FT	PF	PTS
Adams	0	0	4	0
Preboski	1	1	0	3
McGroarty	0	0	0	0
Armstrong	2	3	2	7
Cafone	0	0	0	0
Edwards	3	6	3	12
Linskey	1	1	3	3
Witasek	0	0	5	0
Mullen	0	0	2	0
	7	11	19	25

The season ended for the All Stars much as it had the season before, a close loss in the NBL final plus the added wrinkle of a loss in the final game of the World Professional Tournament. The frustration was mounting for the Oshkosh team, and the hopes were, again, for that elusive title in the 1939-40 season. The league's eight teams had been stable, other than the move from Warren to Cleveland in February. New young players had entered the league and only one player (Milo Shoun of the Firestones) was over 30. There were teams that had difficulties. Cleveland and Pittsburgh still were striving for a better fan base and Hammond and Indianapolis were losing media interest, which could only result in declining fan interest. For the two Wisconsin and two Akron franchises, the fan and media interest remained strong and they would be the foundation upon which the league continued to build.

Changing a Bit, Staying the Same: The 1939-40 Season

The 1939-40 season for the NBL saw a number of changes. In the world, there was the beginning of World War II with Germany's invasion of Poland. The United States would not enter the war for two more years, but the feeling of impending war appeared throughout the newspapers frequently and this would affect the NBL in the next few years as players enlisted to join the war effort. The United States and the world were coming out of the greatest economic depression that had ever hit the country, but there was still high unemployment, and wages were low. Some players were able to make a living playing pro basketball, but most still held some other position such as coaching and teaching that allowed them enough flexibility to maintain their jobs, yet still play basketball regularly in order to get extra income. In the NBL were the two Akron teams that employed their players in the Akron rubber industry, but these were the only teams left still employing their players in this manner.

Akron continued to be the champion of the league, although the banner had switched from Goodyear to Firestone. Oshkosh had won the Western championship once again, only to lose in the finals to the Firestones. These teams would seem too strong, once again, but they would be challenged by new entrants. Both Pittsburgh and Cleveland left the league but were replaced by teams from Chicago and Detroit, belying the hometown image of the league.[1] Detroit had retained Gerry Archibald, the former Warren and Cleveland coach-manager, and he put together a top squad, drawing players from the American Basketball League on the East Coast, his former Cleveland team and young players signed after graduating from college. Detroit had the

The 1939-40 Firestone Non-Skids. Left to right: Paul Nowak, Jack Jennings, Harry Sorensen, Irv Tergesen, "Soup" Cable, Jerry Bush, Johnny Moir, Bob Hassmiller, Jack Ozburn, Tom Wukovitz, Tommy O'Brien, Fred Beretta. (Dick Triptow personal collection.)

potential to be very competitive in the league. Chicago was, once again, the Bruins and owned by George Halas (the owner of the Chicago Bears and a founder of the National Football League), as had been the case in the 1920s when he had owned a team with that name in the American Basketball League when it was a true national, rather than a regional, league. The only relationship that this team had to the old Bruins was the fact that they retained the same name and owner. They signed a number of young players from powerful college teams, many of whom were from Chicago colleges. The old formula of signing top local players in order to draw fans initially was being followed

by the Bruins. Though a big city, there were the same hometown character-
istics being emulated.

The defending champion Firestone Non-Skids had signed a number of
young players over the previous two years and their squad remained virtually the same for the 1939-40 season. The Goodyears, after a disappointing
.500 record in the league the previous year, had altered their roster signifi-
cantly. Only Chuck Bloedorn remained on the team from the previous years
and he was no longer a starter. Ray Morstadt and Floyd Ebaugh were now
starters and three new players— Ben Stephens, Howard Vocke and Gene
Anderson — joined the squad in starting roles.

Oshkosh had also shaken up their roster with only Edwards and Witasek
back from the starting five. Gone were Preboski and Armstrong, the former
having left the league and the latter joining Indianapolis, as well as Frank
Linskey, who had joined the Bruins. In their places were veteran Charley
Shipp from the Goodyears and two rookies— Lou Barle and Connie Mack
Berry. The Oshkosh team also had weathered a financial crisis. In April the
team had sold shares of stock valued at $25 each in order to raise $10,000. In
financial statements, the team indicated that the costs of running it were $1755
per month, $7020 for the season. Total expenses were $15,983 and receipts
were $15,265, a net loss for the season. In order to provide sufficient capital
for operation, it was necessary to sell shares. [2] In another action, Lon Darling,
the Oshkosh general manager and coach, was named president of the NBL
for 1939-40.

Oshkosh began their non-league season in November, playing around
the state of Wisconsin against local teams. They began the NBL season at home
against the Akron Goodyears, before 1500 fans, in their home court, Merrill
Junior High School gym. Unlike some years, Leroy Edwards began the season ready to go and played all 40 minutes of the opener, but the Goodyears
won 39–33. The Goodyears shot better (12–38, 32 percent to the All Stars'
12–70, 19 percent) and made 15 of 19 free throws for the difference. Jim Montgomery and Bill Lloyd had 10 each for Akron, while Witasek and Pederson
led Oshkosh with 8 each.[3] The All Stars continued their rough start with
losses to Detroit, the Goodyears and the SPHAs (non league), before finally
winning on December 4 over Clarksburg, though it was not until December
17 that they won their first league game over Detroit.[4]

The other Wisconsin team, the Sheboygan Redskins, had pretty much
the same roster as the previous year, but they looked to improve after the year
of playing together. The two Indiana teams were headed in the wrong direction. Indianapolis had lost Jim Birr, who formed his own pro team and did
regional touring; John Wooden, who had only played in five league games
the year before; Glynn Downey and Herm Schussler. Ernie Andres was a fine
addition at guard, but the center was George Chestnut, who had returned to

the squad after playing for them two years before. The Hammond Ciesars, the worst team in the league the prior year, had added Bobby Neu and Chuck Chuckovitz and made 22-year-old Lou Bourdreau their coach. Neither the play nor the coaching ever really gelled.

Play Begins with Eternal Optimism in New Cities

In both Detroit and Chicago hopes were high and both teams began their seasons with victories. Detroit defeated Indianapolis 44–40 in the opener with Buddy Jeannette and Urgel Wintermute, a rookie from NCAA champion Oregon, scoring 12 and 10 points, respectively. The Kautskys were led by Homer "Tarzan" Thompson, from Crawfordsville, Indiana, and the University of Kentucky, with 16 and Scotty Armstrong, the former Oshkosh All Star, with nine.[5] In Chicago the emphasis was on former local college players, but a key signee was Eddie Oram, former captain (1937) at USC and a starter on the MGM AAU team that lost in the national finals the year before. Oram, a 6'3" guard was seen as a great passer, defender and coach on the floor who would lead the team. The other starters were from Loyola and DePaul. Frank Linskey (DePaul) was 27 and had been playing pro ball for five years, most recently with Oshkosh. Willie Phillips, also a former Blue Demon, was only 5'8" but lightning fast and a deadly shooter. The real excitement, however, was focused on the two former Loyola stars, Wibs Kautz and Mike Novak, who had led Loyola to 21 straight victories before losing in the finals of the National Invitational Tournament in Madison Square Garden to Long Island University. Kautz, a 6' guard who could shoot and drive, and Novak, a 6'8" center who could score inside and liked to shoot a two-hander from the outside, were seen as the keys to the Bruins. Novak had an uncanny knack of being able to guide the ball into the basket on its downward flight, as well as being able to block the ball on defense on its downward flight. Both were legal at the time, but Novak's talent caused the league later to change the definition of goal-tending.[6]

Home court for the Chicago team would be the 132nd Regiment Armory located at Madison and Rockwell, about two miles west of the present Chicago Stadium. The building could accommodate at least 5,000 fans and was easily accessible by public transportation. The team would play 28 league games (as would all squads, with each team playing the others four times, two home and two away) and the excitement in Chicago was evidenced by the fact that the media coverage was excellent. The *Chicago Tribune* assigned a reporter to the team and the fan attendance was high. This was to be the first professional league basketball team in the city since 1931 when the old Bruins were part of the American Basketball League that folded that year in the midst of financial losses. The new league and team had changed its character, as the *Tribune* writer noted, in that "pro basketball is now as collegiate as professional football."[7] In their first game, the Bruins did not disappoint, defeating Oshkosh 28–19 before a crowd of 3,000. The All Stars were a notoriously slow starting squad, since Leroy Edwards inevitably began the season in terrible shape. He often hurt his knees or simply could not keep up in early games, a pattern that he had followed since his professional years had begun. In the opener he was held to zero points. Charley Shipp, the former Goodyear star from Indianapolis, had seven to lead the lethargic All Stars. Kautz had 11 for Chicago and his former Loyola teammates, Novak and George Hogan, both had seven to give Loyola alumni 25 of the 28 points.[8]

The Bruins won their next two games, both at home, and were the early leaders in the Western Division at 3–0. The second victory was over the Detroit Eagles, who had started out as the Eastern Division leaders at 5–0. The Bruins cooled the Eagles off with a ten-point victory before 2500. The *Tribune* tried to play up the grudge factor in the contest since the Detroit team had Irv Torgoff, the former LIU star, whose team had topped Loyola the year before in the NIT finals. Kautz was the star with 20 of the 34 Bruin points while the Eagles's Nat Frankel, from the ABL's Kingston team of prior years, had seven. "The game also signaled the return to local pro basketball of Umpire Nat Messinger, who combines the best features of a tobacco auctioneer, hog caller and cheerleader in his assessment of penalties."[9] This was the same Messinger who had been seen by some in Akron as Leroy Edwards' protector.

Articles on the Bruins were common both on games days and throughout the week. It was also noted, that the Duffy Florals, the team that had entered the Midwest Conference in 1935-36, played only five league games, but was allowed into the playoffs which they won to become the league champion, were still in existence. Apparently the *Tribune* reporter either did not recall this or did not consider the Midwest Conference a professional league, judging by his comments of the 6th of December. Nevertheless the Duffy Florals were around and playing at the Chicago Teachers College gym at 68th and Normal Avenue. One of their starters was Glynn Downey (Purdue, '37) who had played the year before for Indiana and was now on Hammond.[10]

Meanwhile the Bruins were preparing to play the Firestones in what would be Chicago's third straight victory. Two thousand seven hundred turned out to cheer Mike Novak's 14 points, scored despite the pummeling he took from the Akron team, as they "belabored Novak about the ribs throughout the game."[11] Jack Ozburn led the Firestones with 12.

In the Eastern Division, Detroit, as noted, had started off 5–0. The Firestones could not match their stellar start of the year before, losing to Indianapolis, Sheboygan, Hammond and Chicago in December. The signing of rookie Ernie Andres from Indiana University by the Kautskys proved to be astute, as he led the team in scoring in the second game and maintained his scoring leadership throughout the year. Andres had 12 in the victory over the Firestones while Homer Thompson had 11. Howard "Soup" Cable got 12 and Jerry Bush eight for the Akron squad. Akron then traveled to Hammond, where they were beaten by the Ciesar All-Americans 52–47 as Chuck Chuckovitz, the All-American from Toledo, had 17 points. Unfortunately for Hammond, this would be an atypical night for Chuckovitz in his rookie year as he averaged only six points per game. Indianapolis, meanwhile, entertained Sheboygan at Butler Fieldhouse and was a most ungracious host, edging the Redskins 37–34 behind Johnny Sines' 10 and Jewell Young's nine points. Dancker and Adams had seven apiece for Sheboygan.[12]

The next Kautsky contest would be against the Akron Goodyears, whose roster had a number of former Big Ten players with whom Indianapolis fans would be familiar. These included Gene Anderson, captain and center from Purdue the prior year; Ben Stephens from Iowa; Jack Nagode from Northwestern and William Fox, a 20-year-old who had played at Ohio State. The Goodyears also had a new coach, Ray Detrick. The Goodyears humbled Indianapolis 31–17, with Andres getting nearly half the Kautsky points (8). For Akron, Stephens had 12 and Jim Montgomery, another rookie, from Villanova, had 10.[13]

The Eastern Division leaders, the Detroit Eagles, entertained the Western Division leaders, the Chicago Bruins, on December 26 in Detroit. The Eagles triumphed, as Nat Frankel topped them with 14 and Irv Torgoff 11. Mike Novak had 13 for the Bruins, who then traveled to Indianapolis to face the Kautskys. *The Indianapolis Star* referred to the Bruins as a "giant cage team" because of the presence of Novak (6'9") and two nonstarters, Tony Carp (6'7") and Elmer Johnson (6'4"), as well as a 6'3" guard (Eddie Oram).[14] In the game, played on the 27th, Novak did overwhelm recently re-signed George Chestnut and Homer Thompson, both of whom picked up four fouls covering Novak, who dropped in 17 points in a 41–33 Bruins victory. Johnny Sines had 13 for the Kautskys and Wibs Kautz had 12 for the Bruins. The Bruins' victory put them back over the .500 mark and kept them the marginal leaders in the West. The standings at the start of 1940 were:

Eastern Division		*Western Division*	
Goodyears	6–3	Chicago	4–3
Detroit	8–4	Sheboygan	6–5
Firestones	5–4	Oshkosh	4–6
Indianapolis	3–7	Hammond	1–5

Ben Stephens of the Goodyears led in scoring with 109 points followed by Frankel of Detroit with 95 and Mike Novak with 80.

The Bruins began the new year in Chicago, against the Goodyears, and the Chicagoans won by a 37–30 margin, with Frank Linskey leading the way with 14 and Kautz following with 10. For the Goodyears Ben Stephens had 10 on 10 of 12 free throw shooting, as 46 fouls were called. Akron shot 14 of 25 while the Bruins barely topped 50 percent with 11 of 21.[15] This facet of the game would prove to be their Achilles heel later in the season. Four nights later Sheboygan came to Chicago and defeated the Bruins, 20–19, in what Charles Bartlett referred to as "the wildest contest Bruin fans have witnessed all season, each unsuccessful attempt for a field goal culminating in a football pileup." Despite the rough contest, Bartlett noted that the play "proved quite pleasing to the 2500 fans who attended."[16] The margin of victory was decided by free throws, as the Redskins were eight of 12 and the Bruins three of 15. Both teams were horrid at times from the floor, with Sheboygan going one for 30 in the first half and Chicago not scoring at all for the last 15 minutes of the contest.

The next Bruins foe would be the Kautskys, but before that contest, the Indianapolis team played the New York Rens in Butler Fieldhouse before a crowd of 2500. In a spirited contest, the Rens edged the Kautskys by two points. Tarzan Cooper had 15 to lead a balanced Ren offense while George Chestnut led Indianapolis with 14. Ernie Andres contributed 10. The Kautskys then traveled to Chicago, where they topped the Bruins in another tight contest decided by free throw shooting. Indianapolis was excellent with 19 of 23 free throws while the Bruins continued their awful charity-tossing with a five of 18 mark. The only bright spot for Chicago was the emergence of a new star, Stan Zadel, another rookie from Loyola, who had seven points off the bench to back Novak (13) and Linskey (12). Jewell Young topped all scorers with 16. Wibs Kautz, who had been having shooting problems, was benched in place of George Hogan. George Wilson of the Chicago Bears, who'd not played competitive basketball since high school, was a new signee. Having George Halas as the owner of both teams made Wilson's signing that much easier to accomplish. (Wilson, of course, continued to play for the Bears and, after that, coached the Detroit Lions and Miami Dolphins in the 1950s and '60s.) The Bruins continued their stumbling a few nights later, traveling to nearby Hammond and losing 34–33. Mid-January saw the Bruins tumble to third at 5–6, 2½ games behind Sheboygan's nine wins and five losses. In the East, Detroit led at 10–6, with the Firestones in second with a 7–5 slate.

Chicago played the Eastern Division-leading Eagles on January 17 and won, while solving their free throw problems, to a large degree. The Bruins canned 12 of 22 charity tosses (Detroit was 14 of 18) in the 36–28 victory. Wibs Kautz broke out of his scoring slump and led the Chicago team with 15, followed by Novak with 11. Irv Torgoff, the former LIU star, had eight for Detroit followed by Frankel's seven. That same evening the Kautskys topped

Oshkosh at Butler Fieldhouse, before 2,000 fans, by a 44–40 score. Ernie Andres and Jewell Young had 15 and 13, respectively, for Indy, while Charley Shipp and Leroy Edwards paced the All Stars with 12 and 11 points.[17] The Bruins headed to Wisconsin where they defeated the Redskins 45–37 and lost to the All Stars 53–43. In the first contest, Lautenschlager led all scorers with 14, while Novak and Kautz had double figures with 12 and 11 for Chicago. In the latter contest Leroy Edwards led with 13 and Kautz had 11 for Chicago.[18] The Bruins now had seven wins and seven defeats, halfway through the league season. After defeating Hammond a few nights later, the Bruins had moved back into second in a crowded Western Division race, behind Oshkosh's 9–7 record and just ahead of Sheboygan at 9–9. In the East Detroit had opened a two game lead at 12–7 over the Firestones at 9–6.

The Indiana teams continued to hold down the cellar in the two divisions. The Kautskys played and lost to Oshkosh in Jeffersonville, Indiana, a Louisville suburb, 75 miles south of Indianapolis. They then returned home to upset the Firestones 52 to 46. Despite the surprising victory, the Kautskys had begun to lose the media's interest. For the remainder of the season the Kautskys received only minimal coverage from the *Indianapolis Star*, mostly scores without game accounts or box scores, as high school and college basketball swept the pro coverage off the sports pages. An exception was January 25 when the paper reported on a triple-header played in Butler Fieldhouse before 6,000. The Kautskys lost 42–39 to Detroit, with rookies Wintermute and Torgoff pacing the Eagles with 12 and 9 points, while Indianapolis rookie Andres led his team with 12. The big game, however, was between two top Eastern teams, the SPHAs and the Rens. In a one sided contest, the Rens won 34–21. "Puggy" Bell had 12 and "Pop" Gates had 11 for the Rens, while Mo Goldman led the SPHAs with 10.[19] Later in the month the *Star* covered the Kautskys' loss in Hammond, because there were two Indiana participants, but gave as much coverage to Jim Birr's All Stars who also played that evening.[20]

The Bruins continued to hang close in the Western Division race and the *Tribune* continued to lionize their play through the reporting of Charles Bartlett. In touting the Bruins's next home contest at the 132nd Armory, Bartlett focused on the play of Leroy Edwards.

> Edwards got off to a bad start. In the first four games he made only three baskets. He played into shape and is going at a fast clip. In the last six games he has 92 points—15.3 per game.[21]

The Bruins topped Oshkosh, but Edwards led all scorers with 18 points and was praised by Bartlett. "He favors the pivot and hook shot so much that last night, none of his seven field goals originated in a two handed facing effort." The victory, before 3500 spectators, moved the Bruins back into first place. Zadel and Novak had 11 each for the Bruins.[22] The next weekend the

Bruins defeated the Firestones 40 to 34 while Oshkosh beat Indianapolis and Detroit edged the Goodyears. Oshkosh then went to Hammond, where they were upset by the Ciesar All Americans 37–36 in a contest decided at the free throw line. The All Stars made 12 of 17, but Hammond made 13 of 17 for the final margin of victory. Edwards continued his hot scoring with 18 points while Bobby Neu had 13 for Hammond. [23] The standings as of February 5 looked as follows:

Eastern Division			*Western Division*		
Detroit	14	7	Chicago	10	7
Firestones	10	7	Sheboygan	12	9
Goodyears	10	11	Oshkosh	11	10
Indianapolis	7	15	Hammond	5	13

That evening the Bruins lost to the Goodyear Wingfoots in Akron. The Bruins were without Eddie Oram, their coach on the floor, who would miss the next two weeks with an ankle injury. Oram's defense and floor leadership were sorely missed, as the Bruins lost badly. Ben Stephens and Gene Anderson, the Big Ten rookies, were the only players to get double figures (13 and 11, respectively) in the contest. Two nights later the Bruins faced the Firestones in Chicago and, again, the *Tribune* provided the hype, focusing on owner George Halas and his intended actions during the upcoming contest.

> The contest is expected to be so tight that co-owner George Halas will come down to the sidelines from his regular grandstand seat five minute before the end of the game. Heretofore George has not downed his best shouting uniform until the final three minutes. [24]

Despite the additional exhorting of Halas, the Bruins could not overcome the continued absence of Oram and lost to the Firestones. Howard Cable had nine for Akron while Novak led the Bruins with 15 of their 33 points. [25] The Bruins dropped their third contest in a row, this time to Sheboygan 38–35, before defeating Hammond in Indiana 35–31. With the victory, the Bruins moved back above .500, behind Sheboygan's 13–9. In the East, Detroit continued to have the league's best record at 16–7 with Firestone in second at 12–8.

Returning to the 132nd Armory the Bruins lost to the Goodyears before 2500 fans, despite Wibs Kautz' 17 points. Stephens led Akron with 13 in the 37–34 contest. That same night (February 14), the *Star* covered the Kautsky contest once again and, once again, it was because of their facing Hammond as part of a Butler Fieldhouse doubleheader. In the first game the Jim Birrs lost to the Chicago Crusaders, an African American team from Chicago. The Kautskys then lost 48–41, despite 21 points from Ernie Andres. [26]

Later that week, Sheboygan topped Oshkosh to move into a more solid position as Western Division leader. Rube Lautenschlager, the leading scorer for Sheboygan all year and a product of Oshkosh State Teachers College, led with 14. Leroy Edwards remained unstoppable, as he had 21 points with 11 free throws, but it was not enough as the Redskins won by six.[27] Hammond got a rare victory, defeating Goodyear 48–35.

In Chicago there was anticipation of Eddie Oram returning and the Bruins playing well again. Sheboygan, the next Bruin opponent and the division leader, chartered a special train for its fans to travel to Chicago, 125 miles south, to attend the February 21 contest.[28] Before 3800, the Bruins defeated the Redskins 41–34. Kautz had 18 and Stan Zadel eight for the Bruins. George Hesik had nine and Paul Sokody eight for the Redskins.[29] Sheboygan then traveled to Indianapolis, where the Kautskys hurt the Redskins' divisional hopes by defeating them 44–40 while Oshkosh was beating the Bruins in Wisconsin 57 to 41.

The Western Division race was so tight that the Bruins needed to win every game to stay in the playoff picture, which would include only the top two teams from each division. The Bruins played the two weakest teams and won, beating Hammond 31–27 and Indianapolis 50 to 34, while Goodyear was defeating Oshkosh 42 to 35. In the Hammond game, Willie Phillips paced the team with 8 markers, but in the Indianapolis contest, the familiar tandem of Novak (16) and Kautz (13) led the scoring, helped by Oram's steady floor play. In addition, Oram coached the team in the absence of Coach Sam Lifschultz.[30] Three night later, the bubble burst when Detroit, which had lost to Hammond and the Firestones in the past week to fall from first to second in the East, defeated the Bruins 56–53. Novak (19) and Kautz (18) were again the offense while Detroit was led by Bernie Opper's 19.[31]

The final standing saw the All Stars tie the Redskins for the Western Division title at 15–13 while Chicago finished 14–14. In the East the Akron Firestones had come on strong to pass fading Detroit and win the division with a record of 18–9. Detroit finished at 17–10. The two divisional leaders would meet the second place squads in their own divisions in the playoffs.

In the West Oshkosh pounded Sheboygan in Oshkosh 41–24 to take the best of three series lead. Charlie Shipp had 10 and Edwards nine to lead the Stars.[32] The teams then moved the fifty miles to Sheboygan and Eagles Hall ballroom (capacity 1200) where the Redskins won 43–42 before Oshkosh edged them in the final game of the series by winning 31–29. Before Game Two Lon Darling announced that "the Board of Directors of All-Stars, Incorporated would present $50 to the squad—$5 to each of the team members as bonus for the victory."[33] This must have been quite an incentive.

In the East, the defending champion Firestones had coasted to the finish after defeating Goodyear on February 23 by a 46–36 margin.[34] The Non-Skids then played reserves for the last three games in preparation for the playoffs. In the first playoff game, in Akron, Firestone topped Detroit 48–35. Jack Ozburn scored 25, while Frankel led the Eagles with 14.[35] Detroit won game two in Detroit 49–37 before Akron ended the series in Akron by winning 46 to 35 in a game marred by 34 fouls, but highlighted by Ozburn's 20 markers.[36] This set up an NBL Finals with Oshkosh and the Akron Firestones for the second year in a row. This would be a best of five game series.

The first two games were in Oshkosh. In the first, the All Stars won 46–37 behind 20 by Edwards on eight of 29 field goal shooting.[37] In the second they triumphed again 60–46 as Edwards had 16 points. The Akron writers had predicted that Edwards and his play would be the key to winning the rest of the series as the two teams traveled to Akron. "The big center uses his elbows to advantage — and if he is allowed to operate as he wants, is a tough man to stop — by legal means or foul."[38] In Akron, the Firestones won 35–32, despite great adversity as described by Jim Schlemmer.

> Their reflexes are off. They found it difficult to hold onto the ball at times. They were under pressure all the way; groggy half the time from being hacked, tripped, outrassled ... and still they won.[39]

Ozburn had 11 to lead the Non-Skids while Berry (14) and Edwards (13) led Oshkosh. The next night Akron repeated, with a 41–40 victory to tie the series, despite what the Akron writers continued to see as referee bias toward the All Stars and Edwards. In the last minute of the game Oshkosh was down to only five eligible players, "seven if you count the officials as many fans were inclined to do."[40]

Then on March 16, in Kent, Ohio, rather than Akron, the Firestones edged the All Stars once again 61–60, and repeated as NBL champions. The game was in Kent because the Firestone gym was inadequate for the number of fans, the Goodyear gym was unavailable and the Kent gym could accommodate more than 2000 spectators. In this final game Edwards had 16 to lead all scorers, with Berry (14) and Barle (12) also in double figures. For the victorious Non-Skids, Moir had 15, Cable and O'Brien 13 each.[41]

On that same day Shipp, Edwards and Cable were named as first teamers on the NBL All Star team selected by the coaches and writers. They were joined by Kautz of the Bruins and Stephens of Goodyear. Even with that honor, this latest loss was even harder to take for Oshkosh than the previous year's since the All Stars had held a 2–0 advantage in games, then lost three in a row by a total of five points. The Oshkosh faithful were beginning to feel cursed. Though they were now looking forward to next year, once again, there was still the National Professional Tournament, now in its second year, at the 132nd Armory in Chicago, the Bruins' home floor.

The Bruins were one of three NBL teams that accepted invitations to the tournament, which began March 17, the same day that the National AAU tournament opened in Denver with 56 teams, including the defending champion Denver Nuggets, the Phillips 66 Oilers, the San Francisco Olympians and the Twentieth Century team of Los Angeles.[42] Fourteen teams comprised the Pro Tourney field with the Syracuse Reds and the Washington Brewers drawing byes in the first round. The Bruins added Vince McGowan of the Hammond squad to their roster and defeated the Fort Wayne Harvesters 45–27 in the first round. Kautz and Novak led with 12 and 11, and McGowan chipped in with six. Sheboygan followed with a 44–32 victory over the Rochester Seagrams, with Wilmeth Sadat-Singh and Bob Stewart, both recent Syracuse University stars, in their lineup. The former later played with the New York Rens before his unexpected death while on a military training flight in 1943. Sadat-Singh and Stewart both had nine in the loss while Sheboygan was paced by Otto Kolar's 18 and Paul Sokody's 10.

In Game Three, the Harlem Globetrotters, playing predominately out of Seattle at that time, topped the Kenosha Royals (a hybrid of Kenosha and the Hollywood MGM team) by a score of 50–26. The 'Trotters had three players in double figures—Bernie Price with 14, Babe Pressley with 13 and Sonny Boswell with 12. In another game, the Rens had little trouble in defeating the Canton Bulldogs 42 to 21. Puggy Bell had 13 and Johnny Isaacs 10 to lead the Rens. The last two games saw Waterloo (Ohio) defeat Clarksburg (West Virginia) Oilers and the Oshkosh All Stars cruise by the House of David from Benton Harbor, Michigan, 42–22.[43]

The second round saw the Bruins edge the Western Division champion All Stars 40–38 in overtime, aided by the home court advantage, which included 9,000 fans, the largest armory crowd ever. Wibs Kautz had 24 points to lead all scorers, while Charley Shipp led the All Stars with 12. Leroy Edwards had nine. The Syracuse Reds knocked out the other Wisconsin squad, the Redskins, 38–30, and the Washington Brewers defeated Waterloo 35–21. In another tight contest, the Globetrotters edged the Rens 37–36. Sonny Boswell scored 19 for the 'Trotters with Puggy Bell leading the Rens's scoring with 11.[44] There was criticism for placing the two African American teams in the same bracket for the second year in a row, ensuring that the finals would not have two black teams. This seeding may have been done to prevent that, but the brackets also were arranged so that two NBL teams could not meet in the finals.[45] It would not have been unusual to create bracketing that would allow for a black-white final since the biggest crowds were always found at such encounters. Nevertheless, the closeness of the games did not make it seem extraordinary to have the brackets as they were.

The semifinals were the next day and the Bruins defeated Washington 46–38 while the Globetrotters beat the Syracuse Reds 34–24. The Bruins were, again, led by Wibs Kautz, who had 24 points, followed by McGowan's eight.

The 'Trotters got eight from Pressley and Duke Cumberland, as well as seven from Price. Thus, the Bruins would play in the finals of the World Pro Tournament, capping their up-and-down first year. The Globetrotters spoiled the romantic ending for the Bruins, edging them 31–29 to claim the Pro Tournament title. Sonny Boswell had 12 for the 'Trotters and Mike Novak seven to lead Chicago. Wibs Kautz was held to five points. The Bruins were hurt by Vince McGowan's inability to play in the game.[46]

The World Professional Tournament added to Oshkosh's frustrations for the year, but buoyed Chicago's hopes of a title for 1940-41. Both Firestone and Goodyear looked to be in good shape for another run at the NBL title the next season. There was concern whether all the teams would continue in the league the next year with the two Indiana teams the most likely candidates to withdraw. Nevertheless, the league had been extremely competitive, had drawn generally good crowds in at least six venues, two new squads had pumped additional life into the league and a number of rookies had made an impact on play.

The league champion Akron Firestone Non-Skids had repeated and edged the Oshkosh All Stars. Yet the league had some significant changes, most notably the loss of Pittsburgh and Cleveland, but the additions of Chicago and Detroit as league entrants. Most teams looked financially viable; for the NBL, things were looking up.

5

Wisconsin Rhapsody: The 1940-41 Season

The fall of 1940 looked better for the American economy as the United States continued to move out of the Great Depression. The world stage, however, was decidedly glummer as the war in Europe was in its second year. The British had survived the Nazi air strikes and won the Battle of Britain, but the British needs were still great since the Germans occupied most of Western Europe and affected England's ability to obtain and trade goods. President Roosevelt's Lend-Lease agreement of March 1941 with Prime Minister Churchill would be of monumental importance, but it also provided more indication that it was simply a matter of time before the United States might be forced to enter World War II. A number of Americans were enlisting in Canadian or British military services and this included some professional athletes. Still, the war was only an ominous threat in November 1940, and NBL professional basketball was of heightened interest to the fans of the Midwest.

The 1940-41 season was almost all Oshkosh from the beginning of the year until the World Professional Tournament in Chicago in March. Despite some disappointment at the end, this was the year that the Oshkosh faithful had waited for since the All Stars had begun playing in the mid–1930s. During the off-season, both Indianapolis and Detroit had decided to leave the NBL, turning an eight team, two division league into a six team circuit. Indianapolis decided to play as an independent and some NBL teams would engage the Kautskys during the season. The Detroit Eagles returned to the league in November. They had left because they had no venue in which to play, but that situation was finally resolved and the league swiftly revised the schedules to accommodate a seven team circuit with each team playing two home and away series with the other six teams for a total of 24 league games. The playoffs were to pit the first and third place finishers in one series, while the second and fourth place finishers would meet in the other series, with the winners playing for the championship. The Detroit franchise had attracted new backers and a new coach. The former included a banker, an auto dealer and a Chrysler Motors Corporation executive. The new coach would be Henry "Dutch" Dehnert, the former Original Celtic player.[1]

All of the NBL teams began play in November against various non-league opponents. A number of the NBL's players were not joining their teams immediately because of the initiation of a new all-star game that pitted the collegiate all stars from the prior season against the champions of the World Professional Tournament from the previous March, the Harlem Globetrotters. These rookies included Bill Hapac of Illinois and Stan Szukala of DePaul, both of whom would be playing for the Chicago Bruins; Bob Carpenter of East Texas and Scoop Putnam of Tennessee, signed by Oshkosh; Ed Sadowski of Seton Hall and Bob Calihan of Detroit, both contracted by the Detroit Eagles; Ralph Vaughn of Southern Cal, signed by Hammond; and Jay Pelkington of Manhattan and Marv Huffman of Indiana, both for the Akron Goodyear squad.

The All-Star game, played in Chicago Stadium on November 29, 1940, drew over 20,000 spectators. A preliminary game saw Oshkosh defeat the Chicago Bruins 31–24, despite Lefty Edwards being out with an injured knee and Connie Mack Berry absent while still playing football for the Cleveland Rams. In the feature attraction, Stan Szukala tossed in a long shot at the buzzer to give the collegians an upset victory 44–42 over the Globetrotters.[2] The collegiate all stars then dispersed to their respective professional teams, although the league season had already begun.

Oshkosh began the season with five exhibition games, including two against the Globetrotters, and won all five. In the Globetrotter games played in Oshkosh and Edgerton (about 125 miles south of Oshkosh, just north of the Illinois border), rookies Bob Carpenter and Scoop Putnam led the All Stars in scoring as they both hit for double figures twice. Bernie Price was high scorer for the Globetrotters in the 52–39 and 51–41 games.[3]

The league season began on November 27 with the All Stars defeating Goodyear soundly by a 44–27 score. Edwards was still out and Putnam and Witasek had 12 points each, while Ben Stephens led Akron with seven. The shooting was unimpressive, with Oshkosh going 15 for 59 from the field for 25 percent while Akron could manage only 9 of 59 shots successfully for 15 percent.[4]

December found all the league teams finally in action. The champion Firestones lost to the SPHAs in Philadelphia in a tripleheader evening of basketball. The Phillips 66 Oilers defeated the Penn Athletic Club 46–33 and Kate Smith's Celtics edged the Rens 25–22 in the other contests.[5] The next night the Akron Goodyear Wingfoots topped Hammond by 16 points in Hammond, a bad start for what would be Hammond's last year in the league, a year in which they again finished last in the league. Hammond was led in scoring by rookie guard Ralph Vaughn who would not finish the season in Hammond. Goodyear was scheduled to motor up to Wisconsin to face the Sheboygan Redskins in an exhibition game in Manitowoc, but "heavy snows made the highways all but impassable."[6] Such were the difficulties of a professional league in the upper Midwest in winter with minimal snow removal equipment available. The Firestone Non-Skids, meanwhile, continued their Eastern exhibition swing with another loss, this one to the New York Jewels, before 2500 fans in New York. The Akron newspaper report noted "unusual' circumstances that contributed to the loss. These included "a slippery floor, used for a dance prior to the game and American league rules, which prevent 'screening'.... This cost Firestone possession of the ball no less than 19 times (and nullified three baskets)."[7] In a game where no shot clock was yet considered, possession was vital and turnovers were even more costly than today, so it was no wonder that the Skids went down to defeat. In their return to Akron, they finally played a league contest, defeating Detroit by six points as Tom Wukovitz, another former Notre Dame player on the roster (John Moir and Paul Nowack were the others), led the team with 13 points, followed by Moir's 12. For Detroit, largely fielding a new squad, Ed Sadowski from Seton Hall had 13 while Buddy Jeannette had 11.[8]

Firestone went on to Hammond where they lost to the Ciesars. That same weekend Oshkosh downed the Ciesars to remain undefeated in the league. Lefty Edwards was still favoring his knee and rookie Bob Carpenter, playing in place of Edwards, was leading the All Stars in scoring. The All Stars continued to Akron where the two local squads entertained Detroit and Oshkosh in a doubleheader. The All Stars won handily over Goodyear 43–30 with Edwards and Witasek leading with eight points apiece, followed by a trio of players with seven each. Ben Stephens had eight for Akron. In the second contest Detroit edged the Firestones 34–33. Detroit had signed an aging Rusty Saunders (at 34 he was the oldest player in the league) who had battled Dutch Dehnert and the Original Celtics in the late 1920s in the old ABL. As the new Detroit coach, Dehnert felt Saunders could still play and help with the Eagles. Jim Schlemmer of the *Akron Beacon Journal* had this to say: "Big Rusty Saunders, looking older than his years, heavier than ever before, coached the Eagles from the floor and bigger Dutch Dehnert of the old Celtics, coached them from the bench."[9] Two nights later the All Stars defeated the Firestones 37–32 to remain undefeated for the year. Goodyear went to Philadelphia where they played Washington in the first game of a doubleheader. The Wingfoots lost 33–31 before 6,000 fans, but Ben Stephens led all scorers with 19 points. The Wingfoots returned home to top Hammond with Stephens getting 18.[10]

In Chicago, the Bruins had started slowly once again. Because their court was being remodeled, the Bruins did not play their league opener until December 18. They opened with high hopes. Bill Hapac from Chicago Heights and the University of Illinois would add to the Chicago flavor that George Halas and his co-owner, Bill Bidwell, felt would attract the fans to the Armory. Hapac joined Ray Adams from DePaul, who had been an all-league forward with Oshkosh in 1938-39 and was the De La Salle High (of Chicago) coach; Vince McGowan, who had played at DePaul in the 1930s; George Hogan, Wibs Kautz and Mike Novak from Loyola and Coach Frank Linskey, also from DePaul. The Bruins opened with a victory over the Non-Skids, as the former Loyola teammates, Novak and Kautz, accounted for 12 and 11 points, respectively. Jerry Bush had 11 for Firestone. A crowd of 2500 went home happy, and the Bruins motored up to Sheboygan where they defeated the Redskins the next night 27–20.[11] Barely a month into the season the All Stars and Bruins were undefeated with four and two league victories. Firestone at 1–5 and Hammond at 1–6 were at the bottom of the league. Ben Stephens led the league in scoring with 78 points in 6 games (13 ppg).

The Bruins split home and home games with Hammond, losing in Indiana 41 to 33 and winning in Chicago 50 to 46. In the two games Ralph Vaughn had 19, then 9 for the Ciesar All Americans, while Novak led with nine in the first game and Kautz tossed in 21 in Chicago. The Bruins then traveled to Akron for two contests against the local squads there to end the calendar year. The Akron teams quickly set Chicago back with Firestone winning 46 to 45 and Goodyear edging the Bruins 40 to 38. These close losses were a great disappointment to the Bruins and would be remembered in March when the Bruins missed the playoffs by one game. In the Firestone game, Novak and Kautz were again the offensive catalysts with 16 and 15, respectively. Jack Ozburn and Jack Jennings both had 13 for Akron. In the Goodyear game, Kautz and the rookies, Szukala and Hapac, all had eight points for Chicago while Howard Vocke and Marv Huffman had 13 apiece for Akron.

The Oshkosh All Stars finished 1940 without a loss (not counting the previous season, of course), closing the year with wins over Sheboygan and Detroit. As the new year began, the standings in the league were as follows.

Team	Wins	Losses
Oshkosh All Stars	6	0
Goodyear Wingfoots	5	3
Sheboygan Redskins	6	4
Detroit Eagles	3	3
Chicago Bruins	3	4
Firestone Non-Skids	2	6
Hammond Ciesar All Americans	2	7

The New Year and the Rush for Second Place

The All Stars had a lead that they would never relinquish, but there would be a struggle for the remaining playoff spots over the next two months. Early in the year Sheboygan claimed one position with victories over the Bruins in Chicago and over Goodyear 40–31. The Redskins were led by Dave Quabius with 11 points and Otto Kolar with 10. Jake Pelkington and Howard Vocke topped Goodyear with eight and seven, respectively. Goodyear then traveled to Oshkosh where they practiced on the junior high court, which the All Stars used as a home court. The Goodyear familiarity might have been helpful, but the All Stars still triumphed to remain undefeated in the league at 7–0, and for the season with 18 victories. The 35–33 win was not a hot shooting affair, though the newspaper account called the Goodyear field goal percentage good. (It was nine for 45, a 20 percent mark.) Huffman and Stephens both had 10 for the Wingfoots. The home All Stars got three more baskets, but took 30 more shots (12 of 75 for 16 percent).[12]

Oshkosh continued to set the pace for the league, winning their 22nd game in a row and their eighth NBL contest on January 11 against the Bruins in Oshkosh. Erv Prasse from the University of Iowa led the team with 10 points in a game played before 1900 fans. The next night the All Stars had their winning skein snapped in Hammond by losing to the Ciesars 43–32. Clem Ruh from USC, who scored 77 points in his only year in the NBL, picked up 16 of them in this game.[13] Despite the loss, Oshkosh, at 8–1, maintained a sizeable lead over Sheboygan (7–5) and Goodyear (6–7). After the loss the All Stars continued south to Indianapolis where they lost to the Kautskys 42–41, then defeated the same team in Muncie, 40 miles east-northeast of Indianapolis. The trip was not easy as "icy driving conditions slow(ed) travel to 20 miles per hour."[14] The difficult weather continued as only one of the two team cars made it back the next night for an exhibition against the Rens in Marshfield, Wisconsin, 300 miles from Muncie. The All Stars played with six players but still managed to top the Rens by a 43–24 margin. Bob Carpenter had 18 and Connie Berry had 10 for the All Stars while Sadat-Singh had 9 to lead the Rens.[15]

Sixty years later, Erv Prasse, one of the six All Stars to make it to Marshfield for the game, still remembered the conditions. He noted that Lon Darling was driving his Cadillac and was nervous about the icy roads so he and his "crew" detoured into Chicago and stayed at the Morrison Hotel. The other car was driven by Herm Witasek and had Prasse, Berry, Barle and Carpenter. Prasse recalled that Witasek was a very good driver and drove all night to get to Marshfield. Then, with just the six players, they routed the Rens as "every shot we threw in the air went in."[16]

In Akron, the Goodyears continued their bumpy season with a loss to

Hammond, following the loss to Oshkosh on January 5. In the former game Pelkington and Stephens led the Wingfoots with 17 and 11 points, respectively. The defending champion Non-Skids, who had started the season with losses in six of their first seven league games, began to turn things around. After an exhibition win in Clarksburg, West Virginia, against the Oilers, the Firestone team defeated Sheboygan, then defeated the Goodyears 44–36 to even the city series for the year. In that contest, the Firestones got balanced scoring from Moir (11), Wukovitz (11) and Ozburn (8), but lost Jerry Bush with a compound fracture in his finger which was supposed to sideline him for the remainder of the year.[17] Interestingly, Bush was back in the line-up in a week, either proving his toughness, the wonders of medical science or the inaccuracy of the seriousness of the injury (or maybe all three!). The Non-Skids were also buoyed by the return of Howard Cable, who had retired at the end of the 1939-40 season but was lured back in mid–January.

The Non-Skids continued to improve with two more wins against Detroit 48–42, and a non-league contest against the SPHAs as part of an Akron doubleheader that drew 3,000. Goodyear defeated Detroit in the other contest. The Wingfoots then defeated the Bruins in overtime in Chicago. In the latter game Pelkington and Stephens again paced the Wingfoots, while Kautz and Adams were the leading Chicago scorers. At this point of the season, the league's leading scorers were as follows:

Ben Stephens	Goodyear	13.0 ppg
Ralph Vaughn	Hammond	11.2 ppg
Ed Sadowski	Detroit	9.3 ppg
Wibs Kautz	Chicago	8.7 ppg
Tom Wukovitz	Firestone	8.4 ppg
Jake Pelkington	Goodyear	8.4 ppg

Though Kautz was a leading scorer, Mike Novak's production had slipped. Neft et al. claimed that this was because the addition of Hapac, who liked to play inside, had forced Novak outside where he was less effective. Stan Szukala disagreed. He said that Novak liked to do hook shots in the paint, but wasn't forced outside by Hapac. He said that Hapac mostly shot outside the lane, but did rebound and get points on put backs. Szukala also noted that Novak, despite his size, had good foot speed and set up the fast breaks. Thus, his drop in scoring was less about being forced to the outside and more about the Bruins spreading the scoring around more. The millstone of the previous year, poor free throw shooting, continued to plague the Bruins in the 1940-41 season and Szukala conceded that the Bruins "were not good on free throws."[18]

After the loss to the Wingfoots, the Bruins lived up to their previous free throw reputation in a loss to Detroit 45–43. The Eagles made 15 of 17 free throws, while the Bruins hit five of 13 to spell defeat for Chicago. Kautz had 20, Szukala 12 and Hapac eight for the Bruins while the Eagles were led by Buddy Jeannette and Bob Calihan with 11 each.[19]

The season was at its hottest as Oshkosh prepared for three tough games on the weekend of January 18–19. On that Saturday night the All Stars hosted Firestone, a team that had beaten them for the title the previous two years and now was starting to play well once again. In a "rough game all the way," according to the *Akron Beacon Journal*, Oshkosh edged the Non-Skids 45–43. Leroy Edwards topped the All Stars with 10, including eight for eleven from the free throw line. Ozburn had 14 for the Non-Skids. The game was decided at the line, where the All Stars were 17 of 23 and the Non-Skids 15 of 24 for the final two point margin.[20] The All Stars motored the short distance around Lake Winnebago to Sheboygan for an afternoon game on Sunday against the second place Redskins. Led once again by Edwards with 10, the All Stars defeated Sheboygan by a 34–29 score. They then drove halfway home to Fond du Lac where they met the touring New York Renaissance in a Sunday night game. Once again, Oshkosh was triumphant by a score of 45–37. This was the usual Rens squad—fast, intelligent and seasoned, a squad that would claim a record of 128 wins and 22 losses for the year.[21] The All Stars played a number of players and Tex Mueller and Bob Carpenter led them with eight each while Wilmeth Sadat-Singh had 18 and Puggy Bell eight for the Renaissance. The game drew 900 fans to the local high school gym.

Halfway through the league season the All Stars held a commanding lead with 10 wins and one loss, but the battle for second was still in doubt. Sheboygan was eight and six and Goodyear was eight and seven. Three other teams had seven losses, but only five wins. Oshkosh traveled to Chicago on January 22 to meet the Bruins. The Bruins were eager to return to their home floor where the backboards were rectangular rather than fan-shaped, which they saw as a factor in their recent inaccurate shooting. The *Chicago Tribune* began hyping the game three days before the contest. The day before, they had noted that Edwards had been injured much of the early part of the year. They also noted that "the playing strength of the Oshkosh quintet can be gleaned from the fact that the team has won nine and lost one despite the fact that Edwards was used sparingly until the last two games."[22] The game lived up to the hype. Before 4,000 fans at the Armory, the Bruins closed with a rush to hand the All Stars their second league loss 34–32. Bill Hapac had 11 and Wibs Kautz 8 for the Bruins. Lou Barle and Erv Prasse had nine and eight for the Oshkosh five.[23]

The game inspired 3500 fans to return to the next Bruins's home game where they saw Sheboygan fall to Chicago by a 31 to 22 margin. Wibs Kautz had the flu, but Mike Novak and Bill Hapac carried the scoring load with 14 and eight points. The next night in Sheboygan the two teams met once again, but the Redskins edged the Bruins 31–28, although Novak and Hapac again led the Bruins in scoring with 14 and six. Clearly the two players could co-exist with no detriment to the Chicago squad. At this point, the battle was for third with Goodyear at 10–8, Chicago 7–8 and Detroit at 7–7. Earlier in the week, Detroit and Hammond had engaged in a much faster-paced game in Detroit. The halftime score was 42–21 and the final score, 61 to 52 with Detroit winning. Five players scored in double figures. Detroit was led by Bob Calihan's 19, Ed Sadowski's 16 and Buddy Jeannette's 11 while Dar Hutchins had 16 and Bobby Neu 13 for Hammond.[24]

Wibs Kautz returned for the February 5 game against the Goodyears, a must win for the Chicagoans. Bill Hapac responded by scoring a season record 25 points to satisfy the crowd of 2500 as the Bruins won 42–41. Jake Pelkington had 11 and Ben Stephens 10 for Akron.[25] The victory closed the gap on third for Chicago as the Bruins were 8–8 to Goodyears's 10–9 with Detroit still at 7–7. Sheboygan was 10–8 and second while Oshkosh led with an 11–3 mark. Firestone seemed out of the running at 7–10. Hammond sank deeper into the cellar with five wins and 13 losses. The Firestones had lost some tough non-league games recently, 39–38 to the Indianapolis Kautskys in that city, then a loss to the Kate Smith's Celtics in Memphis before 4300 fans. The Celtics were led by Bobby McDermott with 14, while Tom Wukovitz topped the Firestone five with 12.[26] They then came back and beat the Kautskys in Bedford, Indiana, 66–53 in a game that saw five players from the two teams score in double figures. Firestone then went to Chicago where they beat Sheboygan as part of a doubleheader at the 132nd Armory. The Bruins defeated Goodyear in the second contest. The successes, however, were too few for the Firestones as they stumbled at Hammond, losing 41–38 to the Ciesars. Howard Cable, a month out of retirement, led the Akron team with 11 points and Tommy Wukovitz chipped in with 10. Hutchins and Vaughn led the victorious All Americans with 12 and 10, respectively. The Non-Skids now had eleven losses and with only six more league games scheduled, it looked like the defending champions would not even make the playoffs, let alone repeat as champions.

The Goodyear Wingfoots also were fading, as the season drew to a close. On February 8, they were edged at Detroit 41–40, then, fell at home to Oshkosh three nights later by a 40–36 score. This was their fourth loss in a row and there were expressions of concern in the newspaper account of the game. Then the Bruins also began losing and the Firestones started finally playing like defending champions. They defeated the Bruins in Chicago to close within a game of them as they both battled with Goodyear for the last playoff slot. The Non-Skids then went to Sheboygan and Oshkosh and won both games, before returning home to defeat Hammond on February 18. The loss to the Non-Skids was particularly disheartening to the Bruins as they allowed Firestone to score 12 points in the last two minutes and disappoint 3,000 Chicago fans in the Armory. Goodyear then knocked off the Bruins three nights later, winning in the last minute 41–38. Bill Hapac and Wibs Kautz both scored 15 for the Chicagoans, but Mike Novak was out of the lineup. The Goodyears were topped by their usual duo of Stephens and Pelkington.[27]

That same week Oshkosh officially clinched the NBL title with a 64–45 victory in Hammond against the Ciesar All Americans. Leroy Edwards had 16 and Herm Witasek had 14, while Bobby Neu of Hammond matched Edwards's total. Edwards was finally injury-free and rounding into top form for the playoffs. In his next game he scored 16 once again, this time against the New York Rens as the All Stars edged them in overtime in Fort Wayne, Indiana. Sheboygan had opened a one game lead in second, but three teams— Detroit, Firestone and Goodyear — were all at .500 and tied for third, a game behind Sheboygan. Chicago was two games back and George Halas made one last effort to help his team enter the playoffs. He purchased Ralph Vaughn from Hammond in what was "believed to be the biggest cash outlay (for a professional basketball player) since Halas purchased Nat Holman when he (Halas) held a franchise in the old American Basketball League."[28] Vaughn had been dismissed from the team the week before over economic and disciplinary issues and there was a rumor that he would sign with Firestone. Vaughn stated that he didn't plan to sign with any other NBL team for the remainder of the year, stating that "he does not believe it would be quite the sporting thing to do."[29] Vaughn had played well and scored well in games against the Bruins and the hope was that he would play as well with them as he had against them. Unfortunately, that was not the case. According to Stan Szukala, Vaughn "didn't do anything for the Bruins."[30] He played in three games and scored a total of 16 points — zero, eight and eight. In the first game, he hardly played as the Bruins, led by Hapac (20) and Kautz (16), defeated the champion All Stars 49 to 33 in Chicago. Perhaps the All Stars were less focused for the game since they had little to lose in the contest, as the Bruins clearly did. Nevertheless, Connie Mack Berry, the Cleveland Rams' football player, had occasion to slug Wibs Kautz, opening "a three inch cut over his eye. There was also the possibility that he suffered a broken nose from the blow."[31]

With just a week left in the season, the All Stars had a five game lead on Sheboygan. The Redskins, in turn, led Firestone by a game and the Firestones led Detroit and Goodyear by a game with Chicago another game back. In scoring, Ben Stephens of the Goodyears topped the league with 239 points, Wibs Kautz was 37 behind and the rest of the top five were Ed Sadowski of Detroit, Bill Hapac and Jack Ozburn. Ralph Vaughn was sixth, Leroy Edwards tenth after a slow start, Mike Novak 16th and Stan Szukala 27th.

In their last effort at making the playoffs, the Bruins were to play Hammond and the Firestones. The Hammond game was the final home game of the season and steel bleachers were installed along with 1500 chairs to accommodate 4,000 fans. Two local Windy City league games would precede the Bruins' contest. The Chicago squad kept their hopes and those of their fans alive with a 27–18 win over the Ciesars in a game that was the lowest scoring contest in the league for 1940-41. Bill Hapac again led with 11 but Vaughn, playing in place of Kautz, scored 8. Dar Hutchins topped the Ciesars with 5.[32] The next night the All Stars ended their regular season with a win at Sheboygan, and Detroit eliminated the Goodyear Wingfoots from the playoffs with a 50–48 victory over the Wingfoots. Chicago traveled to Akron to face the Firestones with one slim chance of making post season play, but the Non-Skids ran them out of the gym with a 46–27 victory. With the win, the Firestones made it all the way back, from a disastrous start to a second place tie with Sheboygan. "(U)nder an arrangement decided by a flip of a coin, ... the Non-Skid's second-place tie will be disregarded and the Non-Skids will oppose Oshkosh in the first round of play."[33]

Post Season Play

The playoffs began March 4 with the All Stars triumphing over the Firestones 30 to 28 and the Eagles topping Sheboygan 43 to 32. In the former game Oshkosh was led by their two inside players, Carpenter with nine points and Edwards with seven. The Non-Skids countered with Cable's 11 and Moir's 10, but the rest of the team could only manage seven points. Detroit was led by Ed Sadowski's 13 and Jim Brown's 10, while Otto Kolar was the scoring leader for Sheboygan with 10.[34] Detroit had tuned up for the playoffs by participating with the Rens, the Celtics and the SPHAs in a doubleheader invitational tournament in Cleveland, which was won by the Celtics. Detroit lost to the Rens in the consolation game.

In the second playoff game, the Non-Skids traveled with their hosts to Oshkosh, where the All Stars eliminated the Firestone squad 47–41 in overtime. Before 2000 fans, the All Stars won on free throws. Oshkosh was 19 of 25 from the line, Akron 13 of 19. Both teams had 14 baskets, but neither had sterling shooting statistics with Firestone taking 67 shots for 21 percent and Oshkosh 81 for 17 percent. Leroy Edwards topped all scorers with 18 (six for 25 from the field), but he got strong support from Bob Carpenter's 14 and Herm Witasek's 9 (though he was a horrid three of 21 from the floor). Cable and Nowak led Firestone with 11 and seven points.[35]

Sheboygan tied their series at one when it shifted to Wisconsin, defeating the Eagles 22–19. Then the Redskins made it an all-Wisconsin final when they beat Detroit, 54 to 40. In that game Dave Quabius scored the highest game in his professional career with 23 to lead the way for Sheboygan. Calihan and Jeannette had 13 and 10 for Detroit in defeat.[36]

The Final series was to be best of five and opened in Sheboygan, with Oshkosh winning easily, 53 to 38. Edwards had 18 and was the only player in double figures for either team, but the All Stars shot 34 percent from the field, a good percentage for that time, while Sheboygan could convert only 15 percent of their shots.[37] The second game was closer but the outcome was the same, an All Star victory, this time by a score of 44–38. Again Edwards was high scorer, this time with 14, followed closely by Carpenter's 13. Sheboygan had no one in double figures but did shoot better (14 of 53, 26 percent) than Oshkosh (14 of 67, 21 percent). Edwards had five of 22 from the field and all of his made goals were hook shots.[38]

The 1940-41 National Basketball League season ended the next night with an Oshkosh sweep of Sheboygan and of the playoffs. Again Edwards led the scoring with 14, despite fouling out of the contest midway through the third quarter. The game was not close, however, as the All Stars won by 18. Both teams shot similar percentages, in the low 20s, but Oshkosh had four more baskets and a great advantage in foul shooting, going 18 for 23 while Sheboygan could manage only eight for 21 free throws.[39] The page opposite the account of the game contained a half dozen 3" × 3" and 6" × 9" advertisements congratulating the All Stars from various Oshkosh merchants, reinforcing the long-time support of the Oshkosh business community.

World Professional Tournament

Three days after the National League Playoffs ended, the World Professional Tournament opened at the International Amphitheatre in Chicago. Sixteen teams competed, with the opening rounds going over two days (March 15 and 16). The first round saw the Chicago Bruins humble a squad from Davenport, Iowa, by a 53–17 score. The score was 25–4 at the half and the Bruins substituted freely. Both Stan Szukala and George Hogan had 10 for the Bruins. Both the Detroit Eagles, led by Ed Sadowski and Bob Calihan with 19 each, and the Globetrotters won to complete that day's play and advance to the next round before 8500 fans at the Amphitheatre.[40]

The next day Oshkosh topped Fort Wayne 47–41 as Scoop Putnam and Bob Carpenter paced the All Stars with 13 and 12 points, respectively. This was the Fort Wayne Zollner Pistons' first foray into this tournament, and they had defeated the Fort Wayne Harvesters to earn the Fort Wayne slot in the tourney.[41] The Rochester Seagrams, who had added Al Cervi and Jake Pelkington, lost to Kenosha 40–36, while the SPHAs defeated the Bismarck (North Dakota) Phantoms 48–30. One of the Bismarck players was Johnny Kundla, who would become famous as the Minneapolis Lakers' coach later in the decade. The Toledo White Huts, the only integrated team in the tourney, upset

the Sheboygan Redskins 36–28 as Chuck Chuckovitz had 21 points. Chuckovitz had scored only 6 points a game in 1939-40 while playing for Hammond and he chose to not return to the NBL team. Instead he returned to
Toledo and hooked up with a team there. The Renaissance beat Dayton 43–20.
In the only second round game played that day, the Detroit Eagles upset the
defending champion Globetrotters 37 to 36 as Ed Sadowski had 12.[42]

The rest of the second round games were on the 17th, and upsets continued. Toledo and Chuckovitz knocked the Bruins from the tourney before
9500 fans. Chuckovitz continued his hot scoring, getting 23 points while the
Bruins were led by Mike Novak's 12. Bill Hapac and Stan Szukala had seven
apiece. Oshkosh defeated the SPHAs as Edwards scored 12 to offset the eight
apiece that Petey Rosenberg and Inky Lautman scored to pace the Philadelphia squad. The Rens routed Kenosha 43–15. Dolly King, added for the tournament, had 14 and the Rens were buoyed also by the return of Tarzan Cooper
to their roster for this tourney.[43]

The semifinals of the tournament would pit the Eagles against the favored
Rens, and the Toledo White Huts against the favored, NBL champion, All
Stars. Thus, the likely scenario was an NBL champion versus a former World
Professional Tournament champion, the Rens. In yet another upset, Detroit,
which had gotten hot at the right time, defeated the Rens in a thrilling contest 43–42. Ed Sadowski continued his great play with 16 points and Bob Calihan had eight. The Rens were led by Wilmeth Sadat-Singh and "Pop" Gates,
both of whom scored 11 points. Oshkosh finally cooled down Chuckovitz, to
a degree, holding him to 16 points as they outscored Toledo 40 to 37. Bob
Carpenter had 18 and Erv Prasse six for the All Stars. Howard Cable, the
Akron Firestone star, had 11 for the White Huts. The doubleheader was witnessed by 9,000 more fans. And, as an aside, on the same date, in Denver at
the AAU tournament, Hank Luisetti, considered by many to be the top player
in the country, scored 17 in a win for his Bay Area squad.[44]

The finals were played the next night. In the contest for third, the Rens
pounded Toledo 57 to 42. Dolly King had 23, Zack Clayton 12 and Puggy Bell
11. Chuckovitz had 19 while Jimmy Johnson had 11 and Soup Cable six. In
the championship game, Detroit, which had finished fourth in the NBL with
a 12–12 record, completed its fabulous run and topped the All Stars 39–37.
Sadowski had 11, Jack Ahearn nine and Bob Calihan eight for the Eagles. The
All Stars were led by Bob Carpenter's eight and Connie Berry's seven. Leroy
Edwards went one for 15 from the floor as the All Stars shot just 13 for 78 (17
percent). The Eagles were 13 of 51 for 26 percent and had two more free throws
for the margin of victory.[45]

Despite the joy and satisfaction of finally being NBL champions, the loss
in the World Professional Tournament, especially to a team that had finished
fourth in its league, left the All Stars and the Oshkosh fans with some bitter-

ness about the year. It had been such a great year and now the familiar disappointment had set in once again. The Oshkosh contingent was already thinking of the next season, a season that would again have a seven-team league, but with significant changes in the makeup of the league's members. Then, of course, midway through the season, everything would change as the U.S. entered World War II. But, that was in the future and, despite the omnipresent threat of war, the season had ended on a successful run for the All Stars and their league.

6

The NBL in Peace and (Mostly) War: The 1941-42 Season

November of 1941 was filled with anxiety. Though the U.S. was not yet in the war, there seemed little doubt that it would be soon. Many of the NBL players joined reserve units and a few enlisted into one of the armed services. Many of the armed forces began athletic teams on various bases, both to keep morale of the troops up and to represent the military in a positive manner to the public. The armed forces teams played many of the top college teams as well as other military base teams, but did not play any of the NBL or other professional teams. The armed forces teams did add another level of interest for the media to cover, as well for fans to follow, along with collegiate and professional basketball. In 1941-42, the loss of players to the military was minimal, but it grew as the season went on and the war began to escalate after the American entry on December 8, 1941.[1]

The Oshkosh All Stars, as defending champions, were the favorite in the league, which, again, had seven members, as in 1940-41, but not the same seven. Oshkosh was still smarting over their loss to the Detroit Eagles in the finals of the World Professional Tournament in Chicago in March of 1941 and hoped for revenge in the league battles during 1941-42. Alas, that was not to be, as Detroit's owners were forced to compete as an independent squad with the loss of both the naval armory (where they had played in 1940-41) and the light guard armory (where they had played in 1939-40) to national defense training.[2] It is hard to imagine today that a professional league could have such a tenuous existence that it would have to lose a member because of a lack of a home court, but this was a concern in a number of cities during the life of the league. So Detroit and Coach Dutch Dehnert left the league but had some roster changes along the way. Bob Calihan was sold to Fort Wayne but had enlisted and was part of the Great Lakes Naval Training Station squad. Ed Sadowski chose to move to the Wilmington (Delaware) Blue Bombers of the ABL but then ended up signing with the Indianapolis Kautskys. Rusty Saunders retired at the age of 35, the oldest player in the NBL. Joining the Eagles was Jerry Bush, the former St. Johns' star who had played for three years with the Akron Firestone Wingfoots. The Firestone Company chose to drop sponsorship of a top basketball team as a promotional device for the company, and a number of their players signed with other clubs. Hammond, after another horrid season, also chose to leave the NBL.

Joining the league were the Indianapolis Kautskys, returning to the NBL after a one year hiatus of operating as an independent team; the Fort Wayne Zollner Pistons, in their first year as a professional club under the stewardship of Carl Bennett; and the Toledo Jim White Chevrolets, built around former University of Toledo star Chuck Chuckovitz. The Jim Whites also picked up a number of the former Firestone Non-Skids players for various games including Tommy Wukovitz (3 games), Paul Nowak (1 game), Howard Cable (5 games), Glen Roberts (1 game), Bob Hassmiller (2 games) and Jack Ozburn (3 games), though Ozburn's season was cut short by his being called into military service in December of 1941. So the 1941-42 season, as well as the next two seasons, would often be a function of the war effort in terms of rosters, opponents and venues.

The Zollner Pistons had put together a strong team and wanted to play more challenging opposition, so Carl Bennett contacted Leo Fischer of the *Chicago Herald-American*, who was the NBL president, to inquire about playing NBL teams that season.

> Mr. Zollner, after our first year, wanted to play stronger teams, so I went into Chicago on a train, at that time, and saw Mr. Fischer, who was president of the league and asked him to book some exhibition games with us, so we'd have better competition. And, of course, they were struggling and he said, "why don't you fellows join the league?" And, by golly, he went back to Fort Wayne with me and we talked to Mr. Zollner, and of course it didn't take long to say, "let's do it."[3]

The defending champions, the Oshkosh All Stars, were scheduled to play the College All Stars on November 25, rather than the Detroit Eagles, who had actually won the World Professional Tournament the year before. The Eagles' uncertain roster and future convinced the promoters of the game to invite the All Stars since they had also been the NBL champions. The All Stars played eight contests before the College All Star game, winning seven of them. The lone loss was to the Akron Goodyears, in overtime, before a capacity crowd in Kenosha. The victories included wins over the Chicago Bruins before a full house at the All Stars' home court at South Park Junior High School, two victories against the Globetrotters in Oshkosh and Racine, two wins over the Goodyears in Fond du Lac and Marshfield, Wisconsin, a win over the Flying Clouds from Chanute Air Base and two games against regional squads. The All Stars had added a number of top players to their already potent squad including Gene Englund, a 6'5" center from Wisconsin, where he had led the Big Ten in scoring; Bill Komenich, a 6'3" forward from Marquette, Eddie Riska, a speedy guard from Notre Dame; and Werner Engdahl from Wisconsin State at Superior. Oshkosh had also lost Bob Carpenter, the 6'5" center who backed up Leroy Edwards and was the leading scorer after Edwards, Witasek and Shipp, to the military (naval aviation). He would not return until the 1945-46 season. In the preseason exhibition games, all four rookies showed great potential. Riska scored in double figures in the first game and Komenich had eight points while Engdahl had seven and eight in early games. Englund played regularly behind Edwards and was scoring three or four points a game and playing well.

Akron, too, had a top rookie, George Glamack, a 6'6" center from North Carolina, who had the nickname "The Blind Bomber." Glamack had very poor vision, being nearly blind in one eye, and thick glasses, but he had a great hook shot and scored 17 points in one of the early games against Oshkosh. The Wingfoots also signed Rudy Debnar from Duquesne, who was a good-shooting guard. Akron was still looking to Ben Stephens for big scoring at the guard spot, but center Jake Pelkington signed with the Celtics in November after playing a few games with Akron. Pelkington was reportedly offered a one-fifth interest in the Celtics team as well as a salary.[4]

Pelkington had been with the Wingfoots as they dropped two of three games to Oshkosh in Fond du Lac, Marshfield and Kenosha in early November. Floyd Ebaugh rejoined the Goodyear team after missing a year with a broken neck, an injury so severe it was thought he would never walk, let alone play, again.[5]

The league season opened on November 25 and the All Stars topped Goodyear, 37 to 34. Gene Englund had 10 (or nine, depending on the newspaper account) points and was high scorer in the game, and the Goodyear rookie, George Glamack, led them with nine points. The Goodyears then traveled to Sheboygan and lost to the Redskins by the same 37–34 score with Glamack again the high scorer with 14.[6]

Meanwhile, the Oshkosh squad headed to Chicago and Chicago Stadium where 21,800 fans packed the building for the College All-Star-Professional Champion contest. The game was broadcast back to Oshkosh on station WHBY, which would air many of the team's games back to Oshkosh that year. Before the featured game, the Chicago Bruins met the New York Rens in the first of a four game series. Bill Hapac played for the Bruins, even though he had been called up and was playing for the Chanute Army Air Force Base Flying Clouds, and he led the Bruins with 13 points. For the Rens, Sonny Boswell had 15, with Sonny Woods picking up 11 in the Rens' 45–26 rout of the Bruins.[7] In the nightcap, Oshkosh lost to the former collegians 35–33 with a lot of players playing for both teams. Connie Mack Berry led the Oshkosh squad with 7 while Barle, Edwards, Komenich and Shipp all contributed 5 markers. For the College All-Star contingent, Bob Dietz, Moe Becker and Jack "Dutch" Garfinkel all had five points to lead their team's scoring.[8]

The Rens and the Oshkosh team traveled to Wisconsin Rapids, fifty miles west of Oshkosh, to begin a four game Wisconsin series. For the All Stars, it was a continuation of the tradition of playing the Rens regularly each season as well as a tune up for the NBL season. For the Rens, who would win 115 games and drop only 11 this season, the All Stars would provide some of their best challenges for the year. Both teams would enjoy the capacity crowds that they would draw, although the venues were not large. The All Stars took game one 52–42 as their three "E's" all scored in double figures. The rookies, Gene Englund and Werner Engdahl, led with 14 and 13 points, respectively while the veteran, Leroy Edwards, picked up 12. Sonny Boswell had 20 for the Rens to lead all scorers.[9] The next night the squads met in La Crosse, a 75-mile drive southwest of Wisconsin Rapids, and the Rens triumphed 47 to 36. After spending the night in La Crosse, on the Mississippi River, the teams motored to Richland Center, forty miles to the southeast and the birthplace of Frank Lloyd Wright, where the All Stars turned the tables on the Rens with a 47 to 35 victory. Called a "rough game," the game featured 44 fouls, 23 on the Rens, 21 on the All Stars. Puggy Bell of the Rens was the game's top scorer with 14. Veterans Edwards and Witasick had 12 each for Oshkosh.[10] The last game was played in Antigo, 150 miles to the north, near Wausau, with the Rens evening the series at two games by winning 49–45. Leroy Edwards had 19 and Wee Willie Smith had 11 to top the Rens.[11] They went on to Illinois, Indiana, Kentucky and Ohio with eight games in the next ten days as they completed their Midwest swing and then worked their way across New York.[12]

While the All Stars toured Wisconsin, the Chicago Bruins played Fort Wayne in Fort Wayne's NBL home opener at North Side Gym with the Zollner Pistons victorious 48 to 46 before 2500 fans. Wibs Kautz took game scoring honors with 18, backed by Ralph Vaughn and Mike Novak who had eight each. Curly Armstrong and Carlisle "Blackie" Towery had 11 apiece to top the Piston scoring.[13] Towery had been talked into going to Fort Wayne by Herman Schaefer, who had seen him play at Western Kentucky in 1940-41 when Schaefer played at Indiana. In the fall of 1941 Towery hitchhiked to Bloomington, where he met Schaefer, and the two went on to Fort Wayne where they both signed with the Pistons for the upcoming season.[14] After the victory over the Bruins, the Pistons went to Anderson, Indiana, where they lost to the Indianapolis Kautskys.[15] The Bruins went to Sheboygan where they defeated the Redskins soundly by a 51–38 score. Kautz had 20, Vaughn 12 and Otto Kolar, the former Redskin (and Chicago Duffy Floral player) and a native of Cicero, Illinois (as was Bill Hapac), had 10. Paul Maki, a rookie from the University of Minnesota, led the Redskins with nine.[16]

The Akron Goodyears defeated the touring Celtics on December 4 before 1800 fans. The Celtics led at the half by 10 points, but in the second half, "Glamack started firing the ball from the pivot with both hands" to lead a Wingfoot rally to victory 38–36. Former Wing Pelkington picked up eight fouls trying to stop Glamack as the rules were relaxed on ejections in order to keep the best players in the contest. Glamack finished with 18 and Bobby McDermott had 15 on seven "long rangeshots" and a free throw.[17]

The attack on Pearl Harbor on December 7 and the entry of the United States into World War II on December 8 did not have an immediate effect on the NBL, but it did alter the mood of the country quickly. On the one hand, sports and games seemed to be less important as the United States sent troops to training camps and war theaters overseas. On the other hand, sports did provide both a release valve for defense workers and a morale booster for many people who were feeling depressed over the war and its potential loss of life and liberty. On the day that Pearl Harbor was bombed, the two Wisconsin professional teams met in Oshkosh and the All Stars topped the Redskins handily by a 52–30 score, while Goodyear defeated the Kautskys 46–30 in Akron.[18] Four nights later the two Wisconsin teams met again in Sheboygan, where the result was the same but a lot closer as the Stars won 47–45. In this game Edwards and Shipp were high with 16 and nine points for Oshkosh, while Babe Lautenschlager and rookie George Blacklidge from Delta State (Mississippi) led Sheboygan with 15 and 11, respectively.[19] Blacklidge played in 11 league games for Oshkosh that year, his only appearances in the NBL. One effect of the war on the league was the loss of the Chicago Bruins' home venue. The team had played at the 132nd Regiment Armory previously and was set for its home opener there on December 17 when the Bruins' owner, George Halas, received word that the armory would be closed to sports because of the war and the need to use the facility for training. The *Chicago Tribune* noted that the Bruins would still open on December 17 against Oshkosh, somewhere![20]

The Bruins traveled to Wisconsin to meet the All Stars on December 13, hoping that two starters, Mike Novak and Stan Szukala, would be able to play after being out with injuries. Neither did, and the All Stars stayed undefeated in the league with a 54–46 triumph. A small consolation was that Chicago outshot the Oshkosh team, 29 percent to 28 percent from the floor, figures the *Oshkosh Daily Northwestern* saw as "fine percentages." Oshkosh, with four league victories, got 26 points from Leroy Edwards who took full advantage of the absence of the 6'9" Novak. Charley Shipp had 13 from his guard spot. Vaughn and Kautz led the Bruins' scoring with 16 and 15, respectively.[21] This game got no coverage from the *Chicago Tribune*, merely a score with no box score. The paper didn't even bother to pay a local stringer to call in an account of the game from Oshkosh. This was an indicator that the Bruins would have difficulties in the season with media coverage and, subsequently, drawing large crowds, wherever they played in the Chicago area. The Great Lakes Naval Training Station and the Chanute Army Air Force Technical Training Command games were receiving much more prominent and extensive coverage in the *Tribune*, which did not bode well for Halas' NBL team in Chicago.

Fort Wayne, meanwhile, had made the biggest player personnel move of the year by signing Bobby McDermott from the New York Celtics.

Bobby McDermott

Few players would have the impact of McDermott in a game and at the box office. Fred Zollner, the Pistons' owner, had scored a real coup. McDermott had signed with the Whitestone Separates Juniors, a local semi-pro team, during the 1929-30 season when he was only 15, having played one year of high school basketball for Flushing (New York) High School. He moved up to their major squad the next year and played for them before moving to the Wardlow Athletic Club and then the College Point Nomads for 1931-32, '32-33 and '33-34, as well as a number of other local New York squads. He became a deadly shooter and averaged 20 points a game in the 1932-33 season for the Nomads.[22] In 1934-

Bobby McDermott, NBL all time great, pictured with the Fort Wayne Zollner Pistons, for whom he played from 1941 to the middle of the 1946-47 season. (Dick Triptow personal collection)

35 he played for the Long Island Imperials and was a consistently high scorer before signing with the Brooklyn Visitations of the ABL in February 1934 at the age of 21. The Visitations had been a New York power since the early 1920s, having been formed, and mostly filled, with Irish Catholics from the New York region. The team had played in the Metropolitan League from 1921 to 1928, until the league suspended operations, and again from 1931 to 1933, when the new incarnation also ceased operations. They joined the American Basketball League in 1928 and remained in that national league until 1931. When the league was reborn as a Northeastern regional league, the Visitations were a charter member and remained in that league until 1939.

McDermott's hustle, fine shooting and aggressive defense helped Brooklyn surge to the ABL championship, defeating the SPHAs in a playoff. Then he led Brooklyn in scoring in the five game championship playoffs, defeating the New York Jewels for the title. McDermott remained with Brooklyn until the fall of 1936 when he left to join the New York Celtics, largely a touring team but considered one of the top professional squads in the country, along with the New York Rens and the Philadelphia Hebrews (the SPHAs). McDermott added youth, speed and accurate shooting to the Celtics. Ray Meyer, long time DePaul coach and the advisory coach to the Chicago Gears, the NBL champions in 1944-45, called McDermott "one of the greatest two-handed set shooters of all time."[23] John Isaacs of the New York Rens agreed. Shortly after joining the Celtics, McDermott scored a then unheard of 52 points in a game at Matewan, West Virginia, on 26 field goals as the Celtics beat a team of local college all stars by a 78–61 score.[24] He later topped that with 56 points in one game in Atlanta, including 11 straight shots from the field. McDermott returned to the ABL in 1939-40, but returned to the Celtics in December of 1940. He was constantly trying to balance the money he got from the Celtics by playing 125 to 140 games in a season and getting paid by the game, against the desire to have a more stable home life with his wife, Lillian, whom he had married in 1933, and his two sons, born in 1935 and 1939. The offer from Fred Zollner and his Pistons allowed him to get good money by both playing for the Zollner Pistons and working for the Zollner Piston Company in the off-season and to have a more settled family life. In addition, McDermott would use his nine years of professional experience as another coach on the floor, assisting Player-Coach Herm Schaefer and Manager Carl Bennett.

It should be noted that a basketball job with the Pistons was highly desirable because of year-round employment in the off-season in some aspect of the Zollner Piston industry. Blackie Towery recalled his job.

> I was a machinist, a set up man for the machine shop. We all worked in the machine shop except (Vince) McGovern. He started out working there, and then he went into the office. But the rest of us— Birch, Bush, Pelkington, me, Armstrong, Schaefer, Hamilton — all worked in the factory. After the war Fred

Zollner built a fast-pitch softball stadium that would seat 5,000 people. I worked out there in the stadium during the summer, instead of the factory.[25]

Dick Triptow noted that he, too, worked there as a groundskeeper, along with teammate Johnny Niemiera when they were on the Pistons in the period 1947–49.[26] In return for these jobs, and basketball, the players received a year-round salary which was around $100 a week in the early 1940s, a princely sum at the time. In addition at the end of the year, Mr. Zollner would deduct team expenses, then split any profits with the players. This practice ended when "we went to salaries for players, and that was all they did, play basketball professionally. When we went to that, we did away with the expense and the kitty and stuff."[27]

Most players of the time agreed that McDermott was the best outside shooter in the game. The Zollner Piston offense always went through him. Blackie Towery recalled that most coaches made changes that might have been questioned by players. On the other hand, McDermott was the boss, making all the substitutions and "no one questioned him at all." The offense was fairly simple. Towery and Pelkington often played a two-man game.

We'd open up the middle and then I would get it. Pelkington would get over there, and a man would turn his head on him, looking for the ball or something, and big John would go right on underneath and I'd hit him underneath.[28]

At this point (mid–December), the Oshkosh team was undefeated and in first place. Indianapolis was in second, with no other team having a better than .500 record. Jewell Young of the Indianapolis Kautskys was the league's scoring leader with Chuckovitz of Toledo, Glamack of Akron and Kautz of Chicago next. McDermott and the Zollner Pistons began to make an impact as the Pistons won five games in a row to go to 6–2 and second place. McDermott got nine in his Fort Wayne debut and Player-Coach Schaefer topped all scorers with 23 as Fort Wayne defeated Sheboygan 50 to 35.[29] Despite the Pistons's surge, Oshkosh continued to win and keep their first place spot. On December 17, they defeated the Bruins in Chicago at the Coliseum, Chicago's new home court, after the loss of the 132nd Armory. Connie Mack Berry led the All Stars with 14 in a 42–29 victory while Ralph Vaughn topped Chicago scorers with 13.[30] Oshkosh then topped the Goodyears by a 42–35 score in Akron. The victory was led by veterans Edwards (14 points) and Shipp (13). That same night Chicago traveled to Indianapolis and lost to the Kautskys with Ed Sadowski, former Detroit Eagle, leading the scoring with 11. For the Bruins, Wibs Kautz had 12 to maintain his position near the top of the league's scoring leaders.[31]

Three of the seven teams were under .500 with Toledo at 2–1, which would be its high water mark for the season. Indianapolis and Fort Wayne looked like two of the other contenders for the four-team playoff, along with Osh-kosh. The fourth qualifier had yet to emerge. Goodyear was having a prob-lem drawing fans since they had switched venues from their clubhouse to the local Akron Armory. One game they drew fewer than 400 fans and the lay-out of the court in the armory was blamed by *Akron Beacon* sports editor Jim Schlemmer, who suggested changes for the court's location in the armory to maximize views for more customers.[32] Toledo began its tumble with losses to Sheboygan on December 26 and the next night in Oshkosh. Chuck Chuck-ovitz scored 13 of the 28 Toledo points in the 42–28 loss to Sheboygan, and 22 of the Toledo points in the 48–38 loss to Oshkosh. The latter victory made Oshkosh undefeated in seven league contests. Chicago's venue problems became acutely obvious at that same time, when they drew fewer than 500 spectators to their home loss to the Zollner Pistons as McDermott scored 16 for the winners.[33] The Bruins' record of one win in seven games also was not helping draw fans, especially with the competition from college games, as well as the nearby armed forces teams at Great Lakes and Chanute.

Toledo began a season-long slide that would leave them with only three victories, one of which was a forfeit. Rodger Nelson recounts that "Jim White had the sponsorship of the team because he gave them two station wagons for transportation and bought the uniforms."[34] Chuckovitz did lead the league in scoring but entered the military the next season and never returned to pro basketball.

The Akron Goodyear Wingfoots had finally awakened from their slum-ber and won two games in a row in late December over Chicago and Toledo to move to 5–4, fourth in the NBL, just a half game behind Indianapolis's record of 6–4. The Goodyears were paced by the scoring of Ben Stephens and George Glamack, with support from Floyd Ebaugh and Rudy Debnar.

Indianapolis was enjoying its return to the NBL and was led by veter-ans Jewell Young and Johnny Sines (both from Purdue), Scott Armstrong (former Oshkosh All Star), Frank Baird (now 30) and Bob Dietz (all former Butler players). They had lost John Andres (Indiana University) to military service, but Dietz, Johnny Townsend and Ed Sadowski more than made up for the loss. The new year began for the Kautskys with a win at the Coliseum in Chicago. Young had 15 and Dietz 12, while Dick Evans had 11 for the Bru-ins. The game went to overtime, after being tied at 33, but the Kautskys held the Bruins scoreless in the extra period to win.[35] The victory buoyed the Kaut-skys as they headed to Oshkosh, but the All Stars continued their winning, before 2000 fans who managed to squeeze into their junior high school home floor. Gene Englund had 21 to take game scoring honors while Jewell Young had 15 for Indianapolis.[36] The All Stars then headed to Cleveland where they defeated the touring SPHAs by a 42–41 count before 5,000 spectators. The Kautskys traveled to Sheboygan where they lost to the Redskins.

The All Stars and the Bruins were two teams heading in opposite directions; the Bruins dropped their seventh in a row on January 8 to Akron in Chicago, while the All Stars won their ninth and tenth straight league victories over Fort Wayne (41–33) and Toledo (55–47). In the Oshkosh victories, they also defeated their closest competitor (Fort Wayne) and got continued good scoring from Englund and Shipp in the first game and Edwards in the latter contest. McDermott got 15 to top the Zollner scoring as 4000 fans filled the North Side Gym. The Toledo game saw Chuckovitz score 21 points and Scoop Putnam, former All Star, chip in with seven. The resurgence of Edwards, who was recovering from a knee injury, was heartening as he scored 16 points. Gene Englund missed the contest entirely because of attending a class back at Madison since he had not yet been graduated from the University of Wisconsin.[37]

With about half of the league season over, the All Stars were 10–0, Akron was 7–4 with Fort Wayne at 6–4 and Indianapolis at 6–6. Chuckovitz (Toledo) led in league scoring with 155 points while Young (Indianapolis) had 141, Glamack (Akron) 127, Schaefer (Fort Wayne) 111, Stephens (Akron), 102 and Leroy Edwards (Oshkosh), 99.

In mid–January, Oshkosh and Fort Wayne met for two games in Wisconsin that had all the atmosphere of a playoff. The All Stars kept their league slate clean with a 57–47 victory, making them 11–0 in the NBL. The All Stars also defeated the Zollner Pistons the next day in a non-league game in Fond du Lac by a 44–43 count. In that game (the All Stars's 19th win in a row) McDermott and Shipp each made three long shots in succession in the second quarter, without a miss, to excite the crowd. In the first contest, Gene Englund scored 20 points (including six of six from the free throw line) to grab game scoring honors. McDermott had 16 for the Zollners. In the Fond du Lac game, Edwards had 10 and Blackie Towery 13 to lead their teams. McDermott had 12.[38] That weekend also saw Goodyear defeat the Kautskys to strengthen Akron's hold on second place after their poor start to the season.[39]

In Chicago, there was good and bad news. The bad news was that Stan Szukala had been called up and would be reporting to Camp Grant Army Base. The good news was that the Toledo Jim White Chevrolets were coming to town. The Bruins' string of defeats ended at seven as they trounced Toledo by 22 points. Chuckovitz was again the high scorer with 16, with Kautz leading the Bruins with 14.[40] A week later the Bruins ran their league win streak to two by upsetting the Zollner Pistons in the Coliseum, with a late game rally. George Hogan (19) and Wibs Kautz (17) provided a potent one-two punch while Schaefer (18) and McDermott (14) nearly countered for Fort Wayne.[41] The Pistons had come into Chicago after defeating league patsy Toledo in a game where Chuckovitz had 27 to set a new league scoring mark for the year.

The win moved the Pistons back into second place in a tie with Akron, but the Zollners then defeated the Goodyears to claim second by themselves at 8–5, percentage points ahead of Goodyear's 9–6.

Oshkosh finally lost a league game at home, before 2011 fans, as they dropped a 53–43 contest to the Goodyear Wingfoots. Superior shooting did the trick for Akron as they shot 20 of 61 from the field, 32.8 percent, which was referred to as "almost remarkable" shooting by the *Daily Northwestern.* The All Stars were 13 of 78 for 18 percent. Shipp and Edwards topped the All Stars with 14 and 9, respectively, while Stephens had 16 and Glamack 13 for Akron.[42] The All Stars then traveled to Indianapolis and lost again as Jewell Young (17) and Scotty Armstrong (11) were high scorers.[43] Though their lead was still substantial, the aura of invincibility had been dissipated. The All Stars sought to build their lead back up and they won in Sheboygan before traveling to Rochester, New York, in the last weekend in January for the Rochester Tourney. There the All Stars lost to Rochester, then defeated the SPHAs for third place in the tourney. Rochester looked very familiar to the All Stars since Paul Nowak, Jerry Bush, Johhny Moir and Jack Ozburn (all former Firestone Non-Skids starters from the previous year) were in the starting lineup for the Rochester Seagrams squad. The four starters were joined by former Buffalo Bison Al Cervi. Edwards and Englund were high scorers for the All Stars in the tournament.[44]

As January drew to a close and two-thirds of the season was complete, the standings in the NBL looked as follows:

Oshkosh All Stars	12	2
Akron Goodyear Wingfoots	10	7
Fort Wayne Zollner Pistons	8	6
Indianapolis Kautskys	9	7
Sheboygan Redskins	5	8
Chicago Bruins	3	8
Toledo Jim White Chevrolets	2	11

It was clear that Sheboygan needed a big push to qualify for the playoffs and that any of three teams could finish second, third or fourth. The team that got hot could conceivably ride that momentum into and through the playoffs.

The Zollner Pistons lost at home to the weak Bruins 41–40 but then defeated Sheboygan on the road 49–44 to make Fort Wayne 9–7. McDermott continued to top them in scoring, this time with 18.[45] Sheboygan then traveled to Chicago where they defeated the Bruins 40 to 39. The game was played at Cicero Stadium, which was the third home court of the season for the Bruins. The Oshkosh paper called Cicero "the heart of a basketball 'hot bed,'" having produced Bill Hapac, Otto Kolar and Johnny Drish, all of the Bruins.

In addition, Kautz and Novak had played for amateur teams there.[46] In the Oshkosh contest Wibs Kautz had 17 to rally the Bruins, but, at this point, it was obvious that the Chicagoans were just playing out the league season and looking to salvage some pride in the World Professional Tournament after the end of the NBL season.

The All Stars got rolling again, defeating Toledo in Milwaukee before 3200 fans 55–50. Chuckovitz got 23 and got assistance from Willard Pederson with 11 and George Nelmark with 10, but the All Stars had four players with at least eight points, and better bench scoring to win. Edwards and Englund had 10 each. Oshkosh toyed with Appleton at the losers's court, winning 53–33. Oshkosh later turned a close game at halftime (26–23) into a rout in the third quarter by outscoring the Chicago Bruins 22 to 8 in the third period as they won 61–43. In the contest, Edwards was double teamed in the first half, but in the second, when that tactic was abandoned, he hit six of seven attempts from the floor and finished with 22 points.[47]

At about this time, Fort Wayne made another acquisition to strengthen their team, obtaining Paul "Polly" Birch, former Pittsburgh NBL player in the 1938-39 season, and a New York Celtic who had played for a number of years alongside Bobby McDermott. Birch was 30, but a knowledgeable and capable veteran. His presence in the starting lineup helped Fort Wayne to victories in six of their last eight games to finish 15–9. In his first game as a Zollner Piston, Fort Wayne defeated the All Stars in Fort Wayne 43–30.[48] This left the All Stars with a four game lead over Fort Wayne, Akron and Indianapolis, all with records of 10–7. Sheboygan was 6–9, Chicago 4–10 and Toledo 2–13.

Birch's presence was a big help in getting McDermott free for more shots. As Towery recalled:

> We mostly hit the pivot man or the guards would work it, and McDermott would come around first for a quick two-handed set shot. Paul Birch [who had played with McDermott for a number of years on the Celtics] knew how to set a good pick and McDermott was used to stepping right off his pick. The man [defender] would run right into Birch and McDermott would get his two-handed shot off as quick as a man today gets their [sic] one-handed shot off. Only it would be a lot further out.[49]

At this point the NBL announced that they would play a league all star game at season's end which would pit Oshkosh against the all stars of the other six teams in a contest in Oshkosh (home floor), Milwaukee (biggest venue) or Sheboygan (brand new armory). Details would follow soon.

In an effort to draw more fans (or keep the fans interested after Oshkosh had clinched the league title), the *Oshkosh Daily Northwestern* noted that the upcoming games against Indianapolis would pit John Townsend, Kautsky center, against Leroy Edwards, who had played high school ball with Townsend at Technical High School in Indianapolis, though Edwards was a year ahead of Townsend in school. Townsend then went on to Michigan and Edwards to Kentucky. An interesting twist regarding the second of the two weekend games pitting Oshkosh and Indianapolis was that the second game, on Sunday night, would be a home game for Indianapolis, but played in Fond du Lac, Wisconsin, thirty miles south of Oshkosh, "because the fans of that city requested a league contest."[50] Neither game was close. On Saturday night in Oshkosh, before 1817 fans at South Park Junior High, Oshkosh won 66–42. On Sunday night in Fond du Lac before 691 fans, the All Stars won 38–30. Edwards was high for both games with 14 and 17. Johnny Townsend had only four in the first contest but 11 to lead Indianapolis in their home game. Nine of the 11 were free throws. To make matters worse for the Kautskys, they also played, and lost, on Sunday afternoon in Sheboygan 34–25. Losing three games in 24 hours certainly moves a team down in the standings quickly and this dropped Indianapolis to fourth at 10–10, barely ahead of the Redskins at 9–10.

In an anticlimax, Oshkosh clinched first, officially, on February 11 with a victory over Sheboygan. The All Stars then headed to Memphis, Tennessee, where they played the Celtics, defeating them 52–45. Edwards (15) and Witasick (8) were high scorers. The Celtics were paced by Nat Hickey (15) and Jake Pelkington (13). The former Goodyear center from Manhattan College also picked up seven fouls in the contest, which had modified rules.[51] That same night Chuck Chuckovitz and Ed Dancker both broke Chuckovitz's record for points scored that season in an NBL game. Dancker had 30 and Chuckovitz 33, but Sheboygan won easily 67–38.[52]

By this time the *Chicago Tribune* had pretty much given up on the Bruins's season, if not the Bruins. The newspaper had pulled a regular reporter from the Bruins, failed to cover away games and gave minimal coverage to home games. There were longer features on the upcoming games than the coverage of the games themselves, indicating that the newspaper may have been largely printing materials that it was fed by the team or the league. As noted a number of times earlier, the armed services teams often pushed the NBL coverage further back or off the sports pages. The game between Chanute Army Air Base and the New York Renaissance in Cicero Stadium in mid–February was one good example. The game was hyped early and then the contest was very heated, and the overtime victory of Chanute was marred by a near riot. Chanute's star was Bill Hapac, formerly of the Bruins and a Cicero native. Cicero was later known for its near segregationist attitudes (in the 1960s) and the contest foreshadowed some of that. The floor had to be cleared at least once after fighting broke out. Ultimately the locals were happy with the Chanute victory and Hapac's 16 points and the *Tribune* made the most of the story.[53]

With ten days left in the season, Fort Wayne headed to Wisconsin for its last road trip in the regular season. Hoping to make a statement about the upcoming playoffs, the Zollner Pistons stumbled badly against the All Stars on Saturday, losing 72 to 47. Edwards had 22, Eddie Riska, the Notre Dame rookie, had 14 and no Piston scored in double figures in a game where 65 free throws were attempted.[54] The Pistons did manage to salvage some pride by edging Sheboygan the next afternoon, as McDermott's basket and free throw in the last minute were the margin of victory in the 40–38 contest. The loss pushed Sheboygan nearer to elimination from the playoffs.[55] McDermott had risen to second in league scoring with 223 points, barely ahead of Jewell Young's 222, although Young had played in three more games. Edwards was now fourth with 209. Chuckovitz had 306 to maintain a wide margin in the race.

Fort Wayne moved a game up on Goodyear with a victory over Indianapolis the night after the Kautskys had defeated Akron. The Bruins did Sheboygan no favors by edging them in Cicero before 1200 fans 40 to 36. The old regulars, Novak and Kautz, led the scoring with 15 and 10.[56] Sheboygan did edge Toledo the next night to draw within a game of fourth, but three nights later they lost in Akron and were eliminated. The Akron victory moved them to 13–9 and tied with Fort Wayne behind Oshkosh's 19–3 record with two league games to play for each squad. Fort Wayne won its next two games and Akron won one, leaving one contest for them against Oshkosh to tie the Pistons for second. This came on February 24 since the last contest of the year, Indianapolis at Chicago, was cancelled (probably for lack of interest and because it made no difference in the standings). These kinds of actions made professional basketball seem very *un*-professional and did little to develop fan loyalty to the teams or the league. In a game that meant little to Oshkosh and much to Akron, the Wingfoots won 44–41 behind George Glamack's 11 points. With the victory, Goodyear tied Fort Wayne at 15–9. The final standings were:

Oshkosh All Stars	20	4
Fort Wayne Zollner Pistons	15	9
Akron Goodyear Wingfoots	15	9
Indianapolis Kautskys	12	11
Sheboygan Redskins	10	14
Chicago Bruins	7	14
Toledo Jim White Chevrolets	2	20

The Playoffs

In the Shaughnessy system, the first place team played the fourth place team and the second played the third so all that those teams were merely playing for home court. Through a coin toss, that was awarded to Fort Wayne. The first game was played in Akron and the Wingfoots triumphed 46 to 30. The next two games were played in Fort Wayne and the Zollner Pistons won 51–48 and 49–42 (or 43).

In the other series, Oshkosh disposed of Indianapolis quickly in a weekend, winning 40–35 in Indiana on a Saturday night, then polishing them off in Oshkosh on Sunday night 64–48. In the first game, Jewell Young was game high scorer with 20 but Oshkosh got 16 from Edwards as well as eight from both Englund and Komenich. In the second contest, Townsend (20) and Young (15) combined for 35 points while Oshkosh was led by Barle with 12, Englund with 10 and both Berry and Edwards with nine.[57]

The Playoff Finals, another best of three affair, would open in Fort Wayne, then go to Oshkosh for the last two games. Fort Wayne took game one 61–43 as McDermott with 20 and Schaefer with 12 led in scoring. Leroy Edwards took game scoring honors with 22, followed by Tommy Nisbet's nine and Bill Komenich's 8. The game drew 4,000 fans to North Side Gym. The next day, both teams took the train to Oshkosh and were scheduled to arrive at 6:48 P.M. and then head straight to the gym for an 8:30 P.M. tip-off.[58] The faith, justified as it turned out, in the railroad service to get the teams to Oshkosh on time is hard to imagine today when passenger rail service across the country is sporadic and hardly timely.

The South Park gym was filled with 1,733 fans and they saw Bobby McDermott score 19 points to lead his team. They also saw Leroy Edwards turn in what was the top game played by any player all year in the NBL, particularly impressive because of the magnitude of the game. Edwards scored 35 points, a new league high; he played all 40 minutes, shot 14 for 37 from the field and nine of 10 from the free throw line and led his team to victory 68–60. Nisbet and Riska backed Edwards with nine each. It was a rough contest with 52 fouls called (29 on Fort Wayne, 23 on the All Stars).[59]

The next night 2083 fans managed to squeeze into the junior high and they were not disappointed as Oshkosh repeated as NBL champions with a 52–46 victory. Both teams took extraordinary measures to prevent the other team's top scorer from beating them. Edwards was double teamed the entire game and, rather than force the ball, was content to act as a decoy for his mates. He finished with one point, but Barle had 18 and Charley Shipp and Gene Englund nine apiece. McDermott was hounded the entire game by Shipp and failed to score as Curly Armstrong picked up 23 points and Blackie Towery had 8.[60] Announced that evening was the All League team which included Chuckovitz and Stephens at forwards, Edwards at center and Shipp and McDermott in the backcourt. Chuckovitz won the league's scoring race with 406 points while McDermott finished second with 277. Jewell Young had 263 to edge Leroy Edwards with 262. McDermott won the Most Valuable Player award with Chuckovitz second. The second team consisted of Ralph Vaughn, Jewell Young, Ed Dancker of Sheboygan, Herm Schaefer and George Glamack.

The World Professional Tournament

The All Stars and Zollner Pistons had little time to contemplate their playoff performances as the World Professional Tournament opened at the International Amphitheatre at 42nd and Halsted in Chicago just two nights later. Teams had been signing players for their squads to add needed strength in this toughest of tourneys. Dutch Dehnert, the Detroit Eagles coach, signed Jack "Dutch" Garfinkel to the defending pro championship squad. He and Paul Widowitz would take the place of Bob Calihan and Ed Sadowski from the previous year's championship squad, according to the *Chicago Tribune*.[61]

The tournament opened with the defending champion Detroit Eagles sending the Toledo White Huts out of the tournament 46 to 29. In other first round games the Harlem Globetrotters, the 1940 champion, topped the Hagerstown Conoco Flyers 40–33, and the Oshkosh All Stars defeated the Davenport Rockets 44–29. In an upset, of sorts, Fort Wayne lost its opener to the Aberdeen (Maryland) Army Ordnance Training Center 56–42. The local Chicago Bruins defeated the Detroit AAA team 56–46; Sheboygan topped the Columbus Bobb Chevrolets 56–46; the 1939 champion New York Renaissance knocked off the Northern Indiana Steelers 55–37, and the Long Island Grumann Flyers won over the Indianapolis Kautskys 54 to 32. In these games, Detroit's Eagles failed to suit up Jack Garfinkel but did get Jake Pelkington to join the squad. The Rens got 32 points from Sonny Boswell in their opening game and the Grumann Flyers fielded a most intriguing squad. Grumann was a defense plant and workers there were doing war industry work and not subject to military call-up. The team was a mix of players from a number of top teams and included Irv Torgoff and Nat Frankel, former Detroit Eagle players from the New York area; Dolly King from LIU and the Globetrotters; and Charles "Tarzan" Cooper and William "Pop" Gates from the Rens. This was the first great squad of mixed black and white players to compete in such a venue and it foreshadowed the removal of a color barrier which would erode over the next 20 years.

In the second round Detroit topped the Aberdeen Army Ordnance team 40 to 34 behind 19 points from Buddy Jeannette.[62] The Globetrotters knocked out Sheboygan 37–32. Paul Sokody led the Redskins with 11 while Roosevelt Hudson (12) and Bernie Price (11) topped the 'Trotters. Grumman eliminated the Bruins 48–38 as Dolly King had 12, Irv Torgoff 10 and Pop Gates 9. Oshkosh knocked off the Rens 44 to 38 in a rough game where 52 fouls were called, 27 on the Rens and 25 on Oshkosh, and five players fouled out (Charley

Shipp and Eddie Riska of Oshkosh and Sonny Boswell, Willie Smith and Zack Clayton of the Rens). Boswell had 15 before fouling out to lead the Rens in scoring. Johnny Isaacs played in the two Rens' games after not playing with the squad for nearly two years. Gene Englund led the All Stars with 13.[63]

The semifinals of the tourney would pit Oshkosh against the Globetrotters and the Detroit Eagles against the Grumman Flyers. Before 8,200 fans at the Amphitheatre Detroit went to overtime before edging the Flyers 44 to 43. Jerry Bush had 17 and Buddy Jeannette 10 for the Eagles while Pop Gates led the Flyers with 13, followed by Irv Torgoff's nine and Dolly King's eight. In the second contest Oshkosh, behind 20 points by Eddie Riska, defeated the Harlem Globetrotters 48 to 41. Roosevelt Hudson had 13 to lead the 'Trotters.[64]

The stage was now set for the first and only finals rematch in the World Professional Basketball Tournament, which ran from 1939 to 1948. The All Stars had felt their year tainted by their loss in 1941, even after winning the NBL title. Now they had another chance to win both and did not want to let the opportunity slip away. (And speaking of slipping, "the games were delayed an hour and a half until the custodians mopped and cleaned the floor" which had been excessively waxed.[65]) Before a "near capacity crowd of 7,500,"[66] the All Stars edged the Eagles 43–41. Detroit led only once, at 39–38. Jake Ahearn, Buddy Jeannette and Jerry Bush all had 11 for Detroit. Gene Englund and Eddie Riska were high for Oshkosh with 15 and 11,[67] respectively, but the hero of the contest, according to Wilford Smith of the *Chicago Tribune*, was Leroy Edwards.

> The Oshkosh veteran, Leroy Edwards, probably saved the game. Edwards was in and out at center three times because of his injured knee. In his last appearance and with the score tied at 33 each, Edwards scored five consecutive points[68]

Each Oshkosh player got a gold wristwatch for the win.

In the third place game, Grumman defeated the Globetrotters 43–41, the same score as the championship game. Dolly King had 15 for Grumman while Bernie Strong led the 'Trotters with 11. The all tournament team consisted of Jeannette and Bush of Detroit, Moe Becker of Aberdeen, Sonny Boswell of the Rens, Bernie Price of the Globetrotters, Gene Englund and Eddie Riska of the All Stars, Jack Tierney of the Bruins and Milkovich of the Conocos.

For Oshkosh it was a great ending to a fabulous, dream-like year. They had swept through the league and the tournament and were the undisputed professional champions. There were concerns about Edwards's knee, but he had seven months to heal. For the league there were much bigger concerns, however. They had lost a number of stars to the service — Stan Szukala, Bill Hapac, Bob Neu, Dar Hutchins, Bob Calihan, Ernie Andres, Lee Huber and

Jack Ozburn, to name the biggest stars, and more would be going as the war overseas escalated. Would the league have enough players to continue? Would there be enough teams ready to continue? Would there be any government restrictions that would prevent the league from operating, such as the government takeover of the railroads in World War I? These were questions that could not be answered at that point, but by the fall of 1942, the NBL would return in a much different form.

The NBL Goes to War:
The 1942-43 and 1943-44 Seasons

War changes everything. Materials are no longer available or are in short supply. Scrap drives, shortages, alternative materials— these are all indicators of a war society. Many manufacturing plants may convert to war industries at relatively short notice. Some plants or industries may even be nationalized in some manner. Schools alter curricula to address the war crisis. Restrictions are imposed on travel. Communications may be altered or curtailed. People may take a fatalistic approach to romances and become more promiscuous. Baby booms may ensue immediately after wars. Some industries are shut down totally because of restrictions, lack of customers or lack of materials.

A number of colleges shut down their athletic programs temporarily in the 1940s. Some cut back on the number of teams or games. Professional basketball during World War II was threatened with a lack of players as many of the players were drafted or chose to enlist. The leagues considered shutting down, but the U.S. government encouraged the continuation of athletics as a morale booster for citizens discouraged by wartime cutbacks. The NBL had closed 1942 with six teams, but not all could, or would, continue in the new season. The Indianapolis Kautskys felt that too many players lost to service would make their continuation in the league impossible. George Halas and Bill Bidwell gave up, for the second time, on pro basketball in Chicago and the Bruins folded. The Goodyear Company joined the Firestone Company in discontinuing their sponsorship of a professional basketball team. In addition to not having the facilities for basketball, the companies felt that pro basketball no longer seemed to fit their plans for company advertising and encouragement of good health. So, the league was reduced to four teams— Oshkosh, Sheboygan, Fort Wayne and Toledo. Then the United Auto Workers decided to sponsor a team playing out of Chicago and their massive Studebaker plant that had been converted to a war industry facility. Thus, the league was to begin with five teams and a 24 game schedule.

A new and historic wrinkle in all this was that both the Toledo and Chicago rosters would be populated with a mixture of black and white players. Of course, NBL teams had played the Rens, the Globetrotters, the Chicago Crusaders, the Cleveland Pennzoils and other all-black teams for a number of years, but the league had remained all white except for the appearances of Hank Williams as a member of the Buffalo franchise in the 1935-36 season, when the league operated as the Midwest Conference. Sid Goldberg, the Toledo coach, general manager and part owner; and Danny Serafino, the Studebakers' manager, recruited a number of African American players and put together integrated squads. Goldberg used a number of local Toledo players—Al Price, Bill Jones, Casey Jones and Shannie Barnett.[1] Chicago used players already working at the defense plant and exempt from military service. This led to the notion that the team would remain stable throughout an unstable year. Plant workers included Mike Novak, the former Loyola star and Chicago Bruin; Paul Sokody, former Marquette and Sheboygan Redskins player; Dick Evans from Iowa and the Chicago Bruins; and six former Harlem Globetrotters—Bernie Price, Sonny Boswell, Roosevelt Hudson, Hilary Brown, Tony Peyton and Duke Cumberland. Later Ted Strong and Al Johnson, two other African Americans, joined the squad and the Studebaker plant, though the four players still living in 1992 denied that this was the case. Newspaper accounts belie their denials, a strange function of collective memory.[2]

Toledo's experiment in integrated basketball did not last long. Players came and went swiftly and the franchise, again playing as the Jim White Chevrolets, was forced to disband after four league games in December. The team had expected to have Chuck Chuckovitz back, but that did not happen because of conflicts with his coaching job. They signed rookie Bob Gerber from the University of Toledo who played one game, scored 22 points and went into the service. Jewell Young, the former Kautsky, signed with Toledo but missed the beginning of the season after an operation. By the time he was ready to play, the franchise had folded because of losing personnel to the military and "transportation difficulties."[3] The media coverage, at least in the paper of note there, the *Toledo Blade*, was pitiful, so that certainly had to be a factor in failure. When the Toledo franchise disbanded, they had played all away games against each of the other league opponents and lost them all, so there was no advantage for any of the remaining league teams. The teams merely adjusted their schedules to play seven or eight games against each of their league brethren. During their short tenure in the league, however, Goldberg experienced the discrimination and humiliation that black players and black teams suffered on a regular basis in towns and cities all over the United States. In Oshkosh, according to Robert Peterson, who interviewed Goldberg in the 1980s, the players were not able to stay in a hotel or eat in a restaurant. They slept in the car. They then went on to Sheboygan where a minor league baseball player owned a hotel on the waterfront where the team stayed without incident.[4] Interestingly, in a interview conducted in 2002, John Isaacs, former New York Renaissance player, recalled that the Rens stayed and ate in restaurants without incident in Oshkosh, but were unable to find food or lodging in Sheboygan when the Rens toured Wisconsin in the late 1930s and early 1940s.[5]

The Season of 1942-43

If there was ever an example of going back to the future, this was the year. It resembled the rough and tumble professional basketball years of the early 1920s when players switched teams with impunity and leagues battled externally and internally over players. At that time presidents of three major Northeastern professional leagues tried to hammer out an agreement that would keep players from being signed by another team without due compensation.[6] The four remaining NBL teams had rosters that, at times, resembled the free agent days of the 1920s, before the owners of the Celtics initiated an exclusivity clause in the players' contracts. Fort Wayne had the most stable roster with nine players playing in at least 18 of their 23 league games. The Chicago Studebakers had eight players play in at least 18 games with another five appearing in at least one game. Sheboygan had only five players appear in at least 18 games with another six in at least five games and three others in one game each. Oshkosh was most affected by this revolving door with only three players appearing in at least 18 of their 23 league games. Another 11 played in at least five games and six others were listed for at least one game, a total of 20 players on the roster over the course of the season. Illness was one factor, as was the obligation to be at a regular job, often as a coach, but the biggest factor in not fielding a consistent squad was military service. Oshkosh lost four regulars before the season began, then lost four during the year to military service. The roster was constantly being modified as players came and went. Only Leroy Edwards, Charley Shipp and Ralph Vaughn played in at least 18 games so it was no surprise when Oshkosh did not repeat as champions that year. Simply completing the season with a full roster was a triumph, in and of itself.

For Oshkosh the season began with a game against the Clintonville (Wisconsin) Truckers at South Park Junior High, the home court of the All Stars, on November 7, 1942. This was the first of the home games for Oshkosh on successive Saturday nights into February. In hyping the game, the most amazing comment in the *Oshkosh Daily Northwestern* was that Clintonville wanted an NBL franchise and was trying to put together a team worthy of same. Since Clintonville (located about 40 miles due west of Green Bay and about 40 miles north of Oshkosh) had fewer than ten thousand people, the notion is almost laughable.[7]

The game was not very close as the All Stars coasted to a 55–34 victory, led by Gene Englund's 17 and Ralph Vaughn's 14 as the All Stars built up a 31–12 half time lead. Clintonville shot only 17 percent from the field on 10–60, while Oshkosh was 22–86 for 26 percent, "a fine average," according to the *Oshkosh Daily Northwestern* account of November 8. What was significant in one sense was the inability of Leroy Edwards to play much. "Leroy 'Lefty' Edwards started the game but played only five minutes because of an injury sustained when he dropped a heavy weight on a knee Saturday morning."[8] Erv Prasse, former Oshkosh All Star who played with Edwards in 1941-42 and part of 1942-43, claimed that this was typical Edwards. Leroy liked to claim he was sick and complained of knee injuries, but Prasse didn't think that he really had bad knees. Prasse felt that Leroy would say he was injured when he really didn't want to play.

> The team played a lot of exhibition games and during warm-up, Leroy would sit in the stands talking to the fans. Lonnie Darling, [Oshkosh Manager and coach] would go into the stands to get Leroy, and would have to talk and sometimes bribe Leroy into playing. Darling often offered Leroy a beer for every bucket; then Leroy might rack up 40 or 50 points. Leroy loved to play cards and was always looking for a game. Leroy was also a good drinker![9]

This pattern of malingering, or the appearance of it, was true throughout Edwards' career with the All Stars. He often missed exhibition or nonleague games with phantom injuries— a knee was most common, but ankles, toes and elbows also entered into the equation at times. This pattern did not carry over into important games and, like most superstars, Leroy was a big game player; he rose to the occasion.

Few players had the charisma of Leroy Edwards. He surely led the league in nicknames, being called or referred to in print as Lefty, Cowboy, Moose and Li'l Abner. Erv Prasse said that "he looked like Li'l Abner and could have played the part on stage." But in addition to his folksy demeanor, Leroy Edwards was a tiger, a dominating player. Edwards could hook with either hand, always converted on garbage points and "could make his shots even when he was falling. He was quick, could shoot from the outside and was 'dangerous.'"[10] Edwards was a 6' 4" center and the dominant center in the league, and probably the best in the game in the 1930s and early 1940s. Only Wee Willie Smith of the New York Renaissance had the strength and agility of Edwards and Smith was not the consistent scorer that Edwards was. Smith had Pop Gates, John Isaacs and other high scoring forwards while Edwards was always the All Stars' first option. In the biggest games, he came up large, almost always as the leading scorer (and had rebounding statistics been kept would likely have led that also).

Beginning in 1937-38 Edwards led the league in scoring for three straight years and also led all playoff scorers those same years. In 1940-41 he again led all playoff scorers in points and Oshkosh won the championship. In the 1942 playoffs he scored 22 and 35 points (an NBL record at the time) in the first two playoff finals games, then was double teamed and passed off as the All Stars won again. Edwards led his team in league games played from 1937–40, missed one league game in 1940-41, then played in every league game the next two years. In an era when scoring was low and few superstars were evident, Leroy Edwards was the dominant player of the NBL and fans often came to see him first and the Oshkosh All Stars second.

The All Stars played two exhibitions against NBL foe the Fort Wayne Zollner Pistons in early November. The *Oshkosh Daily Northwestern* described the Pistons as "sponsored by an industry that is engaged 100 per cent in war work with members of the team all employed by the company. (T)he Zollners have lost fewer men to the service than any other league teams."[11] It was also noted that Jerry Bush and John Pelkington, former Akron and Indianapolis players, respectively, were now integral parts of the Zollners. The two teams split the weekend series with Fort Wayne winning on Saturday night 45–42 and Oshkosh the victor in the Sunday USO benefit game. Bobby McDermott had 19 and 15 in the two games for Fort Wayne, while Edwards topped the All Stars with 13 and 11. Vaughn and Nimz also got 11 in the second game as Oshkosh won 55–50.[12]

The big news in the small league was the dedication of the new gymnasium in Sheboygan, where the Redskins would play. The Municipal Auditorium and Armory, with seating for 4,000, made Sheboygan the envy of its league brethren playing at local junior highs or high schools or, as in Chicago's case, playing in various venues around the city. The new gym would open with a game against the Camp Grant squad from Rockford, Illinois, that included former Bruin Stan Szukala. In that opener the Redskins won by 12 points before more than 3,000 fans. Szukala led his team with 10, while Ed Dancker, steadily improving at center, topped the Redskins with 11.[13]

Most of the talk in Midwestern basketball circles in November 1942 was of the upcoming College All Star game against Oshkosh. Despite losing players to the service, Oshkosh would be able to use Eddie Riska and Bud Engdahl, who were to be on leave from Great Lakes Naval Base and Camp Crowder (Missouri), respectively. The Great Lakes team with Riska was being seen as one of the top teams in the country, as it had on the roster Dick Klein, Forrest Anderson, Frosty Sprowl from Purdue, Bob Dietz and George Glamack. Much of the NBL's strength was being siphoned off to the service teams and Great Lakes was the top team. The service teams also began to get top coverage from the media. This would hurt the NBL, as it competed for media and spectator support. As for the NBL, the hope in the league was to survive until the end of the war, then grow again after that by adding teams to make an eight team league.

The All Star contest was November 27 in Chicago Stadium with Fort Wayne meeting Camp Grant in the opener. The Collegians were led by Bob Davies (Seton Hall), Bob Gerber (Toledo) and Don Smith (Minnesota). For the second year in a row, Oshkosh was edged by the college squad, this time by 61–55. Gene Englund led Oshkosh with 13, followed by Eddie Riska's 12. Bob Davies led the All Stars with 12, and he then reported to Great Lakes Naval Base, where he made that team even more powerful. In the first game Fort Wayne topped Camp Grant 39–36. Armstrong, Pelkington and McDermott all had eight while Szukala had 11, and former Bruins' teammate George Hogan had nine.[14]

The NBL season began well for Oshkosh with victories over Chicago and Fort Wayne, before losing to Chicago in Cicero Stadium. Edwards and Shipp had 16 and eight in the victory over Chicago as Leroy had a basket and free throw just before the final gun to edge the Studebakers 41–40. Roosevelt Hudson had 14 and Sonny Boswell 12 for the Studebakers. Against Fort Wayne, Gene Englund had 15 and Shipp 11, while Ralph Vaughn hounded Bobby McDermott all night causing him to shoot four of 25 from the field and got only eight points. Jake Pelkington led the Pistons with 14. In Chicago the Studebakers simply outplayed the All Stars as Bernie Price had 14, Mike Novak 10 and Roosie Hudson 11. "Manager Lonnie Darling had nothing but praise for the fine treatment given the Oshkosh team by the Chicago management, the Union of Chicago Studebaker Corporation which sponsors the team and by the fans themselves."[15]

With this victory the *Chicago Defender* now began weekly coverage of the Studebakers, the first time the NBL had been covered in the top African American newspaper in the country. In describing the game the *Defender* report noted that the Studebakers used "Mike Novak, former Chicago Bruins ace, in center and the white cager contributed four baskets and two free throws."[16] The next week, the *Defender* noted, "The personnel of the team is picked on ability, and race and religion does (sic) not keep a player off the squad."[17] This, of course, was what many African American newspapers and activists had been about for some time — judging a player on his ability and not his race. The references in *Defender* stories to Novak being white were to further the notion of racial harmony and integration.

After their victory over the Oshkosh team, the Studebakers defeated Toledo for their third straight victory 42–30, but shortly after that it was announced that the Studebakers would play their home games in the Michigan Avenue Armory at 16th and Michigan Avenue. This was not a final decision as the Studebakers also played league home games in Cicero Stadium, the Coliseum and even a playoff game in DuSable High School. Such wanderings were not conducive to developing a loyal and stable fan base. Nevertheless the Studebakers began the year with five consecutive home victories but four consecutive away losses. Their initial high scorer was Bernie Price with 63 points in six games, second only to Bobby McDermott, as the calendar year drew to a close. The Studebakers ended the year with losses at Sheboygan before 3,000 fans and at Oshkosh. In the former game Sonny Boswell led both teams with 18 points while Ed Dancker had 17 for the Redskins. The Oshkosh game was marked by poor officiating, according to the hometown Oshkosh media, and led to players "telling off the umpire" but drawing no penalties for these actions. Edwards led the scoring with 14, while Duke Cumberland topped Chicago with eight.[18]

Oshkosh, despite the revolving door of players, was maintaining its position at the top of the league. Besides the service losses, Oshkosh had medical problems. Gene Englund had an infected leg and missed a couple of games, Leroy Edwards had his trick knee examined by a bone specialist and both Englund and Don Smith missed games because of high school coaching obligations. The All Stars added Johnny Townsend, former Indianapolis Kautsky, but attending to his law practice in Indianapolis would impinge upon his playing dates. The All Stars began 1943 by winning in overtime at Sheboygan 61–55 and keeping Oshkosh in first. They had six wins and three losses. Sheboygan was five and four, Chicago four and four and Fort Wayne three and three. The All Star victory was before 3300 fans with at least 200 turned away. The two top centers, Edwards and Dancker, each scored 20 points while Ralph Vaughn had 17 for Oshkosh and Babe Lautenschlager had 15 for Sheboygan.[19] The Oshkosh roster had changed with the addition of Price Brookfield, O'Neil Adams, Gene Lorendo, Dave Quabius (former Sheboygan Redskin), and the possible return of Lou Barle, who had failed his military physical because of a punctured eardrum. Fred Nimz was reporting to Oshkosh when he could from Great Lakes and Ray Krzoska was dropped from the All Star squad. The All Stars extended their lead to two games by beating Sheboygan later that week in Oshkosh, in a game when the Redskins couldn't "throw the ball in the ocean," shooting seven for 65 from the field (11 percent). The three All Star stalwarts, Shipp (9), Edwards (8) and Vaughn (8) led the team, while Lautenschlager had 10 for Sheboygan.[20] The day after that game Sheboygan released their player-coach, Erwin "Moose" Graf, and added Bob Regh of Kenosha and George Jablonski to their roster. Carl Roth, the manager, would also act as coach.

Fort Wayne began a slow climb upward, topping Chicago twice in early January with the second a record-setting affair. The latter game was part of a doubleheader in Milwaukee involving all four NBL teams and promoted by

Bill Veeck. Three thousand five hundred sixty-five fans showed up to watch Sheboygan top Oshkosh 42–33 in a rough contest and Fort Wayne top Chicago 78–62. In this latter game McDermott tied Leroy Edwards' NBL record with 14 field goals (on 31 shots) and the Zollners hit an amazing (for the time) 32 of 66 from the field (48 percent) to win easily. Four players scored 16 points—Pelkington, of Fort Wayne, and Cumberland, Price and Brown (all former Globetrotters) for Chicago.[21] Following this game the Studebakers opened the next game against Oshkosh at Cicero Stadium with five African American starters, as Price replaced Novak at center and Hillary Brown took Price's spot at forward. This was the first time that five African Americans started a game in a professional basketball league. Fifty years later Roosie Hudson recalled that

> the Studebakers played team ball no matter who was on the court. It didn't matter if there were three black players and two white in the game or three whites and two blacks, we played as a team. There was no difference.[22]

That same week the Office of Defense Transportation banned pleasure driving in 17 eastern states to save on gasoline consumption. Buses, trolley and subways were encouraged as the mode of travel. Many rural areas suspended or cancelled games or entire seasons because of the difficulty in getting people to view or participate in games.[23]

By mid–January Oshkosh clung to a one game lead with a 9 and 4 record. Fort Wayne was 7 and 4 while Sheboygan (5–6) and Chicago (4–7) had both slipped below .500. A week later three teams had improved while Chicago had fallen farther behind. The Studebakers had added another former Ren and Globetrotter, Ted Strong, a defensive specialist, in mid–January, but the team continued to sputter. Later accounts of the squad laid the blame on poor race relations among the players, but the coach and players on that team denied that was ever the case. Both Bernie Price and Roosie Hudson said that the differences involved egos, particularly those of Sonny Boswell and Mike Novak. Novak thought Boswell shot too much and didn't share the ball enough.[24] After the league season ended and the team entered the World Professional Tournament in Chicago, Novak and Paul Sokody left the squad.

Fort Wayne began a run in midseason that resulted in winning 12 of their last 14 league contests to finish 17 and six. McDermott's hot shooting was augmented by support from Armstrong with Towery, Schaefer, Birch, Bush and Pelkington providing the rest of the help. At the end of January they moved into first, a ½ game ahead of Oshkosh, as Sheboygan dropped below Chicago in the standings. At the end of January McDermott was the top scorer in the league by far with 207 points in 13 games (15.9 ppg) followed by Lautenschlager (147) and Dancker (145) of Sheboygan, Price of Chicago (127), Vaughn (125), Edwards (124) and Boswell (119).

February began with Chicago upsetting Oshkosh in a high-scoring contest 73–60. Vaughn had 22 and Edwards 14 while Mike Novak had his best game as a Studebaker with 24. Sonny Boswell had 21 and a new addition, Long, had 15.[25] Oshkosh reversed the results later that week in Oshkosh, then Sheboygan topped the Studebakers in Cicero and then again in Sheboygan. Fort Wayne defeated Chicago in Cicero to end the Studebakers' regular season with an 8–15 record.

Meanwhile Fort Wayne had clinched the league title with a rousing victory on February 9. Over 4,000 fans squeezed into the North High gym and thousands were reportedly turned away as the Zollners beat Oshkosh 47–44.[26] Fort Wayne split its last two games with Sheboygan to finish at 17–6. Oshkosh was reeling; after being 10–5, they lost four in a row before beating Chicago.

In the middle of the league season, Fort Wayne, Sheboygan and Oshkosh (joined by the Toledo White Huts) all journeyed to Memphis to play in an invitational tournament where the winner took home $1000 and the second place team $750. Led by Quabius and Vaughn the All Stars (without Englund) defeated the Redskins (without Lautenschlager) 40–36 in the title game before 3,500 fans.[27] The All Stars hoped to improve as they signed former Kautsky Jewell Young to finish the season, but he played in just three games and scored seven points, having little impact on the fortunes of the All Stars. Despite the victory in the Memphis tourney the All Stars continued to tumble and landed in third place on February 15 after losing to Fort Wayne and Sheboygan with a record of 11 and 12.

Sheboygan split their last two games with Fort Wayne to finish in second place with a record of 12 and 11. They would begin the playoffs against Oshkosh while Fort Wayne played Chicago, as all four teams were in the playoffs. Despite the All Stars' plummet at the end of the season, the local paper noted that they were "still very much in the running for the championship of the National Basketball League."[28]

The playoffs were not kind to the All Stars as the Sheboygan Redskins downed Oshkosh in two games that were not close. In the first game in Sheboygan, the score was 50–38 with Ed Dancker topping the scoring with 13. For Oshkosh, Ralph Vaughn had 12 and Leroy Edwards nine. The next day in Oshkosh the score was 56–47. Babe Lautenschlager had 16 while Leroy Edwards and Gene Englund each had 15.[29] A big key for Sheboygan was the insertion of Buddy Jeannette in the Redskins' lineup. Jeannette, after playing for Warren-Cleveland in 1938-39 and Detroit in 1939–42, was playing for the Rochester Eber-Seagrams in Rochester, New York, and working in a defense plant there. As he recalled,

> They wanted me to come out there and finish the season with them. They wanted me bad. I hemmed and hawed and finally said, "Well, I'll take $500 a game." They said, "Be here Saturday."[30]

Jeannette played four regular season games for Sheboygan, scored 62 points, then scored 49 more in five playoff games. He was a major key to the Redskins' playoff success.

In the other series Fort Wayne, led by McDermott's 16 points, cruised past the Studebakers in their first game 49–37 on the Zollner Pistons' court. The second game was played at DuSable High School on Chicago's South Side and the Studebakers won by a 45–32 count. No Piston scored in double figures, but Price (14) and Boswell (12) did for Chicago. Back in Fort Wayne, 3800 fans turned out to cheer the Zollners to a 44–32 victory in the game, and the series. Boswell had 13 and Novak, eight in the loss while McDermott topped Fort Wayne with 12.[31]

Fort Wayne was heavily favored in the finals and, as league champion, had the choice of the three game format, either home, away, home or away, home, home. They chose the former and the series opened on March 1, but the Redskins upset the Zollners 55–50 in overtime. The third quarter proved to be Fort Wayne's undoing. After leading by 27–21 at the half, they were outscored 19–7 in the third quarter to trail 40–34 entering the last quarter. McDermott scored 20 and Ed Dancker again led Sheboygan with 16.[32]

That same day the All-League team was announced and Dancker's excellent season was recognized by his selection as the First Team center, consigning Edwards to the Second Team for the first time in league annals. Also making the First Team were Shipp and Vaughn of Oshkosh and Armstrong and McDermott of Fort Wayne. McDermott had run away with the scoring championship with 314 points in 23 games, for a 13.7 average. Second was Dancker with 247 in 22 games. The rest of the Second Team had Sonny Boswell of Chicago, Jerry Bush of Fort Wayne, Kenny Suesens of Sheboygan and Buddy Jeannette. There was some serious questioning of how a player who had appeared in only four regular season contests could be named to the team, but Leo Fischer, league president, offered no explanation. Babe Lautenschlager who had finished seventh in league scoring was the person most affected by Jeannette being named to the Second Team, but few Sheboygan fans carried their gripes very far. After all, Jeannette had sparked them to the 1–0 lead in the finals that they held.

Game Two in Sheboygan had the Zollners in a very tough spot, but they rose to the occasion. They led 44–42 but Jeannette's heave at the buzzer tied the game for Sheboygan.[33] In the overtime Armstrong scored twice and Towery one for the win 50–45 by Fort Wayne.[34]

Game three in Fort Wayne continued the home disadvantage, although it took a week to be determined. With a court unavailable until March 9, the two teams were stalled. This was again reminiscent of the situation in pro basketball in the 1920s. In the spring of 1921, the champions of the Penn State League, the Scranton Miners, and the champions of the New York State League, the Albany Senators, met in a seven game series to determine the champion of professional basketball. In the middle of that series, it was placed on hiatus so a number of players from each team could compete in another series of games that pitted the Original Celtics of New York against the New York Whirlwinds. Following a 13-day delay, the Scranton-Albany series concluded with a final two games.[35] Though the comparison is not exactly parallel, it illustrates the continued weak and frail state that professional basketball was in during the 1920s and the 1940s. Things had changed, but professional basketball was still a sport that lived from day to day.

Sheboygan played an exhibition game against the Clintonville Truckers on March 5 in which Clintonville had the services of both Connie Mack Berry and Gene Englund of the Oshkosh All Stars. Finally on March 9, the NBL championship was decided when the Redskins, "before a highly partisan crowd and near riot after the final whistle," won 30–29 on a basket from the corner by Ed Dancker with seven seconds left.[36] Though the championship was decided, the league season did not end until March 11 when Fort Wayne, the regular season league champion, defeated the NBL All Stars (players from the other three teams) by a 49–48 score. McDermott had 13 and Pelkington seven for the Zollners, Sonny Boswell (11), Buddy Jeannette (10) and Bill McDonald (10) topped the league players in scoring.

All four league teams would compete in the World Professional Championship in Chicago where the field had been cut back to 12 teams in order to minimize travel.[37] As a warm up, the champion Redskins played the All Stars in Oshkosh. Joining the Redskins was Johnny Kotz, late of the University of Wisconsin Badgers, who led the Redskins with 16 points, while Leroy Edwards had 17.

The World Tournament

The 1943 Professional Tournament opened on Sunday afternoon with the Detroit Eagles topping the Akron Collegians 33–31, which sent the Eagles into a game that night against Oshkosh. Dutch Dehnert, Detroit coach, had signed three University of Notre Dame players for the tournament — Charles Butler, Robert Rensberger and Ralph Vinciguerra,[38] but the latter two did not play, ultimately. Butler, however, led the Eagles in scoring in the Oshkosh game with 16. He was followed in scoring by Paul Sokody, who had left the Studebakers, with nine, and Chuck Chuckovitz, the former Toledo star, who had seven. This was almost all the Eagles' scoring, however, as they fell to Oshkosh 65–36. The All Stars were helped by the arrival of Tommy Nisbet and Bob Carpenter. Carpenter flew in from Norfolk, where he was stationed, to play in the tournament. He had six and Nisbet eight while Englund (11) and Vaughn (10) led a formidable All Star attack.[39]

Other first round games (all played in the Michigan Avenue Armory) saw the Dayton Bombers beat the Chicago Ramblers 46–41; Fort Wayne defeat the Kautskys 57–52; and the Minneapolis Sparklers surprise the Studebakers 45–44. In the next round Dayton upset the Globetrotters, who had a first round bye, 44–34, despite 17 points by "Goose" Tatum of the 'Trotters. The Zollners then avenged their loss in the NBL Finals by topping Sheboygan 48–40. McDermott had 14 for Fort Wayne and Jeanette had 16 for Sheboygan. The Washington Bears, with a number of former Renaissance players on the roster, defeated the Sparklers easily 42 to 21. This set up the semifinals with defending champion Oshkosh against Fort Wayne and Washington against Dayton. The Bears defeated Dayton by a 38–30 count, but the All Stars surprised the Zollners with a 40–39 victory. Charlie Shipp, who led Oshkosh in scoring with seven, hit a long shot in the last 30 seconds for the victory margin. Five other All Stars had at least five points and the Pistons had five players with at least five points, led by Armstrong's 11.[40]

The finals were played in Chicago Stadium and drew 11,000 fans to watch Fort Wayne take third with a 58–52 victory over Dayton. The championship game was all Washington Bears as they "made Oshkosh play their kind of basketball ... centered around a passing attack which kept possession until clear openings were gained or the defense fouled."[41] Three All Stars and two Bears fouled out, though it was noted that pivot plays allowed for body contact at all times, "leaving Cowboy Edwards and Gene Englund practically helpless."[42] Edwards topped the All Stars with seven points while Vaughn had six. Oshkosh shot only 20 percent from the floor (11–56) while Washington was only marginally better with 15 of 64 for 23 percent. Game scoring honors went to Johnny Isaacs with 11 who "was most effective from out on the floor."[43] Pop Gates had nine. For their victory the Bears won $1500, a figure so low that, even sixty years later, John Isaacs found it insulting.[44] The second place All Stars won $1000. Paul "Curly" Armstrong of Fort Wayne was named the tourney MVP, which was voted on before the Finals were played. Shortly after that, Armstrong entered the Navy, as did Herman Schaefer. Many other players would follow and prospects for the next year were not good for the NBL.

It may be instructive to examine how teams were actually doing, financially, at the time. There were different economic situations on the four NBL squads. Fred Zollner employed his players in his Zollner Piston Company and split the basketball profits with them at the end of the year. Each player split several thousand dollars, making them the best paid players in pro basketball and setting the stage for the continued growth of salaries for all pro players.[45] The Studebakers were owned and operated by the United Auto Workers Union at the plant.

Both Oshkosh and Sheboygan were city-wide enterprises modeled on the Green Bay Packers with many community members owning a share of the team.

An April 15 statement of the Sheboygan Basketball Association showed that home games for the team brought in $18,391 in box office receipts; season tickets were another $5,079 in assets for a gross total of $23,471. Taxes claimed $2241 for a net of $21,230 in profit from home games. Away games, exhibitions, league games and the playoff contest brought in $6225.[46] Apparently the use of the Municipal Arena was either gratis or very minimal, leaving travel expenses, equipment and player-staff salaries as the major expenses. Jeanette noted that players were playing for about $50 a game. For 40 games that is about $18,000 for a nine person squad (which is what Oshkosh had). Certainly the staff and equipment was no more than $5000, leaving a minimum profit of at least $4000, a princely sum for what was essentially a public corporation. Actually Coach Frank Zummach had a salary of only $500 from 1939–42 when he also served as the team's attorney (for another $100) and had an outside law practice. This also left money in the bank for emergencies such as a short term hire of someone like Jeannette. In fact, with the additional expenses, the 1943 balance sheet showed a profit of $943.49 for the year. The All Stars were set up in the same way as the Redskins, except that they were a more popular attraction at home (in a smaller venue) and on the road. Thus, they may have generated more income and could pay better salaries.

The 1943-44 Season

The 1942-43 season had ended with four teams, but only two real contenders, the Fort Wayne Pistons and the Sheboygan Redskins. The dominance of the Oshkosh All Stars was a thing of the past as they struggled to keep a complete team of capable players. The ground-breaking Chicago Studebakers had their season end in acrimony, and the team's break-up also led to the loss of support of the UAW, and the team folded. Replacing them was a Cleveland franchise sponsored by the Chase Brass Company. Again the league would have four teams, all of whom would make the playoffs.

In October of 1943 the Zollner Pistons released their schedule for the year, which included games against the Washington Bears, the defending World Tournament Champions, and the Midland Michigan Dow Chemical team, a powerful AAU team. The two games against Dow were to be charity affairs, since it was the only way that the Dow players, many of whom played at the University of Wyoming the previous year under Ev Shelton, who was now the Dow coach, could retain their amateur standing in a game against "out and out professionals."[47] The Pistons would be without two starters from the previous year — Paul Armstrong and Herman Schaefer — as well as Gus Doener, all of whom were in the active military. The addition of Buddy Jeannette, who had been the late season catalyst for Sheboygan as they won the NBL title the prior year, was a great coup for Fred Zollner and the Pistons. Jeannette had been urged by Jerry Bush and John Pelkington to sign with the Pistons and later noted that it was the best move that he ever made.[48] The Pistons also added Chick Reiser from the Brooklyn Eagles of the American Basketball League. Detroit's roster wasn't deep but they had the best starting five of the four teams in the league.

Cleveland emulated the Toledo model of 1941-42, when it was Chuckovitz and four other guys, by building their squad around Mel Riebe, a local legend who had not attended college. Since graduating from Euclid Shore High School in 1934 Riebe had been a tremendous scorer for many teams, professional and amateur. He and his brother, Bill, both 5'11" were joined by Ned Endres, a former University of Akron star, Will Swinhart from Toledo University and Pete Lalich from Ohio University.

Sheboygan had lost Jeannette to the Pistons and Ken Buehler to the military but they added Mike Novak from Chicago as well as two former DePaul players, Tony Kelly and Elmer Gainer. With five players on the roster 6'6" or taller, the Redskins were the tallest team in the league.

Oshkosh had Leroy Edwards and Charlie Shipp, but had lost Ralph Vaughn to the military. Added to the starting five were rookie Clint Wager, a 6'6" player from St. Mary's (Minnesota) who also played pro football for the Cardinals; Ed Erban, a former Marquette player; and Paul Schiewe from Wisconsin.

The Pistons defeated Midland Dow in two close games with good scoring coming from McDermott, Jeannette and Pelkington. Dow was led by Milo Komenich, a 6'7" former All-America center from Wyoming, who would play in the NBL (initially with Fort Wayne) after the war. The Pistons headed east where they beat the SPHAs in Philadelphia, then lost to the Bears in Washington 40–26. Puggy Bell had 15, Pop Gates 12, and the Bears defense held McDermott to eight.[49] On December 2, the Pistons opened the league season in Sheboygan where they topped the Redskins 55–44 behind McDermott's 23 points. Mike Novak had 13 to lead Sheboygan.[50]

The Pistons next faced the Washington Bears, the reigning World Professional Champions, for three games around Indiana and Ohio. The Bears had just lost to the College All-Stars before almost 24 thousand fans and weren't pleased about that.[51] The Bears had beaten Fort Wayne badly 10 days earlier, and the Zollners were eager to play better before their own home fans. On December 6, more than 3,000 fans jammed the North Side Gym to cheer on the Zollners, but the Bears won 54–48 as Puggy Bell notched 24 points and Pop Gates and John Isaacs supported him with 10 and eight, respectively. McDermott had 12 while Towery and Jeannette had 10 each. The Bears shot 36 percent to the Zollners' 26 percent. Two nights later, the teams met in

Defiance, Ohio, just across the Maumee River from Indiana, where the Bears triumphed again by a 53–46 score. Zack Clayton had 12 and Gates and Isaacs 11, while Jeannette had 10 and McDermott 12 for Fort Wayne. The next night, the teams were in Toledo with a closer score (51–49), but the same result. Pelkington topped all scorers with 20 with McDermott picking up 13. The Bears were led by Isaacs (16), Clayton (14) and Bell (10).[52]

Despite these frustrating results, the Pistons remained confident that they could, and would, lead the NBL in wins for the season. They returned home to defeat their closest rivals, the Redskins of Sheboygan, by eight points in a game marred by the ejections of Mike Novak and Bobby McDermott four minutes into the contest for fighting. The Pistons traveled to Oshkosh and topped the All Stars, despite Leroy Edwards leading all scorers with 13 in the 41–37 game. The next week the Pistons topped Oshkosh again, this time at North Side Gym 56–39. The Pistons faced a Cleveland squad which had just won its first game (over Oshkosh) in which Mel Riebe had 30 points.[53] Two victories over Cleveland (home and away) followed. Mel Riebe got 17 and 15 points in the games and Ned Endres scored 19 in the first contest, but the Pistons managed to squeak by 43–42 in Fort Wayne, before coasting 62–44 in Cleveland with McDermott scoring 22 in the latter contest. The games drew 3000 and 3500 respectively.[54] The calendar year ended with Fort Wayne undefeated in the league with six wins. Sheboygan had split four games, while Cleveland had one win in four tries and Oshkosh was winless in their four games.

On January 3, the Pistons finally lost in the league to the All Stars in North Side Gym by a 53–44 score. Charlie Shipp had 14, Clint Wager 11 and Leroy Edwards nine, while McDermott topped all scorers with 16. Oshkosh won two of its next three games while Sheboygan won three in a row. Fort Wayne was now 6–1, with Sheboygan only a game back at 5–2, with Oshkosh at 3–6 but playing better. The Pistons responded with four straight league wins at home and away against Sheboygan, at Oshkosh and at home against Cleveland. McDermott upped his scoring with 21 against Sheboygan and 18 against Oshkosh. Edwards had 16 in the latter game. Since all four teams again made the playoffs, the season was for playoff position, and the Pistons now had a big lead there with Sheboygan two games ahead of Oshkosh for first round home court advantage. Big league news came from Milwaukee in another Milwaukee doubleheader exhibition. Before 3000 fans, Fort Wayne topped the Redskins while Cleveland beat the Chicago Collegians 48–40 behind Mel Riebe's 32 points. This broke the floor record of 31 set by McDermott.[55]

The Fort Wayne win skein ended on January 25 with a decisive loss to the Redskins, a contest in which Ben Tenny of the News-Sentinel observed that "Fort Wayne had a completely bad game, defensively and offensively." Fort Wayne shot zero for 15 in the final quarter.[56] The Pistons had a short bench and certainly could have used Paul Armstrong and Herman Schaefer, both of whom were playing for the Great Lakes Naval team and topping that team in scoring. Great Lakes would end up 34–3 and according to Smith, Rimer and Triptow were rated the country's best team, service or collegiate.[57] By the end of January, the league standings were:

Fort Wayne	11	2
Sheboygan	9	6
Oshkosh	6	8
Cleveland	1	11

The scoring leader was Mel Riebe with 216 points with McDermott next at 198. Despite his lead, Riebe would play only 18 games so McDermott might be able to catch him at season's end, since he was to play 22 league games. Clint Wager was a distant third with 140 points for Oshkosh.

Fort Wayne sewed up the title by winning seven games in a row, beginning with home and away wins over Oshkosh. At that time the league also announced that memberships applications for the postwar NBL had been "received by franchise seekers in Chicago, Rochester, Buffalo, Detroit, Pittsburgh, Milwaukee and two in Hammond." No action had been taken, but with five teams on the inactive list (Goodyears, Non-Skids, Toledo, Indianapolis and Chicago), it was anticipated that there would be the "biggest and strongest professional league in history once world hostilities cease(d)."[58]

Sheboygan continued to play well and was now 10 and seven and leading Oshkosh by 3½ games with the All Stars at 6–10. Teams were essentially marking time until March when the playoffs were to begin. Cleveland made a significant change in their roster in early February when they added Wee Willie Smith, the 32-year-old long-time New York Rens' center.[59] In his first game Smith tied Bill Riebe with eight points behind Mel Riebe's 22, but the Zollner Pistons edged the Chase Brass by a 54–50 score.[60] Smith, who was the only African American in the league, played in four games, scored 24 points and helped the Chase Brass win one of their last five games (the Brass also won their last game, but without Smith) to finish at 3–15. The Pistons played the Washington Bears for the fifth time in the season on February 25 and finally managed to salvage one game from the series by a 40–38 score in Rochester, New York, before 3500 fans. The game was marred by a dressing room fight, after the contest, resulting in McDermott losing a tooth.[61] The Pistons then lost two of their last three league games to finish at 18–4, far ahead of Sheboygan's 14 and 8 record.

The playoffs saw Fort Wayne make short work of Cleveland, first topping them by 64–37 as Fort Wayne featured a "fast-passing, lightning cutting game that swept them under the hoop time and again for easy shots."[62] The Pistons shot 26 of 59 from the field for 44 percent (termed "remarkable") and Cleveland shot 12 of 89 (12 percent). Smith had 10 in this game, his only double figure game of the six league contests in which he played. The game was never close, and the next contest was only a bit closer, 42–31. The contest was played at Cleveland's Cathedral Latin High School before a small crowd on a small court. (Cleveland had played their final league games there or at Euclid Shore High because of the small number of fans attending, making use of the Public Hall an unnecessary expense.) Since the Riebe brothers had attended the latter high school, it was hoped that the gym would be filled for the game. Sheboygan eliminated the Oshkosh All Stars in three games, setting up the expected rematch with the Pistons.

In the best of five series, Fort Wayne topped Sheboygan in three straight to claim the title. Game one was at Sheboygan before more than 3,000 and was close the entire contest before Fort Wayne won 55–53. McDermott had 18 and Dick Schultz led the Redskins with 17. In the next game, again at Sheboygan, the Pistons won 36–26 before the largest crowd in Sheboygan history, 3,700. Jake Pelkington was the only player to reach double figures with 12.[63] In the third game, "the Pistons jumped in front, 33–11 and coasted home, 48–38."[64]

During the finals, the League All Stars were announced and the first team had Mel Riebe, Bobby McDermott, Buddy Jeannette, Clint Wager of Oshkosh and Ed Dancker of Sheboygan. Riebe and McDermott were named co–MVPs. The two had finished atop the league-scoring race with Riebe having 324 in 18 games (17.9 ppg) and McDermott, 306 in 22 games (13.9 ppg).

The World Tournament

After sweeping to the league championship, the Pistons hoped to turn a similar trick in the World Professional Tournament and cap a nearly perfect season. In a tune-up for the tournament, the Pistons played Dutch Dehnert's Brooklyn Eagles squad, one of the favorites for the tourney title, and defeated them 54–45. This foreshadowed tournament play. The tourney in Chicago opened on March 20 with first round games in Chicago Stadium drawing 7,200 spectators. In those games the Dayton Acme Aviators defeated the Akron Collegians 52–38, Brooklyn topped Camp Campbell, Kentucky, by 55–41 and the New York Rens defeated Detroit Suffrins 39–33. In the first game the Collegians were led by former Akron Firestone and Notre Dame star Johnny Moir with 13 points. In the second game, Brooklyn was led by Bob Tough, former St. John's star, with 16. He was aided by Mickey Rottner from Loyola and Camp Grant, who was added to the Brooklyn roster just before the tournament, who scored 11.

The next day the Globetrotters edged the Pittsburgh Corbetts 41–40 to advance, as did Oshkosh, who defeated the Rochester Wings 51–40. Bernie Price, the former Chicago Studebaker, had 17 to top the Globetrotters. In the latter game, Leroy Edwards had 20 points.

Fort Wayne and Sheboygan had been awarded byes so they did not play their first games until March 22 and Fort Wayne defeated Dayton easily by 59–34. The Pistons got 21 from McDermott and eight or nine points from Reiser, Towery, Bush and Jeannette. Sheboygan was beaten by the Brooklyn Eagles 49–43. Mickey Rottner had 16, Dutch Garfinkel 14 and Bob Tough 9, while for Sheboygan, Bill McDonald had 11 and Ed Dancker 10.

In the other games, the Rens (who were "composed mainly of Washington Bears" said the *Fort Wayne News-Sentinel*) routed the Cleveland Chase Brass (without Willie Smith, who was back playing for the Rens) by 62–38. The Rens had repeated as champion of the Cleveland Tournament, held the week before, and were playing dominating basketball. Mel Riebe had 23, but the Rens got 18 from Dolly King as well as 10 from both Sonny Woods and Pop Gates. In the last contest, the Globetrotters won 41–31, according to the *Chicago Tribune* (and most other sources), but the *Fort Wayne News-Sentinel* told a different and more interesting story. They claimed that the game was a forfeit, which would be a 2–0 official score. Lonnie Darling took his team off the floor with three minutes to play and the score 41–31. A fight had broken out with six minutes to play that involved most of the players on both teams. The police restored order, but minutes into the rest of the game, new fights broke out and Darling pulled his team. In the shortened game, Roosie Hudson had 10 for the Globies while Schiewe and Edwards had eight each. Edwards was also referred to by the *Tribune* as "Turk," a new nickname. The games were played before nearly 12,000 fans.[65]

It would be Fort Wayne against the Rens and Brooklyn against the Globetrotters. For the first time since the tournament began in 1939, the two African American teams were not in the same bracket, a placement that some had seen as subtle racism and others saw as ensuring good business by making it impossible for two black teams to meet in the finals. Despite this change, neither of the African American teams won. The Globetrotters had lost a number of players and were not as good as prior years. The Rens were in transition, phasing out some of their older players and bringing in new, younger talent. Fort Wayne was the best team at this time, playing unselfish basketball and relying on McDermott for the extra points. Brooklyn was comprised of players from various military services and the team seemed to disappear after 1944. Fort Wayne edged the Rens 42–38 with balanced scoring once again. Bush and McDermott had nine, each, and Jeannette and Pelkington eight each. For the Rens, Puggy Bell had 14, Sonny Woods, eight. Brooklyn had an easy time with the Globetrotters 63–41 as Bob Tough scored 32 to equal the tourney record set by Sonny Boswell in 1941. Boswell had nine for the

'Trotters and Babe Pressley 12. Tough was helped by Mickey Rottner's 11 points. Both games were officiated by Nate Messinger, a prominent NBL ref, who was assisted by Steve Barak in game one and Dutch Kriznecky in game two.[66]

The championship game of the tournament was not close. At the end of three quarters the score was Fort Wayne 42, Brooklyn 21. The final score was 50–33. Pelkington had 19 and McDermott 14 while Tough and Bernie Opper had 11 each to top the Eagles. Bobby McDermott became the third Piston to be MVP of the World Pro Tournament, joining Curly Armstrong in 1943 and Buddy Jeannette in 1941, when he was a Detroit Eagle. The consolation contest went to the Globetrotters 37–29, although "neither team appeared to be trying, with the Rens especially just going through the motions."[67] Duke Cumberland of the Trotters was the only player to reach double figures with 10 points. In an anticlimactic but fitting ending, the Pistons played one more game, the NBL All Star game at home in North Side Gym. "At half-time of the All-Star game, NBL President Leo Fischer presented the Naismith Cup to Owner Fred Zollner."[68] The final score was 45–39, Zollners, with Pelkington getting 14 and McDermott 12. For the league All Stars, Dancker had 11 and Edwards 8. The All Stars were hurt by their horrendous shooting (11 of 85 for 13 percent), while the Pistons hit 18 of 61 for 29 percent.

Thus ended the greatest year for the Pistons, and, possibly, the lowest point of the NBL's history to date. The hope was that the next year would bring an increase in teams and a better-balanced league. For now the NBL was glad to have made it through the worst of the war years with the league intact. A new arena had opened in Sheboygan and there was hope of one in Oshkosh. Fred Zollner had the leverage to press Fort Wayne for a better arena, but the league had to show that it could grow and that more than 3,500 fans (the full capacity of North Side Gym) would actually attend games in Fort Wayne. And, of course, there was still the war in Europe and the Pacific.

The NBL Begins Regrowing: The 1944-45 Season

After the great success of the Fort Wayne Zollner Pistons in 1944, it was not surprising that they would be the overwhelming favorite to repeat their championship in 1944-45. The heart of the team — Bob McDermott, Buddy Jeannette, Jake Pelkington, Jerry Bush — would return. The major loss was Carlton "Blackie" Towery to the military, but Charley Shipp was added to the roster and Chick Reiser elevated to a starting position. The major opposition appeared to be the Sheboygan Redskins once again. They had Ed Dancker, Mike Novak and Rube Lautenschlager back and added Bobby Holm from the University of Wisconsin, so they seemed to be in good shape to contest with the Zollners. The league had expanded to six teams, adding the Pittsburgh Raiders and the Chicago American Gears. One key change in rules prohibited goaltending by defensive centers. Since most players weren't very tall and jumping above the rim was rare, the rule was not really needed. But now there were bigger, more agile centers like Ed Dancker, Mike Novak and, in college, Bob Kurland and George Mikan. The need to control this kind of basket interference had become more acute.

The Chicago franchise was operated by Maurice White, the owner of the American Gear Company. He added a solid group of players, almost exclusively with Chicago ties, and hired Jack Brickhouse, the future Hall of Fame announcer for the Cubs, as his Gears announcer. The heart of the team would be two rookies, Stan Patrick from the University of Illinois, and Dick Triptow from DePaul. Cleveland changed sponsors and became the Allman Transfers and the Oshkosh All Stars were steady in their continuance. Despite having the most players lost to military service, the All Stars endured, and built their squad, once again, around the great Leroy Edwards, with support from Clint Wager and new additions Pete Pasco and Homer Fuller.

For Oshkosh the season started in the fall with their usual tour of the state of Wisconsin, playing local teams. This was always a good way to spread good will and publicize the squad, though the war had certainly thinned the ranks of teams everywhere. The defending champion Zollner Pistons sought a repeat of their title from the previous year, but they also wanted to have four key triumphs. First, they wanted to win in the College All-Star clash, something no professional team had done yet. Second, they wanted to win the league title once again, followed by victory in the league playoffs. Finally they wanted to win the World Professional Championship in March in Chicago, repeating their triumph of 1944. The goals were high, but they were confident in their ability to reach them.

As a warm-up to the league season, the Zollners went on an eastern swing in late November. They played American Basketball League teams, the Wilmington Blue Bombers, Baltimore Bullets and the Philadelphia SPHAs, as well as a team from Wilkes-Barre (White's Pros), and the Dayton Acme Bombers. The Zollner Pistons won all six of their games (they played Wilmington twice), many played before crowds of 5,000 or more and using ABL rules. The major rule difference was that the ABL played three 15-minute periods, rather than two 20 minute ones, which had some implications for substitutions and fouls. Nevertheless, the closest any of the teams came to the Pistons was four points in Philadelphia against the SPHAs, before seven thousand fans. The Zollner Pistons' scoring was spread around, but McDermott and Pelkington were almost always high scorers for the games with Pelkington getting 25 in the Wilkes-Barre win. The Zollner Pistons squad was ready to meet its first goal by taking on the College All-Stars on December 1, 1944. A boost came from Blackie Towery, who was given a furlough and was able to play in the contest for the Pistons. Before 21,372 fans in Chicago Stadium, the Pistons ended the run of College All-Star victories with a 44–38 triumph. McDermott had 17 and Towery 10 to lead Fort Wayne.[1]

The victory over the All-Stars sent the Zollner Pistons into their first league game against Cleveland with continued momentum and they downed Cleveland 51–36. The Ohio team comprised of a number of the former Chase Brass players from the previous season, but there was a new coach, Jeff Carlin, who had coached for many years at Case University in Cleveland. He told Mel Riebe, in no uncertain terms, that he had to do more than just shoot. Riebe was joined by his brother, Bill, Ned Endress and Frank Garcia from the Chase Brass, but the team was considerably strengthened by the addition of Tommy Wukovitz, the former Notre Dame and Akron Firestone star; Mike Byztura, who had played at Duquesne and LIU under Claire Bee; and John Mills, a 6'8" post player from Western Kentucky. Despite Mel Riebe's small stature (5'11"), most of Riebe's shots were inside, hooks high off the board. Riebe was very quick ("quicker than cats," said Blackie Towery[2]) and shot the ball from a variety of angles. Blackie Towery recalled that in this game Riebe didn't shoot as much (he had only one basket), but the result was the same, a Cleveland loss.

Chicago began its league season with a pair of losses in Wisconsin, first to Oshkosh and then to Sheboygan. In the first contest, the Gears led at the half 27–22, but then went 13½ minutes of the second half before scoring again. By then, they were way behind and lost 47–29. Leading Oshkosh were Leroy Edwards and Howie Hoffman, each with 15, while Chicago's scoring leaders were Swede Roos and Stan Patrick with eight apiece.[3]

Oshkosh began the year playing well and winning, led by Edwards and Pete Pasko. The *Oshkosh Daily Northwestern* noted that Edwards "continued along the comeback trail, playing a good defensive game and displaying a new aggressiveness which will establish him as one of the league's leading centers, if it is continued."[4] After the twin defeats, the Gears did not play a league game again for two weeks, when they had their home opener in the Chicago Coliseum, against the same Oshkosh squad. The results were reversed as Stan Patrick and Dick Triptow led the Gears with 17 and 11 points, respectively, and Hoffman topped Oshkosh with 17 in the 52–46 contest.[5]

Fort Wayne continued its winning ways, following its home victory over Cleveland. The Zollner Pistons traveled to Sheboygan where they defeated the Redskins 55–49 before dropping their first game of the season at Oshkosh 49–45. Sheboygan had replaced their coach, Carl Roth (who was also the team's legal counsel), with former Celtic Dutch Dehnert, who had been coaching the Detroit Eagles. Dehnert's experience, it was hoped, would bolster the Redskins enough to bring an NBL title back to Sheboygan. The Oshkosh-Pistons game was played before 2100 "electrified fans."[6] Bob McDermott scored 22, but no one else provided much scoring, and Leroy Edwards was tops for Oshkosh with 20, including 14 of 15 free throws. Moving on to Cleveland, the Pistons defeated the Allman Transfers, this time in overtime. McDermott, Bush and Jeannette all scored in double figures with 21, 12 and 10, respectively. For Cleveland, Mel Riebe led with 18, followed by Mike Byztura's 12.[7] The Pistons returned home to defeat Sheboygan again and recapture first in the league. At this early point of the season, Fort Wayne had four wins in five league games, Oshkosh was three and one, Sheboygan had split four games and Pittsburgh, Chicago and Cleveland were all under .500.

After an exhibition victory over Cleveland in Youngstown, Ohio, the Zollners defeated Pittsburgh in home and away games. Bob McDermott got 20 points in each game for the Pistons. The league scoring race found Mel Riebe on top with 159 points in eight games, followed by McDermott with 124 in seven, Edwards 104 in seven and Novak with 67 in five games. The Pistons had a 6–1 record, followed by Oshkosh at 4–2 and Sheboygan at 3–2. The Pistons played exhibitions before meeting Chicago in Fort Wayne in their last game of 1944. Behind McDermott's 20 and Pelkington's 11, the Zollner Pistons won 59–50. Triptow had 14 for Chicago followed by Bill McDonald's 12. Stan Patrick was unable to play "because of his coaching responsibilities at De La Salle High School in Chicago."[8] The *News-Sentinel*, however, waxed effusive over the young star of Chicago, Dick Triptow. "Dick Triptow, held scoreless by Bob McDermott in the first half, found the range and gave a great offensive exhibition in the second half." The article went on to call Triptow "one of the fastest and hardest driving young players ever seen here."

Shortly after that game, Chicago bought Connie Mack Berry, the Chicago Bears football player, from Oshkosh after purchasing Bill McDonald and Elmer Gainer from Sheboygan. Maurice White, the Gears' owner, was willing to spend more on his team to make them winners (he hoped). Pittsburgh, at the same time, added 40-year-old Nat Hickey, the former Celtic, to their roster.[9] The Raiders ended the calendar year with a 55–50 loss to Oshkosh, as Pete Pasco and Leroy Edwards scored 20 and 16, respectively, to lead the All Stars. Joe Urso had 12 for Pittsburgh.[10] The year 1944 ended with Fort Wayne at 7–1, holding a slim lead over Oshkosh at 6–4 with Sheboygan right behind at 5–4.

Sheboygan came into Fort Wayne on January 2 hoping to cut the Pistons' lead, but was turned back by Fort Wayne in their cozy North Side gym by a score of 54 to 39. Bob McDermott had 13 and Chick Reiser 11 for the Zollners while Ed Dancker had 15 for the Redskins, who were hurt by the absence of Mike Novak, who was ill. The game was rough, and even more fouls could have been called, but the Pistons won because of better bench strength and better shooting (28 percent to Sheboygan's 19 percent from the field).[11]

The next night the Zollners were in Chicago to face the Gears and the scoring pace was torrid as the teams combined to break the NBL record for points in a contest. Before an enthusiastic crowd of 3,000, the Pistons won by a 73–64 score. Bud Jeannette led all scorers with 27 points, with McDermott supporting with 19. For Chicago, Stan Patrick had 24, Dick Triptow 15 and Bill McDonald 12. The Pistons moved on to Wisconsin, where they defeated both Sheboygan and Oshkosh to go 11 and 1 in the league. The losses dropped Sheboygan to eight and six and Oshkosh to six and six.

The Zollners returned home to again face Oshkosh and were forced to overtime before winning. McDermott's 14, followed by Reiser's and Jeannette's 12 each, led Fort Wayne, while Pasko had 12 for Oshkosh. The Pistons then headed south for a series of exhibitions, which were always big money-makers. In Nashville they defeated the Smyrna Army base team 45–42, and then they defeated teams in Birmingham, Chattanooga and Atlanta before heading back home to face Chicago on January 16. The Gears came into Fort Wayne after losing in Sheboygan (where Dick Triptow had 17 to pace Chicago) and winning in Oshkosh. In this game Triptow scored in the last five seconds to bring the victory to Chicago. The Oshkosh paper called Triptow's shot from just beyond midcourt "one of the greatest shots of the year."[12] He had 14 and Stan Patrick 17, while Leroy Edwards had 16 for Oshkosh.[13] The Gears then moved on to Pittsburgh, where they dropped a game to the Raiders 64 to 49 as Dick Evans scored 21 and Huck Hartman 18 for Pittsburgh and Stan Patrick 21 to pace Chicago. The Gears lost to Fort Wayne 59–49 to end their road trip with one win in four games. Bob McDermott had 16 and Bud Jeannette 12 for Fort Wayne, while Ray Krzoska led Chicago with 14 and Vince McGowan had 11. Stan Patrick missed this game because of his high school coaching duties once again. The Gears were hurt by poor free throw shooting as they went 11 for 24 from the line.[14]

The month of January was a good one for the Allied Forces in both Europe and the Pacific. In mid–January the Belgian Bulge was caving in and would finally collapse, allowing American forces to burst through those lines and on toward Germany. By the end of January the Russian forces were less than 75 miles from Berlin as they advanced from the east. In the Pacific, General Douglas MacArthur's forces won Clark Air Field in the Philippines, then landed near Bataan by the end of the month. The war was rapidly moving toward an end, though there would still be severe casualties over the next seven months before the peace was finally achieved in the Pacific. Soldiers were beginning to return from active duty and the renewed interest in professional sport was affecting the NBL in a positive way. Besides the overwhelming specter of the war, there were domestic issues that plagued the country. One was the terrible disease of polio, which would continue unchecked until the development of polio vaccines by Jonas Salk and Albert Sabin in the 1950s. As part of the battle against polio the Pistons designated their proceeds from their game on January 24 for the Polio Fund of Fort Wayne, which brought in more than $1000 after operating expenses were subtracted.

The Pistons beat Cleveland the night before playing Pittsburgh, then defeated the Raiders. In the first game, characterized by "poor shooting and ragged passing of both fives," Mel Riebe scored 18 and his brother, Bill, 11, to lead the Transfers. McDermott had 12 and Reiser and Bush had 11 each to top Fort Wayne in the game. The next night Jeannette led the Pistons with 18 in the victory over Pittsburgh. Hartman had 14 for the Raiders. McDermott and Pelkington had 11 and 10, respectively, for Fort Wayne.[15]

At this point in the season, the Zollner Pistons had a nearly unblemished league record at 16 wins and one loss. Second was Sheboygan, with 12 wins and six losses, and then the other four teams were below .500, with Pittsburgh and Chicago six and 10, and Oshkosh and Cleveland at six and 12 each. With the playoffs still limited to four teams, it was clear that Fort Wayne and Sheboygan would host the first round contests; the only question was whom would they each be hosting. In individual league scoring, Mel Riebe had a small lead over Bob McDermott with Stan Patrick a distant third.

Patrick's Chicago squad hosted Cleveland in the Coliseum in late January in an effort to make a playoff move. Cleveland led the season series two games to one as the Allmans showed a marked improvement over the prior year's Cleveland team that had played under the Chase Brass banner. In addition to the team game, there were the individual matchups with Riebe leading the league in scoring (282 points in 15 games) and Patrick third (217 points in 14 games). The two did not really match up since, as noted earlier, Riebe liked to play inside, despite his lack of height. Blackie Towery, the former Fort Wayne Zollner Piston, recalled that Riebe played pivot and Towery, at 6'5", would often guard him, playing in front of him.

> He liked to hook with either hand. He'd throw that arm way up there and lay it up on top of those corners on the backboard. It was a little high for me to get up and get it.... He was a good shooter.... No disrespect for the ball club in any way, but if they didn't go to him, they were in trouble.[16]

The Gears topped Cleveland in the Chicago Coliseum 59–50 despite Riebe's 21 points and Byztura's 11. They were more than matched by Chicago's balanced scoring, as Patrick had 16, Triptow 12, McGowan 11 and Gainer 10.[17]

The Pistons arrived in Chicago far in front and the desperate Gears rallied to beat them 52–50 as Stan Patrick tossed in a shot with 30 seconds left for the win. He led the Gears with 16 points and Triptow, Gainer and Bill McDonald had 11 each. Pelkington had 17 and McDermott 14 for the Pistons. The Pistons returned home to top Oshkosh and the Pittsburgh Raiders; in the latter game McDermott had 27 on 12 of 30 from the field. The game was not very intense, apparently, as it was noted that few fouls were called and few players were "bearing down hard enough on defense to do much fouling."[18] With the victories, the Zollner Pistons had 18 wins in 20 league games with Sheboygan at 13 and six. No other team was at .500 with the Gears, the tops of the others at eight wins and ten losses. Pittsburgh was six and 12, Oshkosh seven and 13 and Cleveland six and 15.

Chicago topped Pittsburgh in the Coliseum but then lost to Cleveland in the same building as Riebe had 22 and Tommy Wukovitz, the former Akron Firestone player, had 13, a total matched by Patrick, who led in scoring for the Gears in the game.[19] The Gears went to Fort Wayne where the Zollners avenged their recent loss in Chicago with a 60 to 49 victory. McDermott led all scorers with 27, while Patrick and Triptow topped the Gears with 19 and 17, respectively. The two also continued to wow the Fort Wayne fans. Before a capacity crowd, "Patrick and Triptow showed the big crowd some scintillating firing, especially on the long push shots they like to take."[20]

Four nights later the Pistons lost in Cleveland before 5,000 fans, but McDermott set a league record for scoring with 36, breaking the record of 35 held by Leroy Edwards and McDermott himself. Pelkington had 19, and

Mel Riebe 26 for Cleveland in the 62–61 contest.[21] With the loss the standings looked as follows:

Fort Wayne	19–3
Sheboygan	15–8
Chicago	10–13
Oshkosh	8–14
Cleveland	9–15
Pittsburgh	7–15

With the regular season winding down, the managers of the six NBL clubs were polled to select All-Time Stars of Professional Basketball. The voters were Lonnie Darling (Oshkosh), Jack Tierney (Chicago), Jeff Carlsen (Cleveland), Joe Urso (Pittsburgh), Carl Bennet (Fort Wayne) and Dutch Dehnert (Sheboygan). The selectees were three Original New York Celtics— Nat Holman, Johnny Beckman and Dehnert — who were joined by two modern players, McDermott and Edwards. The second team consisted of two more Celtics— Joe Lapchick and Nat Hickey — as well as three contemporary players, Jeannette, Jerry Bush and Wee Willie Smith. An honorable mention squad consisted of former Celtic Davey Banks, Benny Borgmann and three modern players— Curley Armstrong, Eddie Riska and Ed Dancker. It is interesting to note that of the five first teamers, only one, Leroy Edwards, still remains outside the Hall of Fame.

The selections served as kind of diversion from the runaway lead that the Pistons had in the league. By the 19th of February they were 22 and five and led Sheboygan's 16–9 record. They were followed by Chicago (12–14), Oshkosh (11–16), Cleveland (10–16) and Pittsburgh (7–17). The league-scoring race was still tight between Riebe and McDermott. The last day of the season saw the two meet in Fort Wayne where the game was less important (since playoff positions were already set) than the scoring race. In the Pistons' victory, McDermott had 30 points while Riebe had 29, but Riebe edged McDermott for the scoring title, 607 points (20.2 ppg) to 603 (20.1 ppg). This game also saw the first appearance of Ed Sadowski in the Pistons' lineup. He had been signed to aid in the playoffs and scored 13 points. Assigned to Wright Field in Dayton (125 miles from Fort Wayne), it was hoped that he would be able to get leaves from the Air Corps to play for the Pistons on a regular basis during the playoffs.[22] One other noteworthy feat on that evening was the Chicago Gears' victory over Pittsburgh by a 95–64 score, which broke the league record for points in a game. Stan Patrick set a new individual mark with 38 points. The victory helped Chicago clinch the third spot in the league with a 14–16 record. Cleveland dropped to 13–17 for fourth, with Oshkosh a game behind them. The two best records were by Fort Wayne at 25–5 and Sheboygan with a 19–11 mark. The playoffs would pit the top team (Fort Wayne) against the fourth best team (Cleveland), while the second and third teams battled to reach the finals.

The Playoffs

The Gears opened the playoffs by shocking Sheboygan 50–49 in Wisconsin as Gainer, Triptow and Patrick all scored in double figures (13, 12, 11, respectively). Ed Dancker had 17 and Mike Novak 12 for the Redskins, almost exclusively from inside. The next night the Redskins returned the favor, beating the Gears in Chicago by a 49–36 margin. Dancker and Novak again dominated inside with 18 and 14 points, while Triptow was the only Gear in double figures with 10. Two nights later the Redskins humiliated Chicago by a 57–27 score to send the favored Sheboygan squad into the finals. Novak led with 16 and no Chicago player could score more than six.[23]

In the Eastern semifinals, Fort Wayne, before the "smallest crowd in many weeks" in Fort Wayne, smashed Cleveland 78 to 50, as McDermott, Pelkington and Bush were all in double figures with 18, 12 and 10. Riebe, as usual, led Cleveland with 19 on seven of 25 shooting, which corresponded to his team's floor percentage on 17 of 69 shooting. The Zollners were much better with 32 of 79 floor shots (41 percent).[24]

The second game of the series was also the last as the two teams met in the Cleveland Public Auditorium, where the Zollner Pistons won 58 to 51. Again, Mel Riebe led in game scoring with 22 (8 of 22 for 36 percent), but the rest of his team had only six field goals (on 44 shots for 13.5 percent) while the Pistons shot 32 percent (20 of 63). McDermott led with 20 and Chick Reiser followed with 13.[25] The Zollners headed to Sheboygan, hoping to complete the third phase of their four-phase plan, to win the NBL playoffs.

Sheboygan was not a gracious host, winning both games played there. In the first, played before 3500 in the Municipal Auditorium, Dick Schulz, Ed Dancker and Bobby Holm had 18, 17 and 11 as the Redskins shot 37 percent from the floor to the visiting Pistons' 23 percent. Ed Sadowski led Fort Wayne with 17 and McDermott had 13 on five of 21 shooting in the 65–53 Sheboygan win. Game two was closer (50–47), but the Fort Wayne shooting remained cold, as they were 17 of 77 from the floor (22 percent) and only McDermott had double figures, with 11 (on 4 of 27 shooting). The Redskins shot 33 percent, as Ed Dancker made 12 (of 22) of the 19 Sheboygan buckets in scoring 29 points.[26]

The Zollner Pistons did not panic. Two nights later they faced Sheboygan on the North Side court and won 58 to 47. Scoring was balanced for both teams with Jeanette getting 13 and Pelkington and McDermott each scoring 10. For Sheboygan, Rube Lautenschlager had 11, Ed Dancker 10 and Dick

Schulz 9. Both teams shot about the same (Redskins 24 percent and the Pistons 27 percent). The Zollners' victory prolonged the series another two days, when the result was the same, a Fort Wayne victory, this time by a 58 to 41 score before a packed house of 3500. Ben Tenny noted that there was good play early, but the second half was ragged. McDermott and Tony Kelly of the Redskins were banished for fighting with six minutes left and both Dancker and Pelkington fouled out. So it all came down to one last game two nights later. Before another sold out house, the Pistons topped Sheboygan to cap a great comeback and retain the NBL title. Bob McDermott had 19 points (9 for 23 from the field) and Jeannette 10 while Schulz and Holm each had 11 for the Redskins. Sheboygan played without their coach, Dutch Dehnert, "whose only son was killed in action in Germany and Dehnert returned to New York to be with his wife." It was noted that before entering the service, young Dehnert had been a fine net prospect at Columbia.[27]

The World Professional Tournament

The Zollners entered the World Professional Tournament as the defending champions, as well as having achieved three of their pre-season goals—to win the College All-Star clash, to win the league title in the NBL and to win the NBL Playoffs. All that was left was the World Professional Tournament to cap an unprecedented year for the Zollner Pistons. The addition of Ed Sadowski was clearly an asset, but other squads had also strengthened their teams. With a one and done tournament, a bad night meant no second chances. Five of the six NBL teams were in the 14-team field. Any of them could knock off the Zollner Pistons on a neutral floor, and Chicago was not a totally neutral site for the Gears. The opening game pitted the Gears against the Hartford Nutmegs and the Chicagoans triumphed 58 to 47 behind Patrick's 15 and Triptow's 10. A recent addition, Price Brookfield, contributed seven. Oshkosh followed that game with a win over the Detroit Mansfields 60 to 56 as Leroy Edwards scored 23 points to lead all scorers. In the last game of the day, the New York Rens defeated the Indianapolis Oilers 67 to 59. Both teams had balanced scoring; Roy Hurley led Indianapolis with 18, but Willie Smith (17), Puggy Bell (15), Zack Clayton (14) and Hank DeZonie (13) more than made up for that for the Rens.[28]

The next day another tripleheader was held in the Chicago Stadium. Dow Midland defeated Cleveland 61–46; Pittsburgh topped Newark C.O. Twos 53–50; and Dayton Acmes bested the Grumman Hellcats 43–27. Dow Midland was led by Harvey Martens with 18, but Urgel Wintermute, former University of Oregon and Detroit Eagle star in 1939-40, chipped in 12. The Transfers were led, as usual, by Riebe, with 24, while Byztura had 10. The Raiders' win was paced by Matt Vaniel's 18, with Huck Hartman and Moe Radakovich (just signed for the tournament) contributing 11 each. Mike Bloom and Dutch Garfinkel from the SPHAs had 17 and 13, respectively, for the Newark squad. Bob Tough had 12 and Matt Goukas, Sr., appeared but did not score. Dayton's victory was paced by McNeill[29] with 14 and John Mahnken with 8. The Hellcats had Pop Gates and John Isaacs, but they each scored only one point in the loss. The *News-Sentinel* said that Grumman had "a number of colored and eastern college products."[30]

Day three of the tournament brought 14,702 fans to the Chicago Stadium, many to cheer for the Gears against the Globetrotters, and those fans were not disappointed as Chicago won 53 to 49. The 'Trotters had drawn a bye in the first round, but the Gears, without Stan Patrick, managed to edge the Globetrotters. Dick Triptow had 13, Price Brookfield 12 and Kleggie Hermsen, another recent signee out of Minnesota, had 11. Game two saw the Zollner Pistons, the defending champions, who had also drawn a bye, defeating Oshkosh 63 to 52. McDermott had 18 on five of 21 shooting and Jerry Bush had 14 on six of nine from the floor. As a team, the Zollners were 19 for 60 for 34 percent. Oshkosh's leading scorer was Leroy Edwards with 13 followed by a recent addition to the roster, Des Smith, with 12. The All Stars were 19 of 88 from the floor for 22 percent. Game three had the Dayton Acmes edging Dow Midland 52 to 50 as McNeill (Bruce Hale) had 25 and John Mahken 10. Dow was led by Harvey Martens with 14 and Ray Patterson with 12. And in game four, the New York Rens bested Pittsburgh 61–52. Irv Brenner had 15 for the Raiders while the Rens got double figure scoring from Bricktop Wright (18), Zack Clayton (15) and Hank DeZonie (10).[31]

The tournament was down to four teams and the semifinals were held before 10,000 fans, after an off day for all four teams to rest. In the first semifinal Dayton humbled the Gears 80 to 51, in what was labeled an upset by the *News-Sentinel*. Dayton was again paced by McNeill (Hale) with 23, with John Mahnken scoring 22. The Gears again did not have Stan Patrick, but got 15 points from Price Brookfield and 11 from Ray Krzoka. In the second game the Zollners won easily over the Rens by a 64 to 45 score. McDermott (16), Jeannette (12) and Pelkington (11) were in double figures for Fort Wayne. The Rens' leaders were Bell (16) and DeZonie (12).[32]

Two nights later, on March 25, the games for third and the championship were played in Chicago Stadium. In the third place game the Gears topped the Rens 64–55. In the championship match the Zollners made short work of Dayton, triumphing by a 78 to 52 score. Mahnken and McNeill (Hale) were the Dayton scoring leaders again with 16 and 15, respectively. For the Pistons, Bud Jeannette had 18 on seven of nine shooting from the field. McDermott had 15 as the Zollners shot 40 percent (29 of 72) from the field. Dayton was 20 of 81 for 25 percent. As a result of his solid tournament play, Jeannette was selected tournament MVP (the third straight Piston to be selected, after Armstrong and McDermott, as MVP in the tourney). Joining him on the First All Tourney Team were McDermott, Puggy Bell, John Mahnken and Dick Triptow, although the official tourney program listed Bruce Hale, rather than Bell. The second team was Jerry Bush, Mel Riebe, Chick Rieser, Jake Pelkington and Ray Patterson.[33] Seven of the ten were NBL stars.

The Zollner Pistons had achieved all their team goals for the year and, just to add a bit to them, they defeated the NBL All-Stars two nights later before 3,000 in Fort Wayne to sweep every big game for 1944-45.[34] For the Pistons it was a dream year. Four of their five starters were picked to the First or Second NBL All League teams. McDermott and Jeannette were picked to the First Team along with Leroy Edwards, Mel Riebe and Stan Patrick. Pelkington and Bush were named to the Second Team along with Dick Triptow, Ed Dancker and "Huck" Hartman.

It was apparent that the war would be over soon. Germany fell in April, but it took until August for the Japanese to surrender to allied forces. Nevertheless, the league owners knew that 1945-46 would allow for more of the NBL armed forces players to leave the service and return to the league. How many and how soon that would occur was not clear, but after all the speculation of how many teams would be available after the war, it was clear that there would be an expanded and more competitive NBL in 1945-46. What effect that would have on the Pistons and their incipient dynasty remained to be seen, but more competition than merely Sheboygan would be necessary to reclaim overall fan interest in the NBL.

Enter the Royals: NBL 1945-46

With the end of World War II most of the servicemen were being released and the prospects for a tougher, stronger NBL for 1945-46 were excellent. There were still call-ups, but overall, most of the servicemen were either out by the autumn of 1945, or they were being mustered out in the immediate future, so the season seemed to have great hopes, indeed. The rumors of teams returning to or joining the NBL after the war held true in at least two cases, as the Indianapolis Kautskys and the Rochester Royals were added to the league to make an eight team league with two four team divisions. In the West, the Chicago Gears returned along with the two Wisconsin stalwarts, the Oshkosh All Stars and the Sheboygan Redskins. They would be joined by Indianapolis to round out the division. In the East, defending champion Fort Wayne and the Cleveland Allman Transfers returned, but the Pittsburgh Raiders' franchise was taken over by supporters in Youngstown, Ohio, 40 miles northwest, and would play as the Youngstown Bears. The final team would be the Rochester Royals, owned and operated by Lester Harrison, a longtime basketball aficionado in that city.

Harrison, the son of Russian Jewish immigrants, had organized and played for "teams sponsored by the Ebers Brothers and Seagrams liquor companies."[1] He had played in the 1930s, while operating a local grocery business, and his teams dominated the region and competed against the top professional and semi-professional squads in the northeastern quadrant of the United States. His finest early signee was Al Cervi, from Buffalo, who had begun playing locally right out of high school, appeared in the NBL in the 1937-38 season with the Buffalo Bisons and later signed with Harrison's Seagrams squad in 1939. Cervi entered the service in 1941 but returned in 1945 and re-signed with Harrison's new squad to compete in the NBL. Andrew "Fuzzy" Levane, a teammate of Cervi's for many years said:

He was dynamite. He was very strong and could drive. There was no jump shot then, only a set shot, but he was strong and very competitive. He had an up-and-under shot, a layup. He'd be hit going in but he'd make the shot. He was very tough defensively; he used to shake up Bobby McDermott, who was the best set shooter with the smoothest shot and was the greatest offensive player of that era.[2]

Rochester's team and its owner-general manager and coach, Les Harrison, was a perfect match for the NBL, which was most popular in smaller cities where the top entertainment in professional sports was, indeed, the NBL. Harrison was extremely civic-minded and tried to promote the Rochester team as a civic endeavor and sought support on that basis. Despite Harrison's parents being recent immigrants to Rochester, there was a long Jewish history in Rochester, a city of 325,000 in 1940, but a slowly declining population. The first Jews settled in Rochester in 1843 and successive waves of German, Polish, Russian and Rumanian Jews developed a thriving Jewish community.[3] Harrison was easily accepted, then, as a small businessman in Rochester, rather than a *Jewish* businessman and his efforts at community building were well received. In return for the community's support, Harrison would seek the best talent in order to make the Rochester team one that the community could support with pride. After competing as an independent team with sponsorship, Harrison dropped the liquor sponsorship after being pressured by the dry Gannett newspapers, which were responding to the local Rochester liquor store concerns. The team then competed for a year as the Rochester Pros in 1944-45 before purchasing an NBL franchise for $25,000 in 1945.[4]

The Rochester franchise began its practices on November 1, aiming toward a league opener on November 24. All of the practices were at 7 P.M. allowing players to hold other jobs, as well as Harrison and his coach, Eddie Malanowicz of Buffalo, a longtime friend and playing partner. The team had no name yet and was still using the moniker Pros for the time being. All of the league teams would play 34 contests, 17 at home and 17 away. The first name player that Harrison signed was Otto Graham, the former Northwestern star in football and basketball, who had already announced that he would be playing professional football for the Cleveland Browns. Graham was to be Harrison's playmaker and, according to Harrison, was being paid as one of the top professionals in the game.[5] Al Cervi said that Graham had good hands and played good defense and played well.[6]

One week after signing Graham, Harrison signed George Glamack, the "Blind Bomber," who had previously starred at North Carolina and in the NBL with the Akron Goodyear Wingfoots, before entering the armed forces. Glamack was discharged in the New York City area on November 10 and immediately traveled to Rochester where he agreed to terms with Les Harrison and the newly named Royals.[7] Fuzzy Levane had this to say about Glamack:

That guy always said that he couldn't see, but every time he passed the ball, he'd give you a wink. He was a hook shot artist, and he had that bank board shot. He shot with both hands, left or right. George's hook shot was longer than Mikan's. He hooked toward the baseline because he liked to play the [angle of] the board.[8]

A few days later Al Cervi returned to Rochester from Texas after his four-year tour in the Army Air Force. That same day Harrison signed John Mahnken, formerly of Georgetown and a star in World Tournament games for the Dayton Acmes the previous spring, and Al Nagretti from Seton Hall. Both were due to be discharged from the military imminently.[9]

The Royals were set to open their first NBL season, but the official league opener was on November 22 when Sheboygan defeated the Chicago Gears in Sheboygan by a 53 to 49 score. For the Redskins, Ed Dancker, the steady center, led with 17 markers while rookie Al Lucas from Fordham had nine. The Redskins had strengthened their roster with the addition of Lucas and Al Grennert as well as rookies Kleggie Hermsen from Minnesota and Steve Sharkey. For the Gears, 1944-45 Rookie of the Year, Stan Patrick, had 17, while Nick Hashu had 11. The difference in the contest was free throw shooting as Chicago made only 11 of 23 and Sheboygan countered with 13 of 17.[10]

Before the league opener the Royals added more players, most notably Andy "Fuzzy" Levane from St. Johns and Bill "Red" Holzman from CCNY. Both had also been serving in the military with Holzman having been discharged from the navy within days of his signing.[11] Harrison had sought and signed Levane in 1944 when he was playing in the Coast Guard, both for his play and assuming that he was Jewish, which would appeal to that ethnic group in Rochester. When he found out that he was actually Italian, he asked for a recommendation for a Jewish player and Levane recommended Holzman.[12] This strategy was as old as professional basketball itself, when teams were often formed around ethnic groups, but the Original Celtics were the first to "mix ethnicities" in order to appeal to various groups as well as to strengthen their teams.[13] Levane was still living in New York when he agreed to play with Rochester and he would take a train there for games and would stay in a hotel on late nights if he had to. The team got along well and felt well paid.

> We were millionaires! I was making five grand a year! Before that I didn't know that you could get paid for what we were doing. I got married in 1945 and bought a house in Rochester and we stayed there until 1949.[14]

Neither Levane nor Holzman played much in the opening game because they hadn't worked out much with the Royals, but the team was still able to defeat Sheboygan in the opener 53 to 52, before a turn away crowd of 3500 at the Edgerton Park Arena. Cervi (10), Glamack (9) and Mahnken (9) were the leading scorers for the Royals while Dick Schulz (16) and Mike Novak (10) topped the Redskins.[15] That same evening Oshkosh defeated Indianapolis by 65 to 47. Earlier Indianapolis had spoiled Chicago's home opener with a 40–35 win, as Nat Hickey, the 46-year-old former Celtic, had 15 of the 40 points.[16]

The Kautskys moved on to Cleveland, where the Allmen Transfers defeated them 51 to 44. The Transfers were led by Johnny Moir and Tom Wukovitz, former Notre Dame and Akron Firestone teammates, with 13 and 12, respectively. Missing from the Cleveland lineup was Mel Riebe, who had entered the service and wouldn't return until near the end of the season. For Indianapolis, Roy Hurley had 13 and Jerry Steiner 9.[17]

The Kautskys were a team in transition, as a number of post war squads were. Kautsky had signed former Celtic and Pittsburgh Raider Nat Hickey to coach the team and he even played in 13 games during the season. Most of the players were from the local area where they had starred in high school or college. Jerry Steiner had played at Butler, Roy Hurley at Murray State in Kentucky, and Bob Dietz was from Butler as was Woody Norris. Ernie Andres, from Indiana University, returned to the Kautskys but quit to concentrate on baseball with the Boston Red Sox. Bob Gerber from Toledo University returned from the service to play for the Kautskys.[18] In January they would sign their biggest and best addition, Arnie Risen of Ohio State. A junior from Williamsport, Kentucky, Risen had played a year at Eastern Kentucky University, then transferred to Ohio State.[19] Risen had academic difficulties in this, his junior year, and in January it was announced that he was scholastically ineligible for the second semester.[20] After being sought by a few pro teams, he signed with the Kautskys.

Chicago defeated Oshkosh, also on the 25, in the Gears' second game at Cicero Stadium, as Dick Triptow had 18 and Dick Klein 10 while Bob Carpenter was the only All Star in double figures with 12.[21] The *Rochester Democrat and Chronicle* account noted that Dick Tripton (sic) was "personally responsible for Oshkosh's downfall." The paper was dedicated to covering the league and would soon know the names of all of the players.[22] The Chicago roster had also improved greatly with the additions of Bob Calihan, a former University of Detroit star who had played with the Detroit Eagles before entering the military; George Ratkovicz, 6'7" tall, who had appeared with Chicago's Bruins in 1942 before entering the military; Bob Neu, a former DePaul star who had begun his career in Hammond in 1940; Bill Hapac, who had starred for Illinois and then the Bruins in 1940-41; and Dick Klein, from Northwestern, who much later was one of the owners of the Chicago Bulls in the NBA.

Youngstown opened its season at home with a loss to Sheboygan. The game was marred by a fight, involving Youngstown coach Paul Birch, Mike Novak of the Redskins and Irv Brenner of the Bears. All were ejected. The game drew 2700 fans who saw Press Maravich, former Detroit Eagle and later

LSU coach (as well as father of Hall of Famer Pete), lead his team with 13 points while Ed Dancker tied him for game honors with his 13 for Sheboygan. Free throws were the downfall for the Bears, who hit seven of 23, while Sheboygan dropped 15 of 25.[23] The opening month ended with Oshkosh winning in Sheboygan in one of the old defensive NBL battles. No one scored in double figures as Bob Carpenter of Oshkosh, Dick Schulz and Al Lucas of Sheboygan all had eight points in the 33–30 game.[24] The Western Division leaders were Oshkosh with two wins in three games while Sheboygan had split four games and the Gears and Kautskys had each lost two of three. The Eastern Division teams had played only one or no games as of yet.

Rochester hosted Cleveland to end the month of November and topped them easily before 3000 fans. Glamack, Cervi and Holzman all had 15 in this game. Holzman credited it with making him a starter, rather than just a "Jewish fixture" on the team.[25] Mike Byztura had 14 and Tom Wukovitz had 12 for Cleveland. The next day Oshkosh topped Sheboygan again, this time in Oshkosh by a 47–36 score with Al Lucas getting 10 for Sheboygan while Bob Carpenter (13) and Clint Wager (10) led Oshkosh.[26]

The league was idle on November 30, as the Pistons met the College All Stars in Chicago Stadium before 22,912 fans. The Zollner Pistons picked up where they'd left off the year before with a 63–55 victory, behind McDermott's 13 markers. Pelkington, Jeannette, Jerry Bush and Chick Reiser each had 11. Paul Cloyd from Wisconsin was the only All Star in double figures with 10.[27] The Pistons shot 36 percent from the floor to only 23 percent by the All Stars.

In what was their biggest game as an NBL entrant so far, the Royals went to Fort Wayne and topped the two-time champions by a 56–54 score. Bob McDermott had 15 and Jake Pelkington 12 for the Pistons, but Glamack (17), Cervi (13) and Graham (9) led the way for Rochester. Again, free throws were the key to victory as the Royals were 22 of 30 and the Zollners just 16 of 25.[28] The Royals then defeated Youngstown in Ohio behind Holzman's 14 and Glamack's 13, then topped the Bears once again five days later to begin the league season with five straight wins. In the latter game, John Mahnken (15), Fuzzy Levane (14) and George Glamack (13) led Rochester, illustrating what a multi-weaponed attack Harrison had assembled.[29]

During this same period the two Wisconsin teams played a league doubleheader in the Milwaukee Arena that drew 6500 fans. Sheboygan topped Indianapolis 61–56 while Oshkosh defeated Youngstown 60 to 43. In the latter game Carpenter's 15 points were aided by Leroy Edwards and his 14 points.[30] (These doubleheaders in Milwaukee, and sometimes in Cleveland, were very successful in drawing five to ten thousand fans to the arenas and the concept would be continued into the NBA after the merger of the NBL and BAA in 1949). In Chicago, Fort Wayne won its first league game by a 60 to 51 margin. Bud Jeannette had 23, the league game high for the year, Bob

McDermott had 14 and Ed Sadowski 10 for Fort Wayne. Stan Patrick (17) and George Ratkovicz (10) topped the Gears' attack.[31] The Pistons went on to win at home against the Sheboygan Redskins with the balanced Pistons' attack showing clearly, as Sadowski and McDermott had 11 each, Reiser and Jeannette each had 10 and Pelkington had nine in the 70–52 contest. The Redskins were led by their big men, Novak (13) and Dancker (12), while Dick Schulz had 10. Sheboygan was hurt by its 22 percent shooting from the field, while the Pistons sank ten more baskets, shooting just under 33 percent, considered a very good percentage. The Pistons went on to Youngstown and defeated the Bears by nearly the same score (71–52) with McDermott going off for 25 markers. Press (or Al) Maravich had 13 as did Frankie Baumholtz, the former Ohio University star, who would make a bigger name for himself as a major league baseball player with the Cubs and Reds.[32]

Rochester went to Cleveland and took their sixth league win in a row before 2900 at the Cleveland Auditorium. Despite not having Mahnken and Nagretti, who were not furloughed from Wright Field, the game was not close as George Glamack had 20, Bill Holzman 15 and Otto Graham 11. Oshkosh continued its good start in the league with an easy win in Indianapolis as Carpenter (17), Gene Englund (13) and Leroy Edwards (12) dominated inside.[33]

On December 12, the Royals made another significant acquisition when Les Harrison outbid Sheboygan and Youngstown to sign Bob Davies, the former Seton Hall All American, who had starred for the Great Lakes Naval Training squad and had been the MVP of the 1942 College All-Star game. Levane described the kind of player Davies was.

> Bobby Davies was a great offensive player. He was a flashy player; he would dribble, pass the ball behind his back, but defensively, he couldn't play my grandmother. We used to have to cover for him all the time. Davies always liked to go to the ball. He took chances, but could fly. All around offensive player with great fast break. He had the outside shot and could drive to the basket.[34]

In addition, both Holzman and Levane had found Rochester to their liking (though they continued to commute from New York City) and had decided to not accept good job offers in New York City until at least the end of the season.[35]

At this early juncture of the season, Bob Carpenter and George Glamack had emerged as early scoring leaders with Mike Novak and Al Lucas right behind. Bob McDermott had played only four league games to the others' six, seven or eight so there would be a lot of movement in this list as the season progressed.[36] The Pistons were playing a lot of exhibitions against the Dow Midland Chemicals, Philadelphia SPHAs and the Chicago Collegians, games that would be regretted at the end of the season, despite Pistons victories almost every outing.[37]

Despite the return of so many ballplayers, everything was not going as well in most industries in the United States. Labor demands, often led by veterans who spoke out openly for economic justice, were not uncommon. Whereas during the war everyone pulled together, labor was no longer willing to simply go along with all of the requests of Big Business without what labor considered fair compensation. By the beginning of 1946 strikes were occurring in the largest plants in the country throughout the East, the Midwest and the lower Great Plains. Affected were thousands of glassworkers, steelworkers, Western Union employees, oil refinery workers, autoworkers and electrical workers, just to note the most prominent. By the end of January, 1292 steel plants were shut and 750,000 workers had gone on strike in that industry alone.[38] Most basketball players were still holding other jobs as the NBL teetered on the edge of economic failure even after the war.[39]

By the end of the calendar year Bob McDermott had managed to move into second in league scoring just behind Mike Novak and just ahead of Bob Carpenter, Ed Dancker and Dick Schulz. The standings saw Rochester, with eight wins in nine contests, and Fort Wayne, essentially tied, with nine wins in eleven games. Cleveland and Youngstown were below .500. In the West, Sheboygan had won 11 of 16 league contests to lead Oshkosh at seven and five by two games. Chicago and Indianapolis were below .500 with the Kautskys at only one win in 11 contests. After going winless in their first nine games, the Youngstown Bears had suddenly gotten tougher after adding Huck Hartman from Midland-Dow, defeating Indianapolis, Oshkosh and Chicago, before falling in Oshkosh.

Cleveland had signed Bob Shaw directly after the NFL season ended, where he played for the Cleveland Rams. In his first contest as an Allmen Transfer he led the team with 16 points in a narrow loss to Sheboygan.[40] It was hoped that Shaw's addition might make up for the loss of scoring punch that occurred when Mel Riebe was called up to the navy. He served at Great Lakes and was a star for them for two seasons (1945-46 and 1946-47).

Rochester played exhibitions against two excellent black teams at the end of the year. First were the Chicago Monarchs, who had both former New York Rens and Harlem Globetrotters on their roster, and were mostly a touring squad. The Royals topped them in a high scoring contest as Glamack (18), Cervi (14) and Holzman (11) had double figures. For the Monarchs, Sonny Boswell, who had played in the NBL with the Chicago Studebakers, led with 15, and Pop Gates had 13.[41] The next week the Royals defeated the Washington Bears by a 51–41 score before a disappointing crowd of 1600, the lowest turnout of the season in Rochester's Edgerton Sports Arena. The game had been hyped for more than a week and tickets were only 90 cents for the 1250 general admission seats. The Bears had been champions of the World Professional Tournament in 1943, but only Tarzan Cooper, who was now their coach also, and John Isaacs remained from that squad, and the fans simply didn't show interest in attending the game.

In the last weeks of the year the Royals added Jack "Dutch" Garfinkel, an All America player at St. John's in 1941 and current Philadelphia SPHA, to their roster. It was noted that he would join Holzman and Levane, his former teammate at St. John's, in traveling to Rochester from New York City.[42] The next day, December 22, the nation mourned the passing of General George Patton, who died in his sleep in Germany. The Royals were undefeated until December 29 when the Pistons came into Rochester and defeated the Royals before a crowd of 3800. Glamack led in scoring with 20 and was supported by John Mahnken with 14, while Jake Pelkington (17), Ed Sadowski (16), Jerry Bush (11) and Bob McDermott (11) led the Zollners' attack.[43]

Sheboygan, the Western Division leader, began the new year with back to back losses in Chicago and Oshkosh. The Gears stopped Cleveland to finally climb to .500 in 10 games. The Gears' owner, Maurice White, had initiated an incentive plan at this point that was designed, he thought, to maximize player performance. Each player received $6 per basket and $3 per free throw, payable only if the team won. The players discussed pooling the money and splitting it at the end of the season but they couldn't agree on this. White later added $3 per assist.[44] It was difficult to ascertain the effects of the incentive system; the Gears ended up at 17 and 17 and missed the playoffs, but others did notice the system and commented on it. The Gears lost two in

Al Cervi, star of the Rochester Royals and later the Syracuse Nationals. (Used by permission of Rochester Public Library.)

a row to the top Eastern teams, Rochester and Fort Wayne, both on the road. In Rochester, Otto Graham (13), Red Holzman (12) and Al Cervi (11) topped the Royals while Stan Patrick had 12 for Chicago. In Fort Wayne, Patrick again led with 14 with support from George Ratkovich's 9. McDermott had 11 backed by nine from both Sadowski and Jeannette.[45]

Rochester continued playing well in the beginning of 1946, winning three exhibitions and four league contests in the first two weeks of January, though the hint of potential difficulties arose at that point. Levane, Garfinkel, Mahnken and Nagretti were still on base, not discharged yet as had been projected, and the strain on some of the Royals was showing. In the Royals' victory on January 14 against Youngstown, Cervi, Holzman and Davies all played the entire 40 minutes and Graham would have, had he not fouled out near the end of the contest.[46] Then the Royals lost to the Pistons in an exhibition in Toronto, which drew 12,000 to Maple Leaf Gardens for the contest. Again Levane, Negretti and Mahnken were unable to play. Glamack and Jeannette tied for scoring honors in the game with 19. The Pistons went on to Buffalo and defeated the Wright Field team from Dayton, which had Mahnken and Nagretti, as well as Bruce Hale. Hale led with 24 points, Nagretti had eight and Mahnken only one as the Zollners entertained the 5500 fans with their victory.[47] The Royals and Pistons were slated for two league games following the Canadian exhibition. The feeling in Rochester was that the Royals, man for man, were better than the Zollners, but the Pistons were still "top dogs" because "as a team they function like one of the precision machines which bear their trade name. Individual players don't try to set up plays for themselves; the team looks for its play first."[48] On the 19th the two Eastern leaders met in Rochester where the Royals won 61 to 43 before 4400 fans. The two teams then boarded the train and went to Fort Wayne, where they met the next evening. In that contest Fort Wayne won 58–53 to draw even with the Royals. At this point, the halfway mark of the season, the Royals were 13 and 2 while the Zollners were 15 and 3, giving the Pistons a ½ game edge. In the West, Sheboygan was 14 and 8 with Oshkosh (9–8) and Chicago (9–9) in a battle for the second and last playoff spot.[49] The scoring leaders were McDermott, Dancker, Glamack, Carpenter, Patrick, and Novak, but McDermott had played four fewer games than Dancker, so McDermott's 18-point lead was even more significant, since he would have more games still to play. At this point the Pistons began winning more consistently and the Royals fell into a minor slump. The Royals lost to Sheboygan, Chicago and Oshkosh while Fort Wayne defeated Cleveland and by the end of the month the Pistons had a full two game lead on Rochester. The Royals played some exhibitions against Sheboygan in Waukegan, Illinois (Otto Graham's hometown), and the Rens in Mohawk, New York, and won both of those games to get back into the winning habit, then downing Cleveland in league play in Rochester. The owner of the Allmans grew fed up with the tumble that his team had taken, having dropped 10 of their last 11 contests to drop to 3 and 15. Allman fined Bob Shaw $50 for his listless play, then released him. Shaw was picked up by Youngstown for one game, appeared the next year in eight games for Toledo's NBL franchise, then ended his pro basketball career.

The Pistons' winning was briefly interrupted by an upset loss in Youngstown, where Baumholtz had 19, Moe Becker 15 and recently discharged serviceman Leo Mogus had 14 to pace the Bears in their win. Sadowski (16) and Pelkington (11) were the only Zollners in double figures.[50] The Pistons then went to Chicago and beat the Gears, who had just slipped into second ahead of Oshkosh. The Pistons then defeated Cleveland, Oshkosh, Indianapolis (before 7000 in Butler Fieldhouse), Cleveland again, Indianapolis once again, and Sheboygan, before falling to the Royals in Rochester. In this game, played before a capacity crowd of 4,000, Glamack and Holzman each had 16 while the Pistons were led by Sadowski (14), McDermott (13), Jeannette (10) and Bush (10) in the 58–55 Royals win, described as "mighty rough."[51] The Royals had hit another rough patch with Cervi out with a bad back and both Mahnken and Nagretti still not discharged and missing games because of their service at Wright Field. Rochester and Fort Wayne returned to Fort Wayne, where the Royals won again, this time by a 64–59 margin in North Side Gym. Despite the Fort Wayne lead of two full games with three weeks to go, a prescient article by Ben Tenny in the *Fort Wayne News-Sentinel* questioned whether the Pistons were strong enough to overcome Rochester in the playoffs.[52] Tenny also raised the issue of rough play in his column the next day, comparing the "kneeing, pushing and occasional fist" that the NBL seemed to be moving toward, with the old ABL (a league in which Fort Wayne competed during the life of the league from 1925 to 1931). Tenny said that "fans tired of that (style of play) and the loop fizzled out." In contrast he saw the NBL as one of "high-powered offenses, clean-cut players and good competition" and linked this to the rise in popularity of the league and the professional sport.[53] Tenny's concern was mentioned by George Beahon in his column for the *Rochester Democrat and Chronicle,* where he cited Ed Dancker of the Redskins as the NBL's "bad boy," having fouled out of 10 of his team's 20 games.[54]

At the end of February the Royals played the Rens once again, in Schenectady, New York, defeating them by 14. Davies (13), Levane (12) and Holzman (10) were in double figures for the Royals while Pop Gates and Puggy Bell topped the Rens, scoring with 12 each.[55] The Royals returned home to top the Gears before 3800 fans, then played the next night in Cleveland, defeating the Chicago Colored Monarchs. In the latter game, Sonny Boswell (13), the former Chicago Studebaker, and Wee Willie Smith (9), former Ren and Chase Brass player, led their teams in scoring.[56]

By the end of the month, there were two questions about the playoffs: would the Royals catch the Pistons and would Chicago or Oshkosh be the other team in the Western series? In scoring, Bob Carpenter and Bob McDermott were in a virtual dead heat for the lead, with Carpenter having 412 points in 30 games (13.7 ppg) and McDermott having 407 in a like number of contests (13.6 ppg). The Pistons released three players, including Herm Schaefer, to get the roster down to 10 (called a workable size). They had added Bob Tough to their roster, probably a reaction to the Royals adding Bob Fitzgerald to their roster in mid–February. It was noted that all three released players could continue to work at the Zollner plant if they wished.[57] That same day the Pistons' lead stretched to three games and, on March 3, the Pistons clinched the regular season championship with a victory over Sheboygan, after defeating Cleveland the day before. In the latter contest Mel Riebe returned from Great Lakes Naval Base to score 20 points for the Allmens, but that was not enough to spell victory for his team.[58] To Al Cervi, Riebe's return subtracted as much as it added since Cervi felt Riebe was over-rated, a great shooter but one who played no defense.[59]

The season's last week saw Carpenter still leading Bob McDermott 442 to 430. Leroy Edwards in his 10th professional season and no longer as fast at 30, still managed to be sixth in the league in scoring, averaging 10.5 points per game. More exciting news was the potential addition of George Mikan to the Chicago Gears when the DePaul season ended. If the Gears made the playoffs, he would be able to compete for them. Another note was Bob Davies being announced as coach of Seton Hall, beginning March 15. Davies would succeed his former coach and mentor, John "Honey" Russell, as basketball coach (as well as baseball coach), although Seton Hall had not fielded a basketball squad since 1942-43 because of the war.[60] What effect this would have on him, as a player, was unclear. Despite beating the Pistons for their fifth straight victory, the Gears fell short of making the playoffs as Oshkosh finished at 19 and 15. Chicago was 17 and 16, but with no chance of making the playoffs, lost in Youngstown to the Bears 54 to 38.

The Playoffs

The playoffs began in Sheboygan and Fort Wayne on March 12. Sheboygan defeated Oshkosh 46–45 and Fort Wayne defeated Rochester 54 to 44. In the former contest Bob Feerick, the former Santa Clara star, had 12 for Oshkosh, while Dancker and Novak scored 12 and 10, respectively, to lead Sheboygan. The latter game was notable in that Bob Davies failed to score from the field, going 0 for 14 as the Royals shot 16 percent from the floor. Fort Wayne shot 38 percent, termed "brilliant" by Ben Tenny of the News-Sentinel.

Only the decided advantage by the Royals in free throws (20 of 27 to the Zollners' 10 of 18) kept the game reasonably close.[61]

The next night, before 3,800, Rochester defeated Fort Wayne 58 to 52 in a game where both teams made the same number of field goals, but the superior number of free throws taken and made by Rochester was the difference. They were 18 of 26 to the Fort Wayne crew's 12 of 20. Glamack led three Royals in double figures with 13, supported by Holzman and Davies with 11 each. Sadowski had 14 and McDermott 10 for the Pistons.

On that same day, it was announced that the Royals would not be participating in the World Professional Tournament, slated to open March 25. Earlier Harry Harrin, the promoter of the tournament, and Leo Fischer, editor of the *Chicago Herald-American* and co-sponsor, had journeyed to Rochester to negotiate with Les Harrison in order to get the Royals into the tournament. The Chicagoans offered to pay most of the Royals' expenses, but offered no salaries in return for them playing. Harrison put it to his players for a vote, saying that he would give the players the entire guarantee plus any prize money won, plus proceeds from an exhibition game in Anderson, Indiana, that they would play. The players unanimously accepted the offer, but when Harrison called Hannin to accept, he was told that "the business office refused to okay the deal, the whole thing was off." This had occurred right after the Fort Wayne opening victory and the feeling may have been that the Pistons would knock off the Royals and there was no incentive to get them to Chicago since the Pistons were so popular there anyway.[62]

Ten days later, after the Royals were the new NBL champs, Elliot Cushing, the *Rochester Democrat and Chronicle* sports editor, wrote a blistering column, both praising the great acumen of Les Harrison for creating the Royals from virtually nothing and blasting the organizers of the "pseudo champion Professional Tournament" for its mishandling of the Rochester team. Cushing quoted Ike Duffey, "who operates a jerkwater team in Anderson, Indiana." He noted that Duffey, "for the benefit of the tournament, blasted the Royals as being a 'home-court club' and said Rochester was not a good team because it 'would not win in the West.'" Cushing then went on to claim that most non-partial observers felt that "Johnny Mahnken will run rings around the highly publicized Mikan and that the latter will be just another player in the smart, tough competition next year." Finally he derided the Gears asking for $2500 to come to Rochester for the Royals Appreciation Game that would close the season, especially since the Royals request for half of that had been deemed unacceptable to the Chicago tournament organizers.[63]

Returning to Rochester, the Royals made short work of the Pistons by the same 58 to 52 score, then dominated the Zollners 70 to 54 to eliminate the champions from the playoffs. It was noted that scalpers were getting $5 for a pair of $1.20 seats and $8 to $10 for a pair of $1.80s. In the last game,

Glamack and Davies each had 23 points and Bob McDermott had no field goals in scoring three points. Sadowski (11) and Reiser (10) led the Zollners in scoring. The Pistons blamed their defeats on their having played too many exhibition games earlier in the season and having "nothing left for the last three games won by the Royals."[64]

In the West, Oshkosh took the second game of the series 53–41 in Sheboygan before 3,000 fans. Feerick (17), Carpenter (13) and Dancker (14) were the only players in double figures for the two squads. Returning to Oshkosh, Sheboygan reversed the loss with a 58 to 52 win. Two recent additions, Steve Sharkey, with 16, and Mickey Rottner, with 14, led the Redskins, who played without Ed Dancker, out with a knee injury. Oshkosh held on in the fourth game and routed Sheboygan 68 to 42 as Leroy Edwards had 21 to lead all scorers. The fifth game went to Sheboygan, in their auditorium, by a 65 to 46 score. Ed Dancker had 19 and Dick Schulz 14 to end the All Stars' championship hopes.

The defeat of Oshkosh in the Western Finals was the highlight for Sheboygan, as the Redskins were sent packing, in three games, by the Royals. The scores were 60 to 50, 61–54 and 66–48. Holzman (17), Mahnken (13) and Glamack (11) keyed the first victory. Bob Davies had 22 to top the scoring in Game Two and Holzman, with 16, led the scoring in the final contest as four Royals scored in double figures; Mahnken and Cervi both had 13 and Davies 12. Novak had 12 for Sheboygan.[65]

The World Professional Tournament

The World Tournament opened on March 25 without the NBL champions but with George Mikan, the College Player of the Year. He had signed with Chicago for $60,000 for five years, according to information released by Maurice White, the Gears' owner. White had beaten out both Rochester and Midland Dow for Mikan's services and he debuted in an exhibition game on March 19 in Anderson, Indiana, against the Anderson Chiefs. He scored 17 points, as did Bob Calihan, in leading the Gears to a 68–60 victory, one that Dick Triptow said "came quite easily."[66] Mikan played less than three quarters of the contest as he fouled out with two minutes left in the third quarter. In the next game, Mikan had 20 against the Detroit Mansfields in a game played in Cicero Stadium, which the Gears won 59 to 48.[67] Despite these successes, Mikan expressed his surprise at the differences that he immediately felt in the professional game. "I was a college boy with a substantial reputation, but I was coming into a professional game that had always been populated by a bunch of tough, road-weary, street-wise working stiffs who were anything but All-American boys."[68]

In the opening round of the Pro Tournament in Chicago Stadium on March 25, Anderson defeated Cleveland 59 to 46, Dow Midland topped the Indianapolis Kautskys by 72 to 59 and the Gears defeated the Pittsburgh Raiders 69 to 58. Ed Stanczak, a former Fort Wayne Central Catholic High School star who had not attended college, led Anderson with 21 points, but suffered a serious ankle injury in the game. For Dow, Urgel "Slim" Wintermute had 23 while Arnie Risen led the Kautskys with 20. Mikan led four Gears in double figures with 17 while Calihan (15), Patrick (15) and Szukala (10) supported his effort. A sobering note was the announcement of the death of Pierre "Huck" Hartman, the former Pittsburgh and Youngstown star, at 25, of pneumonia in Youngstown.[69]

On the next night 9520 fans showed up to watch Oshkosh defeat the Detroit Mansfields 60 to 32, the New York Rens crush the Toledo Allmens 82 to 39 and the Baltimore Bullets (the ABL champions) edge the Dayton Mickeys by 61 to 58. Carpenter (12) and Edwards (9) led Oshkosh in scoring. In the second contest, Hank DeZonie had 21 for the Rens while Pop Gates and Sonny Wood had 14 each. In the final game, Bloom and Stutz each had 15 for the Bullets, while Bruce Hale had 19 for Dayton.[70]

Both the Zollners and the Redskins had drawn byes in the first round and they opened their tournament action on March 29 in a quadruple header that drew 16,931 "screaming fans." Fort Wayne edged Dow Midland 67 to 65, with McDermott (14), Reiser (13) and Jeannette (12) leading the scoring. For Dow, Paul Cloyd (former Wisconsin star) had 22 and Slim Wintermute 11. Sheboygan's tourney ended unexpectedly, as they were upset 52 to 51 by the Gears, and their powerful new center, George Mikan. He had 14 and Calihan had nine, but Stan Patrick's two late baskets at the end of the contest sealed the victory. For the Redskins, Dancker had 11, Schulz nine, and Novak eight. Baltimore edged Anderson 67 to 65 as Bloom (17) and Stutz (16) led them again. In the fourth game of the day Oshkosh topped the New York Rens 50 to 44. Balanced scoring by the All Stars was the key to victory as Bob Carpenter had 14, Clint Wager 12, and Leroy Edwards and Fred Rehm 10 each. The Renaissance squad was led by Pop Gates, with 17, and Hank Dezonie, with 10. This set the semi-finals with three NBL teams among the four — the Gears, the All Stars, the Zollner Pistons and the Bullets.[71]

The semi-finals were played on April 3 and it turned into an all–NBL final, as Oshkosh topped George Mikan and the Gears 72 to 66, and Fort Wayne edged the Bullets 50 to 49 in a doubleheader watched by 12,235. Mikan was the game's high scorer with 25, but both he and Dick Triptow fouled out in the third quarter and were followed to the bench on fouls by Stan Szukala and George Ratkovich in the fourth quarter. The All Stars led 36–33 at the half but the Gears put on a furious third quarter to lead 50 to 44 after three. The victorious All Stars got 22 from Bob Feerick, 18 from Bob Carpenter and

10 from Clint Wager to propel them back to the tournament finals for the first time since 1943. The Zollners struggled mightily with the Bullets as Stan Stutz (real name Modzelewski), with 16, and Mike Bloom, with 10, kept Baltimore in the contest until the final gun. Bud Jeannette with 10 and Bob McDermott with 9 topped the Pistons' scoring.[72]

The finals would pit the two NBL teams, one from the West and one from the East, and the Zollners seemed to have everything going for them. They had defeated the All Stars in four straight league contests and in a preseason exhibition, but there was a new wrinkle. After the second round of the tournament on March 29, the All Stars and Zollner Pistons had taken the train to Oshkosh where they met in the final game in Oshkosh for the season. In a first, the All Stars defeated the Pistons 61 to 52 behind Bob Feerick's 15 and Bob Carpenter's 10. McDermott was high scorer for the game with 18 and Bob Tough had 12.[73]

That victory certainly buoyed the All Stars as they nipped the Gears and got set to play the Zollners once again. The championship was to be a best of three series as was the battle for third. The merchants of Oshkosh joined together to sponsor the broadcast of the games on WOSH, in what the merchants said was "the public interest."[74] And the recent victory over the Pistons was the impetus as the All Stars topped the Pistons in Game One 61 to 59 behind the strong showing of the old pro, Leroy Edwards, called "Horse" by the *Tribune*'s Wilfred Smith.[75] Edwards had 12, Carpenter 19 and Feerick 11 to lead Oshkosh while McDermott had 17 on 6 of 22 shooting to lead the Zollners. A crowd of 11,132 enjoyed this game and the opening game, in which the Gears, led by Mikan's 17 points and Calihan's 16, defeated Baltimore by a 59 to 54 score.[76]

The next night Fort Wayne evened the series with a decisive nine-point victory, despite 24 points from Edwards on 10 of 24 from the field. McDermott again led the Pistons' scoring with 13, but his five of 21 from the floor was not impressive. Neither team shot well as Fort Wayne was 19 of 71 (26 percent) and Oshkosh, 16 of 81 (19 percent). The Gears defeated Baltimore for the second straight night by 65 to 50 and 15,000 fans enjoyed seeing Mikan get 27 markers in the victory. The fans also cheered the announcement that the local hero, Mikan, had been named the tournament's Most Valuable Player.[77]

Two nights later, the Pistons won their third straight World Professional Tournament title (tainted by Rochester's absence) by defeating the All Stars 73 to 57 before only 8,440 fans. The attendance was probably lower because the Gears had already finished off the Bullets. The *Tribune* noted, however, that it had been expected that the teams (Chicago and Baltimore) would play three games no matter what, but "Chicago was not available for some reason." Dick Triptow had no recall of Chicago even considering playing, so it may have been a decision by Maurice White. Either way, the first game was between Anderson and Sheboygan, with the Chiefs winning 55 to 52. In the championship final, four Pistons scored in double figures, McDermott (20), Sadowski (14), Bob Tough (10) and Jake Pelkington (10), as the Zollners burned the nets for 40 percent on 29 of 72 shooting. Oshkosh shot 20 of 90 for 22 percent and were led by Leroy Edwards with 24 and Bob Feerick with 19. Edwards, at 31, was the unexpected high scorer of the series with 59 points, 36 percent of his team's scoring.[78]

The season ended for the NBL teams at this, the latest date (April 8) in a year to date. The Zollner Pistons were the World Professional Tournament champions once again, but after their decisive loss to Rochester in the NBL Eastern Division playoffs, it was hard to view them as the undisputed champions. There would be lots of fodder for discussion and speculation during the offseason as the new rivalry between Rochester and Fort Wayne grew. The league had drawn more fans than ever before, and had approached the number of league teams not seen since the 1939-40 season. There was interest in league expansion and the economy continued to grow, so more discretionary spending was likely to lead to higher attendance. Players continued to be discharged from the military and that boded well for even better play for 1946-47. There were problems, however, including size and control of all playing arenas, and these problems would be more pronounced as the NBL faced a new challenge in 1946, a new professional league.

An Explosion of Teams:
The 1946-47 Season

The 1945-46 season had been a great success for the NBL as it had expanded to eight teams in two divisions, the league's largest size since the 1939-40 season. The teams that began the 1945 season had all done reasonably well except for the Cleveland Allmen Transfers and they left the league. The league, however, had attracted five new teams and began the season with 12 teams divided into two six-team divisions. This re-infusion of interest had been predicted in the dark days of the war years when the league had only four teams and was barely surviving, often only with the assistance of Fred Zollner, the bank-rolling owner of the Fort Wayne Pistons. A number of the new teams were teams that had either shut down or cut back on play during the war because of lack of players or capital. Now with the return of both, there was great interest in joining the NBL.

In May of 1946, NBL president Leo Fischer sent an "Official Bulletin" to all NBL clubs. In that bulletin, he prepared the owners for their June 17 meeting in Chicago, which he referred to "as the most important in our history." He had a number of agenda items. The first was expansion, and he noted that the league would operate with at least ten teams. He went on to mention those and his progress in dealing with the applicants from Toledo, Syracuse, Pittsburgh, Milwaukee, St. Louis, Minneapolis, Dayton and Anderson, Indiana. Fischer said that new clubs were paying $1500 and recommended an increase to $2500 or more.

The second issue was financing, and he proposed a budget of $6000 for the league for the next year, with $3000 going to the commissioner as salary, $1000 for publicity, $1000 for postage and printing expenses, $500 for travel expenses and $500 for the league treasurer. He proposed that this money should be generated by having the league receive $30 from the revenues of each league game played.

The next item was a selective draft in order to keep salary costs under control and to limit whom each team might have to outbid for players on teams outside the league. He also recommended that rosters return to a 12-person limit.

Other issues included exhibitions, schedules and officiating with the best situation being a full-time officiating staff. The last note, in bold capital letters was, "Sign your key men as soon as possible to binding contracts!"[1]

At peak strength, the United States had 12,300,00 troops in World War II. There were approximately 300,000 casualties, meaning that over the period of 1945 to 1947 12 million troops, mostly males, returned to civilian life in the United States. These included a very large percentage of NBL players as well as other basketballers who had played in college and the Armed Forces but had not begun professional careers. This influx of talent was a large factor in encouraging owners to pursue franchises in the National Basketball League. The economy was booming, as it had during the war, but now there weren't shortages, and war industries had converted back to more domestic needs. This resurgent economy and the continued interest in basketball as a spectator sport emboldened unsure owner-entrepreneurs to take another shot at basketball in the NBL. In the Eastern Division Toledo was a returning member, with the same management, but now sponsored by Jeep, and the team became the Toledo Jeeps. Buffalo, which had had a team in the Midwestern Conference the first year of the NBL in 1937-38, also returned as the Buffalo Bisons once again. A new entry in the East was a squad from Syracuse, the Nationals.

According to Danny Biasone, the Nationals' owner and the inventor of the 24-second clock a few years later, all he initially wanted was to have the Rochester Royals come to Syracuse for an exhibition game against a local team which Biasone would sponsor. Les Harrison, the Royals' owner, wasn't interested, no matter what the guarantee and Biasone called the NBL office in Chicago to complain. To his surprise, he was offered the opportunity to purchase a franchise and thereby guarantee Rochester would be playing in Syracuse a number of times during the season. So for $5000 (this was Biasone's claim, but, as noted above, Leo Fischer said that $2500 could purchase a franchise) Biasone purchased an NBL franchise, which, over the years, became the Philadelphia 76ers and now is worth more than $100 million.[2] The Nats would soon sign Benny Borgmann, a great pro basketball player from the 1920s and '30s and a scout for the Rochester Red Wings in baseball, as their coach. A team would soon follow.

The new teams in the Western Division were the Anderson (Indiana) Packers and the Detroit Gems. The Packers had been playing many of the NBL teams, and owner Ike Duffey decided to pursue a league affiliation. Detroit was a new squad in a city where the NBL had tried once before (in 1940) but where basketball seemed to be popular enough to make a real go of it. The Gems were owned by a Dearborn jeweler named Maurice Winston. His associates included King Boring and Ben Maron, who would serve as the coach of the team.[3]

Anderson, as noted, was new to the league and to major league sports, and the entry into the league was trumpeted as a major coup for the city, which quickly embraced the Packers as the city's team. Anderson was a city of 42,000, about the same size as Oshkosh and Sheboygan. At their opening game the Packers had as their guests the lieutenant governor of Indiana; Leo Ferris, the president of the Buffalo entry of the NBL; Frank Kautsky and Paul Walk, the co-owners of the Indianapolis Kautskys; Lon Darling, coach of the Oshkosh All Stars and secretary-treasurer of the NBL; all members of the Oshkosh squad who would play in Indianapolis the following night; Keith Brehm, the NBL publicity director; C.D. Rotruck, the mayor of Anderson; and other city officials.[4]

Other leagues and teams were forming or re-forming as a result of the new atmosphere of confidence that pervaded post-war America. The NBL owners tried to cooperate with a number of these leagues and they all signed an agreement not to infringe on each other's territory. The New York State, New England and American Leagues all were part of these. This had also been proposed by Leo Fischer in his May 1946 "Bulletin," saying, "I believe that the time is ripe for us to work with the American League and minor league groups on observance of contracts and regulation of tournaments and exhibitions games."[5] One notable non-participant was a new league that was formed in the spring of 1946 by owners or operators of large northeastern sports arenas where hockey (mostly the NHL, but also the AHL) was played. Led by Walter Brown of Boston and Max Kase of New York (and the *New York Journal-American*), these arena operators ended up forming a league that had teams in 11 major cities and was named the Basketball Association of America. The feeling was that there were more than enough players to go around, these arenas were available (and they wanted to put them to more use), and fans would come to almost any good sporting event in the euphoria of post-war America. The BAA chose to be in Washington, Philadelphia, New York, Boston, Providence, Toronto, St. Louis, Cleveland, Detroit, Pittsburgh and Chicago so there would be a direct turf challenge in only two cities, Chicago and Detroit. Considering Detroit and Pittsburgh's dismal appeal to fans in these cities as NBL entrants, it was surprising that ownership in these cities signed on, but arena owners saw an opportunity and were willing to give this new league a try.

Meanwhile, the older, more established NBL began with its teams playing exhibitions around their regions. The Pistons, perhaps fearing lack of interest because of the BAA, decided to forego their pre-season Eastern swing and stayed in the Midwest, playing a number of exhibitions against Midland (Michigan) Dow, a strong squad in the region. They had attempted to join the NBL in the summer of 1946, but the league was already set for the new season and agreed to allow them to join in 1947-48. They would then schedule games against all 12 NBL teams in 1946-47, preparatory to joining the league as a full member in 1947.[6] The Dows played and lost an exhibition to Oshkosh, then the Zollner Pistons played Dow Midland in five straight evenings in Peoria, Illinois; Springfield, Illinois; St. Louis; Decatur, Illinois; and New Haven, Indiana, with the Pistons winning three of the five contests. During that run, the NBL officially opened with Syracuse losing to Toledo, before 4100, at the University of Toledo Fieldhouse 57–43.[7]

Chicago and Rochester began their exhibition season with a game in Schenectady, New York, won by the Royals 55 to 50. George Mikan, now in his first official year as a Gear, scored 19 and Bob Davies had 16 for the Royals. Both would miss vital games for their respective teams as the season progressed, Davies in fulfilling his new position as coach of Seton Hall, his alma mater, and Mikan in a contract dispute. Sheboygan chose to become the "first basketball team to travel by air" in heading to California to play the California Red Devils.[8]

The League Season Opens

Shortly before the NBL teams opened their seasons, the first judgment of the Nuremburg war trials was announced. The effects of the war continued to be felt, even as the United States and its Soviet allies entered the Cold War.[9]

The Chicago Gears began their league season on the road, losing to Oshkosh in Wisconsin. The Gears would be forced to play their first six league games on the road because their home venue, the International Amphitheatre, was being used for livestock exhibitions, locking the Gears out of the building until December 11. In the Oshkosh contest, the All Stars got 19 points from Gene Englund and 14 from Leroy Edwards as they muscled their way past the young George Mikan, who had 10. Bruce Hale led the Gears with 14 with Stan Patrick scoring 12.[10] Oshkosh then traveled to Indianapolis to open the Kautskys' league season with an Indianapolis victory 51–47. Anderson started its league debut with three straight victories and was the early leader in the Western Division. For Fort Wayne, the league opener was November 17 and they defeated the Youngstown Bears at home in an "unimpressive" victory before a "near capacity crowd." The winning Pistons shot 29 percent from the floor and the Bears, 23 percent. It should be noted that a "near capacity" crowd in Fort Wayne would have been something less than 4,000. Meanwhile in the

The 1947-48 Fort Wayne Zollner Pistons. Front row, left to right: Curly Armstrong, Bob Tough, Carl Bennett (General Manager/Coach), Richie Niemiera, Walt Kirk. Back row, left to right: Ken Menke, Carlton "Blackie" Towery, Bob Kinney, John Pelkington, Milo Komenich, Jack Smiley, Ralph Hamilton. (Dick Triptow personal collection.)

new BAA they were drawing as many as 17,000 to New York's Madison Square Garden.[11] The real battleground, however, would be in Chicago, where the two teams were in competition. The new Chicago Stags had an advantage in playing their home games early in November at Chicago Stadium and getting the chance to build up a fan base for at least a month before the Gears would play in Chicago.

By the end of November every team had played at least one game, although Chicago had played only one while Anderson had played six and led the Western Division with a record of five wins and one loss. Rochester led the East with four victories in as many games. Detroit was already one and five and Youngstown one and six in the Eastern Division cellar.

At this point the annual game pitting the College All Stars against the defending World Professional champions was held. With the Stags now using the Chicago Stadium for their home games, this would be a singular appearance for an NBL team (the Zollner Pistons in this case) on that floor. The contest resulted in a victory for the former collegians by a 57 to 54 score, in overtime, in front of more than 20,000 fans (23,778 claimed Jim Enright of the *Chicago Herald-American*).[12] The All Stars were led by George Mikan, late of DePaul and now a Gear with 16; Leo Klier from Notre Dame and now on Indianapolis with 12; and Freddy Lewis, former Eastern Kentucky star now on Sheboygan, also with 12. Despite Mikan being high scorer, Enright was most impressed with Klier, whom he called "a ball of unchained lightning with his blind passing and ball hawking talents."[13] For the Pistons McDermott had 22 and Chick Reiser 11. Worth noting is that almost all of the All Stars who would play professionally that year would play in the NBL. The game also had an opening contest to attract fans, and this pitted the Globetrotters against the NBL's Anderson Duffey Packers. Led by Howie Schultz with 20 and Bill Hapac, the former Chicago Bruin, with 13, the Packers won by 56–52. The 'Trotters were led by Goose Tatum with 17 and Ermer Robinson with 10.[14]

Two days later the Gears, on a seemingly interminable road trip, handed the Royals their first defeat 65 to 64 as Price Brookfield hit a shot with 17 seconds to go for the win. The Chicagoans had three players in double figures led by Mikan with 20, Stan Patrick with 16 and Brookfield with 13. The Royals were led by their guard tandem of Al Cervi (17), Bob Davies (16) and Bill "Red" Holzman (11).[15] The Gears moved on to Syracuse, where they topped the Nationals 69 to 59 behind Mikan's 21. The Royals traveled to Indianapolis, where they lost to the Kautskys before 8300 people by a 59–58 score. The Gears went on to play, and lose to, Syracuse, three nights later in Moline, Illinois, in what was probably termed a home game for the Gears. 4,000 people attended the contest and that relatively high number was probably a factor in what was the subsequent defection, three weeks later, of the Buffalo Bisons, as they moved their franchise to the Tri-Cities area of Moline, Rock Island and Davenport.

The Buffalo move meant that James "Pop" Gates, signed by Buffalo and a native New Yorker, would now be playing in small town America, where integrated sports teams were certainly unusual. Gates, Dolly King (Rochester) and Bill Farrow (Toledo) became the first African Americans in the NBL since the 1943-44 season. It may have been that the signing of Jackie Robinson (who also played for a pro basketball team in California, the Red Devils) by the Dodgers to a contract with the Montreal Royals, and his Rookie of the Year performance for Montreal in the International League, was influential in the NBL owners signing black players, but that seems less compelling than the fact that African Americans had been playing regularly against top white professional teams since the Rens began in the late 1920s. These teams had been very successful and they were popular with both black and white audiences. Clearly, the black players were just as capable as the white players, but, during the war, pro league basketball was not as much of a money-maker as playing on independent black teams, so more integration did not occur.

The Buffalo franchise had been hurting financially, only averaging 2500 fans per game. The competition with professional hockey, boxing and college basketball in the region was too much for the Bisons and they lost $25,000 on their first six league games. At that point they began considering moving to Milwaukee, Minneapolis or Moline. They ultimately chose Moline because of the success of the Chicago-Syracuse game that drew 4,000, played in Moline on December 6. Once the decision was made to move, the Bison management sold 40 (of the 100) shares in the team for $375 each. Most of these shares were purchased by small-business owners in the Tri-Cities region. In return, they received a season ticket for the remaining 16 home games as well as their investment in the team, which was re-named the Blackhawks on January 1, following a naming contest held for two weeks. The team was quickly embraced by the fans of the Tri- Cities area, and the first home games drew more than 3,500 fans to each contest, despite horrible weather conditions.[16] The Wharton Fieldhouse in Moline was a great place to play, according to both Dick Triptow and Stan Von Nieda. The latter recalled that the atmosphere was "quite raucous, a hometown crowd. They were really great fans, very supportive and there was no question that the team was a great source of community pride."[17]

On December 11 the Gears played their first home game against the Oshkosh All Stars, the first chance for the local fans to see George Mikan in a Gears' uniform. The 7,900 fans who attended the game at the International Amphitheatre left disappointed after Oshkosh dumped the Gears by a 44–41 score. Mikan had only nine with Stan Patrick (11) and Bob Calihan (10) topping the scoring. Bob Carpenter had 14 for Oshkosh. Even greater disappointment was revealed the next day as Mikan announced that he was retiring. Mikan said that "his heart isn't in the game under present conditions." The team also played without their new coach, Davey Banks, the former New York Celtics' great. Reports said that he and the team "weren't hitting it off well."[18] Banks was let go by owner Maurice White after compiling a record of 4 and 4. His dispute was also about money, too, at least in part. He had been hired for $7500, but was then told that he was being paid on a 52-week contract, instead of one where the season and, his agreement, ended March 9.[19] Dick Triptow says that Bruce Hale handled the coaching duties for the next three weeks until Bob McDermott was signed, but the official coach was the general manager of the Gears, Harry Foote, with assistance from Swede Roos, the previous year's coach.[20] So the Gears had no coach and had lost their biggest star.

The issue with Mikan was precipitated by money, not lack of interest. White was attempting to get Mikan to accept $6500, rather than $12000 for his salary, because White was having money problems. He had already cut four ballplayers without warning when they went to board the train heading to an away game. One of them was Mikan's older brother, Joe, so this latest action by White was not well received, to say the least, by George Mikan. He elected to sue the Gears and White for breach of contract and the unilateral nature of the contract.[21]

Mikan Returns to a Different Squad

The Mikan case went on for six weeks and he did not appear in a game again until February 1, 1947. Mikan was represented by two attorneys, Stacy Osgood and noted labor lawyer Arthur Goldberg, who was later appointed to the U.S. Supreme Court. The lawyer for the Gears was David Fisher, who was also the son of Judge Harry Fisher who was hearing the case. The two sides were encouraged by Judge Fisher to find an amiable settlement and it seemed that they had in mid–January, but it all fell apart. The hearings were covered regularly in the sports pages of Chicago's papers as if they were a sporting event and finally were settled, very quietly, it should be noted, on January 29. Two nights later Mikan was back in the lineup at the International Amphitheatre before 3,700 fans where he scored 22 points in leading the Gears to a victory over the Syracuse Nats.[22]

The team that Mikan joined was in fifth place in the division with a record of 13 and 14. With only four teams in each division making the play-offs, the Gears would have to step up the pace to even make the playoffs. The standings at that point looked like this:

Eastern Division			*Western Division*		
Rochester	20	5	Indianapolis	19	7
Toledo	16	12	Oshkosh	16	9
Fort Wayne	15	12	Anderson	16	13
Syracuse	9	16	Sheboygan	14	12
Tri-Cities (Moline)	9	17	Chicago	13	14
Youngstown	9	21	Detroit	4	22

In addition, the team was not quite the same as the squad that Mikan had left. On January 3 the Gears had signed Bobby McDermott as their player-coach after the Pistons had agreed to give him his release.

The Zollner Pistons had started off the league season playing uninspired basketball, and by December 20 they had seven wins and seven losses and had dropped six of their last seven league contests. Following their loss at Syracuse, McDermott, Charley Shipp and Milo Komenich got into an argument over a craps game aboard the New York Central's overnight sleeper. A fight ensued and Carl Bennett was awakened from his berth to break up the altercation. Later he talked with each player separately to get his version of the events, then talked to Fred Zollner about it when the team returned to Fort Wayne. Zollner suspended all three of the players as a result of "insubordination to team's management."[23] This was done on December 21 (Merry Christmas!). Ben Tenny made an interesting comment at this time regarding McDermott, who had led the Pistons to two NBL titles and three World Professional Championship Tournament titles. "(F)ans here never took the long-shot artist to their hearts ... one of the paradoxes of local sports history."[24]

Ultimately, Shipp ended up in Anderson and Komenich was reinstated. McDermott was given his outright release and allowed to make his own deal after all the NBL clubs waived on him. He then went to Cleveland to investigate the offer of the Cleveland Rebels of the BAA, who were coached by his old friend and former Celtic teammate Dutch Dehnert, but rejected it, and signed with the Gears as their player-coach on January 2, 1947.[25]

At about this same time, the Buffalo owners decided that they could not keep their franchise from hemorrhaging money without some sort of change, and that was a relocation to the Tri-Cities area of Illinois-Iowa. Despite being the furthest west city in the league, the Hawks, as they were now called, continued to play in the Eastern Division. The leaders of that division were the defending champions, the Rochester Royals, who were leading by 3 games at year's end. The Royals were still led by Bob Davies, Al Cervi, Bill Holzman and George Glamack, but they had signed Dolly King, the former Long Island University star, and were now getting regular and excellent play from Fuzzy Levane, the former St. John's star who had finally been mustered out of the Coast Guard. King, an African American, was signed by Les Harrison only after he had raised the issue with his team, noted that the squad needed players, that he had played with blacks before, and felt that they should be accepted to the team. When the team agreed, King was signed on October 15, 1946.[26]

The Royals were not big or very rugged, but they were fast and excellent shooters. By the first of the year they led the league and Al Cervi was the league's leading scorer. The Royals' coach, Eddie Melanowicz, had been a great player in Buffalo, but Les Harrison, the Royals' owner, often called himself co-coach, and in later years, according to Al Cervi, Harrison "stole" Melanowicz's win record as his (Harrison's) own.[27] Arnie Risen, who joined the Royals near the end of the 1947-48 season, said,

> Les Harrison was a good judge of personnel and what it took to win, but he was not good at coaching. Back then there was not much coaching at the pro level; the guys just got together and did it. There weren't a lot of plays. The coach decided who needed rest.[28]

After leading the division by five games at the beginning of February,

The 1946-47 Rochester Royals. Front row, left to right: Dutch Garfinkel, Al Cervi, Red Holzman, Bob Davies, Fuzzy Levane. Back row, left to right: James Quinlan, Arnie Johnson, George Glamack, Dolly King. (Dick Triptow personal collection.)

the Royals hoped to stay healthy and, maybe, add another big man to help them in the playoffs in March. The team did not have the same cohesiveness night after night that had been evident the previous year, mostly because of the loss of Bob Davies to his Seton Hall coaching much of the time. In a mild upset, the Zollner Pistons defeated the Royals in Rochester in early February. The Pistons had added a Texan named Frank Gates late in the season and got a big boost from Bob Kinney, a 6'6" inside player from Rice. In the victory over the Royals, Pelkington had 11 with Gates and Kinney both chipping in with 10. The Royals got 27 from Al Cervi, 13 from Levane and 11 from Holzman, but they shot only 25 percent from the floor (to the Pistons' 35 percent).[29] Davies' absence was strongly felt. The Royals then traveled to Anderson, where the Duffey Packers beat them before the Royals finally righted themselves in Indianapolis. There, before 11,000 in Butler Fieldhouse, the Royals won 50 to 47. Bob Davies flew in from New Jersey for the contest and tied George Glamack for high scorer with 12. Leo Klier led the Kautskys with 10.[30] The next night, the Royals played their third game in three nights in Indiana and absorbed another defeat, this time to the Pistons. Four Pistons were in double figures, led by Kinney and Chick Reiser with 15 each. Glamack, with 17, and Holzman, with 15, topped the Royals, who had Bob Davies once again.[31]

The Pistons to hoped to catch the Royals, but their last gasp fell short in Toledo, on February 23, where the Zollners lost 60 to 54. Two nights later, in Syracuse, the Nats ended Moline's seven game win streak with a 53–47 victory. In the last five minutes of the contest a fight broke out between "Pop" Gates of Tri-Cities and Chick Meehan of Syracuse. Meehan had been an all around athlete in high school in Syracuse and was popular with the local fans. He was a good-looking guy who prided himself on being able to stop hot shooters. The Hawks and Gates were hot, riding their seven game winning streak. The game was rough and Gates was leading the team in scoring with 11. A loose ball at the top of the key found Meehan and Gates dashing for the same object. In the jostling Gates pushed Meehan and he went straight to the floor where he "hit his face hard and made a noise like a bowling ball striking a pin."[32] Meehan arose, faced Gates with his fists up and Gates floored him with a punch. From there, the fight escalated to include players and fans, before Gates was surrounded by police and rushed out of the armory. Gates's account was that Meehan had gotten "chesty" with him and had twice thrown him (Gates) to the floor before the incident. Gates later sent a letter of apology to Meehan (dated March 11, 1947) in which he noted that they had been friends before and that the trouble never should have started and that he was sincerely sorry.[33]

Despite both Gates and Meehan saying that the incident had nothing to do with race, the feeling was that the fans' involvement did and there was a fear among some owners that the continued use of African American players might be bad for the league. By the next year there were no African Americans on NBL rosters, though that would change the next year after that (1948-49). Still, many white owners feared for their profits and some saw the continued inclusion of blacks as simply not comfortable to them.

Contention for the playoffs was still tight and the last weeks of the season would be crucial (and draw fans, it was hoped). In the East, Rochester had a 3½ game lead on Fort Wayne with Syracuse, Toledo and Moline all within a game of each other for the last two playoff spots. In the West, Oshkosh and Indianapolis were fighting for the top spot, with Chicago, Anderson and Sheboygan all close behind, within a game of each other. The real fight in both divisions would be for fourth, making the playoffs. In the individual scoring race, Al Cervi of the Royals had taken the top spot in scoring and scoring average (13.9) with Hal Tidrick and George Sobek of Toledo second and third, followed by Arnie Risen of Indianapolis and Bill Holzman of Rochester. About fifteen spots below them was George Mikan, but having played in 17 fewer games, he had the best scoring average (17.3). Down a bit further was Leroy

Edwards who, despite being in his tenth professional season (unusual for the time), could still average 9.4 points per game.

The last two weeks of the season saw teams jostling for position in the league and making roster changes to carry them through the playoffs and the World Professional Tournament. The Rochester-Chicago game of February, in which the officials had decided to use a sudden death format for the second overtime, was replayed from the start on March 15 and the Royals pounded the Gears 75 to 55. The Gears, however, put on a rush at the end of the season and managed to tie Sheboygan for third in the division behind Oshkosh and Indianapolis, leaving Anderson and Detroit out of the playoffs. In the East, Toledo and Syracuse came on at the end and finished over .500, while Tri-Cities faded to 19 and 25. The Youngstown Bears were far behind. Cervi led the league in scoring topping Fred Lewis of Sheboygan by 47 points with Arnie Risen only three behind Lewis. The All Star teams had the following (in order of points received in the voting):

First Team	Second Team
Al Cervi	Bob Carpenter
Bob Davies	Bob Calihan
George Mikan	Arnie Risen
Fred Lewis	Red Holzman
Bob McDermott	Hal Tidrick

The MVP of the league was Bob Davies, despite missing 12 of his team's 44 games. This was a source of contention between Harrison and Al Cervi, who was still angry about not having Harrison's support for 1947 MVP sixty years later.[34] Davies was not well liked as a player, even by his own teammates. Stan Von Nieda recalled when his team, the Tri-Cities Blackhawks, and the Royals were traveling together by train from Moline to Rochester,

> We were playing back in the club car and we were playing rummy. It was a couple of the Rochester guys playing and a couple of our guys, maybe four or five of us playing. Bob Davies walked in and said, "Deal me in," and when he said that, the two Rochester guys got up and left. He wasn't very well-liked.[35]

Lon Darling was voted Coach of the Year for bringing the Oshkosh All Stars from a 19–15 record in 1945-46 to the Western Division title in 1946-47. The Rookie of the Year was Freddie Lewis of Sheboygan. The other rookies on the All Rookie team were Hal Tidrick, Leo Klier, Don Otten and Jerry Rizzo.[36]

The Playoffs and the World Professional Tournament

The playoffs opened with the Pistons facing Toledo, the Royals facing Syracuse, the Gears against the Kautskys and the All Stars facing the Redskins of Sheboygan. The Pistons opened at home against the Jeeps and won easily 65 to 38 in Game One as the Jeeps hit just 20 percent from the field. Game Two was not much closer as Fort Wayne won by 51 to 34 and the Jeeps sank even lower in their shooting to 12 percent on 9 of 76 field goals for the game.[37]

Game Three was in Toledo and the Jeeps managed to improve their play considerably. The conditions were not ideal, as a driving rain caused water to drip onto the floor of the Toledo Fieldhouse throughout the contest. Nevertheless, it was a fast, hard contest before 4000 fans, who braved the adverse elements to view the game and the Toledo victory. Tidrick (18) and Sobek (12) led the Jeeps while Chick Reiser with 11 was the only Piston in double figures.[38] The fourth game saw the Pistons lead most of the game but fade in the last six minutes after leading 49–41 at that mark. The final score had Toledo winning 58 to 53 as Bernie Meehan, acquired in the last week of the season from Youngstown, got 20 to lead the attack. Curly Armstrong had 19 for the Zollners.[39] The final game was played in Fort Wayne and was not close, as the Pistons finally put the Jeeps away with a 64–46 win. Chick Reiser led a balanced attack with 17 while George Sobek of the Jeeps was the only other player in double figures with 12.[40]

In the other Eastern series, the Royals were heavily favored against the Nationals and they defeated them three games to one, although the games were surprisingly close; the Royals won Game One in overtime, Syracuse won Game Two by three points, and the Royals won the last two games by six and five points, respectively. Davies and Cervi were in double figures for each game with Levane scoring double figures in three of the games. Rizzo and Chaney had fine series for the Nationals.

The Western series between the two Wisconsin squads was very tight. Sheboygan surprised Oshkosh by winning the first two games of the series in Sheboygan in two low scoring games. With their backs to the wall, the All Stars went to work in Oshkosh. First they won 54 to 44. Then they evened the series with a 53–45 victory with Englund, Wager and Edwards getting 13, 10 and 9, respectively, inside. The Redskins hurt their cause by making only five of 18 free throws.[41] The All Stars took a tightly contested final game by a 49 to 47 score as Gene Englund and Al Lucas led their teams with 15 points each.

Meanwhile the Gears and Kautskys were going at it. Despite the Kautskys' slightly better record, Mikan's presence made the Gears the favorite in the series and the first two games seemed to bear that out. In Indianapolis the Gears edged the Kautskys 74 to 72. Mikan and Arnie Risen put on a good show, scoring 26 and 25, respectively. Herm Schaeffer, Gus Doerner, Ernie Andres and Leo Klier all had 11 to support Risen, while Price Brookfield had 12 for Chicago.[42] A controversial in-bounds play turned the ball over to the Gears, and Stan Patrick scored with 15 seconds left for the win. The Kautskys

George Mikan (left), Patricia (Pat) Mikan, Helen Triptow, and Dick Triptow during the 1946-47 season. (Dick Triptow personal collection.)

protested but it was disallowed.[43] Two nights later the Gears won again, although Risen took game honors with 27 points. Mikan had 22 and McDermott 11, but both fouled out. A big factor in the victory was the Gears' hitting 17 of 18 free throws.[44]

The series then moved to Chicago with the Gears a prohibitive favorite to end the series in Cicero Stadium. Instead, the Kautskys, before 2200 fans, edged the Gears 68 to 67 as Risen, Doerner, Klier and Schaefer all scored in double figures, led by Risen's 18. Mikan and Calihan had 15 and Hale 13, with Triptow and McDermott right behind with eight each.[45] The next game was equally stunning, with the Kautskys winning again by a 55–54 score before 3,000 in the International Ampitheatre. Risen and Doerner with 16 and 15, respectively, led the Kautskys while Hale (16) and Mikan (10)[46] led Chicago. According to Dick Triptow, Risen "was giving Big George (Mikan) all kinds of trouble in the pivot."[47]

The series came down to one game, played in the International Amphitheatre (which had a court of over 100 feet, rather than the 94 feet of regulation courts) and the Gears managed to win in a rough, bruising game. Mikan scored 26 points, held Risen to nine (he fouled out in the third quarter) and was supported by Calihan's 17 in the 76–62 Gears' win. Herm Schaefer led the Kautskys with 17. Player-coach Bob McDermott was ejected for "roughing up" referee Norris Ward and a fight broke out in the crowd before order was established and the game resumed.[48]

In the Western Finals, the Gears would face Oshkosh in a best of three series and the Gears would not have Bobby McDermott on the floor for the first two games as a result of the incident in the Kautskys' final game. McDermott was also fined $100 but was allowed to coach from the bench. Even without Mac, the Gears swept the All Stars in two games by 60–54 in Chicago and 61–60 in Wisconsin. In Game One Mikan and Calihan had 18 and 17, respectively, while holding Edwards to zero. Gene Englund had 18 for Oshkosh. In Game Two Mikan (22) and Calihan (14) led Chicago while Ralph Vaughn, the All Star guard who had played for the Chicago Bruins in 1941-42, led Oshkosh with 21. Edwards did not play and Carpenter had 14. The Gears shot 32 percent from the field to the All Stars' 29 percent in the final game.[49]

Despite their loss, the All Stars still had the World Professional Tournament to look forward to and, as a tune-up to those games, they renewed their old rivalry with the New York Renaissance. Over the period from 1935 to 1939 the two teams met 24 times with the All Stars taking 13 of the contests. Since then the series had been dormant, so this game was a great draw in Oshkosh. In a strong ending, the Rens won and both teams headed to Chicago for the tournament. The Rens were led in scoring by Nathaniel "Sweetwater" Clifton with 20; he later was one of the first African Americans to integrate the NBA in 1949-50.[50] The Rens moved on to Fort Wayne, where they defeated the Zollners 48–42, led by Clifton and George Crowe, who would later play for the St. Louis Cardinals and the Cincinnati Reds in a respected Major League Baseball tenure.[51]

The Eastern Finals again pitted the Zollner Pistons against the Royals, with the feeling that this was the real championship series, that either of these teams would beat Chicago or Oshkosh. The two teams split the opening games with Rochester winning 58 to 49 in Rochester and the Pistons winning 56 to 49 in Fort Wayne. The shooting was not good for either team in either game with the top percentage being the 33 percent that the Royals had in Game 2. At about that time, the All Star, MVP and Coach of the Year awards were announced and new MVP Bob Davies was quoted as saying that "Al Cervi is basketball's best finisher." Since Cervi had gotten more votes for the All Star team than Davies, he may have felt the need to be politic in his good fortune and assuage the feelings that Cervi might have had regarding the MVP result. That was probably wise, since even nearly 60 years later Al Cervi was still apoplectic over what he considered a rigged vote that cost him the MVP award.[52] The Royals also had strong opinions about the coaching award, feeling that either Nat Hickey of the Kautskys or Benny Borgmann of the Nationals "deserved the award more than Darling."[53]

The decisive third game was played in Rochester and was a Royal rout

76 to 47 as four Royals (Holzman, Cervi, Davies, King) scored in double figures to key the triumph. Aroused by what the Royals saw as vile, racist epithets against Dolly King, the team played with anger and determination. King had been the "target of a sulpherous and slanderous attack from the Fort Wayne bench which was a disgrace to democratic America.... Victory was a triumph for American sportsmanship."[54] By contrast the *Fort Wayne News-Sentinel* saw the crowd as "the most vociferous, even dangerous, crowd we believe we have ever seen at a sports event" and the key to the win in which the Royals hit 48 percent in the first half to assure the rout.[55]

The Royals' win assured them of the home court advantage in the Championship Finals against the Gears. The first contest was in Rochester, and it went to the Royals in a game in which six players went out on fouls—Hale, Mikan, Patrick, McDermott of the Gears and Nagretti and Glamack of the Royals—as 58 fouls were called. Bob Davies had 23 for game honors with six others in double figures—Dolly King (16), Mikan (14), Hale (12), Patrick (12), Levane (11) and Cervi (10).

As an aside, the Chicago Stags defeated the Washington Capitols in D.C. that same evening before 4,357 fans.[56] There were already rumors of the BAA having difficulties at this point. Elliot Cushing, *Rochester Democrat and Chronicle* sports editor, averred that Cleveland would leave the BAA because of poor attendance and that Chicago had taken a considerable loss. New York, Philadelphia and Washington had all done well. In the NBL the Kautskys had drawn over 150,000 fans to Butler Fieldhouse to lead the league, and Rochester would have drawn more than the 100,000 that they did draw had there been more parking space as "the clamor for tickets gets louder every day." Cushing went on to note that there was a "crying need for an assist column in National league scoring records," an obvious oversight, one can say in hindsight, as was the lack of a rebounding column.[57]

The Gears and Royals met again in Rochester on April 5 and the Gears upset the Royals 67 to 63. George Mikan had 27 points while Al Cervi had 22 for the Royals. King (13) and Davies (11) were in double figures for the Royals as was Price Brookfield (12) for Chicago.[58]

The World Professional Tournament

The World Professional Tournament began on April 5, which meant the two top NBL teams would not be able to compete. In addition, none of the BAA teams were competing and the BAA playoffs were also still going on at this time. Thus, playoffs for both Chicago teams, and the World Tournament, were happening in the Chicago venues. It would be interesting to see how much basketball the fans would actually view in person during this period of time and how the Chicago Stadium would be able to provide for both the BAA Playoffs and the World Tournament. The tournament's first day drew 10,731 fans and they saw two NBL teams, Oshkosh and Anderson, advance by defeating Herkimer, New York, and the Pittsburgh Pirates, respectively. The next night the tournament, before 11,230, had a full slate of games with three more NBL teams defeating their opponents and one NBL squad, Syracuse, losing. Sheboygan defeated the Portland (Oregon) Indians 62–48; Moline beat the Baltimore Bullets of the ABL, with Buddy Jeannette (who scored 19 points), by a 57–46 score; Dow Midland defeated Syracuse by 71 to 39 and Toledo topped the New York Rens by 62 to 59, despite four Rens— Sonny Wood (16), Hank DeZonie (12), Nat Clifton (10) and George Crowe (10)— in double figures.[59]

The NBL Finals shifted to Chicago and the International Amphitheatre on April 7, where the Gears took a two games to one lead with their 78 to 70 victory before 4,700 fans. As in game one, 58 fouls (31 on the Gears, 27 on the Royals) were called. The referee was Chuck Chuckovich, the former NBL star, who certainly had an insider perspective on the game. The Royals had better balance with five players— Davies (19), Cervi (13), Holzman (12), Glamack (11), and King (11)— in double figures, but the Gears had Mikan (23) and Calihan (22) to offset that.[60]

That same evening, a couple of miles away, the World Professional Tournament continued, before 14,295, with another Stadium quadruple-header in which four NBL teams moved to the semi-finals, eliminating three NBL teams and the Dow Midland squad. Fort Wayne defeated Anderson 52 to 40; Oshkosh topped Sheboygan by 53 to 44; Toledo eliminated Dow 59–55 and Indianapolis won over Moline by 65 to 56.

The next night, the Stags won in the Stadium with no attendance given, probably indicating that it was low. It was also announced that the NBL would be withdrawing from the Professional Basketball group that had been formed before the season began. NBL commissioner Ward "Piggy" Lambert claimed that only the NBL and the ABL were living up to the agreement. Lambert also charged that the BAA had a "raid list" wherein Don Otten of the Moline Blackhawks and Bob Davies of the Royals were designated for the Celtics. Leo Ferris, general manager of the Blackhawks and vice president of the league, threatened court action if the BAA tampered with Otten.[61]

The NBL ended its season on April 9 as the Gears stopped the Royals 79 to 68, to win the title before a crowd of 7,200 in the International Amphitheatre. Both teams had balanced scoring. For the Royals, Glamack and Holzman had 15, Cervi 12 and Davies 10. For the Gears Calihan had 22, McDermott 15, Mikan 14, Hale 11 and Patrick 10. Mikan had four fouls halfway through the second, sat for the third and played until there was a minute left in the game.[62] Despite winning the series, the Gears were not NBL champions for

The Chicago Gears celebrate their victory in the NBL playoffs of 1947. Kneeling, left to right: Max Morris, Jack Goldie (Trainer), Bobby Goldie (Jack's son), Bob Calihan, Stan Szukala. Standing, left to right: Price Brookfield, Dick Triptow, Art Stoefen, Harry Foote (General Manager), George Mikan, Bobby McDermott (Player-Coach), George Ratkovicz, Stan Patrick, Bruce Hale. (Dick Triptow personal collection.)

that year, at least officially, since the league commissioner, Piggy Lambert, had decided, for unexplained resaons, that the regular season champion would be the league champ. So the Gears were merely the winners of the playoffs.

Meanwhile, a few miles away, Indianapolis topped Oshkosh 59–38 in one semi-final and Toledo surprised Fort Wayne 61–56 in the other. Herm Schaefer, with 19, and Arnie Risen, with 13, led the Kautskys. Toledo was led by Hal Tidrick, with 17, and Bob Gerber, with 13, in their victory. The all-NBL doubleheader drew 11,839 fans to Chicago Stadium, meaning over 19,000 fans viewed pro basketball in Chicago that night involving six NBL teams.[63] The next night, before 14,413, the Kautskys defeated the Jeeps 62–47 to win the title while Fort Wayne defeated Oshkosh 86–67 for third. Of particular note were the 26 points that the Pistons got from rookie Ralph Hamilton, who was signed just before the tournament began, out of Indiana.[64]

Three nights later the Chicago Stags drew only 2025 to the Stadium for their game against the Capitols. The NBL seemed to be the best game in town to the fans. As noted earlier, there were BAA successes, one of which was Joe Fulks. He finished the BAA regular season with 1389 points in 60 games, an average of 23 points per game. Including his playoff totals (222 more), he finished with 1611 points which broke what was claimed to be the former season point total of 1404 points set by Willie Kummer in 1912 when he played for Connelsville, Pennsylvania, of the Central Pro League, which operated in six western Pennsylvania towns— Johnstown, Uniontown, Charleroi, Washington and Pittsburgh, as well as Connelsville. Kummer, 61, attended the record-breaking game and congratulated Fulks.[65]

The end of the NBL season was not the end of the season for either of the two squads. Les Harrison, owner of the Royals, and Maurice White, owner of the Gears, cooked up a three game series that would culminate in Rochester and be the opportunity for the Rochester fans to thank the Royals and bid them farewell for the year. Harrison, a noted tightwad, paid only three of his players and got the others to play as part of their regular contracts. Maurice White had his players under contract until April 15, but offered the players $1000 each if they could take two of the three games. In a letter to Dick Triptow, Al Cervi recalled the Royals players' attitudes toward the games.

> The series was really a joke. Most of the guys didn't even want to play. Three of us got $300 apiece and the others, nothing.... I would have liked to get a part of the $1,000 that White gave you guys.[66]

Even 60 years later, Cervi was still angered by Harrison's cheapness.[67] The Royals took the first game, played in the Hershey Arena on April 11 before 3,499, by a score of 76–73, despite Mikan's 21 points, which led all scorers. The next night the Gears won in Schenectady, New York, in overtime by a 75–74 score. Mikan again led the Gears with 17 while Bob Davies had 22 for the Royals. On April 13, the Gears won the series in Rochester before 4,000 fans, many of whom also attended the appreciation dinner for the Royals. The score was 65–60 with Mikan again high scorer with 27.[68] Fuzzy Levane led the Royals with 15. In recalling the season, Levane noted that he thought the Royals were as good or better than the Gears, but the difference was always George Mikan.[69]

George Mikan and the Chicago Gears were the biggest story of the 1946-47 NBL season, but the birth of the BAA was a larger story for professional basketball. The BAA venue owners had, as noted, a mixed season of success, and their league was going to have to make significant changes to stay afloat. The NBL, too, would be adjusting to its rival, and the 1947-48 season would also bring structural changes to the NBL. The continued vitality of both leagues was in jeopardy since early indications were that two major, professional leagues were probably one too many, as far as the talent pool and the public acceptance was concerned. How, and when, the two leagues adjusted to that reality, would affect the next season, and beyond.

The Lakers Bring Dominance to the NBL: The 1947-48 Season

By 1947 the world was seemingly war free, but there was significant tension and fighting in the Middle East as the Jewish Haganah attempted to pressure the British to agree to create a Jewish state of Israel in the British territory of Palestine. On November 29, 1947, the newly created United Nations determined that there should be two states created out of Palestine, one Jewish and one Arab. The Jews accepted the partition; the Arabs did not and fighting began for territory between the two groups. In Europe the communist control of Eastern European nations, dubbed the Iron Curtain in March of 1946 by Winston Churchill in a speech at Westminster College in Fulton, Missouri, continued. Czechoslovakia's government was becoming less stable, due to communist efforts to suppress all opposition.

In the United States big labor began to flex its muscles. Whereas labor and big business had pulled together without much disagreement during the war, things now had rapidly changed. During the war most able-bodied men were at war and women first entered the labor ranks in large numbers. Factories were converted to war needs. After the war there was prosperity in the United States, as Europe struggled to rebuild its factories and businesses. The G.I. Bill allowed many returning soldiers to enter colleges, rather than return immediately to factories, and a labor shortage allowed unions to gain leverage in the potentially boom economy. In politics, President Truman was seen by many as a lame duck president, having succeeded Franklin Roosevelt in April of 1945. Truman was unpopular in his own party, particularly in the South, as he supported his party's efforts at pursuing equal rights for African Americans.

People had more time and money to spend on entertainment, and professional basketball was part of that. The fall of 1947 began what was probably the high water mark of the National Basketball League. The prior season had ended with 12 teams but Youngstown chose not to return. Detroit's franchise was sold to owners from Minneapolis who transferred the franchise to that city. The Midland-Flint Dows, who had applied too late for entry into the league the previous year, were added to the NBL, keeping the number of teams stable at 12. In 1946 players were still being gradually released from service, but as the season of 1947-48 began, the talent pool had swelled to its greatest capacity ever. It was possible that two leagues, in this case the NBL and the BAA, might both be able to prosper with this additional talent and the leagues made efforts at cooperating. They had been rivals in only two cities, Chicago and Detroit, though the efforts of both squads in Detroit were too sad to be called a rivalry. In Chicago, where the Stags and the American Gears played, serious competition for fans was not evident. Talks held in June of 1947 between BAA and NBL officials were moving towards a number of peaceful coexistence measures, including a common draft, a prohibition from raiding the other league's team rosters for players, possible doubleheaders with the NBL and BAA playing teams in their own leagues at a common site and time.[1] Later there was talk of a possible "championship series" between the two leagues.[2]

Whether this truce would have lasted or not became moot when Maurice White, the owner of the NBL champion Chicago American Gears, decided to pull his team out of the NBL and form his own professional league. According to Dick Triptow, White wanted to be the president of the NBL and, when that didn't occur, he pursued the creation of a new 32-team league with him as president and initial financial backer. This was pared to 16 teams, including the Gears who had a few players go to other teams in the new league, the Professional Basketball League of America, as player coaches. White made these moves in late summer and by October his league was ready to play.[3]

With the announced formation of the PBLA, the NBL revised its own schedule to accommodate 11 teams and drafted the players from the Gears in case the league were to fail. The feelings were strong that this league would self-destruct and the NBL owners wanted to be prepared to swiftly re-assign the Gears players as well as any other NBL players who chose to jump to the PBLA. The NBL owners did vote to suspend any jumpers for five years, but they still wanted to clarify who had the rights to these various players.

With the loss of the Chicago team in the NBL, relations between the NBL and the BAA became even more cordial. With no fighting over turf, the Chicago Stadium became a place where the two teams might mutually meet and make money. Beginning on November 15, 1947, a series of 22 doubleheaders would be held in the stadium pitting the Chicago Stags against a BAA opponent and two NBL teams battling one another in the other game. The leagues agreed to modify the financial distribution system to allow for all four teams to be given a percentage of the gate. Formerly, only the home team got gate receipts. This new agreement was great for the BAA since it helped boost interest in the league in Chicago and brought out more fans. The gains for the NBL were a bit more hopeful. Since the Stadium had a capacity of over 16,000 and crowds for the World Professional Tournament (played in the Stadium) were consistently over 10,000, it was felt that NBL teams would be able to make money with such an arrangement.

The PBLA began play on October 24, 1947, when the Atlanta Crackers defeated the Oklahoma Drillers. Three weeks later, on November 12, 1947, the league declared itself bankrupt, having lost $600,000 in that time. (This was at a time when the average house cost just under $7000.) The question of what happened to the Gears team then arose. Initially the implication was that there was a good chance that the Gears could return as a team as long as there was a new owner (other than Maurice White) for the franchise. It was noted specifically that the players had not been assigned to various clubs (as had been rumored), but would be assigned according to the league's draft law.[4] On November 16 it was reported that the Minneapolis franchise had withdrawn its opposition to the return of the Gears. Then, at a meeting at the Morrison Hotel in Chicago later that day, the owners voted 11–0 to reject the bid of the Gears to return to the league that year. The league also said that the Gears players would be reassigned to a Chicago franchise were one to enter the league in 1948-49. This was an unbelievable tale and, since no Chicago franchise did enter the next year, could never be truly disproved. Instead the Gears players were "subject to a previous draft" and reassigned to various NBL clubs.[5] In addition, White was clearly disliked by the other owners, despite his creativity and innovation, which was ahead of its time. The feeling was to eradicate any notion of his team and that was done.

The biggest prize, George Mikan, was assigned to the Minneapolis franchise. Bob Calihan went to Flint, Price Brookfield to Anderson, Bruce Hale to Indianapolis and Bob McDermott to Sheboygan. The other players went to the various teams, other than Fort Wayne who had not drafted any of them. The dissolution of the Gears destroyed a potential dynasty, felt Dick Triptow, and it altered the balance of power in the entire league and, later, all of professional basketball.

At the time of the PBLA implosion the NBL teams had completed no more than five games. Minneapolis had started by splitting two games but the teams had no legitimate center. The Lakers had signed local stars, mostly from the University of Minnesota or Hamline College, and were interested in more. In particular they expressed an interest in Howie Schultz, who was on the Anderson Duffey Packers and was a former Hamline player. Clearly, the Lakers sought to be a hometown team. Bill Carlson of the *Minneapolis Star* noted, upon the signing of another local high school and Minnesota Gopher star, that the Lakers were "the best home-town club in the circuit."[6]

Despite this hometown pride, the team was clearly dying for a real center. Beginning in mid–October the Lakers' pursuit of a center was chronicled on an almost daily basis. It appeared that either Jim Pollard, a natural forward, or Bob Gerber, a former Toledo cager signed on October 29, would have to handle the center chores until November 13, when it looked as if Mikan would fall into the Lakers' lap. Despite the NBL claim that there was no list, the *Minneapolis Star* noted that Mikan was on the Lakers' list as the PBLA folded.[7]

It is hard to imagine that the NBL owners, particularly Ben Berger and Maurice Chalfen, who had drafted Mikan when the PBLA was formed, ever seriously considered allowing the Gears to return to the league. First, Maurice White was disliked by most, if not all, of the other owners. He was willing to spend too much and his behavior was often loud and boorish. Many people acknowledged that he had a drinking problem, which Dick Triptow addresses briefly in his account of the Gears. Certainly his creation of a rival league warranted permanent excommunication from the NBL and shunning from the owners, but punishing the Gears' players didn't necessarily follow. The success of the Gears did concern the owners. Mikan's rapid development and growing dominance in the league was aided by the excellent supporting cast that the Gears had. McDermott was seen as the greatest player in NBL history, by many, and its best overall outside shooter. Triptow was considered the fastest player in the league and a great driver to the basket. Calihan was a great shooter and scorer. Hale was a fine shooter from anywhere on the floor and a smart tactician. Ratkovicz was a burly back-up to Mikan and Brookfield, Szukala and Patrick were excellent shooters and all-around players who understood the concept of team play. Although Rochester and Fort Wayne had consistently strong teams, there certainly were worries that the dominance of the Gears could lead to a lack of interest in the NBL, when they were engaged in a heated struggle in Chicago with the Stags of the BAA for fan interest and media attention. By giving up Chicago the NBL could work more harmoniously with the BAA and possibly abet notions of a merger, leading to a situation parallel to that which baseball followed at the turn of the century when the American League and the National League agreed to a World Series and a jointure of the leagues.

The Lakers then went through a courtship of Mikan, who was concerned with leaving Chicago and his nearly completed law studies.[8] He signed a contract on November 18 for what was reported to be $15,000 per year for four years, but he notes that it was actually $12,500. (This was only about five times the average income of an American worker at the time, a far cry from the percentages of today.) Two nights later, he played his first game as a Laker, and the result was a disappointing loss to the Sheboygan Redskins by 56 to 41 on the winner's floor, before 2500 fans. Mikan had 16 points, but wasn't used to his teammates as of yet and it showed.[9] Mikan noted that the Lakers and Kundla "weren't used to playing with a big pivot player, so their idea was to feed me the ball every single time they got it." The Redskins caught on to this quickly and the result was that they simply smothered Mikan and totally broke down any Laker offense.[10]

It should be noted that the game and its players were much improved over the NBL of five years, three years or even one year before. The return of players from the service and the addition of new young stars from college forced many of the older, established stars on a number of the clubs from starting roles to backup roles, and many other players into retirement or to teams in other, less competitive leagues. For example, Rube Lautenschlager, the veteran Sheboygan star, decided that, at age 30 and as a teacher at a Sheboygan junior high school, he simply couldn't travel as much, now that the league had expanded. The influx of new players also hastened his departure, as it did the departure of other veterans, some of whom signed with the BAA. The 11 NBL teams probably had 90 percent of the top professionals in the United States at the time. The BAA had Joe Fulks, a fabulous shooter; Howie Dallmar, a fine playmaker from Stanford; Ed Sadowski, a former NBL player, now 30; Carl Braun, only 20 but with great potential; Buddy Jeannette, the 30-year-old player-coach of Baltimore; Max Zaslofsky, a fine shooter; and Bob Feerick, but little else to draw crowds to the games.

The League Is Reshaped

The addition of the various Gears players made strong teams even better and provided more help for weaker squads in the league. The Lakers weren't the only team seeking a stronger center. The Eastern Division champion Rochester Royals had let George Glamack go to the Indianapolis Kautskys and his replacements, Arnie Johnson, Andy Duncan, LeRoy King and the recently acquired former Gear, George Ratkovicz, did not have the offensive strength to provide an inside presence. The Royals were still a guard oriented team built around Bob Davies, Al Cervi, Bill "Red" Holzman and Andrew "Fuzzy" Levane. Still, the team was expected to repeat in the division, and, with the exit of the Gears, was one of the favorites for the NBL championship.

The Royals started their exhibition season with victories over NBL rivals Toledo Jeeps and Indianapolis Kautskys before losing to the Philadelphia Warriors of the BAA in Philadelphia. The Royals then lost to the new Flint-Midland entry in the NBL and twice to the BAA Baltimore Bullets, whom they defeated a week later. In between they played the Warriors again, this time topping them by 13, holding Joe Fulks to just 14 points. The Royals still had question marks as they prepared for their opener on November 11 in the Edgerton Arena of Rochester.

The other league teams had started their seasons already and an early surprise was the Anderson Duffey Packers. The Packers had entered the league the year before and compiled a 24 and 20 record, and played to mostly good crowds in the local Anderson, Indiana, High School gymnasium, which seated over 4600. Ike Duffey, owner of a meat packing plant in Anderson, hired Murray Mendenhall, considered the dean of Indiana high school coaches, from Fort Wayne Central High School to coach the team. In 1946-47 he was voted coach of the year in the NBL. Duffey and Mendenhall signed a number of new players to the team for 1947-48 including John "Shotgun" Hargis from the University of Texas, who had also been in the Marines during the war. Joining him as rookies were Frank Brian from LSU and Charlie Black from the University of Kansas. Both had been in the service and were in their mid–20s. Howie Schultz, the 6'6" center from Minnesota, returned after leading the team in scoring in 1946-47 with 11 ppg.

Anderson started the season winning eight of their first nine league contests and shot out to the lead in the Eastern Division over both Rochester and Fort Wayne. The Zollner Pistons had added Ralph Hamilton, a 25-year-old rookie from Indiana University who had starred in the service. A native of Fort Wayne, Hamilton played at South Side High and had joined the Pistons briefly at the end of the 1946-47 season, appearing in the World Professional Tournament in Chicago where he scored 26 points in the Pistons' third place victory over Oshkosh. Also added to the roster was 24-year-old rookie Jack Smiley, who had played at the University of Illinois on the "whiz kids" squad of 1943 before going off to war, then returning to the university to complete his college career in 1947.

Fort Wayne played exhibitions mostly against other NBL clubs, keeping their travel to a minimum. They began the league season with wins against Sheboygan, with their 24-year-old rookie center, Marko "Mike" Todorovich from the University of Wyoming, and in Syracuse against the Nationals, the latter a 52–52 victory in which Jake Pelkington had 20 points.[11] The Pistons faced Anderson after losing in Dayton to the Dayton Metropolitans, a team led by Duke Cumberland and Nat Clifton, African American stars who had 24 and 11 points, respectively, in the Dayton victory. In the Anderson game the Pistons scored 69 points, but lost 82–69 as NBL shooting and scoring accelerated across the league. The three rookies, Brian (19), Hargis (17) and Black (16), as well as Schultz (17), all scored in double figures for the Packers.[12] The Pistons faced Mikan and his new Lakers' teammates in Fort Wayne on consecutive nights in early December and came away with two losses. Led by Mikan, with 20 and 24 points in the two games, and Jim Pollard, with 18 and 10, the Lakers had no trouble with Fort Wayne in either contest. Even at that early date in the season, the Fort Wayne writers were questioning the possibilities of Pistons success that season.[13]

Fort Wayne then defeated the Tri-Cities team in Moline before losing to Rochester in Fort Wayne. The Royals got 13 points from Andy Duncan on the inside to complement the guard play of Cervi (11), Holzman (16) and Levane (10), while the Zollners were led by Curly Armstrong (14), Jake Pelkington (13) and Walt Kirk (12).[14] The Pistons then traveled to Chicago where they defeated the Lakers in the second game of a Stadium doubleheader following the BAA opening contest. Mikan got 22, but the Pistons held the Lakers to 24 percent shooting, while shooting 33 percent themselves, but 46 percent in the first half when the game was really won.[15]

By the end of November the league standings showed Anderson in front in the East at eight wins and one loss, with Fort Wayne and Rochester both two games back, and Syracuse, Toledo and Flint all under .500. The Flint-Dow team was particularly disappointing, having lost eight of their first nine. After being denied admission the prior year because of a late application to the league, the Flint-Midland Dows were optimistic. They had looked adequate in the preseason, but once the season began, so did the losing. The additions of Stan Patrick and Bob Calihan from the Gears' break-up were helpful, as Calihan led the team in scoring and Patrick was third in that department, but the team never learned how to win, and their losses were often not close. They ended the year with only eight victories in 60 games and left the league soon after the season ended.

In the Western Division, all five teams were bunched together near the .500 level with the Lakers the best at four wins in seven games and the Oshkosh All Stars, last at five and seven. The Lakers were trying to find the right combination to augment Mikan. Clearly Jim Pollard would be the second starter and "Swede" Carlson seemed secure at another spot. Rookie Jack Dwan seemed to be a fourth starter, but the team needed a floor leader and they got one in late November when they signed Herm Schaefer, who had been dropped by the Indianapolis Kautskys after just three games. Viewed as too old by the Kautskys, Schaefer proved to be just right for the Lakers.[16] His impact, however, was not immediately apparent. The Lakers lost five in a row on the road and dropped to the bottom of the tight Western Division early in December. Part of the Lakers' problem was the All Star game against the World Professional Tournament champion Kautskys. Pollard was the high scorer in that contest, played November 28 in Chicago Stadium, with 19 points, as the College All Stars won 68 to 62. Pollard traveled with the team to Syracuse on a Thursday, took a train back to Chicago for the Friday night game, then traveled back to Rochester for a Saturday game. The team then went on to play and lose at Flint, though Mikan had 23 and Pollard 13. The traveling was wearing to all the players, but especially Pollard. Pollard was seen as the first of the great leapers in professional basketball by Stan Von Nieda, who recalled, "He was the first guy I ever saw, in practice (he wasn't allowed to in the game), dunk from the foul line on the dead run. He could really get up there."[17]

The Lakers finally broke their losing streak in Huntington, Indiana, 30 miles southwest of Fort Wayne, by a score of 56 to 42, defeating the Zollner Pistons. Mikan hit 14 of 15 free throws in totaling 24 points.[18] The Lakers returned home but continued to stumble against Oshkosh, losing 44 to 38, as none of the players on either team scored in double figures.

In terms of individual scoring at that point, rookie John Hargis of Anderson led the league in points with 211 in 16 games, followed by Mikan, Al Cervi of the Royals, Frank Brian, another Anderson rookie, and Bob Davies of Rochester. Mikan had played in only 10 league games but was averaging 20.4 points a game, just short of Mel Riebe's 20.5 record average that had led the league in 1944-45. Within a week, Mikan had improved that average to a record 20.7 ppg, and led the league in points, followed by Cervi, Hargis and rookie Marko Todorovich of Sheboygan.

In mid–December, Dick Triptow, the former Gear, went from Tri-Cities to Anderson in a cash deal, then was traded to Fort Wayne for Milo Komenich in a deal that "has the league wondering," according to Bill Carlson, the *Minneapolis Star* reporter.[19] Other roster changes were common, but most involved dropping players and signing new ones. Few major trades transpired. At about this same time, global issues interceded directly with the NBL. Phil Fox, a popular NBL referee from Brooklyn, was rumored to be through for the season and was set to travel to Palestine with a "hand-picked band" of fighters to join the Haganah. Three weeks later it was noted that his trip to Jerusalem and Tel Aviv had been sidetracked and he was back refereeing.[20]

The Lakers were beginning to assert themselves, particularly on the defensive end of the court, and they hosted the Eastern Division leaders, Anderson, with the intention of establishing their overall superiority. That hope proved ill founded, or at least premature, as Anderson topped the Lakers 57 to 53 on December 17. Two of the top Duffey Packer scorers, Howie Schultz with 18, and Rollie Seitz with 14, were Hamline College alumni and they enjoyed the return to the Twin Cities. Mikan had 27, but he got little help from his teammates, as Pollard was next with eight.[21] This loss seemed, however, to arouse the Lakers, who began winning consistently.

The Lakers closed out the calendar year with league wins over Tri-Cities, Sheboygan, and Indianapolis, as well as an exhibition victory over a St. Cloud Moose team in St. Cloud (Minnesota). They ended the calendar year with a record in the league of 14 wins and 9 losses and looked to be the class of the Western Division. George Mikan continued to score consistently in the 20-point range and was the most dominating presence inside that the league (or professional basketball) had ever witnessed. Stan Von Nieda noted that playing against Mikan was a lost cause

> It was hopeless; you hoped not to get caught in a switch with him, but every now and then, you did. I would make a fake at blocking the shot, which was impossible, but I would put my hand over his eyes, so he couldn't see the basket too well, and he used to cuss me for that.... What was I going to do with a 7-footer, 6'11" guy? He was a tremendous competitor. He could play in today's basketball game just because of his Competitiveness. He just wouldn't let anyone outrebound him.[22]

The only other team over .500 in the Western Division was the Sheboygan Redskins, led by their rookie, Mike Todorovich; Chicago acquisitions Bobby McDermott and Max Morris; as well as veterans Paul Cloyd, Ed Dancker and Fred Lewis. In December McDermott was sold to Tri-Cities because of differences with Sheboygan management. McDermott had been made player-coach in Sheboygan and Doxie Moore was kicked upstairs, but after the Redskins won three of seven games under McDermott, he was replaced by Moore and then sold to Tri-Cities, where he was made player-coach, replacing Nat Hickey. After McDermott's departure, the Redskins played poorly, ending up 23 and 37 and far out of the playoffs.

The Tri-Cities Blackhawks went from 8 and 12 under Nat Hickey to 22 and 18 with Bobby McDermott to finish 30 and 30, second in the West. The Blackhawks were led by 7-footer Don Otten; Billy Hassett, a quick guard from Notre Dame; and Stan "Whitey" Von Nieda, a fine shooter from Penn State, all of whom averaged in double figures in scoring, as did McDermott. Von Nieda recalled that McDermott was at the end of his career and "his legs were starting to give on him and he couldn't drive to the basket anymore and all he had was the set (shot), but sometimes that was enough."[23]

Von Nieda elaborated on his view of McDermott ten years after his discussion with Neil Isaacs:

> One thing that I found out about Bobby, he was very loyal. If you played for him and really put out for him, that was all he ever asked. And he had that great two-handed set shot, the best I think I have ever seen.... He knew the game. The set shot was his. That was the main thing. He would set it up; he would drive, on occasion, but he would rather shoot the set. I loved playing with him because he was very appreciative of effort and a very, very fierce competitor.
>
> As a coach, he had some set plays. He had some plays that would work to Otten's advantage, or for his advantage, or for my advantage. Primarily there was one play: he would pass the ball down the side, and Billy [Hassett] would bring the ball up the court. Otten was in the post, at that time we had the smaller key, but Otten would go to the other side of the post and leave it a little more blank, at one time, so Billy would pass down the side, come over and set a little pick for me and I would come barreling down the middle, going on

The 1947 Indianapolis Kautskys. Front row, left to right: Gus Doerner, Lowell Galloway, Arnie Risen, Bill Closs, Homer Thompson. Back row, left to right: Woody Norris, Ernie Andres, Bob Dietz, Leo Klier, Herm Schaefer. (Dick Triptow personal collection.)

a return pass, and take a little hook shot. We did that almost very game and we would get a bucket out of it. We would do things like that, we would set very specific things and we would set up Bobby's set shot, too. We would have a double pick for him outside.[24]

At the bottom of the West at this time were Oshkosh and Indianapolis, both of which had had good seasons the year before, finishing first and second in the division. For the World Professional Tournament champion Kautskys, this was quite a comedown. The team had cut Herm Schaefer, and Ernie Andres had retired, but the team had obtained Fred Lewis from Sheboygan and Bruce Hale from the Gears' break-up. Arnie Risen and Leo Klier were solid returning starters. Nevertheless the team didn't click and they were 11 and 19 by early January. The Oshkosh All Stars had the same record despite the return of their rugged front line of Carpenter, Edwards and Englund. The loss of guards Eddie Riska (to injuries) and Ralph Vaughan (to retirement) was difficult for the team to overcome, although they played better in the latter part of the season and squeezed into the playoffs with a 29 and 31 record, good for third in the division.

In the Eastern Division Anderson's hot start had led to a cooling, and by early January the Rochester Royals were in front with a record of 21 wins and five losses. Anderson held second at 20 and seven with the Pistons a distant third with 14 wins and nine losses. Syracuse, led by Paul Homer and Mike Novak, the former center for Sheboygan and Chicago NBL teams, was at 10 and 16, while the Toledo Jeeps were at eight and 16. Flint was deep in the cellar with four wins in 24 games.

Welcome 1948

The playoff positions appeared set in the Eastern Division, other than the fourth, and final spot, which looked to be between Toledo and Syracuse. Only Minneapolis and Sheboygan were sure things in the West with the other five teams scrambling for two playoff positions. Nineteen forty-eighty began for the Pistons on a good note as they defeated the Lakers in Minneapolis before a record crowd of 7,086 by a score of 46 to 41, stopping the Lakers' win streak at five. The Pistons got double figure scoring from Paul "Curly" Armstrong with 14, and Jack Smiley with 11. Mikan had 22, but second leading scorer Jim Pollard was one of nine from the floor and had only four points.[25]

The Pistons used the victory over the Lakers as a springboard to continued success as they won three more games in a row over Sheboygan, Oshkosh and Sheboygan once again. In those games their scoring was nicely distributed, with five different players scoring in double figures in the three victories. The team concept that Fort Wayne had often exhibited in previous years was again on display. Hopes were high, then, as the Pistons prepared to face their nemesis, the Rochester Royals, in two games on January 13 and 14. The Royals had edged the Pistons in mid–December by a score of 62–58, in Fort Wayne, to take the Eastern Division lead and they had held it ever since. The Pistons were then blown out of the gym in Rochester, losing to the Royals by a score of 75 to 48. Only Bob Kinney and Jack Smiley could score in double figures, both with 11, and the Royals were led by Holzman (18 points), Duncan (16), Davies (13) and Wanzer (11). Al Cervi continued to be in and out of the lineup with injuries, but the Royals did not seem to miss him much at this point of the season.[26] Immediately after the game the two teams took a night train from Rochester to Fort Wayne, where the two squads met again the next night. The Pistons turned the tables on the Royals, defeating them by a 70 to 56 score. This was a game that the Pistons needed much more than the Royals, who had already won 22 games. The Pistons were still struggling to catch the Eastern leaders and had a 16 and 10 record heading into the contest. The Royals had no one in double figures in the game and the Pistons were led by Pelkington with 17, Armstrong with 15 and Dick Triptow with 11.[27]

The Pistons continued their home play defeating the Toledo Jeeps four nights later by 54–49. In a game called, "listless" by Ben Tenny of the *Fort Wayne News-Sentinel*, the Pistons had no one in double figures and the Jeeps were led by Dick Meehan and Harry Boykoff, the 6'10" rookie from St. John's, both of whom had 11 points.[28] This listlessness carried over to the short road trip to Moline, Illinois, where the Blackhawks defeated the Pistons by 10 points. Pelkington, with 15, and Ralph Hamilton, with 11, topped Fort Wayne, but they couldn't match the scoring of the Tri-Cities' Von Nieda with 22, Don Otten with 19 or player-coach McDermott with 11.[29] The contest was played in Wharton Field House in Moline, which Von Nieda recalled as one of the better facilities, seating about 6,000 people and "we'd fill the place when we played the big teams" like the Pistons.[30]

With their loss the Pistons fell 1½ half games behind the second place Royals. Fort Wayne had the same number of losses as Rochester, but three fewer wins. Syracuse had now edged in front of Toledo for the last playoff spot.

In the Western Division the Lakers, with a record of 23 wins and 12 losses, had opened up a lengthy lead on Tri-Cities and Oshkosh, both with 16 and 16 records. Sheboygan was three games ahead of Indianapolis for the last play-off spot. The Lakers had won 12 of 15 games and George Mikan had stretched his leading point total to more than 600 points (20.3 ppg) by mid–January, more than 150 points better than his nearest rival, Don Otten, with 434 points (14 ppg). Mikan was supported by Jim Pollard's 405 points (12.3 per game), which ranked fifth in the league. In Rochester, on January 18, Mikan scored 41 points in a 75–73 Lakers victory. His 41 points broke the league record of 40 set by Bob Carpenter of Oshkosh two years before and his 17 field goals topped McDermott's record of 16 set in 1945 when he was with Fort Wayne.[31]

At about this time an event occurred that aroused the ire of many of the league owners and led to calls for the resignation of NBL commissioner Ward "Piggy" Lambert. The Kautskys were foundering in last place and, likely because of this, were not drawing nearly as well as usual to the large Butler Fieldhouse. Frank Kautsky was looking for a way to cut his costs and agreed to sell his center, Arnie Risen, to the Rochester Royals and their owner, Les Harrison. Since letting George Glamack go, the Royals had continued to struggle for an inside presence on the court. The Royals were within a game or two of the first place Anderson Duffey Packers, and Harrison felt that the addition of Risen would put the Royals into first by season's end and make the Royals able to compete more closely with George Mikan and the Lakers in the playoffs. So on January 21 Risen was sold to Rochester for $25,000. The Lakers' general manager, Max Winter, immediately protested the action because it violated the NBL bylaws prohibiting players being obtained for the playoffs. The trading deadline had been more than a week earlier, but Lambert okayed the deal and the cries for his resignation began.[32] The sale was made the day before the Royals were to play the Lakers in Chicago as part of the BAA-NBL doubleheaders and this made the timing even more irritating to Winter and the Lakers management. On the court, however, the Lakers seemed unaffected. They defeated the Royals before 6,500 fans as Mikan scored 23 points and tied Al Cervi's record of 632 in an NBL season set in 44 games. With 25 games to go, Mikan would not just beat the record, he would totally obliterate it. Risen, the object of the controversy, picked up four fouls in the first half and finished the game with 12 points. Bob Davies led both teams with 27 points.[33]

Much of the Lakers' turnaround was keyed by the presence of Herm Schaefer in the lineup. Mikan noted, "He was a stabilizing factor for the team, deliberately and methodically dribbling down the court to start all the plays.... Herm played with his head — he was a very smart player,"[34] and he got Mikan to see that he needed to move the ball out of the pivot more in order to get the defense moving off him so that Mikan could then get the ball back and score. The Lakers won 27 of their last 33 regular season games and coasted into the playoffs, 13 games ahead in the Western Division. One of those games was actually televised over a Minneapolis television station and was duly noted, in amazement, by Elliot Cushing.[35]

An interesting side note at this time was the release of a poll of NBL coaches that indicated that there was wide disparity among them as to how long it took a new professional to develop into a "top-notch pro star." Three coaches, Kundla of the Lakers, Doxie Moore of Sheboygan and Bruce Hale of Indianapolis, thought one season was sufficient while two, Benny Borgmann, the old ABL star and coach of the Nationals, as well as Julie Rivlin of Toledo, felt two years were needed. Murray Mendenhall of Anderson, Les Harrison of Rochester and Carl Bennett of Fort Wayne thought that three years were necessary, while Lonnie Darling of Oshkosh felt five years of professional experience were needed for a top player to develop into a professional star.[36] Darling at that time also had the oldest starting lineup in the league with Bob Carpenter (30), Gene Englund (30) and Leroy Edwards (33) comprising his back line, and this may have colored his judgment.

February began with the Lakers now six games in front of Oshkosh and seven in front of Tri-Cities, with Sheboygan a game behind the Blackhawks. In the East, Anderson had regained the lead by two games over Rochester with Fort Wayne 4½ back. Syracuse held fourth, 13 games back of the leader and 1½ games ahead of Toledo. The Zollner Pistons had improved their play, especially at home where they were undefeated from December 14 until February 19 (17 straight victories). Many players found the Pistons' home court, North Side High School, both intimidating and annoying. For visiting teams that liked to run, the shorter court negated that opportunity. Whitey Von Nieda noted, "I didn't like the small court in Fort Wayne because I was a running man, that was my best game."[37] Dick Triptow hated playing there as a visiting player, but "later on when I became a Zollner, it was heaven."[38] The gym seated 3500 and sometimes as many as 4000 were jammed into the venue with fans almost on top of the players. It was a difficult place to play for anyone but the Pistons. In their home win streak they defeated every NBL team and came within a game of first place. Their leading scorers in those games included Ralph Hamilton, Curly Armstrong, Bob Kinney, Jake Pelkington, Johnny Niemiera, Dick Triptow and Bob Tough, indicating the manner in which the Pistons distributed the ball, not relying on one or two players to ensure victory.

The Royals, too, had a variety of offensive weapons: Bob Davies, Al Cervi, Bill Holzman and the recent addition, Arnie Risen; all were leading scorers and Andy Duncan also contributed consistently. Both squads were well balanced. Anderson, the division leader, had a number of options, but their big three scorers were almost always Frankie Brian, Howie Schultz and John Hargis. All three teams won consistently through February and, as March began, were bunched at the top. Anderson and Rochester had records of 36 and 14, with Fort Wayne at 34 wins and 14 losses.

In mid–February the individual scoring leaders reflected the team balance of those teams in that no one from the three Eastern leaders was in the top five in individual scoring. George Mikan had expanded his lead to nearly 200 points over Don Otten of Tri-Cities. Mikan had 764 points in 38 games, for an average of 20.1 points per game. Otten had 578 in 42 games (13.8 ppg). The next three were Hal Tidrick of Toledo with 548 (13.2 ppg), Arnie Risen, who had played for Rochester for only a bit over two weeks, with 547 (13.7) and Bob Calihan, of the hapless Flint Dows, with 530 points (13.9 ppg).[39] The scoring was much increased over previous years in the NBL, and even more so over the previous generation of professionals. Advances in equipment, better facilities, and better preparation in college were all key factors in this. Joe Lapchick, however, saw another factor that made the current era's professionals better scorers and all-around players. Lapchick, who had been the star center for the great New York Celtics teams of the 1920s, had turned to coaching in the 1930s and was successful at St. John's University before returning to the professional ranks as the coach of the New York Knicks of the BAA in 1947-48. He felt that the competition was so intense that it was every man for himself, and team interest was subjugated to such tactics.[40]

And on the subject of tactics, external political forces were taking new directions in the United States and the world at this time. The dissatisfaction with President Truman among Southern Democrats led to wholesale secession from the party in South Carolina. Ultimately, this would lead to the formation of the States' Rights Democratic Party, or Dixiecrat Party, with Strom Thurmond, their candidate for president in 1948, receiving 39 electoral votes.

In Czechoslovakia the Communists imprisoned seven opposition leaders in February, leading to the dissolution of any semblance of democracy in that nation.[41]

And then there were Mikan and the Lakers. Clearly the dominant player in the league, Mikan listened to Herm Schaefer and made his team and his teammates better by not attempting to do all the scoring when teams dropped two or three men on him. Jim Pollard was an excellent second scorer and Don "Swede" Carlson also was a good shooter. Carlson was injured for much of January, but returned in February as the Lakers streaked to the end of the season. The month began with the Lakers playing in the 10,000-seat Minneapolis Armory where they routed the Kautskys 85 to 55. Pollard (19), Mikan (17), Tony Jaros (14) and Jack Dwan (10) all had double figure scoring for the Lakers as they coasted to the win.[42] Lakers team management was thrilled with the Lakers' success, both on the court and at the box office, but they were still calling for the ouster of "Piggy" Lambert as commissioner, for "malfeasance of office." No details were offered but the Risen sale was believed to be the prime factor in this situation.[43]

The Lakers and the 'Trotters Meet

These management concerns seemed to have little effect on the team as they continued to crush opponents. They beat Syracuse by 14 (Mikan had 24), they beat Oshkosh by 22 (Mikan and Jaros had 20 each), and they won in Indianapolis with Mikan getting 21. And during this period it was announced that "the Lakers had contracted with the Harlem Globetrotters for a two-game series, the first game at Chicago Stadium ... and the second game here (Minneapolis) some time next year."[44] The game would likely sell out the stadium since the Lakers were playing so well, led by Mikan, the top player in professional basketball, and the Globetrotters were on a 93 game winning streak.[45] Now, admittedly the 'Trotters played a lot of patsies, but their games were not the rigged entertainment exhibitions that they became famous for from the 1960s forward. The Globetrotters were a formidable squad and had won the World Professional Tournament in 1940 over the Chicago Bruins. That team had been led by Sonny Boswell, Duke Cumberland, Bernie Price and Babe Pressley, but only Pressley and back-up player Ted Strong remained from that squad. The new Globetrotters were a much younger squad led by Ermer Robinson, Marques Haynes and Reece "Goose" Tatum. The Globetrotters had two squads, an East and a West squad, that played around the country and their coach and owner, Abe Saperstein, combined the two squads for the clash against the Lakers on February 19, 1948.

The Lakers and 'Trotters met in Chicago Stadium as the opening game of a BAA doubleheader (featuring the Chicago Stags) before 17,853 fans with the Globetrotters winning 61–59 on a shot by Ermer Robinson that was in the air as the final gun sounded. The Lakers were led by Mikan with 24 points, and Pollard with 18. The 'Trotters got 17 from Robinson, 15 from Marques Haynes, 12 from King and nine from "Goose" Tatum, who fouled out covering Mikan. Mikan's seven missed free throws (of 11 shot), a rare occurrence for him, were a key factor in the Lakers' loss.

As George Mikan recalled, the game was more a point of pride for the players than a financial gain, since they weren't paid for it, since it was an unscheduled contest, and NBL teams didn't pay their players by the game anyway. Exhibitions were just part of the "landscape." Still, "every one of us wanted to show who the better team was."[46]

The Lakers were upset over the loss, particularly the refereeing, and looked forward to a rematch, which could not be scheduled initially but finally led to a total of eight games over the next three years. The two referees had been supplied by Saperstein, noted Mikan, and, after losing to the 'Trotters again the next year, the Lakers' manager, Max Winter, said that in subsequent games, each team would supply a referee. The Lakers didn't lose to the 'Trotters again.[47]

The Minneapolis papers claimed that the noise of the crowd had obscured the sound of the gun and that the last shot was too late, but made little else of the game. The *Fort Wayne News-Sentinel* paid no attention to the game since it was just another exhibition game to them. After all, the Globetrotters and the Rens, the top two African American teams, had been playing the NBL teams since the 1930s. The *New York Times* ignored the contest, although they did cover the second game in the Stadium doubleheader, the Chicago Stags and the New York Knicks. The *Chicago Tribune* gave the Laker-'Trotter contest coverage on the first page of the sports section with a photograph of the game, but devoted only two paragraphs to the contest with another two on the second game of the doubleheader.

By far the greatest coverage was by the *Chicago Defender*, the most respected and widely read African American newspaper in the United States. The *Defender* was a weekly, and the game was not covered until February 28, but at that time, the paper provided an extensive account of the game, nearly bucket-by-bucket coverage of the scoring as well as the fouls.[48] The game was clearly a step on the road to full acceptance of whites and blacks playing basketball together (at least on the same court), but just as important or more so were the earlier NBL integrations of teams. Later in 1948 the Lakers and Rens met in the finals of what would turn out to be the last World Professional Basketball Tournament in Chicago. The Globetrotters-Lakers contest in February of 1948 was no bigger than that contest yet some writers, now in retrospect, most notably John Christgau, argue for the watershed nature of that game.[49]

Back to the NBL Race

At this point the Royals, who had dropped four games in a row in early February, turned things around, although they continued to be plagued by recurring injuries. Starting on February 17, the Rochester Royals defeated the Blackhawks at home, the Flint Dows in Flint, the Toledo Jeeps in Ohio, the Dows once again in New York, the Syracuse Nationals in Rochester, Toledo at home, the Blackhawks in Moline, Fort Wayne at home and the Kautskys in Chicago Stadium, before finally losing to the Tri-City Hawks in Moline on March 9, three weeks after their last loss. The Royals' victory skein propelled them into the Eastern Conference lead by a game over the Anderson Duffey Packers, who had led the East since the opening of the season. The Royals were 40 and 15 while Anderson had 39 wins and 16 losses, with Fort Wayne third at 37 and 17. During the Royals' string of wins they enjoyed being in the best shape, in terms of injuries, that they had all year. Al Cervi, who had been bothered by knee problems, returned to the lineup at the beginning of the win streak and was instrumental in its accomplishment. The acquisition of Arnie Risen, and his place in the lineup, was now more comfortable to the players and that was also a big factor in their success. Red Holzman was a steadying influence throughout this as he maintained an iron man streak of not missing a game for nearly three full seasons. Fuzzy Levane was still in and out of the contests with various ailments, and Bob Davies was still having some knee problems, but the Royals felt confident that they would be able to repeat in the Eastern Division and as NBL champions.[50]

One unusual incident during this run occurred in the Chicago Stadium doubleheader on March 7. The Royals arrived in Chicago via overnight sleeper train from Rochester and took the floor just 13½ hours after leaving the Edgerton Arena in Rochester. Both the Royals and the Indianapolis Kautskys came out on the floor in the visiting blue uniforms. The Royals had been designated the home team for this game in Chicago and did not have those uniforms, so they wore the white of the Chicago Stags of the BAA (who beat the Providence Steamrollers in the second game of the doubleheader). The Kautskys had not played a league contest since February second when they had ended the Lakers' 12-game win streak by defeating them in Indianapolis, 83 to 63. Despite the Kautskys being rested and on a high after the win over the Lakers, the Royals won 61 to 46 behind Risen, Cervi, Davies and Andy Duncan, all of whom had 12 points in the win. George Glamack with 13 and Leo Klier with 11 led the Kautskys.[51]

The heated race in the NBL was certainly matched by the heated politics of the U.S. at the time. President Truman was faced by numerous strikes[52] or the threat of strikes and had to decide whether it was appropriate for him to intervene, either unofficially through jawboning or officially, as he ultimately did, with the steel strike that led to the government taking over the steel mills for a time in 1952. Truman's troubles led to speculation that he might not run for election in 1948, but in March he told party leaders that he would indeed run if nominated. On that same day, General Douglas MacArthur, still in Japan, said that he would run if asked, but would not seek the nomination for president.[53]

The Lakers, after winning 12 league contests in a row, lost two games in Indiana, to the Kautskys and the Duffey Packers, before getting back on the winning track. One highlight of their win streak occurred in Chicago on February 29. It was "George Mikan Day" in Chicago, and he was presented with numerous gifts including a new, 1948 Chrysler. Seven thousand two hundred seventy-seven fans showed up at the Stadium to help celebrate and the Lakers obliged by topping Syracuse 66 to 56. Mikan had only 14 as Jim Pollard topped the scoring with 16. Jim Homer had 18 for the Nats and Paul Seymour, a 19-year-old in his second year in the league, had 14.[54] Seymour would continue to play for Syracuse until 1960, becoming a fixture of the franchise. After the two losses, the Lakers then won five of the final seven games of the season. Their only losses were to Rochester on March 16 in New York 66–63, and to Tri-Cities, on the final game of the season, as the Hawks captured second place in the Western Division by finishing at 30 and 30, 13 games behind the Lakers' record of 43 and 17.

The big personal story in the league was George Mikan, who went about shattering scoring records for the league. (Since rebounds weren't kept as a statistic in professional basketball until 1950, it is impossible to tell what havoc he also was wreaking in this area.) The record for points scored in a season had been set the year before by Al Cervi of the Royals with 632. Mikan tied that record on January 22 in a win against the Royals in the Chicago Stadium. He scored 19 in his next game on January 26 to establish a new record for an NBL season, then proceeded to extend it beyond any competitors. In February he passed 700, then 800, then 900 points. On March 7 he scored 38 points and passed the 1,000 point mark in a win in Sheboygan against the Redskins. In his next game he got 30 points and had a total of 1039 points with his closest competitor, Don Otten of the Tri-Cities Blackhawks, second with 739 points. On March 13 he had set a new NBL one game record with 42 points against Fort Wayne in a 92–64 Laker win.[55] At season's end Mikan had scored 1195 points, an average of 21.3 points per game.

The Lakers coasted into the playoffs, although there was a fight for the other three positions in the Western Division. Tri-Cities edged Oshkosh by one game for second and the Indianapolis Kautskys managed to grab the fourth spot by 1½ games over the last place Redskins. The Eastern Division was a bit tighter. On March 3 the Royals finally caught the Packers for the lead in a win over Toledo. Three nights later, the Royals took the divisional lead in a win over the Lakers as Anderson lost to Toledo. The Packers then retook the lead, only to have both teams tied again on March 13. That night the Royals defeated the Packers in Rochester to take a one game lead. Arnie Risen had 18, but Al Cervi was acclaimed the difference in the game as he stole numerous balls and picked up 13 points.[56] The Royals went on to extend that lead to two games by season's end. Fort Wayne, which had been two games back of the leaders on March 2, lost their final two regular season games to Tri-Cities and Oshkosh to finish in third, four games off the pace. Syracuse took the fourth playoff spot in the East.

The Playoffs

The Royals and the Lakers were the two hottest teams in the league heading into the playoffs and in their first round games that pattern continued. Rochester had the bigger challenge, facing the Fort Wayne Zollner Pistons, and the series opened in Indiana on March 23. The Royals upset the Pistons on the North Side Gym court by a 65–56 score, as Al Cervi had 18, Bob Davies 12, and Arnie Risen 11 to lead the Royals. Johnny Niemiera (13) and Bob Kinney (12) led the Pistons, who shot only 10 of 17 free throws to Rochester's 23 of 30. It was the first home loss for the Pistons since December 16 (21 games).[57] The second game of the five game series went to the Zollners by a 68 to 64 score. The game was rough, the crowd was rowdy, and the ill feelings of the previous year's contests were evident once again. After the game, the players from both teams, as well as the referees, took the same sleeping car train to Rochester, where they all got together the next evening on the Edgerton Arena Court in Rochester.

The first game in Rochester found the Royals shorthanded, as Al Cervi was out with the flu, but the Royals got an unexpectedly strong game from Fuzzy Levane, who had been out with intestinal ailments. He had 14 points, as did Red Holzman, to lead the Royals to a 64 to 47 win. Jake Pelkington had 12 for Fort Wayne.[58] Two nights later the Royals eliminated the Pistons with a 71 to 62 victory. Arnie Risen had 25 points, with support from Bob Davies (12) and Andy Duncan (10), while Al Cervi again missed the game. Armstrong and Kinney led Fort Wayne with 18 and 17, respectively. The Royals shot 42 percent from the field compared to the Zollners' 28 percent.[59] During this series, strong rumors resurfaced that the BAA was still trying to get four NBL clubs (Rochester, Indianapolis, Fort Wayne and Minneapolis) to join the BAA.

The Royals would play Anderson, who eliminated Syracuse in three straight games. During the playoffs the NBL announced the All League teams and they were dominated by Rochester and Minneapolis on the first team, which consisted of Mikan, Pollard, Cervi, Holzman and Marko Todorovich of Sheboygan. The second team was Bob Calihan of Flint, Bob McDermott and Don Otten of Tri-Cities, Bob Davies of the Royals and Frankie Brian of Anderson. The obvious MVP was Mikan.

In the West, Mikan and his Lakers defeated Oshkosh, three games to one. Mikan averaged 20.5 points per game in the series and got lots of support from Jim Pollard, Jack Dwan and Herm Schaefer. Leroy Edwards, the old (33 but a 12 year pro) veteran, had some of his last double figure scoring games. In Game One of the series he picked up 12, but fouled out (as did Gene Englund and Clint Wager) trying to stop George Mikan, and in Game Four Edwards had 13 to tie for the team lead with Englund. In the one All Star win, Englund had 26 points to lead the team over the Lakers by a 69 to 51 score.[60]

The Lakers awaited their next opponent in the other series, which would be the Tri-Cities Blackhawks, who topped the Kautskys in four games behind the scoring of Don Otten, Stan Von Nieda and Bob McDermott. The rookie, Von Nieda, averaged just over 16 points per game to lead the scoring. For the Kautskys, player-coach Bruce Hale led the team with 64 points in the four game series.

The second rounds of the playoffs were only best of three series and the Lakers made short work of the Blackhawks in two straight. The first game was played before a record crowd of 5,569 in Moline's Auditorium, but the game wasn't close as the Lakers won 98 to 79. Game Two was even more of a rout before 7,433 in Minneapolis, the final score being 83–59 Lakers. Besides being overmatched, the Blackhawks were hit with key injuries in the game. Stan Von Nieda dislocated his shoulder in the first quarter and Billy Hassett fell on his back and sustained a spinal injury in the second quarter. Don Otten had 16 points, but the Lakers got 23 from Mikan, 22 from Tony Jaros and 16 from Jim Pollard to win the Western Division Playoffs going away.[61]

The Eastern Division Finals began March 30 in Anderson. The Royals stayed at the Claypool Hotel in Indianapolis, then took a bus to Anderson, 40 miles to the northeast. Anderson had been nearly unbeatable on its home court, characterized by George Beahon of the *Rochester Democrat and Chronicle* as being "nearly as wide as it is long." Surprisingly, the Royals were able to beat the Duffey Packers by a 71 to 66 score. Bob Davies had 19, Arnie Risen 13 and Andy Duncan 12 to lead the Royals, while Howie Schultz with 16, Rollie Seitz with 13 and John Hargis with 10 topped the Packers.[62]

Game Two was four nights later in Rochester, two nights after the Lakers had ended their series. For the first time in three years, Red Holzman missed a game and the Royals compounded his loss with poor defense, losing by a 76 to 69 score. Hargis (22), Charlie Black (13), Ralph Johnson (12) and Frankie Brian (11) led the Packers. The day before Hargis, Brian and Black had all been named to the NBL All-Rookie team, the former two on the first team and the latter on the second team. Mike Todorovich was named top rookie with Pollard and Von Nieda joining the two Packers on the first team. The second team also had Ralph Hamilton of Fort Wayne, Jim Homer of Syracuse, Harry Boykoff and Fran Curran of Toledo besides Black. The Coach of the Year was Murray Mendenhall of the Anderson Duffey Packers.[63]

The next night the Royals defeated the Packers, easily, by a 74 to 58 score with Davies scoring 17 to lead the team. The win, however, was very costly to the Eastern Division champions. In the fourth quarter, Howie Schultz, who had his back to the basket and was being guarded closely by Arnie Risen, spun and dipped his shoulder into Risen, cracking him directly in the jaw. Risen toppled to the floor and was removed from the game after which it was determined that his jaw had been broken in two places. In the dressing room after the game Schultz refused to deny that the blow was deliberate, answering only, "Ask Risen."[64] The consensus of the Royals' players was that Schultz was a clean player and that it had to have been an accident. The next day it was rumored that Risen might play against the Lakers because the Lakers had committed to the World Professional Tournament in Chicago which was being held April 8 to April 11 and that would delay the start of the NBL Finals until April 13.[65] In a separate column that same day Elliot Cushing said that he had managed to talk to Schultz before the Packers left town and Schultz had said that he had been upset because Risen had been holding him all evening, mostly by the belt, and continued to do so even though his team was up by 25 points. Schultz also had been elbowed by Risen in the previous game and had stitches in his lip from that encounter. Schultz said that his intent was to brush off Risen "like a mosquito," thinking that he would hit him in the chest and push him back, but that somehow Risen was in a lower position and he lowered his shoulder directly into Risen's jaw. Schultz said that he had no intention to injure him.[66]

The delay in finishing the playoffs brought criticism of Commissioner Lambert, this time from Rochester. Elliot Cushing said that the Finals were delayed by a "pseudo World Tournament" and that Lambert, "who is paid $10,000 a year as Commissioner, regards the synthetic Chicago affair more important than the deciding of the championship of his own league."[67] The delay in the beginning of the Finals also allowed the NBL to hold its own meetings in Chicago (since five of the NBL's eleven teams were in Chicago for the World Professional Tournament) and rumors once again flew regarding the potential loss of four franchises to the BAA and the granting of new franchises for 1948-49. One story noted that seven bids had been made to join the NBL from parties in Denver, Des Moines, Chicago, Louisville, Dayton, Wilkes-Barre and St. Paul.[68] The *Minneapolis Star* had other rumors. Continuing their push to see Lambert out of the commissioner's job, they noted that he would resign after the Finals and floated the names of two possible successors. One was Chet Roan of the University of Minnesota, who seemed to be the favorite. The other was Doxie Moore, the manager-coach of the Sheboygan Redskins. He seemed less likely, it was noted, because he was held in some disfavor in Sheboygan as well as at least two other NBL cities (not specified).[69] Two days later the *Star*'s Carlson had more rumors, this time about the jumping to the BAA and the franchises that might enter the league in 1948. In a column in that same paper, Charlie Johnson reiterated the view expressed earlier in the season when the rumors about the four teams jumping to the BAA began. He noted that fans in Minneapolis wanted to be in a big name city league with New York, Washington, Philadelphia and Chicago. He went on to predict, however, that if the Lakers withdrew from the NBL, "it might ruin the league." Pro ball, he said needs both leagues to talk about a merger.[70] And in Fort Wayne the merger possibilities were also raised.[71]

The World Professional Tournament

What would turn out to be the last World Professional Tournament opened play on April 8. There were only eight teams and five of these were from the NBL; the others were the Wilkes-Barre Barons, the Bridgeport (Connecticut) Newfield Steelers and the New York Rens. In the first round the Tri-Cities Blackhawks ousted the Zollner Pistons by a 57 to 50 score. Dick Triptow was the only Piston in double figures with 12 while Stan Von Nieda with 15 and Don Otten with 12 topped the Hawks. The Rens, led by Nathaniel "Sweetwater" Clifton's 28 points, eliminated Bridgeport 67 to 51. Anderson defeated the Kautskys 59 to 53 and the Lakers routed Wilkes-Barre by a 98 to 48 margin. The only question in that game was whether the Lakers would top 100 points.[72] In the semi-finals, played before 13,652 in the Chicago Stadium, the Rens defeated Tri-Cities 59 to 55. The Rens had great balance as Clifton had 19, Sonny Wood had 11, Jim Usry had 10 and George Crowe chipped in nine. Don Otten had 20 and "Whitey" Von Nieda 11 for the Hawks. In Game Two the Lakers edged Anderson by a 59 to 56 margin as Mikan had 21, Carlson 12 and Schaeffer 10. Brian (13) and Hargis (11) led Anderson.[73]

While this was going on, the Royals, who had turned down a bid to play in the World Professional Tournament, were playing a two game set in Rochester as part of the season ending Royal Appreciation Games. Les Harrison managed to put together an impressive group of NBL All-Stars to provide the opposition including Bob Calihan and Stan Patrick of Flint, Leo Klier and Bruce Hale of Indianapolis, Gene Englund of Oshkosh, Hal Tidrick and Fran Curran of Toledo and Mike Novak and Jerry Rizzo of Syracuse. In the first game on April 10 the Royals won by 72 to 61 and in the second the Royals again won by 74 to 64. A total of 5,604 fans turned out for the two games.

It was hoped that Risen might appear in one of these games as a warm up for playing the Lakers, but on April 11 it was announced that three other small fractures had been discovered in his jaw and he was definitely out of the NBL Finals.[74]

In the final of the World Professional Tournament, Anderson edged Tri-Cities for 3rd place with a 66–64 victory. In the championship game the Lakers topped the Rens by a 75 to 71 score as free throws, the downfall of the Lakers in the Globetrotter loss in February, proved to be the difference in this contest. The Lakers hit 19 of 22 from the line while the Rens were only 15 of 29 to spell doom for them. Clifton again led the Rens with 24 followed by "Pop" Gates with 16, "Duke" Cumberland with 14 and Crowe with 12. Mikan had 40 for the Lakers followed by Pollard with 14.[75] Mikan was voted MVP of the tournament. Unlike previous years, the season did not end for at least two teams with the conclusion of the tournament. The Lakers returned to Minneapolis where they were prohibitive favorites to defeat the Royals, who were crippled by the loss of Risen and Al Cervi, who had re-injured his knee in a shooting drill in Rochester on April 12. In addition, Red Holzman was still hobbling.

The NBL Finals

Game one was surprisingly close, considering the Royals' limited line-up. Eight thousand one hundred forty-three fans, a record in the Minnesota State Armory, saw the Lakers win 80 to 72 as Mikan took advantage of Risen's absence with 26 points. Mikan was supported by Pollard, Jaros and Schaeffer, all of whom had 14 points. The patchwork Royals were led by Bobby Wanzer with 16, Andy Duncan with 14, Bob Davies with 13, George Ratkovicz with 11 and Arnie Johnson with 10.[76] Game two, played before 7540, was more of the same with the score 82–67 Lakers. Mikan again led with 25, but Herm Schaeffer was close behind with 24. Don Smith (11), Jim Pollard (10) and Jack Dwan (10) all contributed. The Royals got 23 from Davies and a very surprising 16 from Arnie Johnson.[77]

Following the game both teams boarded the train and headed to Rochester. Game Three found the Lakers still sleeping (or so it seemed), as the Royals stole a game by a 74 to 60 score. Mikan had 32 for the losers but Schaeffer was the only other Laker in double figures with 10 as the Lakers were outplayed in all aspects of the game. Andy Duncan (18) and Bob Davies (16) topped the Royals, but the big surprise was the contribution of rookie Bill Calhoun, a former teammate of Laker Jim Pollard on the AAU Oakland Bittners, who scored 13 points and held Pollard to one basket in the game. Wanzer also had 10 and Holzman returned to score nine, despite a heavily taped leg.[78]

The Lakers loss was only delaying the inevitable and that proved to be the next night as the Lakers took the title by a 75 to 65 score before an overflow crowd of 4,200 in Edgerton Park Arena. George Mikan had 27, Jim Pollard 19, and Jack Dwan 10 for the Lakers while Davies (20), Johnson (18) and Duncan (10) were high for the Royals.[79]

The Season Continues

What should have ended the NBL season really didn't because of the continued uncertainty surrounding the four potential jumping teams, the addition of new franchises and the possibility of the NBL collapsing. On May 10 the NBL (and BAA) owners met (separately) in Chicago at the Morrison Hotel to discuss plans for the following season. At that time a new NBL franchise was awarded to Detroit and there was an announcement of potential legal action, based on a resolution passed in April in which all the NBL teams concurred (including Minneapolis, Indianapolis, Fort Wayne and Rochester). That resolution stated that if any NBL club withdrew from the league without league permission, the players would become league property and the NBL would seek injunctions against their players, claiming ownership of their contracts. There was indifference from the BAA at this statement and a spokesman from Indianapolis said, "They may not be in business long enough to worry about next season."[80] This was the crux of the issue. The NBL had top players that the BAA needed and was willing to steal four clubs, from either larger cities or with access to larger arenas, to get them, believing that the NBL would collapse and make any legal efforts moot.

The BAA's commissioner, Maurice Podoloff, had met earlier in the spring with Carl Bennett at his home in Fort Wayne where he had formally made the proposal to have three clubs (Minneapolis, Indianapolis and Fort Wayne) join the BAA, and Fred Zollner, the Pistons' owner, approved the proposal the next day. The two leagues formalized the proposal on the 10th of May, although by that time "Les Harrison of the Royals had cajoled an invitation from the BAA.... Both Oshkosh and Toledo applied for BAA franchises but their bids were tabled."[81] At that point, Ward Lambert resigned as NBL commissioner, Doxie Moore was named the new commissioner, Leo Ferris of Tri-Cities replaced Paul Walk of Indianapolis as NBL president and Carl Bennett was named to the BAA Executive Committee.

The NBL was left with seven squads and pending applications as well as the new Detroit franchise. The NBL threatened legal action as well as a bidding war for players coming out of college. In July an effort was made to seek some reconciliation, at a meeting of Ike Duffey, Carl Bennett, and Maurice Podoloff. The tone was cordial but no progress was made; when Duffey left the room a note was found in his handwriting, which was apparently a telegraph message that Duffey intended to send to other NBL owners. In it the note stated that no progress was possible and that the owners should feel free to raid BAA rosters for players.[82] That was essentially a declaration of war between the leagues and the BAA informed its owners that they had the same latitude. In August, reconciliation was tried again, but was unsuccessful. By then the NBL had accepted new franchises and was preparing for a new season with nine teams, four of which were new franchises. Despite the loss of their heart, the body of the NBL continued to live.

Back to the Future:
The Hometown League Reappears
for the 1948-49 Season

The ultimate loss of four of the best teams and many of the top NBL stars to the BAA was a blow, but the NBL and its owners tried to put the best face on the difficult situation. The league had a number of franchise applicants for entry into the league for 1948 and the hope was that the NBL could sustain itself and, possibly, make a deal of some sort with the BAA that would lead to a truce and help both leagues. Obviously the BAA had helped itself mightily, and many in that league believed that the NBL was essentially dead with the gutting of the NBL's top squads. Until then there had been hope that the two leagues could reconcile their differences and join in a manner similar to major league baseball in having a real basketball world series at the end of the season. That would likely have doomed the World Professional Tournament in Chicago, but many viewed this as collateral damage. The BAA had always eschewed the tournament, and with the movement of the Lakers, Pistons, Kautskys and Royals to the BAA (the three past World Professional Tournament champions), the future of the tournament already looked shaky.

Of greater concern to the NBL, of course, was its own future and, after examining the franchise applications, the new NBL chose four new squads to join the league. Besides the four defectors to the BAA, the NBL had also lost Toledo and Flint-Midland, both of which dropped from the league for financial reasons. That left five continuing franchises, and these were joined by Calumet-Hammond (Indiana), Waterloo (Iowa), Detroit and Denver. Waterloo and Denver would play in the Western Division, joining Tri-Cities, Oshkosh and Sheboygan. The Eastern Division would be Syracuse, Anderson, Hammond-Calumet and Detroit.

Waterloo, a small city of about 50,000 on the Cedar River in Iowa, was a strong Three-I League franchise in baseball's minor leagues and had had a respected independent basketball team for a number of years. The team would play in a 7,500-seat arena, called the Hippodrome, and that capacity was exceeded in an early season game, indicating initial strong fan interest. The Hawks had signed Charlie Shipp to be their player-coach. The 35-year-old Shipp had been in the NBL since the mid–1930s, when he had come out of Cathedral High in Indianapolis to play for the Akron Goodyear Wingfoots, and he had played for Fort Wayne, Oshkosh and Anderson. Shipp had Harry Boykoff, Dale Hamilton and Dick Mehen from Toledo, Rollie Seitz from Anderson and Les Deaton from Sheboygan. Prospects were not good.

Denver, the other Western Division entry, had been an AAU power for a number of years and Denver was the site of the National AAU Tournament from 1935 to 1968. The fans and writers of Denver felt that their city was one of, if not the, capital of basketball in the Western United States[1] and their rabid interest would rival any eastern city.[2] It should be noted that Denver of 1948 was much different than the Denver of today. Basically it was still "a little back-water town in 1948," according to Dolph Schayes, who was a rookie in the NBL that year.

> I don't remember that Denver was noted for anything but having a tuberculo-sis center. I remember that it was a real cowboy town. It didn't seem like much of a town, but I recall the Brown Palace Hotel, where they had a good steak.[3]

The team would be coached by Ralph Bishop, an All-America player at the University of Washington in the 1930s. He had been the only college player on the 1936 U.S. Olympic team, the first year that the sport was in the Games. The team would be led by Ace Gruenig, Jack Cotton and Harold Hutcheson. One intriguing member of the squad was Morris Udall, who would gain much greater fame as a politician than as a basketball player. As it turned out there was another interesting aspect to the Denver home games in the NBL, the referees.

> I remember the referees out in Denver had a very different style, and the NBL didn't send eastern referees out there. They just used a couple of local guys, maybe from the Mountain League. I remember that their style was similar to football. When there was a foul, they would throw a handkerchief, like they do in football. That was how they would referee. I remember that. I guess Denver was a hotbed of basketball.[4]

Denver also would mean long trips by the teams who would come out to play two games in three nights, then return east. In many cases, the visit-ing teams would be run out of the gym in the first game because of the ele-vation, but by the next game, two nights later, they would be able to be more

The 1948-49 Denver Nuggets, including future Congressman Morris Udall. Left to right: Coach Ralph Bishop, Ace Gruenig, Jack Cotton, Ward Gibson, Harold Hutcheson, Guy Mitchell, Morris Udall, Al Guokas, Leonard Alterman, Jimmy Darden, Gene Lalley. (From the 1948-49 NBL Yearbook, author's collection.)

competitive. Stan Von Nieda recalled that when they played their first game there, he "thought the court was about a mile and a half long. I had never played at elevation before."[5]

Calumet-Hammond, Indiana, would be one of the two new Eastern Division franchises and its entry was reminiscent of the old Whiting-Hammond team that had competed in the NBL in the 1930s. Calumet had signed Bob Carpenter, the former Oshkosh star, as its player-coach, and its ownership followed the Wisconsin model practiced by Oshkosh, Sheboygan and the Green Bay Packers NFL team. The Calumet Buccaneers were "owned by 200 fans (at $100 per share) residing in the Indiana cities of Hammond, Whiting, East Chicago, and Calumet City, Illinois. With a team backed by so many people from so many urban localities, it is obvious that there must be real enthusiasm about professional basketball."[6] This whole process had been orchestrated by Ike Duffey, the president of the NBL and owner of the Anderson Packers. When it was obvious in the summer of 1948 that the Toledo Jeeps were hurting financially and would not be able to continue, Duffey bought the franchise and then appealed to Walter Thornton, a local northern Indiana businessman, to sell the team to backers in the region. Thornton was successful in doing so and also became the team's business manager.[7]

The Buccaneers would be led on the court by Carpenter; George Sobek, who came from the Toledo roster after they left the league; Stan Patrick, who had been on the Flint-Midland Dows; and Clint Wager from the Oshkosh All Stars.

The Detroit Vagabond Kings (one of their co-owners, King Boring, had been a partner in the Detroit Gems of the 1946-47 NBL season) were the other new squad but they were thwarted in an attempt to find a home court on which to play. Many of the players had been on the Flint roster the previous year. The Kings looked for scoring from John Sebastian and Ollie Shoaf at the guard slots with Del Loranger to help on the inside.

> They had intended to play in the Forum, a new athletic arena on the outskirts of Detroit, with a seating capacity of 10,000. However, building difficulties have delayed its completion and King Boring and Ernie Pabis were forced to go elsewhere. The result was that they never did find a suitable location, and were forced to withdraw from the league.[8]

It did not help that the Kings had a record of 2 wins and 17 defeats at the time of their withdrawal. Dolph Schayes recalled that "they had a terrible team."[9] One account said that the Kings were expelled from the league, in fact.[10] Between having a hard time finding where the team was playing home games and then seeing them lose consistently, the fans stayed away in droves. The withdrawal of the franchise in late December put the league in a difficult spot. If they simply dropped the Kings and their scheduled games, it would make an even more unbalanced schedule. A better solution, it was thought by new Commissioner Doxie Moore and President Ike Duffey, was to find an existing team and convince them to enter the league, picking up the Kings' record and schedule. The Detroit players would be divided among the other league teams. Duffey and Moore managed to convince Bob Douglas, the owner of the New York Renaissance, and Eric Illidge, their manager, to enter the league in late December. Earlier in the season, the Rens had lost to the Anderson Packers by three points before 20,000 spectators in the preliminary game to the Minneapolis Lakers-College All-Star game. The Rens had also played a few games in Dayton, Ohio, and had developed a small following there. Thus, on December 17, the Rens agreed to enter the NBL and play as the Dayton Rens. The Rens would also continue an extensive traveling schedule.[11] This Rens squad would be coached by "Pop" Gates and led on the floor by him, Hank DeZonie, George Crowe and Sonny Wood. The *Philadelphia Inquirer* noted that the "Rens had played a series of exhibition games earlier this season at Dayton, where the promoter, Elwood Parsons, is a Negro."[12] The Dayton press was thrilled to finally land a big league franchise, even if the team would play as the Dayton Rens only at home. Because of the reputation that the Rens had established as a road attraction, they were to continue to play as the New York Rens when on the road.[13] The African American press was less sanguine about the team's entry into the NBL. Whereas the *Chicago Defender* had covered the Chicago Studebakers in the 1942-43 NBL season, the Rens were not as favored in 1948-49. The *Defender* provided just three paragraphs on the Rens' entry into the NBL and never covered them again during the NBL season.[14] In contrast the Harlem Globetrotters were covered regularly each week. In April of 1949 Fay Young, in his *Defender* column, did note that the Globetrotters needed new players, a real "housecleaning," as they were no longer as prepared to play the game the fans expected now that they (the 'Trotters) had reached "the top rung of the ladder of basketball," behavior that the Rens had also fallen victim to in the years where they were dominant.[15]

There were also changes among the established clubs in the league, the most notable being that All-Pro Al Cervi went from the Eastern Champion Royals to the Syracuse Nationals as player-coach replacing Hall of Famer "Bennie" Borgmann as the coach. Cervi and Les Harrison had many disagreements in the years that Cervi played for the Royals. Both men were stubborn, headstrong and had easily aroused tempers, so their frequent disagreements were no surprise. David Ramsey felt that the source of the disagreement that led to Cervi leaving the Royals was not explained by either man,[16] but in interviewing Cervi, it was obvious that he felt lied to and double-crossed by Harrison. Cervi found out that Harrison was paying other players, such as Bob Davies, more money for 1946-47, after telling Cervi that he was getting as much as anyone on the team. In addition, Harrison asked Cervi to step aside and Harrison pushed Davies for the MVP in the NBL in 1947 (he was awarded it), despite the fact that Cervi had led the league in scoring and not missed a game. Then Harrison accused Cervi of faking a knee injury during the 1947-48 season. Cervi, even more than 50 years later, called Harrison a liar and said that he couldn't stand him and wouldn't play for him anymore.[17] So Harrison let him go to Syracuse as the Royals departed for the BAA.

In addition to Cervi, the Nationals had an outstanding rookie in Dolph Schayes, from NYU, who would become an offensive force with the Nationals, retiring in 1964 as the NBA's all time leading scorer (a mark since broken). Billy Gabor, another rookie, was from Syracuse University, and his presence on the team brought many fans to the Nationals' games. Help was also expected from returnees Paul Seymour, Jim Homer, John Chaney and Jerry Rizzo.

The Anderson Duffey Packers, who started off the prior season with the best record in the league and led the East for most of the season, replicated that beginning in 1948-49. They had, essentially, the same strong team that finished the 1947-48 season with Frankie Brian, John Hargis, Howie Schultz, Ed Stanczak and Milo Komenich, but added Bill Closs from Indianapolis. They would be tough to beat and would not have to play either Rochester or Minneapolis in the playoffs since they had gone to the BAA.

The Tri-City Blackhawks had had an excellent second half the previous year and finished second to the Lakers in the West. They retained Stan "Whitey" Von Nieda, Don Otten, Billy Hassett, Joe Camic, and added George Ratkovicz, whom the Royals had let go, and rookie Murray Weir from the University of Iowa, where he led the Big Nine in scoring. Bob McDermott, the future Hall of Famer, returned as player-coach.

Oshkosh had lost Carpenter and Wager in an apparent effort to control salaries. Leroy Edwards, the all time leading scorer in the NBL, had slowed enough to play in only 10 games and retired at the end of the season. The All Stars added Alex Hannum, a big defensive specialist from USC who would later become a Hall of Fame coach; Gene Berce, a fine rookie from Marquette; Jack Burmaster from the University of Illinois; and Bob Mulvihill from Fordham. They joined returning starters Gene Englund, Glenn Selbo, Walt Lauterbach and Eddie Riska. Replacing Carpenter's scoring would be a prime issue with the All Stars, still coached and managed by Lon Darling.

Sheboygan, the other Wisconsin squad, had replaced Doxie Moore, who moved into the league commissioner's chair, with Kenny Suessens as player-coach. The top returning players were Marko Todorovich, Paul Cloyd and Max Morris, with new players Bobby Cook and Noble Jorgensen looked to for immediate help. The veteran Rich Dancker had retired and it was hoped that Milt Schoon, late of the Flint-Midland Dows, could take his place.

The Season Begins

The NBL season began on the first of November. It was a chaotic time in the United States as Election Day was November 2. The favored candidate, Republican challenger Thomas Dewey, was defeated soundly by sitting president Harry Truman, despite the added candidacy of Strom Thurmond whose Dixiecrat ticket managed to capture 38 electoral votes from Truman's formerly solid Democratic base. Even with that, Truman still totaled 304 electoral votes to Dewey's 189. Dewey and his endorsers, like the *Chicago Tribune*, appealed to all citizens to back President Truman after the election, indicating strong support for the president.

The BAA and its commissioner, Maurice Podoloff, criticized the NBL as no longer being a major league, similar to the comments made by some BAA members after the defection of the four NBL squads had been announced the previous spring. On November 4, NBL commissioner Doxie Moore traveled from the league offices in West Lafayette, Indiana, to Chicago where he met reporters at the Drake Hotel to answer the BAA's recent charge that the NBL was a minor league. This latest charge had arisen after the BAA and NBL leadership had met in late October and the NBL refused to endorse a BAA proposal for each club to have a $45,000 cap on salaries and to ban exhibition games. Said Moore, "Our payroll in Sheboygan last year was $60,000 and our club was by no means tops."[18] The NBL, with its smaller arenas, vitally needed the exhibition games and they had larger salaries than the requested cap. Podoloff said that he had been "offering the olive branch" to the NBL in search of a working agreement, but Lon Darling, the Oshkosh All Stars' manager and coach, said that the BAA "wants everything its own way." In addition, the NBL had added Denver, with a 6700-seat arena, and Hammond, with an arena seating 6,000, so their capacities would begin to be on a par with the BAA.[19]

Darling's team retained its city-wide popularity, the hometown status that brought civic pride to the fore in support of the All Stars. At the onset of the new season, 17 different local Fox Valley merchants sponsored a full page "good luck" message in the *Oshkosh Daily Northwestern* which included photographs of all the ballplayers and Coach Darling.[20] It was this kind of enthusiastic support, that also was seen in Sheboygan, Anderson and Moline (Tri-Cities), that the league hoped to have emulated in Denver, Hammond, Waterloo and Detroit.

In the first week of the season the All Stars benefited from playing the Detroit Vagabond Kings in three of their first five league games and Oshkosh won them all. It was a new Oshkosh team with only Gene Englund and Glenn Selbo and Floyd Volker being significant contributors from among the returning veteran players. Rookies Gene Berce, Jack Burmaster, and Alex Hannum were instrumental in the early victories. Berce scored in double figures in three of the four opening victories. It was obvious that Detroit had strength in their guards with John Sebastian and Ollie Shoaf, but the teamwork and rebounding left something to be desired. In the first month Detroit lost 12 of its 13 games, most of which it was forced to play on the road because of venue difficulties in Detroit.

Detroit firmly settled into last in the Eastern Division while Oshkosh jumped into first in the West. Rivaling Detroit for futility were the Denver Nuggets, who were forced to play long road trips, followed by home stands almost as long. The Nuggets began with bright hopes; the story that preceded their opening game was an inspirational portrait of Morris Udall, a rookie from Arizona, who had lost an eye at the age of 6 but had overcome that to lead his law school class academically and become all conference three years in a row at the University of Arizona. He had also managed to finagle his way into the service and had been in Iwo Jima and Guam for three years during World War II before his discharge.[21]

Denver would fly to almost all their initial road games in the east before taking trains between eastern cities. They began the season with seven straight on the road and lost them all. Ward Gibson was their big scorer and was in the top three in league scoring, but the Nuggets didn't have enough depth or rebounding to secure a victory. New to the league and to professional basketball after great success in the AAU, the losing was not familiar to Denver fans and the team may have lost some of the fans before even appearing at home. They wouldn't be sure until the Nuggets' first home game on November 15. The first Denver loss was also the first game (and victory) for the Hammond-Calumet City Buccaneers. The game was very well-attended with between 4,000 and 5,600 fans in the Hammond Civic Center for the contest, won by Hammond 58 to 39.[22]

The Oshkosh early success was matched by the Waterloo Hawks, who were getting good scoring from Harry Boykoff, Dick Mehen and Rollie Seitz. By December 2 the Hawks had won nine of ten league contests and led the All Stars by 1½ games. The only blemish on Waterloo's record was a loss in Moline to Tri-Cities 67–63, where Stan Von Nieda tossed in 19 points to lead his mates and offset the scoring of Boykoff with 17, Mehen with 16 and Leo Kubiak with 15.[23] A week later in Waterloo, the tables were turned as the home team won 61 to 59. Most impressive was the crowd of 7536 that turned out to watch Kubiak (19), Mehen (16) and Boykoff (12) offset the 18 from Don Otten and the 16 from Whitey Von Nieda to edge Tri-Cities.[24] Sheboygan, led by Marko Todorovich and Paul Cloyd, was inconsistent and had a record of seven wins and eight losses in early December. One surprise in the West was the announcement of Lon Darling that he was resigning as coach after the All Stars dropped five in a row, three of them league games. He announced that Gene Englund and Eddie Riska would take over as player-coaches.[25]

In the Eastern Division the Syracuse Nationals started out fast, winning eight of their first ten league games and opening a small lead on Anderson, which began with seven wins in 12 games. The Packers dropped their first league contest in Syracuse on November 12 when Billy Gabor, with 14, and Jerry Rizzo, with 12, led the Nats to victory. The Nationals were drawing well. Two nights later they attracted over four thousand fans to the Syracuse Coliseum to watch them defeat Sheboygan 53 to 48. Rookies Dolph Schayes and Gabor topped the scoring with 14 and 10, respectively, while Sheboygan was led by rookies Bob Brannum, from Michigan State (11), and Merlin Gilbertson, from Washington (10).[26] Hammond was six up, six down into December, under Bob Carpenter, who was slowed by a foot injury but still was scoring adequately, as was George Sobek, the former Toledo star. In late

November Hammond topped Syracuse in a game where three players on the two team (Schayes, 20; Sobek, 24; Carpenter, 21) had 20 or more points.[27]

At the end of November the College All-Star contest drew 19,345 to Chicago Stadium to watch the Minneapolis Lakers pound the former collegians and rub salt in the wounds of the NBL as they saw the best team in basketball now a BAA power. One consolation was that most of the College All-Stars were signed to NBL teams, including co-leader in points Don Ray with Tri-Cities.[28]

Despite World War II having ended more than three years previously, the world was not at peace. Truman's labor troubles of his previous three years were not immediately obvious, but they continued to linger beneath the headlines. The Middle East was simmering, despite the conclusion of the Arab-Israeli War, which had broken out following the establishment of the Jewish state. The United Nations warned the Arab countries to recognize both that they had lost the war and that Israel had a right to exist. In Europe there was anger on the part of the United States, England and France and much of Western Europe at the closure of the Russian section of Berlin by the Russians. The closure in June of 1948 had resulted in the Berlin Airlift, which lasted until September of 1949 with tensions in the city at a constantly high level. In China the Communists were bearing down on Nanking and the government of Chaing Kai-Shek. The cold war was making the entire world increasingly nervous.

The cold war between the NBL and the BAA also continued. The NBL struggled to overcome the derision of the BAA, but the NBL's foundation was shaken by the collapse of the Detroit franchise in mid–December. As noted earlier, the franchise was hampered by limited venue access, minimal fan support and a poor team. Attendance figures were often not reported but, when they were, they hardly ever exceeded 1,000 customers in Detroit. The best players on the Vagabond Kings were redistributed, just as the Gears' players had been the previous year, when Maurice White's Professional Basketball League of America folded in three weeks. John Sebastian, Ollie Shoaf and Hal Devoll went to Hammond, Dillard Crocker went to Anderson and Ben Schadler to Waterloo. Del Loranger and Dave Latter decided to stay in the Detroit area and left professional basketball. There was little interest in the rest of the roster.

Dayton entered the league, but was immediately saddled with both a horrible record (2–17) and a venue problem. The schedule would not allow for the Rens to use the Dayton Coliseum because it was already booked. Thus, a number of the home games of the Rens would be played in Springfield, Ohio, in a venue that could accommodate about 1200.[29] As it happened that would turn out to be sufficient. The first home contest drew only 397 fans as Anderson, behind Frankie Brian's 25 points, defeated the Rens 82–61. "Pop"

Gates, player-coach and former Tri-Cities player, had 18 to lead the Rens' scoring.[30]

The other bottom team in the league, Denver of the Western Division, had finally won a game. After going winless in their first seven contests on the road, the Nuggets returned to Denver where they lost their first three home games. The home debut was against Oshkosh, which chartered a special railroad car for the team, 30 officials of Oshkosh manufacturing firms as well as sportswriters and broadcasters.[31] Almost as disappointing as the loss was the fact that only 1240 fans paid their way to see the contest. Certainly losing their first seven games was not a great incentive for fans, but Denver had prided itself on basketball knowledge and support of its teams, so this was a surprise.[32] The Nuggets dropped two more home games before finally defeating Tri-Cities 60–51 before 2,056 fans. Ward Gibson had 25 to rally the Nuggets to victory.[33] The Nuggets then began playing decent basketball and by the end of December they were still last, but had nine wins to go with 19 losses. Ward Gibson continued to lead them in scoring but missed a few games with a mysterious stomach ailment. A celebrated addition to the Nuggets was Robert "Ace" Gruenig, a long-time star for various Denver AAU teams and still a fine player at the age of 35. (Gruenig was elected to the Naismith Memorial Basketball Hall of Fame in 1962, based almost exclusively on his performances as an AAU player.)

The top teams continued to play well. By mid–December, Anderson and Syracuse were the only two Eastern Division teams above .500, both with records of 13 wins and five losses. Oshkosh with a record of 14 and seven had a slight lead on Tri-Cities (12–7) with Waterloo at 10 and nine and Sheboygan 11–11.

Near the end of the month Syracuse came to Denver, having just dropped a one-point decision in Moline before 4,400 spectators. There had been a lot of criticism of the referees throughout the season, but the Nationals felt that they had been "homered" in this game and were noticeably upset.[34] That angst seemed to carry over into the Denver contest when calls did not go the Nationals' way. In the first quarter, player-coach Al Cervi, a fiery competitor, was angered by a call and shoved the referee. Later, near the end of the contest won by the Nuggets 60–54, Jerry Rizzo punched the referee and was tossed from the contest in which he was the leading Syracuse scorer with 15 points.[35] David Ramsey, in his history of the Syracuse franchise, said that referee Jerry Fowler was surrounded by a group of angry Syracuse players and, seeking to escape the encirclement, tried to break through via Jerry Rizzo who punched him in the face. He quoted Rizzo who said, "He pushed me, and I hit him. That's all."[36] The next day, it was announced that Rizzo was suspended by NBL commissioner Doxie Moore for the rest of the season and Al Cervi had been fined $50 for the two technical fouls, one of which was given for shoving the referee. Jack Carberry, in his "Second Guess" column, called for Rizzo to not be signed by the BAA and tried to encourage this incident to be a kind of impetus for more NBL-BAA cooperation. He noted that earlier in the season Bob Doll had quit the Nuggets and signed with the Boston Celtics of the BAA, even though he had left the St. Louis Bombers of that league to go to Denver. Carberry saw these player personnel actions as needing to be addressed by some joint agreement between the two leagues.[37]

Syracuse again played at Denver the next night and the Nationals defeated the Nuggets before 3,149 fans, a number enhanced, most likely, by the controversy over the fisticuffs in the last game. Despite the loss, the *Post* was effusive in its praise of veteran "Ace" Gruening, noting, "Gruening played a magnificent game, both on the boards and at the post." He scored nine, second to Gibson's 13, both outscored by Schayes (17) for the Nats.[38] Other games that night saw the Rens take a rare win 56–53 in Hammond and Waterloo top Anderson in Iowa by a 50–45 score. The former game saw George Crowe get 17 for the Rens and George Glamack, the "Blind Bomber," pick up 16 for Hammond.[39]

A few nights later Syracuse lost its first home game to their Eastern Division rivals, the Anderson Packers, by a 73 to 57 score before 5,111. The size of the crowd was heartening to Syracuse ownership, but Anderson was too tough on the court, led by Komenich's 15 and Frank Gates's 14. Syracuse got most of its scoring from player-coach Cervi (14), Schayes (13) and Gabor (12).[40]

Welcome 1949

Nineteen forty-nine began with heightened tension in the Middle East as Jewish and Arab armies clashed in the region. The Communist Chinese push continued and the Nationalists were fleeing to the East. Berlin remained blockaded and the continued subject of the Berlin Airlift with supply planes landing and leaving Tempelhof Airport every ninety seconds around the clock.

In the NBL, Anderson was three games in front of Syracuse in the Eastern Division. Hammond was five behind Syracuse and Dayton 6 behind the Buccaneers. In the West, Oshkosh had a one game lead on Tri-Cities and a two game lead on Sheboygan. Waterloo had gone 3–13 after their 9–1 start and they were now two games out of third. Denver had rallied to move within four games of the Hawks. Shortly after the first of the year Bob Carpenter resigned as coach of Hammond and was able to return to Oshkosh. In an unusual arrangement, Carpenter had actually been rented to Hammond by Oshkosh with the stipulation that he couldn't be sold elsewhere. If Hammond didn't want him, he was to be returned to Oshkosh. George Sobek was named to replace Carpenter as Buccaneers' coach.[41] In a related action, the All Stars asked waivers on Ed Dancker, who never actually played for them. Dancker, now 34, had been a mainstay for Sheboygan for a number of years but had been sold to Syracuse at the end of the 1947-48 season. Dancker refused to report to the Nats, who then released him and he joined the Milwaukee Shooting Stars, an independent team, which often played in Milwaukee against and as part of NBL doubleheaders in that city that involved Sheboygan and Oshkosh. Dancker was employed by a large industrial firm in Milwaukee and found the 75 mile commute to Oshkosh for games difficult, something that had been easier when he played in Sheboygan, just 40 miles north.[42]

In an embarrassing page from the NBL past, Oshkosh lost a game in Syracuse on January 6 when the All Stars were forced to use three players, and the Nats were allowed to use two players, who had fouled out, in order to complete the game. Subsequently the three Oshkosh players were banished after six fouls, while two of their teammates still had five. There were 64 fouls called in the game. With limited rosters (10 players), these kinds of events were becoming more possible and certainly were instrumental in the NBA changing to a six foul rule shortly after the formation of the league in 1949.[43] A interesting note that week was that Jerry Rizzo, the suspended Syracuse player, had signed with Saratoga Springs of the New York State League, a minor league basketball operation. In his first game he scored five points as his team lost to Glens Falls.[44]

At this time, about halfway through the season, the individual scoring leaders were:

Gene Englund, Oshkosh	14.7 ppg
Ward "Hoot" Gibson, Denver	14.7 ppg
Don Otten, Tri-Cities	13.9 ppg
Dick Mehen, Waterloo	13.6 ppg
Al Cervi, Syracuse	12.6 ppg
Dolph Schayes, Syracuse	12.5 ppg
Harry Boykoff, Waterloo	12.1 ppg
Ollie Shoaf, Hammond	10.6 ppg
John Sebastian, Hammond	9.9 ppg
Bob McDermott, Tri-Cities	9.9 ppg

By the end of the season two of these had been traded to other teams. Two (Shoaf and Sebastian) were already playing on their second NBL team of the year after the Detroit franchise failed.

Continued Efforts at Mergers and Warring Words

Despite the small size of the new NBL cities, good-sized crowds continued to be the norm for Waterloo, Tri-Cities (Moline, mostly), Hammond and

Syracuse. Hammond was regularly drawing 3,000 to 5,000 fans, Syracuse 4,000 to 6,000 and Waterloo more than 5,000 at some contests. On January 16 the Tri-Cities Blackhawks defeated Syracuse in Moline 83–72 before 5,675 spectators with another 1,000 turned away at the door. Syracuse returned the favor on January 27 when they hosted Tri-Cities before 4,506 fans who saw a 58–55 Syracuse victory.[45] Three nights later the Nats defeated Dayton before 3,220 fans.[46]

There were disappointments, however. Dayton's constantly shifting venues and the lack of real connection to the city resulted in many small crowds in the Springfield, Ohio, gymnasium (which seated only 1,500, anyway). The occasional wanderings of the Wisconsin teams to various regional venues sometimes brought smaller crowds than anticipated. Sheboygan's home game in Rockford, Illinois, on January 17 attracted only 800 to the site, for example.[47] Nevertheless the NBL seemed to be doing better, financially, as a league than the BAA and rumors continued to fly regarding the demise of the BAA or the abandonment of some of its unhappy teams. On February 2 Jack Carberry, in his column, "The Second Guess," discussed reports that some BAA and American Basketball League clubs were "seeking, some in desperation, to go into the NBL fold." He cited rumors that the Washington Capitols would move to Indianapolis and join the NBL and that the current Indianapolis franchise would withdraw from the BAA. He also repeated rumors, noted earlier in the season, that the Fort Wayne franchise was seeking admission to the NBL and that the Minneapolis franchise would move to Des Moines for the next season.[48] Certainly the latter rumor was unfounded (and Carl Bennett says that it was); the Lakers drew well at home and were probably the saving force of the league while on the road. Everyone wanted to see George Mikan, who was simply the dominant player in basketball at the time.

Mikan was leading the Lakers to the Western Division lead of the BAA (though the Rochester Royals were tied or in the lead, at times, and subsequently won the title by one game) and was leading the league in scoring. By the end of January he led runner-up Joe Fulks by 100 points, but Fulks had some scoring explosions and caught Mikan less than three weeks later. Mikan then put on his own scoring spree, retook the lead a week later and finished the year with a record 1698 points, 138 points ahead of Fulks. Mikan averaged 28.3 points per game and Fulks 26.0.

Other rumors about the BAA's troubles had at least a grain of credibility and had been heard before. On January 25, the *Dayton Daily News* headlined an article drawn from the *Baltimore Sun* that claimed that Fort Wayne and Indianapolis were contemplating a return to the NBL. At the time the two squads were fifth and sixth, respectively, in the Western Division of the BAA. No source for the rumor was identified.[49]

Just over a week after Carberry's column appeared in the *Denver Post*, he was contacted by Maurice Podoloff, the BAA commissioner. He sought to use Carberry as a kind of intermediary with the NBL. In a letter to Carberry, which he reported in his column on February 11, Podoloff reiterated a position he had stated earlier in negotiations with the NBL and its president, Ike Duffey. Podoloff asserted that the BAA, NBL, ABL and other minor basketball leagues should follow the model of baseball and hockey in having a unified working agreement among the leagues, one that would also lead to a real "world series of basketball."[50]

Carberry's mediating function continued, apparently without success, judging by his column of the next week. In that he noted that Ike Duffey saw no conciliation possible and that it would be "war to the end." According to Carberry, Duffey rejected the "peace offering" of Podoloff saying, "flatly and finally" that the BAA would fold as the Indianapolis, Chicago, St. Louis, Boston, Providence, Philadelphia and Washington clubs "can't go next year." Duffey went on to say that the NBL had saved the BAA twice in the past, once with the working agreement that they had signed the prior year and which, Duffey claimed, the BAA had consistently violated, and again with the "theft" of the four NBL teams by the BAA. Now he saw the BAA as needing the NBL once again since the BAA was "on the verge of collapse." Duffey had recently attended a BAA game at Chicago Stadium where only 353 customers (of over 3,000 total) paid to enter. He also said that a recent Warriors game in Philadelphia had fewer than 200 paid admissions. He noted that the NBL was better off playing before very good crowds in what is called "the small town." He reiterated the fine attendance figures of Waterloo, Moline and Hammond as examples of what he was referring to.[51]

There were other rumors about the NBL also, some less rosy for certain franchises. One had the Oshkosh squad moving to Milwaukee and merging with that city's independent team, the Shooting Stars. This would have been a direct reflection of the fact that Oshkosh, despite its great community support, was still playing its contests in a local junior high school where barely 2,000 customers could squeeze into the stands. The Oshkosh team had not been drawing as expected and the club was in the red. There were also supposedly 11 applications for new NBL franchises, including Milwaukee, Rochester, Indianapolis (the latter two readmissions), Des Moines, Cedar Rapids, Baltimore, Grand Rapids, Louisville, Cincinnati, Wilkes-Barre and Rockford.[52]

A week later Podoloff replied with a brief comment that the statement that the BAA was hurting financially was not worth commenting upon. He then did comment, anyway, saying, "I would wonder whether Duffey can be so naïve as to believe that his bombast and the sputtering of his Commissioner, Doxie Moore, can persuade any graduating college player contemplating a professional career that the Basketball Association of America has less to offer than a league which has teams in Anderson, Oshkosh, Sheboygan and a cooperative team in Denver."[53] This, then, was really the crux of the issue, proper posturing to sign the best available college seniors. It is clear from all indications that Duffey was right, the BAA was in financial trouble, and that would continue for another six or seven years after the NBA was formed with the merger of the two leagues. Nevertheless the charge and argumentation was vital in convincing new players to enter the league in 1949-50, the subsequent merger no longer seeming to be a realistic possibility at that time.

The next day there was a final word on this war of words when Lon Darling weighed in with this statement:

> The NBL will last a lot longer than the other league, as teams are owned by civic organizations, whose only interest is in giving fans entertainment and advertising the city. The BAA is interested in nothing but money.[54]

Darling's comments would be prophetic in many ways in the future, but their impact was not really much at that time.

The League Races Tighten

February brought changes to the teams and the races in both the Eastern and Western Divisions of the NBL. Oshkosh slipped into second in the West behind Tri-Cities and Syracuse moved ahead of Anderson as of February 7. Oshkosh released veteran Eddie Riska on February 9. Since he had also been serving as coach with Gene Englund after Darling gave up that position, a replacement was needed, and Babe Lautenbach was named to fill that slot. Glen Selbo was then named team captain to replace Lautenbach.[55] Shortly afterward, the All Stars retook first place in the division and began to widen their lead over Tri-Cities and Sheboygan.

By the 17th of February the All Stars had a record of 29 wins and 20 losses and the Redskins were 24 and 20, while the Blackhawks were 25 and 21, a 2½ game margin for the All Stars over both teams. Despite their early successes, Waterloo had slipped below .500 with a record of 21 and 24. The Nuggets continued to sputter. After their 0–10 start, they had gone 12 and 20, much better, but they were still deep in the Western Division cellar and this would greatly affect attendance in Denver, where the Nuggets were playing in the new University of Denver Fieldhouse.

The *Denver Post* writers, particularly Claire Jordan, the Nuggets beat writer, continued to note that Denver was a great basketball town, but that the fans had become accustomed to winning after the successes of Denver in the AAU, and the losing of the Nuggets began to eat into attendance. A new

AAU team sponsored by the Denver Chevrolet dealers was playing well in the National Industrial Basketball League (NIBL) and that also hurt interest in the Nuggets. In mid–February the Nuggets sold their leading scorer, Ward Gibson, to the Tri-Cities Blackhawks for what the Nuggets' business manager, Hal Davis, called "one of the top prices paid for which a basketball player has been sold."[56] There were a number of reasons for the sale. First was a need for cash by the Nuggets since they weren't drawing as well as expected. Second was the fact that Gibson wanted to play with a winner and the Nuggets accommodated him by sending him back to the Midwest. He had starred at Creighton in college and was from Des Moines, so a move to Moline was comfortable for him. Finally, there was Gibson's reluctance to fly. The Nuggets, being nearly 1,000 miles from the next nearest NBL team (in Waterloo, Iowa) would fly to the Midwest or the east and then have seven or eight game road trips, before flying back to Denver for extended home stands. Gibson's fear of flying meant that he would have to take trains and, occasionally, was unable to make a game because of this. Moving him back to the Midwest would alleviate this problem.

Gibson's acquisition by Tri-Cities allowed Hawks owner Ben Kerner to sell McDermott to Hammond when McDermott asked Kerner for a raise.[57] McDermott was always difficult, although his on-court abilities were never in question. Both McDermott and Kerner were stubborn and pugnacious and the match simply got sour. Sending McDermott to Hammond (strictly as a player) did not help them much and didn't seem to have an adverse effect on Tri-Cities. They picked up Roger Potter, a former Moline high school coach, and continued playing well for the rest of the season.

The end of February brought good news for both the BAA and the NBL. George Mikan attracted 9,184 fans to Madison Square Garden where he scored 48 points to lead the Lakers to a 101–74 victory over the Knicks. The NBL seemed to be on the verge of signing top collegian "Easy" Ed Macauley of St. Louis University, who was supposedly being offered the highest salary ever paid to a pro basketball player.[58]

In addition, Israel and Egypt ended their war so there was some easing of tension in the Middle East. That was offset by the Russian replacement of their foreign minister Molotov, one of the last original Bolsheviks, by Vishinsky. There was uncertainty in the West as to what Stalin's rationale was and this made Americans more ill at ease about the ramifications for world peace.

March saw Anderson extend its lead in the Eastern Division greatly over Syracuse and the lead was eight games by season's end. Hammond finished 20 games below .500, but that was enough to finish third ahead of Dayton who had been hampered from the beginning by the horrendous start of Detroit, which the Rens had to carry with them for the rest of the season. The NBL decision was to have three teams from each division make the playoffs and

Hammond was in. In the West, Oshkosh and Tri-Cities were within a game in mid–March with Sheboygan two games behind. Waterloo was fading out of the playoff picture and Denver, after recovering, somewhat, from their 0–10 start had climbed to within six games of Waterloo before closing the season with 11 consecutive losses.

Because of cancelled games during the severe winter of 1948-49 the Sheboygan Redskins played day-night doubleheaders on Sunday, March 13, and on Sunday, March 31, both against the Dayton Rens. By splitting with Dayton, Sheboygan fell to third, one game behind Tri-Cities, rather than tied with them for second. Oshkosh was in first and finished there, one game up on Tri-Cities when the season ended.

During that final week NBL honors were announced. Don Otten of Tri-Cities led the league in scoring with 13.8 points per game. He was followed by Dick Mehen of Waterloo (13.4 ppg), Gene Englund of Oshkosh (13.2 ppg), Ward Gibson of Denver, then Tri-Cities (12.8 ppg) and Dolph Schayes of Syracuse (12.8 ppg, but eight points less than Gibson). Otten was also named Most Valuable Player in the NBL. He, Mehen, Englund, Frankie Brian of Anderson and Al Cervi of Syracuse were named to the All League 1st Team. Marko Todorovich of Sheboygan, Stan Von Nieda of Tri-Cities, Ward Gibson, and Bill Closs and Ralph Johnson, both of Anderson, comprised the Second Team. The 1st All Rookie Team was Schayes, Jimmy Darden of Denver, Don Ray of Tri-Cities and Jack Burmaster and Gene Berce of Oshkosh. The 2nd team was Billy Gabor and Ed Peterson of Syracuse, Leo Kubiak of Waterloo, Alex Hannum of Oshkosh and Dee Gibson of Tri-Cities. Schayes was named Rookie of the Year and Al Cervi Coach of the Year.[59]

The NBL Playoffs

In the first round of the Western Division series, Tri-Cities made short work of Sheboygan, winning 75–60 in Moline and by 59–51 in Sheboygan to capture the best of three series in two straight games. Otten and Von Nieda were the top scorers, but were assisted by rookie Murray Weir, who had 16 in Game One.[60]

The second round of the Eastern Playoffs pitted Syracuse against Anderson. Though Anderson had finished eight games ahead of the Nationals, these were still the two teams with the best records in the NBL in 1948-49. Oshkosh and Tri-Cities, who were separated only by a game in the standings, would square off in the West. This latter series opened in Wisconsin with the All Stars winning 68–66. Four Oshkosh players scored in double figures while Otten, with 19, was the only Blackhawk to do that.[61] Game Two, also played in Oshkosh, was an even more decisive All Star victory, 73–59 behind 15 points from Marshall Hawkins, 11 from Jack Burmaster and 10 from Bob Carpenter. Leroy Edwards, who had missed many games and appeared in only 10 games in his 15th professional season, had a revival, of sorts, in the playoffs. He had six in this contest against the Blackhawks.[62] The teams went to Moline where the Blackhawks won 70 to 64, with Dee Gibson getting 18 markers. The All Stars came back in the next contest in Moline to win 70 to 69 and move into the NBL Finals. Don Otten had 22 for Tri-Cities and was backed by 15 from Dee Gibson and 11 from Don Ray. For Oshkosh, Floyd Volker was the unexpected scoring leader with 20 while Gene Englund (14) and Bob Carpenter (13) also were in double figures. It was also noted that Leroy Edwards had been a big factor in the victories over Tri-Cities, but that he had re-injured his knee and would not play in the Finals.[63]

In the Eastern Division Finals, Anderson defeated the Nationals in Syracuse in their first contest by a score of 89 to 74. Frankie Brian had 17 to lead six Packers in double figures. For the Nats, Cervi had 14, Bob Calihan, a late season addition, had 13 and Dolph Schayes 11.[64] The Packers, who were the precursor of later NBA "run and gun" basketball, played 10 men regularly in their games and kept pushing the ball, exhausting their opponents who had shorter benches. The Packers had an excellent rotation but their egos seemed to be held in check by Coach Murray Mendenhall. Frankie Brian, Bill Closs and Ralph Johnson won all-league honors, but Milo Komenich, Ed Stanczak and Howie Schultz, with better scoring averages than Johnson or Closs, could also have been selected. John Hargis, an All-Rookie player the year before, could have also been mentioned in league honors. This was a great team and the results were consistent with that team concept.

Game Two was also in Syracuse and resulted in the Nats' only victory of the series 80–62. Schayes went off for 24 points to take game honors, but was supported by Ed Peterson, Billy Gabor (each with 12) and Paul Seymour with 10. Johnson (15), Komenich (14) and Hargis (10) were in double figures for the Packers.[65] The return to Anderson turned the series into a one-sided affair as the Packers won the final two games by scores of 76–59 and 90–84. Both games were very rough. In Game Three, 72 fouls were called and six Syracuse players fouled out. In the final contest, the Packers hit 42 of 51 free throws to set a new NBL playoff record on both accounts. The home court advantage certainly had an effect. Five Packers were in double figures, led by Brian's 19. Schayes led four Syracuse players in double figures with 15.[66]

The NBL Championship Finals would pit the top team in the league against one of the pioneer NBL franchises. The series was close, with three tight contests, but Anderson won them all to take their first NBL championship and, as it turned out, the last NBL championship. In Game One in Oshkosh, Anderson won in overtime 74–70 behind Ralph Johnson's 23, Brian's 14 and Hargis's 12. Oshkosh countered with Englund (18), Carpenter (15) and

Berce (10). Game Two, also in Oshkosh, was 72–70 with Milo Komenich (19), Frank Gates and Bill Closs (each with 14) pacing the Packers. The All Stars were led by Marshall Hawkins (20), Englund (12) and Burmaster (10).[67]

Despite the close contests, the BAA Finals were getting more coverage, mostly because of the game's superstar, George Mikan. Mikan and his teammates had finished second to Rochester in the Western Division of the BAA, but had defeated the Royals in two straight contests to take the Western Title. In the BAA Finals, the Lakers got out to a three games to none lead when Mikan broke his wrist early in the game in a loss to Washington. Mikan finished the game shooting left-handed and scored 15 points. Game five also went to the Capitols as Mikan, playing with his hand wrapped, because officials wouldn't allow him to play with a cast, had 22 points, mostly on left-handed hooks. Game Six returned to Minnesota, but to the Saint Paul Arena because the Minneapolis venues had been booked. Mikan had 29, the Lakers won by 21 and were seen as the best in basketball.[68]

The Packers, meanwhile, finished off the All Stars in Anderson in another foul-plagued contest; 69 fouls were called and 83 free throws shot. Anderson was 30 of 45, Oshkosh 26 of 38. Brian led Anderson with 17 and Gene Englund was the only All Star in double figures with 21. Worth noting was the final (and unexpected) appearance of Leroy Edwards, who had six points off the bench. Edwards was the only player to play for the entire life of the NBL and playing in its last official contest was certainly fitting.[69]

In the NBL awards ceremony, Ike Duffey's father, Isaiah, congratulated his son for bringing a championship to Anderson. Frankie Brian recalled, "Our championship was a championship for the little guys, the little towns. After those teams moved from our league that year, I think it was important for us to win and show that a small town could produce a champion."[70] And the hometown spirit that created the NBL still lingered at its last championship.

Looking To 1949-50: What About the NBL?

The newspapers had been filled with rumors of the uncertain futures of the BAA and various teams in that league as well as of potential expansion of the NBL or possible franchise movement. In April one rumor proved true when the Indianapolis Jets (the former Kautskys) of the BAA went into receivership with $20,000 in debts. In addition, George Glamack was seeking $50,000 in damages from the Jets, who had dropped him eleven games into the season. (The next month Glamack was joined by Leo Mogus and Walt Kirk in a suit that sought a total of $4662.51 owed the three from the Jets.[71]) The Jets had finished in last in the Western Division and had alienated their fans greatly through poor management and administration, personified by owner Paul Walk. Walk tried to sell the franchise to Ike Duffey, which infuriated Maurice Podoloff for obvious reasons, but ultimately the NBL did better. They waited until the Jets expired, then, in May, performed a great coup by awarding Indianapolis an NBL franchise with a twist. The team would be comprised mostly of the University of Kentucky players who had recently represented the United States in the 1948 Olympic Games in London and play as the Indianapolis Olympians. This brought instant interest and credibility to the franchise, which would be owned and operated by the players.[72]

Beginning in June, NBL and BAA owners and league administrators met sporadically in an effort to find a way to merge and put an end to their war, which threatened to sink both leagues. Though the NBL appeared healthier, Ed Stanczak contended that Ike Duffey "really kept the NBL going there for a while.... He put up money for many of those clubs like Oshkosh, Hammond, Sheboygan to keep them going."[73] The BAA was also not doing well financially and a number of clubs, as Ike Duffey well knew, were not reporting accurate gates. Without a merger it was not clear if the BAA could sustain itself another year.

Finally in August representatives from both leagues met in New York and agreed to join forces as one league that would be called the National Basketball Association. The agreement was not without many second thoughts on the part of the NBL owners. Robert Peterson claims, "On July 1 Leo Ferris, Ike Duffey and Magnus Brinkman of the NBL told the BAA's Executive Committee that eight of their teams wanted a merger."[74] This may have been so, but it is curious since there were only nine NBL teams and Dayton was really the New York Rens, who must have been ambivalent, at best, about such a merger. It would have seemed that Waterloo and Oshkosh and probably Hammond might have had their doubts, also. Todd Gould repeats this version and it probably came from Peterson, but neither author cites a source for the statement.[75] Interestingly, Magnus Brinkman is quoted on August 3, the day of the merger announcement, as being much more ambivalent than the prior attributions would have led one to believe.

> Magnus Brinkman, president of Sheboygan, Wis, Redskins, said Sheboygan, Anderson, Hammond, Waterloo and Denver favor remaining in the National League. Moline and Syracuse, he said, are committed to the merger with the B.A.A. Dayton and Oshkosh haven't committed themselves.

In that same article, Ike Duffey was quoted a saying, "The merger must come, sooner or later, or both leagues will be ruined."[76]

So the decision was a fait accompli. Now there would be the question of sorting all the details out. The announcement on the third of August noted that 18 teams would form the league. From the BAA, two teams, Providence and Indianapolis, had succumbed so they would bring ten teams to the new

NBA. From the NBL there would be eight teams; neither Hammond nor Dayton would continue in the league and the Oshkosh franchise would move to Milwaukee under new ownership since the All Stars had been a community enterprise. The rosters of the clubs were frozen and details would emerge at an organizational meeting to be held in Chicago on August 11. For the next year or two, the plan was to maintain the old structures with two divisions, each comprising a former league, rather than to re-structure along geographic lines. The model was the way major league baseball had formed in 1900 with the merger of the American and National Leagues, which maintained their independent integrity.[77]

A week later the new league announced that there would indeed be two divisions, an American and a National, and that they would be re-divided into Eastern and Western entities. The question of who would get the signing rights to players that had been drafted by teams from both leagues and remained unsigned was to be decided by coin tosses. Players signed would remain with that team.[78]

In later reporting of the merger and the formation of the league in his 1968 history of the NBA, Leonard Koppett discussed another issue, that of African Americans in the league. The BAA had none and never had in its three years of existence. The NBL, of course, had a history, though uneven and minimal, of African Americans in the league, capped by having an entire team of African Americans in 1948-49. The BAA had been hesitant to draft and sign "Negroes" because of the close financial relationship that the BAA owners had with Abe Saperstein, owner of the Harlem Globetrotters. The Globetrotters appeared in doubleheaders with BAA teams in BAA venues and were often the reason for the BAA's largest crowds. Saperstein wanted all the top African American players for his team and the BAA was reluctant to offend him. To the BAA it was less a social issue and more about money. This would be re-examined and changed in the NBA's second year.

Some of Koppet's claims and analyses do not stand up under scrutiny, however. He claimed that the NBA gathered itself into three divisions at the time of the merger and that Denver and Waterloo had not finished the NBL season but were invited to join the league anyway. He also noted that 17 teams were to begin the season. These claims were simply false and create a revisionist tone to the early history of the league.[79]

What did happen is not entirely clear but the results were. The owners of the Oshkosh franchise that was transplanted to Milwaukee did not feel that they could succeed and withdrew from the league between August and October. The initial 18 team, two subdivided divisions became a scheduling nightmare. Originally each of the old BAA teams was to play each other six times for 54 games and then play home and home games against the NBL's former squads for a total of 16 games and a schedule of 70 games. The NBL teams would play each other seven times and the BAA teams home and home for 69 games. The schedule would be unbalanced but workable. The loss of Milwaukee and the scheduling and travel issues made this schedule impossible, apparently. Instead the league was divided into three divisions. The Eastern had six teams, five from the BAA, and Syracuse. The Central Division had five teams, all former BAA squads. The Western Division contained six teams, all former NBL squads. "Generally speaking, each team will play about 34 games at home and on the road."[80] That ended up being true and the initial desire by Podoloff to have NBL teams playing mostly NBL teams and BAA teams playing mostly BAA teams, was also true, except for Syracuse.

That was in the future; the present was that the NBL and its 12 (or 14, if one counts the Midwest Conference) year existence was over. There was an effort in 1950-51 to revive another league when the NBA was reduced to 11 teams. Sheboygan, Anderson and Waterloo, all NBA dropouts, combined with Kansas City, Louisville, St. Paul and Grand Rapids (all former Professional Basketball League of America franchises) to form the National Professional Basketball League. These teams were joined by a new Denver franchise as it, too, dropped out of the NBA after a year. This new league sought to capture the old NBL magic, but it was not to be, and by the end of the year the league was down to four squads, all former NBL franchises (although Denver had shifted to Evansville, Indiana, near the end of the season). Thus, the NBL and its remnants succumbed, but the NBL legacy was and is a significant part of the NBA.

NBL Lessons
and Accomplishments

From 1937 until 1948 the National Basketball League was the undisputed premiere professional basketball league in the United States. Of course, there were only two leagues during much of that time, and the American Basketball League was content to stay regional and sign regional players from New York, New Jersey and Eastern Pennsylvania to populate the league. The reach of the ABL was not extensive and the result was a league that played under the radar of many of the media outlets of the time, even on the Eastern Seaboard. The BAA began in 1946, but except for a few top players there was little comparison between the overall quality of the two leagues. Players in the NBL were from across the nation and it was clear that the NBL was the closest thing to a true national league around.

One indicator of the NBL's dominance was the list of invited participants in the World Professional Basketball Championship Tournament, which was held in Chicago from 1939–1948. The first year saw 12 teams, two from the NBL. The next year there were 14 teams, with three from the NBL. In 1941, the figures were 16 and five (of seven NBL teams.) The next year, all seven of the 16 NBL teams were invited and two NBL teams met in the Finals. In 1943 all three of the remaining NBL teams were among the twelve teams and in 1944 all four NBL tams were again invited as the Pistons began their three-year skein of tournament championships. In 1945 five of the six NBL teams were among the 14 teams in the tournament and in 1946 six of the 14 participating teams were from the NBL with two NBL teams (Fort Wayne and Oshkosh) meeting in the Finals. In 1947 nine of the 14 teams were from the NBL with two (Indianapolis and Toledo) again meeting in the Finals. The last year of the tournament five of the eight teams were NBL squads. Of course, the lack of participation of the BAA teams hurt the tournament and made the statement of NBL dominance in the last years of the tournament difficult to quantify with assurance.

The NBL had been constructed on the remnants of the old ABL, which had begun in 1925 and lasted until 1931 in cities from New York to Chicago. Cities which had been in the ABL and subsequently joined the NBL, some time between 1937 and 1947, included Chicago, Fort Wayne, Cleveland, Toledo, Rochester, Detroit and Buffalo. Sometimes these teams had been successful ABL franchises and other times not so successful, but there was a record from which the subsequent league could learn.

The success of the NBL, however, was premised upon a different model than the ABL, relying more on the appeal to middle-size urban areas for growth and development, rather than the traditional large cities than had characterized most major leagues in American professional sports. If there were any model team, it would have been the Green Bay Packers in professional football, a squad that thrived with total community involvement and continues to do so. The most successful NBL franchises, for the most part, were similar to the Packers, and this was both the source of success in the league and a large factor in the league's demise. The league grew in a completely different setting and social milieu from earlier professional basketball leagues and from other professional sports leagues. For the earlier ABL the league had been a byproduct of good economic times when consumer spending grew. The owners of the teams were often people from other professional sports who wanted to have a team in another sport's league. These owners probably enjoyed basketball but saw it as another opportunity for making money first and enhancing the sport of basketball second.

In contrast to that, the initial owners, and many throughout the history of the NBL, had much different goals. These owners, for the most part, had two interests that led them to pursue professional basketball ownership. One was a love of the game itself, and second was a desire to use the game to promote their communities. In some cases, it was also a convenient way to advertise their products or companies, but that notion was less important than the former two factors. Frank Kautsky was the epitome of the former interest and Fred Zollner was a good example of the latter.

The fact that the league grew and developed in the midst of the Great Depression was also much different, and the appeal was not to a culture with lots of money to spend, but rather to a culture with little money and more time, mostly because of under- or unemployment. Players sought basketball as a supplement to low wages in most other areas of the economy. Basketball often became the key to gaining steady employment in a factory or business. It was this economic situation that sometimes drove top players away from professional basketball, per se, and to Amateur Athletic Union (AAU) basketball, a universe wherein basketball was a part of one's employment, but not one's employment, as such. Top players like Hank Luisetti and Bob Kurland never played professional basketball because they made more money and felt more secure linking AAU basketball with their employment. In the later years of the NBL, World War II was a significant factor in the size and scope of the league. Indeed, the history of the league can be easily divided into three segments: the Great Depression, World War II and post–World War II. The league took on new qualities with each new era that it embraced.

One of the most significant changes in professional basketball as it progressed from the American Basketball League and through the history of the NBL was the composition of the players. Whereas the ABL was largely populated by players who had not graduated from or even attended college, the NBL was markedly different. Over the first nine years of the league, approximately 350 players are listed with 305 having identified colleges, 45 having no college. This was a radical departure from earlier years of professional basketball and much of that change must be attributed to the Great Depression. During the last three years of the league that ratio grew in favor of college attendees. The value of a college education, on and off the court, was recognized by both players and owners. It also helped the league in providing fans with players with whom they were more familiar because of their college stardom. Some of the greatest early players were not college graduates, however. Bob McDermott, Leroy Edwards, Charley Shipp, Ed Dancker, Mel Riebe, and Al Cervi all jumped directly into professional basketball, although Edwards did play one year of varsity basketball at Kentucky (where he led the team in scoring). These players were so good that they would have starred in any situation; college may have helped them, but the times dictated to them that they needed to pursue financial gain as quickly as possible.

It should be noted that Edwards and Shipp should also be recognized for being the only two players to participate in the entire history of the NBL. Edwards began his professional career with the Indianapolis U.S. Tires team of the Midwest Conference in 1936-37, then joined Oshkosh. Oshkosh joined the NBL in its initial year, though not quite at the beginning of the season, and Edwards played with the All Stars until the league ended. That, interestingly enough, was also the end of the All Stars as a professional team since they did not join the NBA when that league commenced operations in the fall of 1949. The failure to include Edwards in the Naismith Memorial Basketball Hall of Fame is shameful. The entire NBL is diminished by his absence. Interestingly, there are only 10 players in the Hall of Fame who played in the NBL. Alex Hannum and Red Holzman are enshrined as coaches. Of those ten, only two played their professional basketball exclusively in the NBL. Even that is really not true since Bob McDermott played for the Celtics for a number of years. John Wooden is the other player, and he played in the two years of the Midwest Conference and two years of NBL ball. He is likely there for his college playing since he only was in 46 league games as a professional in four years, despite leading the Midwest Conference in scoring one year. It seems amazing that in 12 years of professional existence there could be no NBL players who played in only that league deserving of Hall of Fame enshrinement. Edwards' absence, of course, is the most egregious.

Charley Shipp, like Edwards, was a native of Indianapolis. He attended Cathedral High and Edwards attended Technical High and they graduated two years apart. Shipp began his professional career with Akron, playing for the Goodyear Wingfoots, which also got him a position in one of the factories. He joined Oshkosh in 1939 and played on the same team with Edwards until 1945 when he was wooed by the Zollner Pistons and Fred Zollner's better pay. He remained with Fort Wayne until late in the 1946-47 season when he was traded to Anderson. In the last year of the NBL, 1948-49, he was the player-coach of the Waterloo Hawks.

Another significant change from the earlier leagues to the NBL was the increasing number of big men in the league. Robert Peterson discusses this, noting, "When the National Basketball League began its first season in 1937, the players on the thirteen teams averaged about 6-feet 1-inch, but there were only six men over 6-foot-5." By 1940, he observes, "The NBL had nine players who topped 6-foot-5."[1] This trend continued. Edwards was seen as the first good, big man in the league and he dominated inside in the early years of the league at 6-foot-4. By 1941 every team had a player 6'4" or more, and a number of them were good players. These included Gene Englund (Oshkosh) at 6'5", "Blackie" Towery, 6'4" and Elmer Gainer, 6'6" (Fort Wayne), Floyd Ebaugh, 6'7", and George Glamack, 6'6" (Akron Goodyears), Scott Armstrong and John Townsend, both 6'4" (Indianapolis), Ed Dancker, 6'7" (Sheboygan), Mike Novak, 6'9", George Ratkovicz, 6'6", and Vince McGowan, 6'6" (Chicago) and assorted players from Toledo, none of whom lasted very long. The point is that the league's big men were getting bigger and the type of game being played utilized that size more. Reductions in the number of jump balls allowed the game to flow more quickly and freely and the agile big man became more instrumental in a team's success. Some teams, such as Oshkosh, put together a big (for the time) front line and attempted to overpower teams. World War II put these and other long term plans to rest, but, after the war, Oshkosh returned with a starting five where the smallest player was 6'3". Sheboygan countered with Novak, Dancker and Kleggie Hermsen, all 6'7" or more, but neither could top guard-oriented Rochester in 1946. Still, every team felt that it needed a good, powerful, big man after the entry of George Mikan into the NBL. Mikan's teams not only won, but he was also the top drawing card in the professional game, and every team sought another Mikan. (Actually, there was another Mikan. That was George's brother, Ed, who was 6'8" and played at DePaul after George. He played in the NBA starting in 1949 and finishing in 1954 with lifetime averages of 6.7 ppg and 5.5 rebounds per game).

In addition to the change in the game's play, there were also many more games being played. When the NBL began, the league members played between 13 and 20 league games and another 15 to 25 exhibition games. In 1941 each of the seven league members were to play 24 league games and some played as many as 30 more outside the league. In 1945-46 each of the eight teams played 32–34 league games and the next year each of the 12 teams played 44 games with about 30 exhibitions. The 1947-48 season found 60 games as the league standard with some playing another 30 during the season. Clearly the game had become much more physically demanding, for both play and travel, and a player could no longer even contemplate holding another job, even part-time, during the basketball season. Salaries climbed to meet the rising demand for players as the NBL competed for players with the newly formed Basketball Association of America starting in 1946.

Founding Principles of the League

It cannot be emphasized enough that the NBL was founded to promote basketball and the communities that sponsored teams in the league. Though not unimportant, making money was not an initial concern of the owners in the league. They didn't want to lose money, but profit was less of a concern for them than amity and sport. This was in contrast with the BAA, which, as Ike Duffey noted, was most interested in making money. The owners of many of the teams in the NBL had gotten into the league either because they had a real interest or love of the game or saw the league as good for their community. In the former category were people like Frank Kautsky of Indianapolis; Paul Sheeks, the manager of the Akron Firestones; Gerry Archibald of the Warren Penn Hyvis Oilers; Fred Zollner of the Fort Wayne Zollner Pistons; Les Harrison of the Rochester Royals; Maurice White of the Chicago Gears and Ike Duffey of the Anderson Duffey Packers. In the latter category were again Kautsky, Harrison, Zollner, Eddie Ciesar of Hammond's Ciesar All-Americans, Frank Zummach of Sheboygan and Lon Darling of Oshkosh. These latter two weren't really owners since the teams were owned by many community members, as were the Hammond-Calumet City Buccaneers. Of course, there were also corporate entities that sponsored a number of NBL teams, particularly in the earlier years, and these businesses saw this as much a civic duty as a way to gain free advertising. Firestone, Goodyear, Kautsky's Grocery, Jim White Chevrolet of Toledo, Zollner Pistons, Columbus Athletic Supply, Hyvis Penn Oil, King Clothiers, Chase Brass, Allmen Transfer, Jeep,

American Gear Company, Duffey Meat Packing and Dow Chemical were all involved in teams at various times in the league's history.

It should also be noted how many communities saw the professional team in their midst as *their* team and, in some cases, it truly was. Sheboygan used the Green Bay model and had 120 business and professional men as shareholders in the team. The Hammond-Calumet City Buccaneers also followed this model, as did the Denver Nuggets, to a lesser degree. The Tri-Cities squad from Moline (Illinois), Rock Island (Illinois) and Davenport (Iowa) also used community support; their 31 stockholders represented most of the major businesses in the region, and smaller businesses also contributed. In addition the professional basketball venue was a place to be seen, and it was expected of community leaders in towns like Fort Wayne, Oshkosh, Rochester, Waterloo, Moline and Anderson. In Akron and Fort Wayne, the workers for the local industries that sponsored the teams came to the games in force and were encouraged by the companies' weekly magazines or newsletters to support the teams. Fans came in sport coats and ties (and dresses for the females) and cheered their teams unceasingly. Advertisements in the local papers at the beginning and end of the seasons exhorted or congratulated their teams for their performances. The games were the chief entertainment in these small cities and were a source of universal pride throughout the region.

Players were readily identified in the community and easily integrated into these small cities. Dick Triptow, Blackie Towery, Fuzzy Levane, Arnie Risen and Dolph Schayes all commented on their comfort and community fit into Fort Wayne, Rochester or Syracuse. Oshkosh and Rochester, among others, had special exhibition games and banquets at the end of the season to honor their teams, much like those that occurred in many towns and honored their high school teams. The local heroes were often the idols of their young local fans. In the Sheboygan County Historical Center in Sheboygan Falls, there are no fewer than three scrapbooks that have been contributed that illustrate the fervent affection of the local youngsters for the Sheboygan Redskins.

These descriptions, however, were not as true of the big city teams in places like Detroit, Chicago, Pittsburgh and Cleveland. In those venues the NBL was lucky to get media coverage, let alone strong support. These cities supported major league baseball and had for more than 40 years. Professional basketball was not a widely supported enterprise and it was not surprising that basketball teams in these cities came and went, not lasting in a single format. Denver, as a new city on the frontier, was more like the smaller hometowns, and the coverage and pride in its first major sports franchise was obvious, but AAU basketball had a longer, stronger tradition there that hurt attendance and interest in the Denver Nuggets franchise. Minneapolis longed for big league status and the owners and media of that city were very vocal in pushing the NBL to merge with the BAA and the big-time teams. The Minneapolis management began calling for a BAA-NBL merger almost as soon as the Lakers entered the league. They had, of course, the biggest drawing card in professional basketball in Mikan and knew that his appearance could and would pack even the biggest of the big city arenas. The Lakers also had no history in the league and little appreciation or understanding of the base upon which the league had been born and raised. They had an inordinate amount of influence because of Mikan, and this was surely a factor in the acquiescence of the other owners for a merger. I am sure that the long-time franchise owners and operators saw the seeds of their own destruction in the merger that would utterly change the character of the league but were powerless to stop the process once it had been set in motion. Almost all parties began to say that it was not a matter of if, but, rather, when, regarding a merger of the two leagues. Once the NBL was merged, it was not long before the smaller town franchises would be unable to compete in the new NBA, at least financially and usually on the court. Within a year, the NBA was reduced from 17 to 11 teams and, of the six dropouts four were prominent former NBL franchises—Anderson, Sheboygan, Waterloo and Denver. In another year, Tri-Cities moved to Milwaukee, forsaking another NBL city. The hometown appeal that had fostered the league's growth now worked to its disadvantage in the NBA.

One big factor in the locales of franchises was the character of the venues where the teams played. The BAA had big arenas and wanted big arenas in all the NBA franchises in order to allow for a larger potential income from ticket sales. This worked against the inclusion of Oshkosh, which was never able to build an arena and maintained its home court at one of the local junior high or high schools. Sheboygan had a new Civic Auditorium but it seated fewer than 4,000 so it was, ultimately, unacceptable to many league franchises. The idea of building a larger facility so soon after the opening of this auditorium was unacceptable to the Sheboygan shareholders and community. Anderson played at a local high school. Admittedly, it seated over 4,500, but that was still not enough for the new NBA. Fort Wayne was still playing in the North Side High School gym, but the approval of a new arena in the city allowed it to continue as a viable franchise. That arena did not open until 1955 and it was still too small for the NBA, precipitating the franchise's move to Detroit in 1957. Thus, the hometown appeal was antithetical to the need for larger and larger venues in larger and larger cities.

Part of the coverage in the hometowns was radio coverage, something that began because it allowed the local stations to be more involved with the community and to get more programming. Initially, the teams received nothing for the right to broadcast their games and a number of broadcasters became respected fixtures behind the microphones. These included Hilliard

Gates, WKJG in Fort Wayne; Milt Marks, WOWO in Fort Wayne, and Art Bramhill in Sheboygan. Oshkosh, Anderson, Waterloo and Denver also had regular radio coverage of their NBL contests.

Travel and Scheduling

The NBL was one of, if not the first, professional basketball league to have centralized scheduling and a real league office. The NBL offices shifted from Akron to Chicago to West Lafayette as the commissioners changed, but as the league grew and expanded, it also began to realize that it needed to control media coverage. At one time some teams had so little local coverage by the organized media and the league was so loosely controlled that some NBL teams could claim that they were in the thick of the NBL race when they were doing quite the opposite. So, in the early 1940s, the league office in Chicago began producing weekly media summaries of information, which were distributed to local newspapers in each of the league cities. These included league standings, scoring leaders and events like trades or signings. By the last years of the league a publicity director had a small staff to handle this function for the league on a daily basis.

The NBL started with a loose agreement on scheduling in the 1930s, with teams making their own arrangements for games with their league brethren, the only qualification being a minimum number of games in the league. As the league office became more developed, the league made the schedules and tried, sensibly, to coordinate a team's schedule with reasonable traveling. Road trips would usually not be more than four or five league games. Teams also could schedule exhibition contests around gaps in the league schedule.

Initially, the league teams traveled, almost exclusively, by automobile. Some might have seen the need to take the train, which would have been more expensive than traveling in two autos for eight players and a coach. The far western reaches of the league in the late 1930s were Oshkosh and Sheboygan with Buffalo, Warren and Pittsburgh the greatest distance from those western outposts. An occasional train trip might have been necessary, but most of the time teams worked their way east or west, playing different squads in league or exhibition contests. A big factor in this was the Depression, which made every team and player reticent to spend any more money than was really necessary. Train travel was a luxury except when it was a necessity. By the early 1940s the league's geographic parameters had contracted and car travel was more frequently used than ever. Some teams invested in oversized station wagons (kind of the minivans of the era) and were able to save money by using just one vehicle (after absorbing the cost of the initial investment for the purchase of the vehicle).

After the war ended, the league re-expanded and stretched from Wisconsin to Rochester, meaning train travel (usually overnight trains after games) was again common. Economic conditions had also improved greatly in the postwar period, so train travel was no longer viewed as a luxury that could not be afforded. In the last year of the league, the Denver Nuggets were the first team to travel regularly by airplane, setting the standard for future professional teams. The Nuggets would fly a charter flight to the East, then travel by train to the various venues on their seven game road trips. Then, the Nuggets would fly back to Denver, again via chartered aircraft. After they joined the NBA, the Fort Wayne Zollner Pistons purchased an airplane for team travel, possibly being the first professional team to do so.

Integrating the League

The NBL teams played many of the African American teams in exhibitions. The Rens made annual trips through Wisconsin and Indiana, often hooking up with the All Stars or the Pistons and playing their way across the state or the region in the 1930s and 1940s. Most of the fans, black and white, liked the novelty of the top black teams playing the top white teams, and it cannot be denied that the undercurrent of racism had to be present. The successes of the Renaissance team, as well as the lesser successes of such teams as the Chicago Crusaders and the Cleveland Pennzoils, made white fans and media accept the high quality of the play on the part of these black teams. This had to have reduced stereotyping and prejudice among knowledgeable basketball fans. In the first year of the Midwest Conference, one African American player was in the league.

The NBL remained all white until 1942 when both the Toledo Jim White Chevrolets and the Chicago Studebakers added African American players to their rosters. The Toledo franchise folded four games into the season, but the Studebakers played the entire season with seven African Americans and five European Americans on the roster at various times. This was the first fully integrated team to compete in a major professional league in the United States. Most of the African Americans were former Harlem Globetrotters and some returned to the Globetrotters at the end of the season or the next season. That next season, 1943-44, Willie Smith, the former New York Renaissance center, played four games at the end of the season for the Cleveland Chase Brass.

For two years after that the NBL was an all-white league, but in 1946-47 three more African Americans played in the NBL — Bill Farrow for Youngstown, Dolly King for Rochester and William "Pop" Gates for the Buffalo Bisons, who moved to Moline early in the season and became the Tri-

Cities franchise. Gates, a New York City native and former Rens' star, had surely not counted on playing in the Midwest, but when the franchise moved, he stayed with them and was the second leading scorer on the team. A altercation with Chick Meehan of Syracuse was made into a racial confrontation, which both players denied was the case. Dolly King was subjected to some racist taunting in isolated incidents, most notably in Fort Wayne, and these incidents involving the two players were probably instrumental in their not being offered contracts in the NBL the next season.

Both Gates and King returned to all black squads the next season, as the NBL was all white for another season. Then, in 1949, the last season of the league, the New York Rens took on the slot of the Detroit Vagabond Kings when they left the league in mid–December. Unfortunately, the Rens, playing as the Dayton Rens and coached by player-coach Pop Gates, also took on the record of the Kings. Since this was 2–17, the Rens were too deep in the hole to have a prayer of making the playoffs, but they did become the first all-black team to play in a major professional league. These unique NBL accomplishments should be honored by the NBA, but, instead, they are ignored, as is much of the NBL's history by the NBA. Old NBL-NBA players are almost universal in their decrying of this, but the NBA seems unmoved. Former NBL players often point out that the first six NBA champions were all former NBL teams. Not until 1956 did a former BAA team win an NBA championship.

Many of the NBL's accomplishments noted in this chapter foreshadowed the NBA's later decisions and events like integration, plane travel, expanded media coverage, local players on local teams (cf. the NBA's territorial draft), players coming from college to the pros as a matter of course, national expansion, et al. Had the NBL been able to last a bit longer it would have, possibly, been able to survive with its community focus and integrity intact, thanks to a national television contract. That took until the 1960s, however, and even then was not a regular source of real income until the 1970s.

The NBL is the greatest professional league in the United States that few people really know much about. This book was written to change that.

Appendix 1:
NBL Standings, 1937–1949

1937-38

Eastern Division
Akron Firestone Non-Skids (14–4)
Akron Goodyear Wingfoots (13–5)
Pittsburgh Pirates (8–5)
Buffalo Bisons (3–6)
Warren Penns (3–9)
Columbus Athletic Supply (1–12)

Western Division
Oshkosh All Stars (12–2)
Whiting Ciesar All-Americans (12–3)
Fort Wayne General Electrics (13–3)
Indianapolis Kautskys (4–9)
Richmond King Clothiers (1–2)*
Cincinnati Comellos (2–5)
Kankakee Gallagher Trojans (3–11)
Dayton Metropolitans (2–11)

Richmond franchise moved to Cincinnati during season

Goodyear won Eastern Playoffs 2 games to 0 over Firestone. Oshkosh defeated Whiting in two games.

Goodyear defeated Oshkosh in Championship Playoffs, 2 games to 1.

1938-39

Eastern Division
Akron Firestone Non-Skids (24–3)
Akron Goodyear Wingfoots (14–14)
Warren Penns (9–10)*
Cleveland White Horses (5–4)
Pittsburgh Pirates (13–14)

Western Division
Oshkosh All Stars (17–11)
Indianapolis Kautskys (13–13)
Sheboygan Redskins (11–17)
Hammond Ciesar All-Americans (4–24)

Warren moved to Cleveland in February 1939.

Firestones topped Oshkosh in championship series 3 games to 2.

1939-40

Eastern Division
Akron Firestone Non-Skids (18–9)
Detroit Eagles (17–10)
Akron Goodyear Wingfoots (14–14)
Indianapolis Kautskys (9–19)

Western Division
Oshkosh All Stars (15–13)
Sheboygan Redskins (15–13)
Chicago Bruins (14–14)
Hammond Ciesar All-Americans
   (9–19)

   Akron Firestones defeated Detroit for Eastern Championship 2 games to 1.

   Oshkosh defeated Sheboygan 2 games to 1 for Western Championship.

   Firestones won NBL championships, defeating Oshkosh 3 games to 2.

1940-41

Oshkosh All Stars (18–6)
Akron Firestone Non-Skids (13–11)
Sheboygan Redskins (13–11)
Detroit Eagles (12–13)
Akron Goodyear Wingfoots (11–13)
Chicago Bruins (11–13)
Hammond Ciesar All-Americans
   (6–18)

   Oshkosh defeated Firestones in Championship Semifinals 2 games to 0.

   Sheboygan defeated Detroit in Championship Semifinals 2 games to 1.

   Oshkosh won Championship over Sheboygan 3 games to 0.

1941-42

Oshkosh All Stars (20–4)
Akron Goodyear Wingfoots (15–9)
Fort Wayne Zollner Pistons (15–9)
Indianapolis Kautskys (12–11)
Sheboygan Redskins (10–14)

Chicago Bruins (8–15)
Toledo Jim White Chevrolets (3–21)

   Fort Wayne defeated Goodyears in Championship Semifinals 2 games to 1.

   Oshkosh defeated Indianapolis in Championship Semifinals 2 games to 0.

   Oshkosh defeated Fort Wayne in Championship series 2 games to 1.

1942-43

Fort Wayne Zollner Pistons (17–6)
Sheboygan Redskins (12–11)
Oshkosh All Stars (11–12)
Chicago Studebakers (8–15)
Toledo Jim White Chevrolets (0–4)*
Dropped out of league.

   Sheboygan defeated Oshkosh in Championship Semifinals 2 games to 0.

   Fort Wayne defeated Chicago 2 games to 1 in Championship Semifinals.

   Sheboygan defeated Fort Wayne in Championship Series 2 games to 1.

1943-44

Fort Wayne Zollner Pistons (18–4)
Sheboygan Redskins (14–8)
Oshkosh All Stars (7–15)
Cleveland Chase Brass (3–15)

   Fort Wayne defeated Cleveland in Championship Semifinals 2 games to 0.

   Sheboygan defeated Oshkosh in Championship Semifinals 2 games to 1.

   Fort Wayne won Championship 3 games to 0 over Sheboygan.

1944-45

Eastern Division
Fort Wayne Zollner Pistons (25–5)
Cleveland Allman Transfers
(13–17)
Pittsburgh Raiders (7–23)

Western Division
Sheboygan Redskins (19–11)
Chicago American Gears (14–16)
Oshkosh All Stars (12–18)

Sheboygan defeated Chicago in Championship Semifinals 2 games to 1.

Fort Wayne defeated Cleveland in Championship Semifinals 2 games to 0.

Fort Wayne defeated Sheboygan 3 games to 2 to win Championship.

1945-46

Eastern Division
Fort Wayne Zollner Pistons (26–8)
Rochester Royals (24–10)
Youngstown Bears (13–20)
Cleveland Allman Transfers
(4–29)

Western Division
Sheboygan Redskins (21–13)
Oshkosh All Stars (19–15)
Chicago American Gears (17–17)
Indianapolis Kautskys (10–22)

Sheboygan defeated Oshkosh in Championship Semifinals 3 games to 2.

Rochester defeated Fort Wayne in Championship Semifinals 3 games to 1.

Rochester defeated Sheboygan 3 games to 0 for Championship.

1946-47

Eastern Division
Rochester Royals (31–13)
Fort Wayne Zollner Pistons
(25–19)
Syracuse Nationals (21–23)
Toledo Jeeps (21–23)
Buffalo Bisons (5–8)*
Tri-Cities Blackhawks (14–17)
Youngstown Bears (12–32)

Western Division
Oshkosh All Stars (28–16)
Indianapolis Kautskys (27–17)
Chicago American Gears (26–18)
Sheboygan Redskins (26–18)
Anderson Duffey Packers (24–20)
Detroit Gems (4–40)
Transferred to Tri-Cities in January 1947.

Fort Wayne defeated Toledo 3 games to 2 in Eastern Semifinals.

Rochester defeated Syracuse 3 games to 1 in Eastern Semifinals.

Oshkosh topped Sheboygan 3 games to 2 in Western Semifinals.

Chicago defeated Indianapolis in Western Semifinals 3 games to 2.

Chicago defeated Oshkosh in Western Finals 2 games to 0.

Rochester defeated Fort Wayne in Eastern Finals 2 games to 1.

Chicago won Championship 3 games to 1 over Rochester.

1947-48

Eastern Division
Rochester Royals (44–16)
Anderson Duffey Packers (42–18)
Fort Wayne Zollner Pistons (40–20)
Syracuse Nationals (24–36)
Toledo Jeeps (22–37)
Flint-Midland Dow A.C.s (8–52)

Western Division
Minneapolis Lakers (43–17)
Tri-Cities Blackhawks (30–30)
Oshkosh All Stars (29–31)
Indianapolis Kautskys (24–35)
Sheboygan Redskins (23–37)

Rochester defeated Fort Wayne 3 games to 1 in the Eastern Semifinals.

Anderson defeated Syracuse 3 games to 0 in the Eastern Semifinals.

Minneapolis defeated Oshkosh 3 games to 1 in the Western Semifinals.

Tri-Cities defeated Indianapolis 3 games to 1 in the Western Semifinals.

Minneapolis defeated Tri-Cities 2 games to 0 in the Western Finals.

Rochester defeated Anderson 2 games to 1 in the Eastern Finals.

Minneapolis defeated Rochester 3 games to 1 for the Championship.

1948-49

Eastern Division
Anderson Duffey Packers (49–15)

Syracuse Nationals (40–23)
Hammond Calumet Buccaneers (21–41)
Detroit Vagabond Kings (2–17)*
Dayton Rens (14–26)

Western Division
Oshkosh All Stars (37–27)
Tri-Cities Blackhawks (36–28)
Sheboygan Redskins (35–29)
Waterloo Hawks (30–32)
Denver Nuggets (18–44)

Dropped out of league, franchise transferred to Dayton.

Tri-Cities defeated Sheboygan 2 games to 0 in Western Semifinals.

Oshkosh defeated Waterloo 2 games to 0 in Western Semifinals.

Anderson defeated Dayton 2 games to 0 in Eastern Semifinals.

Syracuse topped Hammond 2 games to 0 in Eastern Semifinals.

Anderson defeated Syracuse in the Eastern Finals 2 games to 1.

Oshkosh defeated Tri-Cities in the Western Finals 2 games to 1.

Anderson won Championship, defeating Oshkosh 3 games to 0.

Appendix 2: Scoring Leaders in the Midwest Conference and NBL, 1935–1949

Official NBL data were not always kept or kept accurately. There are discrepancies here from newspaper accounts and from that later complied from *Total Basketball*. League leaders were determined by total points at that time, but I have chosen to list them by points per game average (ppg), the figure used today.

Midwest Conference

1935–1937

Both years the number of games was not standardized around the league, but the best averages were by John Wooden and Leroy Edwards.

NBL

1937-38		Games	Points	PPG
Leroy Edwards	Oshkosh	13	182	14
John Wooden	Whiting	10	107	10.7
Bob Kessler	Indianapolis	10	103	10.3
Jack Ozburn	Akron Non-Skids	15	144	9.6
Vince McGowan	Whiting	15	144	9.6
Scott Armstrong	Fort Wayne	17	147	8.6
1938-39		Games	Points	PPG
Leroy Edwards	Oshkosh	28	334	11.9
Howard Cable	Non-Skids	24	262	10.9

Jewell Young	Indianapolis	26	264	10.2
Paul Birch	Pittsburgh	22	221	10.0
Jack Ozburn	Non-Skids	19	184	9.7
Johnny Sines	Indianapolis	23	215	9.3

1939-40		*Games*	*Points*	*PPG*
Leroy Edwards	Oshkosh	28	361	12.9
Ernie Andres	Indianapolis	27	292	10.8
Ben Stephens	Akron	28	295	10.5
Mike Novak	Chicago	28	293	10.5
Wibs Kautz	Chicago	28	273	9.8
Jewell Young	Indianapolis	28	260	9.3

1940-41		*Games*	*Points*	*PPG*
Ben Stephens	Akron	24	265	11.0
Wibs Kautz	Chicago	21	227	10.8
George Glamack	Wingfoots	24	256	10.7
Ed Sadowski	Detroit	24	256	10.7
Bill Hapac	Chicago	24	227	9.5
Bob Neu	Hammond	22	195	8.9
Ralph Vaughn	Chi/Hammond	23	195	8.5
Leroy Edwards	Oshkosh	23	190	8.3

1941-42		*Games*	*Points*	*PPG*
Chuck Chuckovitz	Toledo	22	406	18.5
Bob McDermott	Fort Wayne	21	277	13.2
Jewell Young	Indianapolis	23	263	11.4
Leroy Edwards	Oshkosh	24	262	10.9
Ed Dancker	Sheboygan	24	243	10.1
Ben Stephens	Wingfoots	24	222	9.3
Ralph Vaughn	Chicago	21	190	9.0

1942-43		*Games*	*Points*	*PPG*
Bob McDermott	Fort Wayne	23	314	13.7
Ed Dancker	Sheboygan	22	247	11.2
Sonny Boswell	Chicago	22	229	10.4
Jake Pelkington	Fort Wayne	23	236	10.3
Ralph Vaughn	Oshkosh	22	222	10.1

1943-44		*Games*	*Points*	*PPG*
Mel Riebe	Cleveland	18	324	17.9
Bob McDermott	Fort Wayne	22	306	13.9
Clint Wager	Oshkosh	22	230	10.5
Ed Dancker	Sheboygan	22	192	8.7
Buddy Jeannette	Fort Wayne	22	184	8.4

1944-45		Games	Points	PPG
Mel Riebe	Cleveland	30	607	20.3
Bob McDermott	Fort Wayne	30	603	20.2
Stan Patrick	Chicago	28	458	16.4
Leroy Edwards	Oshkosh	30	407	13.6
Huck Hartman	Pittsburgh	30	327	10.9

1945-46		Games	Points	PPG
Bob Carpenter	Oshkosh	34	473	13.9
Bob McDermott	Fort Wayne	34	458	13.5
George Glamack	Rochester	34	417	12.3
Arnie Risen	Indianapolis	18	219	12.2
Ed Dancker	Sheboygan	33	393	11.9
Bill "Red" Holzman	Rochester	34	363	10.7
Al Cervi	Rochester	28	300	10.7

1946-47		Games	Points	PPG
George Mikan	Chicago	25	413	16.5
Al Cervi	Rochester	44	632	14.4
Bob Davies	Rochester	32	462	14.4
Fred Lewis	Sheboygan	44	585	13.3
Arnie Risen	Indianapolis	44	582	13.2
Hal Tidrick	Toledo	44	579	13.2

1947-48		Games	Points	PPG
George Mikan	Minneapolis	56	1195	21.3
Bob Calihan	Flint-Midland	56	806	14,4
Don Otten	Tri-Cities	60	824	13.7
Al Cervi	Rochester	49	655	13.4
Arnie Risen	Indpls-Rchsr	61	805	13.2

1948-49		Games	Points	PPG
Don Otten	Tri-Cities	64	899	14 (13.8)
Dick Mehen	Waterloo	62	841	13.6(13.4)
Bob Englund	Oshkosh	63	850	13.5 (13.2)
Ward Gibson	Dnvr-Tri-Cit	62	805	13.0 (12.8)
Dolph Schayes	Syracuse	63	809	12.8

Appendix 3:
NBL All League Teams and MVPs, 1937–1949

1937-38

First Team
Leroy Edwards, Osh*
Scott Armstrong, FtW
John Wooden, Whit
Charlie Shipp, AkG
Chuck Bloedorn, AkG

Second Team
Soup Cable, AkF
Jack Ozburn, AkF
Bob Kessler, Inds
Vince McGowan, Whit
Bart Quinn, FtW

1938-39

First Team
Paul Birch, Pitt
Leroy Edwards, Osh*
John Sines, Inds
Jerry Bush, AkF
Barney Cable, AkF

Second Team
Jack Ozburn, AkF
Johnny Moir, AkF
Jewell Young, Inds
Chuck Bloedorn, AkG
Charlie Shipp, AkG

1939-40

First Team
Ben Stephens, AkG
Wibs Kautz, Chi
Leroy Edwards, Osh*
Charlie Shipp, Osh
Barney Cable, AkF

Second Team
Jack Ozburn, AkF
Ernie Andres, Ind
Rube Lautenschlanger, Shb
Otto Kolar, Shb
Nat Frankel, Det

1940-41

First Team
Ben Stephens, AkG*
Ed Sadowski, Det
Buddy Jeannette, Det
Leroy Edwards, Osh
Charlie Shipp, Osh
Jack Ozburn, AkF

Second Team
Wibs Kautz, Chi
Bill Hapac, Chi
Ralph Vaughn, Chi/ Ham
John Pelkington, AkG
Bob Calihan, Det
Bob Neu, Hamm

1941-42

First Team
Chuck Chuckovits, Tol*
Ben Stephens, AkG

*Most Valuable Player

242

Leroy Edwards, Osh
Bobby McDermott, FtW
Charlie Shipp, Osh

Second Team
Ralph Vaughn, Chi
Jewell Young, Inds
Ed Danker, Shb
Herm Schaefer, FtW
George Glamack, AkG

1942-43

First Team
Ralph Vaughn, Osh
Paul Armstrong, FtW
Ed Danker, Shb
Bobby McDermott,
  FtW*
Charlie Shipp, Osh

Second Team
Sonny Boswell, Chi
Buddy Jeannette, Shb
Leroy Edwards, Osh
Ken Suesens, Shb
Jerry Bush, FtW

1943-44

First Team
Mel Riebe, Clev
Clint Wagner, Osh
Ed Danker, Shb
Bobby McDermott,
  FtW*
Buddy Jeannette, FtW

Second Team
Rube Lautenschlanger,
  Shb
Jerry Bush, FtW
John Pelkington, FtW

Charlie Shipp, Osh
Ken Suesens, Shb

1944-45

First Team
Mel Reibe, Clev
Stan Patrick, Chi
Leroy Edwards, Osh
Bobby McDermott,
  FtW*
Buddy Jeannette, FtW

Second Team
Dick Triptow, Chi
Ed Danker, Shb
John Pelkington, FtW
Jerry Bush
Huck Hartman, Pitt

1945-46

First Team
Bob Carpenter, Osh
Red Holzman, Rch
George Glamack, Rch
Ed Danker, Shb
Buddy Jeannette, FtW
Bobby McDermott,
  FtW*

Second Team
Mike Novak, Shb
Jerry Stiener, Inds
Bob Calihan, Chi
Leroy Edwards, Osh
Frank Baumholtz, Youn
Al Cervi, Rch

1946-47

First Team
Al Cervi, Rch

Bob Davies, Rch*
George Mikan, Chi
Fred Lewis, Shb
Bobby McDermott, Chi

Second Team
Bob Carpenter, Osh
Bob Calihan, Chi
Arnie Risen, Inds
Red Holzman, Rch
Hal Tidrick, Tol

1947-48

First Team
Jim Pollard, Mpls
Marko Todorovich, Shb
George Mikan, Mpls*
Red Holzman, Rch
Al Cervi, Rch

Second Team
Bob Calihan, Flin
Bob Davies, Rch
Don Otten, TriC
Frank Brian, And
Bobby McDermott, TriC

1948-49

First Team
Gene Englund, Osh
Dick Mehen, Wat
Don Otten, TriC*
Frank Brian, And
Al Cervi, Syr

Second Team
Stan Von Nieda, TriC
Marko Todorovich, Shb
Ward Gibson, TriC
Bill Closs, And
Ralph Johnson, And

Chapter Notes

Introduction

1. Much of this is described in more detail in Chapter 1 of M. Nelson, *The Originals: The New York Celtics Invent Modern Basketball* (Bowling Green, OH: Bowling Green State University Popular Press, 1999).

2. See A. Grundman, *The Golden Age of Amateur Basketball*, for a detailed history of that tournament.

Chapter 1

1. The best source of this kind of data would be the various *Reach Basketball Guides* published by the A.J. Reach Company of Philadelphia beginning in 1900 and going through 1927. The data are uneven but often include descriptions of various teams and the origin of their players.

2. Again the best source for this is the Reach Guides. For example, in the 1922-23 Guide, Editor William Scheffer discusses some of the differences in college and professional play on pages 6–7. *Reach Official Basketball Guide 1922-23* (Philadelphia: A.J. Reach, 1922).

3. C. Wilkes, "Bourdieu's Class," in R. Harker, C. Mahar and C. Wilkes, *An Introduction to the Work of Pierre Bourdieu* (London: Macmillan, 1990), p. 118.

4. See P. Bourdieu, "Sport and Social Class," *Social Science Information* 17.6 (1978).

5. S. Reiss, *City Games: The Evolution of American Urban Society and the Rise of Sports* (Urbana: University of Illinois Press, 1989), p. 185.

6. J. Hargreaves, as discussed in D. Harris, *From Class Struggles to the Politics of Pleasure: The Effects of Gramscianism on Cultural Studies* (London: Routledge, 1992), pp. 154–158.

7. A. Guttmann, *Sports Spectators* (New York: Columbia University Press, 1986), p. 104.

8. E. Genovese, "The Politics of Class Struggle in the History of Society: An Appraisal of the Work of Eric Hobsbawm," in P. Thane, G. Crossick, and R. Floud, eds., *The Power of the Past: Essays for Eric Hobsbawm* (Cambridge: Cambridge University Press, 1984).

9. Guttmann, p. 111.

10. R. Peterson, *Cages to Jump Shot: Pro Basketball's Early Years* (Lincoln: University of Nebraska Press, 2002), p. 113.

11. M. Nelson, *The Originals*, p. 174.

12. T. Gould, *Pioneers of the Hardwood* (Bloomington: Indiana University Press, 1998), p. 57.

13. Telephone interview with Phil Dietrich, former *Akron Beacon Journal* sports writer in the 1930s-1960s, 2/18/02.

14. Interestingly such information was commodified by the league with the passage of time. By 1949, in the league's final year before merging with the BAA, the National Basketball League *Official Pro Magazine* claimed that each league member in 1935 had to play eight games. It also incorrectly listed some of the teams in the 1936 to 1937 season as well as one of the contestants in the 1936-37 season championship game.

15. See *Indianapolis Star* and *Akron Beacon Journal* in January 1935.

16. Gould, p. 50.

17. See, for example, P. Levine, *Ellis Island to Ebbets Field: Sport and the American Jewish Experience* (New York: Oxford University Press, 1992).

18. Peterson, p. 201.

19. F. Carlton, "Labor in the Twentieth Century," in Carl Wittke, ed., *History of the State of*

Ohio (Columbus: Ohio State Archaeological and Historical Society, 1943).

20. J. Schlemmer, "Wingfoots, Skids Groom Stronger Cage Outfits," *Akron Beacon Journal*, 11/14/35, p. 24.

21. "Firestone in New Mid-west Basketball Loop; Season opens Dec. 4," *Firestone Non-Skid* 20, no. 20 (11/13/35): 4.

22. J. Wooden (as told to J. Tobin), *They Call Me Coach* (New York: Bantam Books, 1973).

23. J. Schlemmer, "Nonskids Spanks Dayton in Midwest Conference," *Akron Beacon Journal*, 12/5/35, p. 27.

24. "Jump is Doomed Says Cage Official," *Akron Beacon Journal*, 1/25/37.

25. J. Wooden to Murry Nelson, personal correspondence, 9/29/01.

26. "Conference Rules Add Zest to Game," *The Wingfoot Clan* 25, no. 46 (12/23/36): 7.

27. "Renaissance Five Shades Kautskys," *Indianapolis Star*, 1/17/36, p. 36.

28. Gould, p. 80.

29. "Kautskys Repulse Akron Five, 31–24," *Indianapolis Star*, 2/10/36, p. 12.

30. Gould, p. 49.

31. "Kautskys defeat U.S. Tires, 36–32," *Indianapolis Star*, 2/3/36, p. 12.

32. "Kautskys Triumph in Ragged Battle," *Indianapolis Star*, 3/2/36, p. 19.

33. "Kautskys here For Cage Tilt Dec. 27," *Firestone Non-Skid* 20, no. 23 (12/24/35): 8.

34. Peterson, p. 131; K. Shouler, B. Ryan, S. Smith, L. Koppett, and B. Bellotti, *Total Basketball: The Ultimate Basketball Encyclopedia* (Wilmington, DE: Sport Classic Press, 2003), p. 23.

35. "Nonskids to Play Pittsburgh YMHA," *Akron Beacon Journal*, 1/30/36, p. 18.

36. "Nonskid Cagemen Face Windsor in League Tilt Here Wednesday," *Akron Beacon Journal*, 1/28/36, p. 22.

37. The extent of this rivalry is most evident in the newsletters of 1935–39 for the two companies, *The Wingfoot Clan* from the Goodyear Company and *The Firestone Non-Skid* from the Firestone Company.

38. Box scores in the *Akron Beacon Journal* in 1935-36 are the best source of these data.

39. "All Factory Basketball Tourney Huge Success," *Firestone Non-Skid* 20, no. 6 (4/1/35): 1.

40. John Wooden to Murry Nelson, personal correspondence, November 18, 2001.

41. Peterson, p. 113.

42. Wooden, p. 51.

43. Peterson, p. 114.

44. Wooden, p. 51.

45. Gould, p. 83.

46. E. Butler, "Nonskids Battle Deans in Wednesday Headliner," *Akron Beacon Journal*, 3/3/36, p. 22.

47. "Kautskys Lead in Standings," *Indianapolis Star*, 3/2/36, p. 14.

48. J. Schlemmer, "Nonskids Take Eastern Title in Midwest Loop," *Akron Beacon Journal*, 3/2/36, p. 15.

49. E. Butler, "Nonskids Battle Deans in Wednesday Headliner," *Akron Beacon Journal*, 3/3/36, p. 22.

50. "Nonskids Prepare for Playoff Series," *Akron Beacon Journal*, 3/5/36, p. 26.

51. Lester Harrison to Murry Nelson, phone interview, 10/4/94.

52. "Nonskids Prepare for Playoff Series," *Akron Beacon Journal*, 3/5/36, p. 26.

53. "Postpone Midwest Tournament Series," *Akron Beacon Journal*, 3/7/36.

54. "Kautsky Team Victor, 50–32," *Indianapolis Star*, 3/21/36, p. 16.

55. "Firestone Nonskids Win 3rd Place in Midwest Conference," *Firestone Non-Skid* 20, no. 6 (4/1/35): 8.

56. "Chicago Five Wins Conference Crown," *Indianapolis Star*, 3/23/36, p. 13. Kessler's signing and status was noted in "Kautskys to Meet Notre Dame Stars," *Indianapolis Star*, 3/20/36, p. 17. The same situation arose in 1946 when George Mikan signed with the Chicago American Gears on March 16, 1946, shortly after his career at De Paul had ended. Shortly after that the NCAA responded by threatening sanctions against institutions that allowed players to be signed and play professionally in the same season that they had played college ball. Professional basketball leagues and teams (and their representatives) were threatened with being barred from campuses and the leagues responded by outlawing such behavior on the part of their member teams. It was seen as another "Mikan Rule," one of many that his play stimulated; in this case, Mikan was not the first to sign in this manner, but the landscape of the game had changed in 11 years.

57. Telephone interview with Robert Luksta, 7/24/03.

58. "Chicago Five Wins Title in Midwest," *Akron Beacon Journal*, 3/24/36, p. 26.

59. Peterson, p. 114.

60. Peterson, p. 124.

61. See L. Koppett, *24 Seconds to Shoot: The Birth and Improbable Rise of the NBA* (New York: Macmillan, 1968).

62. "Goodyear Seeking Opening Cage Foe," *Akron Beacon Journal*, 11/21/36, p. 17.

63. "Edwards Added To Kautsky Quintet," *Indianapolis Star*, 1/31/37, p. 23.

64. "Quaker City Team Defeats Kautskys," *Indianapolis Star*, 2/4/37, p. 15.

65. "U.S. Tire Cagemen Strengthen Lineup for Opening Game," *Indianapolis Star*, 11/28/36, p. 14.

66. Peterson, p. 201.

67. "Local Teams Lose to Negro Quintets," *Indianapolis Star*, 1/21/37, p. 15.

68. "Renaissance Conquer Tires; Fistic Outbreak Mars Game," *Indianapolis Star*, 3/4/37, p. 21.

69. "Goodyear Becomes Midwest Member," *Akron Beacon Journal*, 12/4/36, p. 49.

70. Ibid.

71. "Goodyear Plays Two Strong Clubs This Week," *The Wingfoot Clan* 25, no. 44 (12/9/36): 4.

72. "Wingfoots Start Over," *Akron Beacon Journal*, 12/12/36, p. 16.

73. "Clifton 'Lefty' Byers Appointed Goodyear Basketball Team Coach," *The Wingfoot Clan* 25, no. 45 (12/16/36): 6.

74. "Goodyear Becomes Midwest Member," *Akron Beacon Journal*, 12/12/36.

75. The Rens supported a number of teams at different levels. These players never played for the "A" squad but might have been on one of their developmental teams.

76. "Fort Wayne Tops Skids," *Akron Beacon Journal*, 12/16/36, p. 23.

77. E. Butler, "Firestone Scores 40–34 Win Over Chicago Team," *Akron Beacon Journal*, 12/30/36, p. 17.

78. E. Butler, "Wings Beat Chicagoans," *Akron Beacon Journal*, 1/5/37, p. 17.

79. Ibid.

80. J. Schlemmer, "Firestone in Danger," *Akron Beacon Journal*, 1/12/37, p. 27.

81. "Goodyear Wins, 31–27, Over Firestone Team," *Akron Beacon Journal*, 1/20/37, p. 19.

82. "Fans Already Ordering Wing-Firestone Tickets," *Akron Beacon Journal*, 1/21/37, p. 21.

83. "Skids Take Double Loss," *Akron Beacon Journal*, 1/28/37, p. 25.

84. J. Schlemmer, "Fans Shout Business," *Akron Beacon Journal*, 1/30/37, p. 25.

85. J. Schlemmer, "Even Sheeks Laughs," *Akron Beacon Journal*, 2/1/37, p. 21.

86. "Standings," *Akron Beacon Journal*, 2/3/37, p. 20.

87. "Firestone, Goodyear Open Playoff Feb. 17," *Akron Beacon Journal*, 2/8/37, p. 17.

88. J. Schlemmer, "A New Forgotten Man," *Akron Beacon Journal*, 2/10/37, p. 20.

89. J. Schlemmer, "Goodyear Has Easy Time Topping Nonskids, 40–24," *Akron Beacon Journal*, 2/22/37, p. 17.

90. J. Schlemmer, "Wings' Season Short," *Akron Beacon Journal*, 2/26/37, p. 37.

91. "Goodyear Takes Honors as Champs of the Midwest," *Akron Beacon Journal*, 3/2/37, p. 28.

92. "Wings Play Final Game," *Akron Beacon Journal*, 2/25/37, p. 27.

93. R.S. Lynd, and H.M. Lynd, *Middletown: A Study in Contemporary American Culture* (New York: Harcourt Brace, 1929); R.S. Lynd, and H.M. Lynd, *Middletown in Transition* (New York: Harcourt Brace, 1937).

94. Lynd and Lynd, *Middletown in Transition*, p. 242.

Chapter 2

1. D. Neft, R. Johnson, R. Cohen, and J. Deutsch, *The Sports Encyclopedia: Pro Basketball* (New York: Grosset and Dunlap, 1975), 20.

2. "All Stars Join National Basketball League," *Oshkosh Daily Northwestern*, 12/8/37, p. 15.

3. Quoted in Peterson, *Cages to Jump Shots*, p. 125.

4. Ibid.

5. Ibid., p. 132.

6. W. O. Rumlow, *The Oshkosh All Stars and the NBL* (Self-published, 1979).

7. M. Strasser, "Lonnie Darling: Dream Chaser," in *Oshkosh All Stars* (Oshkosh, WI: Oshkosh Daily Northwestern, 1979).

8. Ibid., "All Stars Enter Wacky, Shaky World,"

9. "All Stars Lift Lid in Basketball in Turkey Day Test," *Oshkosh Daily Northwestern*, 11/24/37, p. 13.

10. Ibid.

11. "All Stars Join National Basketball League," *Oshkosh Daily Northwestern*, 12/8/37, p. 15.

12. John Isaacs, phone interview, May 18, 2002.

13. Mikan, George, and Joseph Oberle, *Unstoppable: The Story of George Mikan* (Indianapolis: Masters Press, 1997).

14. "Pro Cage Loop Will Retain Center Jump," *Oshkosh Daily Northwestern*, 12/13/37, p. 14.

15. "All Stars Beat Celtics: Play at Bay Tonight," *Oshkosh Daily Northwestern*, 12/23/37, p. 13.

16. "All Stars Lose to Celtics at Bay by 44–39 Score," *Oshkosh Daily Northwestern*, 12/24/37, p. 17.

17. "All Stars Defeat Dayton in Initial National loop Tilt," *Oshkosh Daily Northwestern*, 1/3/38, p. 13.

18. "All Stars 'Pour it on' Kankakee Gallaghers," *Oshkosh Daily Northwestern*, 1/5/38, p. 13.

19. "All Stars Win Two...," *Oshkosh Daily Northwestern*, 1/10/38, p. 12.

20. See Nelson, M. *The Originals*, chapter 5.

21. "All Stars Drop League Game to Whiting Five," *Oshkosh Daily Northwestern*, 1/11/38, p. 12.

22. Ibid.

23. "All Stars Beat Chicago Duffy Florals Twice," *Oshkosh Daily Northwestern*, 1/17/38, p. 12.

24. "Enzo Jels Defeat Oshkosh All Stars in a Hectic Battle," *Oshkosh Daily Northwestern*, 1/20/38, p. 15

25. "All Stars Take Lead in National Cage League," *Oshkosh Daily Northwestern*,1/31/38, p. 12.

26. Ibid.

27. "All Stars Defeat Sheboygan, Lose to Whiting," *Oshkosh Daily Northwestern*, 2/7/38, 13.

28. "Set New Scoring Record in National Basketball Loop," *Oshkosh Daily Northwestern*, 2/9/38, p. 13.

29. "Stars Beat Whiting, Play Goodyears Tonight," *Oshkosh Daily Northwestern*, 2/28/38, p. 12.

30. Firestone Gets Four New Basket Players," *Akron Beacon Journal*, 11/17/37, p. 25.

31. "Fort Wayne's Thrilling Rally Defeats Goodyear Cagers by 29–25," *Akron Beacon Journal*, 12/24/27, p. 12.

32. "Firestone Tops Columbus...," *Akron Beacon Journal*, 12/30/37, p. 16.

33. Telephone interview with Al Cervi, 5/20/04.

34. B. Elliott, "Firestone beats Oshkosh 42–37...," *Akron Beacon Journal*, 1/13/38, p. 20.

35. B. Elliott, "Wings Win 42–40 Tilt," *Akron Beacon Journal*, 1/14/38, p. 29.

36. J. Schlemmer, "Hot Industrial Series Seen as Firestone Wins" *Akron Beacon Journal*, 1/17/38, p. 17.

37. "Nonskids in 41–28 Romp," *Akron Beacon Journal*, 1/20/38, p. 24.

38. J. Schlemmer, "On Basketball," *Akron Beacon Journal*,1/25/38, p. 22.

39. B. Elliott, "Nonskids Beat Phillips Outfit...,"*Akron Beacon Journal*,1/27/38, p. 21.

40. "Firestone's Big Rally Defeats Goodyear, 43–42," *Akron Beacon Journal*, 2/1/38, p. 25.

41. "Goodyear-Renaissance Contest End in Fisticuffs in Four Minutes," *Akron Beacon Journal*, 2/10/38, p. 23.

42. Interview with John Isaacs, March, 2004.

43. "Rens Gain Second Win Over Nonskids," *Akron Beacon Journal*, 2/22/38, p. 21.

44. Neft, Johnson, Cohen and Deutsch in *The Sports Encyclopedia: Pro Basketball* have Edwards with a 16.2 points average and Wooden with 11.0. The discrepancy is probably due to the failure to count certain games as league games against a league opponent or a mistake in determining whether a player actually was at a game that his team played.

45. "Wingfoots Defeat Skids in First Playoff Game," *Akron Beacon Journal*, 2/25/38, p. 27.

46. E. Butler, "Goodyear Comes from Far Back to Beat Firestone, Capture Series," *Akron Beacon Journal*, 2/26/38, p. 15.

47. "All Stars Lose Opener," *Oshkosh Daily Northwestern*, 3/1/38, p. 12; "Goodyear Defeats Oshkosh, 29–28...," *Akron Beacon Journal*, 3/1/38, p. 21.

48. "National Basketball Championship at Stake at Goodyear Tonight," *Akron Beacon Journal*, 3/4/38, p. 28; "All Stars Defeat Goodyear, To Play Rens Here," *Oshkosh Daily Northwestern*, 3/4/38, p. 17.

49. "All Stars Lose the Crown," *Oshkosh Daily Northwestern*, 3/5/38, p. 13; "Goodyear Defeats Oshkosh, 35–27, Retain National Cage Honors," *Akron Beacon Journal*, 3/5/38, p. 14.

50. "All Stars Lose the Crown"

51. Isaacs interview.

52. "All Stars Defeat Famed New York Rens Again," *Oshkosh Daily Northwestern*, 3/11/38, p. 18.

53. "Rens Beat Stars in Final Contest of Series," *Oshkosh Daily Northwestern*, 3/14/38, p. 15.

54. "All Stars Battle Whiting Tonight in Final Contest," *Oshkosh Daily Northwestern*, 3/26/38, p. 13.

55. "All Stars Defeat Whiting, Badger Collegians," *Oshkosh Daily Northwestern*, 3/28/38, p. 12.

56. "Oshkosh All Stars: A Commemorative Souvenir Magazine 1937-1938 Season," (Oshkosh, WI: 1938), p. 2; National Basketball League File, Naismith Memorial Basketball Hall of Fame, Springfield, MA.

57. National Basketball League File.

58. Ibid., p. 6.

59. Ibid., p. 8.

Chapter 3

1. "All Stars Beat Globe Trotters By 44–30 Score," *Oshkosh Daily Northwestern*,11/18/38, p. 19.

2. "All Stars Trounce Akron Firestones, 37–19," *Oshkosh Daily Northwestern*, 11/23/38, p. 13.

3. "All Stars Have 'Off" Night and Lose By 42 To 30," *Oshkosh Daily Northwestern*, 11/25/38, p. 19.

4. W. Blaine Patton, "Local Pro Quintet Wins First League Tilt From Akron Goodyears," *Indianapolis Star*, 11/29/38, p. 13.

5. "Kautskys Top Wings," *Indianapolis Star*, 11/29/38, p. 20.

6. "Goodyear Defeats Hammond 33–30 In Cage League Opener," *Akron Beacon-Journal*, 11/26/38, p. 11.

7. "All Stars Beaten By Warren, 38–37, In Overtime Game," *Oshkosh Daily Northwestern*, 12/5/38, p. 13.

8. "All Stars Win At Madison," *Oshkosh Daily Northwestern*, 12/12/38, p. 13.

9. "Leading Scores," *Indianapolis Star*, 12/18/38, p. 27.

10. "Kautskys Wallop Pro League Rival...," *Indianapolis Star*, 1/3/39, p. 13.

11. W. Blaine Patton, "Ren's Brilliant Attack Humbles Kautsky Quintet By 47 to 33 Margin," *Indianapolis Star*, 1/10/39, p. 13.

12. "Indianapolis Five Wins Game, Takes Second in League," *Indianapolis Star*, 12/13/38, p. 15.

13. "All Stars Split Two-Game Series with Rens," *Oshkosh Daily Northwestern*, 12/19/38, p. 17.

14. John Isaacs, telephone interview, 11/15/02.

15. "On the Sidelines With The Sports Editor," *Oshkosh Daily Northwestern*, 12/20/38, p. 15.

16. "All Stars Skyrocket Back Into First Place," *Oshkosh Daily Northwestern*, 12/24/38, p. 17.

17. "Nonskids Play Eight Contests on Eastern Basketball Junket," *Akron Beacon Journal*, 12/29/38, p. 22.

18. "All Stars Lose Thriller to Akron, Beat Hammond," *Oshkosh Daily Northwestern*, 1/16/39, p. 11; "Nonskids Triumph at Oshkosh, 46–44," *Akron Beacon Journal*, 1/15/39, Sec. C, p. 12.

19. "Reserves Carry Wings to 43–28 Win Over Buffalo," *Akron Beacon Journal*, 1/4/39, p. 15.

20. J. Schlemmer, "Firestone beats Goodyear, 43–41, In Series Opener," *Akron Beacon Journal*, 1/19/39, p. 25.

21. W. Blaine Patton, "Ren's Brilliant Attack Humbles Kautsky Quintet By 47–33 Margin," *Indianapolis Star*, 1/10/39, p. 13.

22. W. Blaine Patton, "Kautsky All Americans Fail in Bid for Western Division Pinnacle," *Oshkosh Daily Northwestern*, 2/13/39, p. 12.

23. "Wings Beaten By Indianapolis as Chuck Bloedorn is Injured," *Akron Beacon Journal*, 2/17/39, p. 33.

24. "Akron Firestones Sweep Kautsky Quintet in National League Contest," *Indianapolis Star*, 2/21/39, p. 13.

25. "Celtics Rap Rens by 36–33 Margin," *Indianapolis Star*, 2/28/39, p. 12.

26. "All Stars Prove Packers' Master in the Cage Sport," *Oshkosh Daily Northwestern*, 2/13/39, p. 13.

27. "Stars Beat Redskins, Play Here On Thursday," *Oshkosh Daily Northwestern*, 2/22/39, p. 11.

28. "Oshkosh All Stars Take Fifth Straight From Redskins 49–36 In Game Marred By Fisticuffs," *Oshkosh Daily Northwestern*, 2/24/39, p. 15.

29. "Oshkosh Conquers Firestone Combine," *Akron Beacon Journal*, 3/5/39, Sec. C, p. 1.

30. "Stars Beat Firestones, Clinch Western Title," *Oshkosh Daily Northwestern*, 3/6/39, p. 13.

31. "All Stars Atone For Sunday's Loss With 56–41 Win," *Oshkosh Daily Northwestern*, 3/7/39, p. 13.

32. "11,000 To See Nonskids Play," *Akron Beacon Journal*, 2/13/39, p. 15.

33. "Goodyear Opposes Oshkosh Thursday," *Akron Beacon Journal*, 3/1/39, p. 18.

34. "Goodyear Halts Firestone Streak With 40–37 Win," *Akron Beacon Journal*, 2/16/39, p. 35.

35. "Nonskid Five Topples Rens," *Akron Beacon Journal*, 3/6/39, p. 17.

36. "Rens Top Nonskids In 28–26 Clash," *Akron Beacon Journal*, 3/7/39, p. 26.

37. "Nonskids Beaten By Rens," *Akron Beacon Journal*, 3/14/39, p. 27.

38. J. Schlemmer, "Nonskids Toy With Oshkosh in Winning First, 50–38," *Akron Beacon Journal*, 3/15/39, p. 21.

39. J. Schlemmer, "Oshkosh Beats Skids, 38–36, To Tie Playoff Series," *Akron Beacon Journal*, 3/16/39, p. 40.

40. "Oshkosh Beats Nonskids, 49–37, Evens Playoff Series," *Akron Beacon Journal*, 3/18/39, p. 11.

41. The *Oshkosh Daily Northwestern* said that he made two buckets; the *Akron Beacon Journal* claimed he netted three.

42. "Pro Basketball Title Tourney Opens Today," *Chicago Tribune*, 3/26/39, pt. 2, p. 3.

43. "Oshkosh Plays in Series Semifinal Tonight," *Oshkosh Daily Northwestern*, 3/27/39, p. 15.

Chapter 4

1. "Chicago Is New Member Of National Basketball League," *Oshkosh Daily Northwestern*, 6/5/39.

2. Financial Statements of Oshkosh All Stars, Oshkosh, Wisconsin, Public Museum.

3. "Goodyears Beat All Stars in League Opener," *Oshkosh Daily Northwestern*, 11/24/39, p. 17.

4. "Oshkosh All Stars Are on Their Way to The Top(?)," *Oshkosh Daily Northwestern*, 12/18/39, p. 17.

5. "Kautsky Beaten in Opener, 44–40," *Indianapolis Star*, 11/30/39, p. 16.

6. Telephone interview with Carlisle "Blackie" Towery, 10/16/03.

7. C. Bartlett, "Bruins to Start Pro Basketball Season Tonight," *Chicago Tribune*, 12/6/39, p. 36.

8. C. Bartlett, "Bruin Quintet Wins, 28 To 19, Over Oshkosh," *Chicago Tribune*, 12/7/39, p. 28.

9. C. Bartlett, "Bruins Whip Eagles, 34–24; Kautz Stars," *Chicago Tribune*, 12/14/39, p. 35.

10. "Renaissance, Duffy Florals Play Tonight," *Chicago Tribune*, 12/17/39, part 2, p. 2.

11. C. Bartlett, "Bruins Beat Firestones by a Novak, 31–29," *Chicago Tribune*, 12/21/39, p. 29.

12. "Kautsky's Win From Sheboygan," *Indianapolis Star*, 12/14/39, p. 21.

13. "Kautsky Netmen Drop Pro Contest," *Indianapolis Star*, 12/21/39, p. 17.

14. "Kautskys to Face Giant Cage Team," *Indianapolis Star*, 12/24/39, p. 18.

15. C. Bartlett, "Bruins Lead All the Way, Defeat Akron," *Chicago Tribune*, 1/4/40, p. 20.

16. C. Bartlett, "Sheboygan Five Rallies To Beat Bruins, 20 to 19," *Chicago Tribune*, 1/8/40, p. 19.

17. "Local Pro Team Shades Oshkosh," *Indianapolis Star*, 1/18/40, p. 17; "Bruins Trounce Eagles, 36–28, as Kautz Stars," *Chicago Tribune*, 1/18/40, p. 23.

18. "Oshkosh Whips Bruins, 53 to 43; Edwards Stars," *Chicago Tribune*, 1/21/40, pt. 2, p. 2.

19. "Detroit and Rens Win Pro Contests," *Indianapolis Star*, 1/25/40, p. 16.

20. "Birr Team Wins, Kautskys Beaten," *Indianapolis Star*, 1/29/40, p. 15.

21. C. Bartlett, "Bruins Seek To Handle Oshkosh Tomorrow Night," *Chicago Tribune*, 1/30/40, p. 19.

22. C. Bartlett, "Bruins Wallop Oshkosh 38–33, Take First Place," *Chicago Tribune*, 2/1/40, p. 30.

23. "Oshkosh Five Beaten 37–36 By Hammond," *Chicago Tribune*, 2/5/40, p. 22.

24. C. Bartlett, "Bruins Battle Akron; Bid For Pro League Lead," *Chicago Tribune*, 2/7/40, p. 25.

25. C. Bartlett, "Firestone Five Triumphs Over Bruins, 39–33," *Chicago Tribune*, 2/8/40, p. 25.

26. "Local Pro Fives Drop Encounters," *Indianapolis Star*, 2/15/40, p. 16.

27. "Redskins Beat Oshkosh Stars By 42–36 Margin," *Chicago Tribune*, 2/16/40, p. 33.

28. "Oram's Return Raises Bruins Playoff Hopes," *Chicago Tribune*, 2/20/40, p. 21.

29. "Bruins Whip Sheboygan In Noisy Battle," *Chicago Tribune*, 2/22/40, p. 27.

30. C. Bartlett, "Bruins Victors 50 to 34: Stay in Pro Title Race," *Chicago Tribune*, 3/2/40, pt. 2, p. 2.

31. "Detroit Knocks Bruins From Title Race, 56–53," *Chicago Tribune*, 3/6/40, p. 26.

32. "All Stars Win the Opener in Playoff Series," *Oshkosh Daily Northwestern*, 3/8/40, p. 15.

33. "Redskins Even Series," *Oshkosh Daily Northwestern*, 3/9/40, p. 13.

34. J. Schlemmer, "Firestone Romps," *Akron Beacon Journal*, 2/25/40, p. C1.

35. J. Schlemmer, "Ozburn Gets 25 as Skids Blast Detroit, 48–35," *Akron Beacon Journal*, 3/7/40, p. 26.

36. "Firestone Defeats Detroit 46–35 to Win Playoffs," *Akron Beacon Journal*, 3/10/40, p. C1.

37. "All Stars Win Opener," *Oshkosh Daily Northwestern*, 3/12/40, p. 19; "All Stars Win Second Game by 60–46," *Oshkosh Daily Northwestern*, 3/13/40, p. 13.

38. "Firestone Battles Oshkosh Tonight," *Akron Beacon Journal*, 3/14/40, p. 36.

39. J. Schlemmer, "Fighting Nonskids Defeat Oshkosh, 35–32, Keep Series Alive," *Akron Beacon Journal*, 3/15/40, p. 41.

40. J. Schlemmer, "Nonskids Battle Oshkosh Tonight at Kent for National Toga," *Akron Beacon Journal*, 3/16/40, p. 11.

41. "Firestone Wins 61–60, to Keep National Title," *Akron Beacon Journal*, 3/17/40, p. C1.

42. "National AAU Tourney Opens Today," *Chicago Tribune*, 3/17/40, pt. 2, p. 2.

43. "Rens, Bruins Win Openers in Pro Meet," *Chicago Tribune*, 3/18/40, p. 25.

44. "Bruins Win in Overtime; Rens Lose to Harlem," *Chicago Tribune*, 3/19/40, p. 25.

45. See discussion by S. Rayl in "The New York Renaissance Professional Black Basketball Team, 1923–1950," Ph.D. dissertation, Pennsylvania State University, August 1996, pp. 270 and 286.

46. "Globetrotters and Bruins Win: Reach Finals," *Chicago Tribune*, 3/20/40, p. 31; "Harlems Beat Bruins To Win Basket Title," *Chicago Tribune*, 3/21/40, p. 29.

Chapter 5

1. "Detroit Eagles Back in National Basketball Loop," *Oshkosh Daily Northwestern*, 11/7/40, p. 19.

2. W. Smith, "All Stars Beat Pros 44 to 42 in Overtime," *Chicago Tribune*, 11/30/40, p. 29.

3. "Oshkosh All Stars Beat Globe Trotters Twice," *Oshkosh Daily Northwestern*, 11/25/40, p. 12.

4. "All Stars Win Opening National League Game," *Oshkosh Daily Northwestern*, 11/28/40, p. 19; "Nonskids Score Double Win, Wingfoots Beaten," *Akron Beacon Journal*, 11/28/40, p. 30.

5. "Firestone Nonskids Beaten By Spha Pro Quintet, 37–35," *Akron Beacon Journal*, 12/1/40, p. C1.

6. "Wings Crush Hammond by 54–38 Margin," *Akron Beacon Journal*, 12/2/40, p. 18.

7. "New York Jewels Hand Skids Second Straight Loss," *Akron Beacon Journal*, 12/2/40, p. 18.

8. "Skids Trump on Detroit, Win, 41–35," *Akron Beacon Journal*, 12/5/40, p. 35.

9. "Oshkosh Tops Wingfoots 43–30: Eagles Edge Nonskids, 34–33," *Akron Beacon Journal*, 12/14/40, p. 10. "Stars take Victory," *Oshkosh Daily Northwestern*, 12/14/40, p. 13.

10. "Washington's Big Rally Tops Wings, 33–31, at Philadelphia," *Akron Beacon Journal*, 12/15/40, p. C1; J. Schlemmer, "Oshkosh's Rally Trips Nonskids, 37–32," *Akron Beacon Journal*, 12/17/40, p. 30; "Stars Defeat Defending Champs, 37–32," *Oshkosh Daily Northwestern*, 12/17/40, p. 15.

11. C. Bartlett, "Bruins Trounce Akron, 44–36 in Opening Game," *Chicago Tribune*, 12/19/40, p. 27; "Chicago Bruins Record 44–36 League Win Over Nonskid Foe," *Akron Beacon Journal*, 12/19/40, p. 40; "Bruins' Deadly Aim Triumphs in Rally, 27–20," *Chicago Tribune*, 12/20/40, p. 31.

12. "Oshkosh Noses Out Goodyear in Last Minute," *Oshkosh Daily Northwestern*, 1/6/41, p. 13; "Oshkosh's Late Rally Drops Wings, 35–33, in League Fray," *Akron Beacon Journal*, 1/5/41, p. C1.

13. "stars [sic] Winning Streak Ends," *Oshkosh Daily Northwestern*, 1/13/41, p. 12; Hammond Five Ends Oshkosh Streak, 43–32," *Chicago Tribune*, 1/13/41, p. 14.

14. "All Stars Beat Kautskys," *Oshkosh Daily Northwestern*, 1/15/41, p. 13.

15. "Stars Beat Rens By 43–24 Score; To Play at Fondy," *Oshkosh Daily Northwestern*, 1/16/41, p. 19.

16. Erv Prasse, telephone interview with author, July 10, 2003.

17. "Nonskids Even City Series," *Akron Beacon Journal*, 1/8/41, p. 16.

18. Stan Szukala, telephone interview with author, 3/19/03; D. Neft et al., *The Sports Encyclopedia: Pro Basketball*.

19. Eagles Defeat Bruins, 45 to 43, on Free Throws," *Chicago Tribune*, 1/18/41, p. 16.

20. "Oshkosh Tops Nonskid Quint in 45–43 Fray," *Akron Beacon Journal*, 1/19/41, p. C1.

21. S. Rayl, "The New York Renaissance Professional Black Basketball Team, 1923–50," unpublished doctoral dissertation, Pennsylvania State University, 1996, p. 504.

22. "Preliminary on Bruin Card Wins Fans' Attention," *Chicago Tribune*, 1/21/41, p. 18.

23. H. Barry, "Bruins' Closing Rush Wins Over Oshkosh," *Chicago Tribune*, 1/23/41, p. 17; "Bruins Stop Stars in Chicago Game by 34 to 32 Score," *Oshkosh Daily Northwestern*, 1/23/41, p. 19.

24. "Detroit Eagles Beat Hammond Quint, 61 to 52," *Chicago Tribune*, 1/24/41, p. 20.

25. "Hapac Stars as Bruins Win, 42–41, Over Goodyears," 2/6/41, p. 19.

26. "Nonskids Beaten by Celtics," *Akron Beacon Journal*, 2/1/41, p. 10.

27. "Firestones Win From Bruins in Rally, 46 to 37," *Chicago Tribune*, 2/13/41, p. 24; "90 Seconds Left, Goodyears Beat Bruins, 41 To 38," *Chicago Tribune*, 2/16/41, pt. 2, p. 3.

28. Hammond Sells Vaughn to Bruins..." *Oshkosh Daily Northwestern*, 2/21/41, p. 14.

29. J. Schlemmer, "Nonskids Nip Wings in Overtime," *Akron Beacon Journal*, 2/23/41, p. C1.

30. Szukala phone interview, 3/19/03.

31. "Hapac and Kautz Lead Bruins to a 49–33 Triumph," *Chicago Tribune*, 2/25/41, p. 21.

32. "Bruins Win 3rd in Row; Defeat Ciesars, 27–18," *Chicago Tribune*, 2/27/41, p. 19.

33. E. Butler, "Skids Top Chicago 46–27; Gain National League Playoffs," *Akron Beacon Journal*, 3/1/41, p. 10.

34. "All Stars Defeat Firestones By 30 to 28," *Oshkosh Daily Northwestern*, 3/5/41, p. 13.

35. "Skids Bow at Oshkosh in Overtime," *Akron Beacon Journal*, 3/7/41, p. 36; "All Stars Eliminate Firestones, 47 to 41," *Oshkosh Daily Northwestern*, 3/7/41, p. 17.

36. All Wisconsin Pro Finals Will Open Tonight," *Oshkosh Daily Northwestern*, 3/10/41, p. 14.

37. "Stars Beat Redskins in Opening Game, 53 to 38," *Oshkosh Daily Northwestern*, 3/11/41, p. 13.

38. "All Stars Need Win Tonight to Clinch Crown," *Oshkosh Daily Northwestern*, 3/12/41, p. 13.

39. "Oshkosh Is Champion of National Cage League," *Oshkosh Daily Northwestern*, 3/12/41, p. 20.

40. "Bruins Swamp Davenport Five in Tourney, before 8500 at International Amphitheatre-Pro Tourney, 53–17," *Chicago Tribune*, 3/16/41, pt. 2, p. 3.

41. R. Nelson, *The Zollner Piston Story*. (Fort Wayne, IN: Allen County Public Library Foundation, 1995).

42. "Detroit Upsets Globetrotters in Meet, 37–36," *Chicago Tribune*, 3/17/41, p. 20; "Stars Win Opening Round in Tournament," *Oshkosh Daily Northwestern*, 3/17/41, p. 12.

43. "All Stars Advance to Semifinals in Tourney," *Oshkosh Daily Northwestern*, 3/18/41, p. 13; "Bruins Put Out of Tourney By Toledo, 43 to 33," *Chicago Tribune*, 3/18/41, p. 20.

44. "Stars Meet Detroit Tonight for Championship," *Oshkosh Daily Northwestern*, 3/19/41, p. 13; "Oshkosh Beats Toledo, 40 to 37 in Pro Tourney," *Chicago Tribune*, 3/19/41, p. 27.

45. "Detroit Eagles Win World's Pro Cage Tourney," *Oshkosh Daily Northwestern*, 3/20/41, p. 25; "Detroit Beats Oshkosh for Pro Crown," *Chicago Tribune*, 3/20/41, p. 24.

Chapter 6

1. The history of armed forces basketball is only really covered in a self-published volume by Seymour Smith, Jack Rimer and Dick Triptow entitled "A Tribute to Armed Forces Basketball, 1941–69." The volume has no date but was done in 2003.

2. J. Schlemmer, column. *Akron Beacon Journal*, 11/5/41, p. 23.

3. Carl Bennett telephone interview, 10/27/03.

4. "Pelkington to Face Wingfoots," *Akron Beacon Journal*, 11/30/41, p. 4-C.

5. "Takes More than Broken Neck to Stop Goodyear's Ebaugh," *Akron Beacon Journal*, 12/18/41, p. 43.

6. "Wings Cagers Are Beaten," *Akron Beacon Journal*, 11/28/41, p. 43.

7. "Stars, Rens Begin Four Game Series," *Oshkosh Daily Northwestern*, 11/29/41, p. 13.

8. "Oshkosh Cagers Lose College All Star Game," *Oshkosh Daily Northwestern*, 11/29/41, p. 13.

9. "Stars Beat Rens in First Battle of Series, 52–42," *Oshkosh Daily Northwestern*, 12/1/41, p. 13.

10. "All Stars Avenge Loss By Beating Rens By 47 to 35," *Oshkosh Daily Northwestern*, 12/3/41, p. 14.

11. "Rens Take Final Game of Series From All Stars," *Oshkosh Daily Northwestern*, 12/4/41, p. 23.

12. S. Rayl, "The New York Renaissance Professional Black Basketball Team."

13. "Bruins Lose to Fort Wayne in 2D Half, 48 to 46," *Chicago Tribune*, 12/2/41, p. 24.

14. R. Nelson, *The Zollner Piston Story*, p. 114.

15. Ibid., p. 115.

16. "Bruins Win Game with Fast Finish," *Oshkosh Daily Northwestern*, 12/5/41, p. 19.

17. E. Butler, "Wingfoots' Second-Half Offensive Defeats Celtics, 38–36," *Akron Beacon Journal*, 12/5/41, p. 42.

18. "Wings Beat League Foe By 46 to 30," *Akron Beacon Journal*, 12/7/41, p. 1-C.

19. "Stars Edge Sheboygan: Will Meet Bruins Here," *Oshkosh Daily Northwestern*, 12/12/41, p. 21.

20. "Bruins Call Off Home Opener — No Place to Play," *Chicago Tribune*, 12/9/41, p. 27.

21. "Edwards Leads Stars to Victory Over the Bruins," *Oshkosh Daily Northwestern*, 12/15/41, p. 13.

22. R. Meyer, *The First Mr. Basketball: The Legend of Bobby McDermott* (Roxboro, MA" self-published, 2000). Most of the details of McDermott's career are drawn from Meyer's research and writing.

23. Richard Triptow, *The Dynasty That Never Was* (Lake Bluff, IL: self-published, 1997), p. 151.

24. R. Meyer, op. cit., p. 8.

25. Towery interview.

26. Dick Triptow and the author have had scores of discussions between 1999 and the present and this has arisen more than once.

27. Telephone interview with Carl Bennett, 10/27/03.

28. Telephone interview with Carlisle "Blackie" Towery, 10/16/03.

29. "Sheboygan Loses to Fort Wayne By a 50 to 35 Score," *Oshkosh Daily Northwestern*, 12/18/41, p. 25.

30. C. Bartlett, "Oshkosh Whips Bruins, 42 to 29 for 5th in Row," *Chicago Tribune*, 12/18/41, p. 33.

31. "All Stars Return After Win Over Goodyears, 42–35," *Oshkosh Daily Northwestern*, 12/22/41, p. 21; "Chicago Bruins Beaten, 38 to 31, By Indianapolis," *Chicago Tribune*, 12/22/41, p. 25.

32. J. Schlemmer, column, *Akron Beacon Journal*, 12/19/41, p. 42.

33. C. Bartlett, "Zollners Beat Bruins, 47–38; 500 at Game," *Chicago Tribune*, 12/26/41, p. 18.

34. R. Nelson, op. cit., p. 119.

35. "Kautskys Deal Bruins Another Defeat, 37 to 33," *Chicago Tribune*, 1/1/42, p. 35.

36. "Indianapolis Falls Before Oshkosh By 56–44," *Oshkosh Daily Northwestern*, 1/5/42, p. 13.

37. "All Stars Win Ninth Straight Loop Victory," *Oshkosh Daily Northwestern*, 1/7/42, p. 13; "Stars Keep Slate Clean, Win No.10 From Toledo Five," *Oshkosh Daily Northwestern*, 1/8/42, p. 17.

38. "Stars Keep League Record Clear of Defeat," *Oshkosh Daily Northwestern*, 1/12/42, p. 12.

39. "Goodyears Defeat Kautskys by 54–44," *Oshkosh Daily Northwestern*, 1/12/42, p. 12.

40. "Bruin Defeats End at 7; Beat Toledo 53 to 31," *Oshkosh Daily Northwestern*, 1/15/42, p. 23.

41. "Bruins Rally, Whip Fort Wayne Quintet, 51 to 47," *Chicago Tribune*, 1/22/42, p. 20.

42. "Oshkosh Win String Snapped By Akron," *Oshkosh Daily Northwestern*, 1/19/42, p. 12.

43. "Kautskys Defeat All Stars, 43–36, at Indianapolis," *Oshkosh Daily Northwestern*, 1/19/42, p. 12.

44. "Stars Lose to Rochester, But Defeat Sphas," *Oshkosh Daily Northwestern*, 1/26/42, p. 14.

45. "Sheboygan Loses to Hoosier Quint in Overtime Game," *Oshkosh Daily Northwestern*, 1/30/42, p. 14.

46. "Move Chicago-Akron Game Up to Tonight," *Oshkosh Daily Northwestern*, 2/3/42, p. 13.

47. "All Stars Defeat Chicago Bruins By 61 to 43," *Oshkosh Daily Northwestern*, 2/2/42, p. 12.

48. "Stars Lose Game By 43–30 Score to Fort Wayne," *Oshkosh Daily Northwestern*, 2/3/42, p. 13; R. Nelson, *The Zollner Piston Story*, p. 119.

49. Telephone interview with Carlisle "Blackie" Towery, 10/16/03.

50. "Oshkosh Pro Five to Play All-Star Cage Aggregation," *Oshkosh Daily Northwestern*, 2/4/42, p. 11.

51. "Celts Bow to Stars, Zollners Here Saturday," *Oshkosh Daily Northwestern*, 2/13/42, p. 15.

52. "Chuckovitz Sets Scoring Mark, But 'Skins Beat Toledo," *Oshkosh Daily Northwestern*, 2/13/42, p. 15.

53. "Chanute Over Rens in Cicero, 39–37, in OT," *Chicago Tribune*, 2/14/42, p. 24.

54. "All Stars Snow Under Fort Wayne By 72 to 47," *Oshkosh Daily Northwestern*, 2/16/42, p. 11.

55. "Sheboygan's Playoff Chances Grow Dimmer," *Oshkosh Daily Northwestern*, 2/16/42, p. 11.

56. "Redskins Lose Tilt in Chicago, 40 to 36," *Oshkosh Daily Northwestern*, 2/19/42, p. 19.

57. "All Stars Defeat Indianapolis Two Straight," *Oshkosh Daily Northwestern*, 3/2/42, p. 12.

58. "Stars Lose Opener, Must Win at Home Tonight or Else...," *Oshkosh Daily Northwestern*, 3/5/42, p. 19.

59. "All Stars, Zollners Play for Title Tonight," *Oshkosh Daily Northwestern*, 3/6/42, p. 12.

60. "All Stars Repeat As National Loop Champs," *Oshkosh Daily Northwestern*, 3/7/42, p. 13.

61. "Detroit Eagles Add Garfinkel fro Pro Tourney," *Chicago Tribune*, 3/3/42, p. 22.

62. "Detroit Beats Army Quint in Pro Meet," *Chicago Tribune*, 3/9/42, pt. 2, p. 2.

63. "Stars Meet Globetrotters in Semi Finals," *Oshkosh Daily Northwestern*, 3/10/42, p. 13.

64. "Detroit Plays Oshkosh for Pro Title Tonight," *Chicago Tribune*, 3/11/42, p. 25.

65. R. Triptow, *The Dynasty That Never Was*, p. 15.

66. W. Smith, "Oshkosh beats Detroit, 43–41, For Pro Title," *Chicago Tribune*, 3/12/42, p. 21. The *Oshkosh Daily Northwestern* claimed 11,500 fans at the game but the *Trib* writer knew the building better and is probably more accurate. By contrast the 1941 game in Chicago Stadium with a much larger capacity had 21,821 fans to watch the same two teams.

67. These scoring numbers were the same in both the *Tribune* and the *Daily Northwestern*, but Bill Himmelman in Peterson's *Cages to Jump Shots* had Englund with 17, Riska with nine, Jeannette with 14 and Bush with eight.

68. Ibid.

Chapter 7

1. A number of writers have included Zano West as an African American player, but Rich Lerner of Toledo has noted that this assertion was inaccurate.

2. M. Funke, "The Chicago Studebakers: How The UAW Helped Integrate Pro Basketball and Reunite Four Players Who Made History," *Solidarity*, 35, no. 7 (July 1992): 16–19.

3. This was never fully explained. "Toledo Out of Pro Loop," *Toledo Blade*, 12/23/42, p. 29.

4. R. Peterson, *Cages To Jump Shots*, p. 130.

5. Telephone interview with John Isaacs, May 18, 2002.

6. See M. Nelson, *The Originals: The New York Celtics Invent Modern Basketball*, pp. 81–100.

7. "All Stars Open with Game Saturday," *Oshkosh Daily Northwestern*, 11/6/42, p. 13.

8. "Stars Win By 55–34 Score in Season's Opener," *Oshkosh Daily Northwestern*, 11/9/42, p. 11.

9. Telephone interview with Erv Prasse, July 10, 2003.

10. Ibid.

11. "Stars to Face Strong Foe Here," *Oshkosh Daily Northwestern*, 11/10/42, p. 13.

12. "Stars, Zollners Split Two Games," *Oshkosh Daily Northwestern*, 11/16/42, p. 13.

13. "Redskins Win Season's Opener By 46 to34 Score," *Oshkosh Daily Northwestern*, 11/19/42, p. 11.

14. "College Stars Rally to Beat Oshkosh, 61–55," *Chicago Tribune*, 11/28/42, p. 19.

15. "All Stars Split Even in Two League Games," *Oshkosh Daily Northwestern*, 12/7/42, p. 13.

16. "Oshkosh Five Defeated By Studebakers," *Chicago Defender*, 12/12/42, p. 21.

17. Photo caption of Bernie Price, *Chicago Defender*, 12/19/42, p. 19.

18. "Chicago Five Bows to Oshkosh By 44 to 33 Score," *Oshkosh Daily Northwestern*, 12/28/42, p. 13.

19. "All Stars Defeat Redskins in Overtime Game," *Oshkosh Daily Northwestern*, 1/2/43, p. 11.

20. "All Stars Increase League Lead to Two Games," *Oshkosh Daily Northwestern*, 1/4/43, p. 11.

21. "Skins Beat Stars; Hoosiers Win 78–62, To Play Here Tonight," *Oshkosh Daily Northwestern*, 1/9/43, p. 11.

22. M. Funke, p. 19.

23. "Patrons Still Attend Sporting Event," *Oshkosh Daily Northwestern*, 1/9/43, p. 10.

24. R. Peterson, *Cages to Jump Shots*, p. 130–131; M. Funke, "The Chicago Studebakers," p. 19.

25. "Studebakers Over Oshkosh in 73–60 Game," *Chicago Tribune*, 2/1/43, p. 20. Long is not listed in any encyclopedias or books as competing for the Studebakers.

26. "Fort Wayne Clinches First in National Loop," *Oshkosh Daily Northwestern*, 2/10/43, p. 11.

27. "Stars Beat Redskins in Tourney in Memphis," *Oshkosh Daily Northwestern*, 2/6/43, p. 11.

28. "Stars Begin Quest for Loop Championship," *Oshkosh Daily Northwestern*, 2/20/43, p. 11.

29. "Redskins Defeat All Stars in Two Straight," *Oshkosh Daily Northwestern*, 2/22/03, p. 11.

30. R. Peterson, p. 134.

31. "Fort Wayne Five Wins First of Playoffs, 49–37," *Chicago Tribune*, 2/21/43, pt. 2, p. 4; "Fort Wayne is Defeated, 45–32, by Studebakers," *Chicago Tribune*, 2/23/43, p. 18; "Zollners Beat Studebakers in Playoff Final," *Chicago Tribune*, 2/24/43, p. 20.

32. "Sheboygan Beats Zollners in Playoff Battle," *Oshkosh Daily Tribune*, 3/2/43, p. 11.

33. Tickets for these games in Sheboygan were $1.40, $1.00 and 85 cents for reserved seats.

General admission was 70 cents with "children on the stage" paying 30 cents.

34. R. Nelson, *The Zollner Piston Story*, p. 124.

35. This is discussed in detail in M. Nelson, *The Originals*, pp. 98–99.

36. "Sheboygan Wins National Loop Championship," *Oshkosh Daily Northwestern*, 3/10/43, p. 13; R. Nelson, *The Zollner Piston Story*, pp. 125–126.

37. "Pro Finals Will be at Stadium," *Oshkosh Daily Northwestern*, 2/23/43, p. 11.

38. "Detroit Pros Sign Three Irish Stars for Tourney," *Chicago Tribune*, 3/13/43, p. 18.

39. "All Stars Down Detroit, Premeet Favorites," *Oshkosh Daily Northwestern*, 3/15/43, p. 11.

40. "All Stars Seek Second World's Title Tonight," *Oshkosh Daily Northwestern*, 3/17/43, p. 13.

41. W. Smith, "Washington beats Oshkosh for Pro Title," *Chicago Tribune*, 3/18/43, p. 27.

42. Ibid.

43. Ibid.

44. John Isaacs, telephone interview.

45. R. Peterson, *Cages to Jump Shots*, pp. 135–136.

46. Financial reports found in Sheboygan Redskins archives, Box 3. Sheboygan County Research Center, Sheboygan Falls, WI.

47. "Zollner Pistons' Home, League Road Schedules are Completed," *Fort Wayne News-Sentinel*, 10/27/43, p. 19.

48. R. Nelson, *The Zollner Piston Story*, p. 128.

49. "Pistons Split on Trip East: Open at Home Tuesday Night," *Fort Wayne News-Sentinel*, 11/29/43, p. 9

50. "Pistons' Late Spurt Defeats Sheboygan, 55–44, in Loop Tilt," *Fort Wayne News-Sentinel*, 12/3/43, p. 26.

51. "23,825 See College Stars Defeat Pros," *Cleveland Plain Dealer*, 12/4/43, p. 16.

52. "Bears, Bell's Sniping Too Much for Piston Cagers Beaten Out By World's Champs," *Fort Wayne News-Sentinel*, 12/7/43, p. 11; "Pistons Lose to Bears, Try Again Tonight," *Fort Wayne News-Sentinel*, 11/9/43, p. 27; "Bears Nose Pistons in 51–49 Clash," *Fort Wayne News-Sentinel*, 12/10/43, p. 30.

53. A. Zirin, "Riebe Tallies 30 as Chase Bag First Pro Victory, 56–51," *Cleveland Plain Dealer*, 12/23/43, p. 14.

54. "Pistons Beat Cleveland Twice, Lengthen Their Lead in League," *Fort Wayne News-Sentinel*, 12/27/43, p. 9.

55. "Pistons try to Stow Riebe, Cleveland Seeks to Halt Zollners," *Fort Wayne News-Sentinel*, 1/18/44, p. 20.

56. B. Tenny, "Sheboygan Humbles Pistons By 41–29: Cleveland Here Sunday," *Fort Wayne News-Sentinel*, 1/26/44, p. 10.

57. S. Smith, J. Rimer, and R. Triptow, *A Tribute to Armed Forces Basketball* (Lake Bluff, IL: self-published, 2003), p. 82.

58. "Pistons, Oshkosh to Renew Hostilities at North Side Gym Tonight," *Fort Wayne News-Sentinel*, 2/8/44, p. 9.

59. "Chase Lose to Sheboygan, 46–45," *Cleveland Plain Dealer*, 2/7/44, p. 12.

60. "Pistons Need Only One Win to Clinch League Championship," *Fort Wayne News-Sentinel*, 2/14/44, p. 9.

61. "Pistons Take Bears; Fight is Aftermath," *Fort Wayne News-Sentinel*, 2/26/44, p. 10

62. "Pistons Trounce Cleveland, 64–37, in Opener," *Fort Wayne News-Sentinel*, 3/6/44, p. 15

63. "Pistons Two Up, Hope to End Series Tuesday," *Fort Wayne News-Sentinel*, 3/13/44, p. 9.

64. R. Nelson, *The Zollner Piston Story*, p. 131.

65. "Fort Wayne, Rens to Meet in Semi Finals," *Chicago Tribune*, 3/23/44, p. 24. "Pistons Win, Face Rens in Semi Finals of Tourney," *Fort Wayne News-Sentinel*, 3/23/44, p. 14.

66. "Fort Wayne Five, Brooklyn Gain Stadium Finals," *Chicago Tribune*, 3/25/44, p. 20.

67. B. Tenny, "Pistons Rule Professional Basketball Realm for 1944," *Fort Wayne News-Sentinel*, 3/27/44, p. 9

68. R. Nelson, *The Zollner Piston Story*, p. 131.

Chapter 8

1. B. Tenny, "Pistons Prove Greatness with 44–38 Victory Over All-Stars," *Fort Wayne News-Sentinel*, 12/2/44, p. 12.

2. Carlisle Towery, phone interview, 10/16/03.

3. "Oshkosh Stars Defeat Chicago Quintet, 47 to 29," *Chicago Tribune*, 12/3/44, pt. 2, p. 2.

4. "Red Hot Oshkosh Team Whips Chicago in Thriller, 47 to 39," *Oshkosh Daily Northwestern*, 12/4/44, p. 11.

5. "Gears Defeat Oshkosh Pro Five, 52 to 46," *Chicago Tribune*, 12/21/44, p. 19.

6. "It's Really True! Oshkosh Stars Trim Zollners by 49 to 45," *Oshkosh Daily Northwestern*, 12/11/44, p. 11.

7. "Pistons Lose to Oshkosh, Then Take Overtime Clash," *Fort Wayne News-Sentinel*, 12/11/44, p. 11.

8. R. Triptow, *The Dynasty That Never Was.*

9. "Chicago Buys Connie Berry," *Fort Wayne News-Sentinel*, 12/29/44, p. 11.

10. "Oshkosh Five Top Pittsburgh Rivals, 55 to 50," *Chicago Tribune*, 12/31/44, pt. 2, p. 3.

11. "Pistons Beat Sheboygan: Face Three Road Clashes," *Fort Wayne News-Sentinel*, 1/3/45, p. 15.

12. "Stars Lose 52–50: Triptow's Sensational Field Goal is Clincher," *Oshkosh Daily Northwestern*, 1/15/45, p. 9.

13. "Gears Lose to Redskins Again, 52–48," *Chicago Tribune*, 1/12/45, p. 22; "Gears Defeat Oshkosh, 52–50 in Last Minute," *Chicago Tribune*, 1/14/45, pt. 2, p. 2.

14. "Pistons Outlast Chicago to Turn in Victory by 59–49; Spurt in Last Quarter Takes Clash," *Fort Wayne News-Sentinel*, 1/17/45, p. 11.

15. "Pistons Keep Going By Downing Cleveland in 50–42 Clash; Mel Riebe Outscores McDermott," *Fort Wayne News-Sentinel*, 1/24/45, p. 11. "Pistons Make Pittsburgh 55–41 Victim; Eye Heavy Schedule Starting On Saturday Night," *Fort Wayne News-Sentinel*, 1/25/45, p. 15.

16. Telephone interview with Carlisle "Blackie" Towery, 10/16/03.

17. "Gears Defeat Cleveland Pro Quintet, 59–50," *Chicago Tribune*, 1/25/45, p. 21.

18. "Pistons Trim Raiders, 63–53: Chicago Next Home Foe," *Fort Wayne News-Sentinel*, 1/31/45, p. 11.

19. "American Gears Five Defeats Pittsburgh, 62–60," *Chicago Tribune*, 2/1/45, p. 21; "Gears Quintet Lose, 66 to 40 to Cleveland," *Chicago Tribune*, 2/2/45, pt. 2, p. 2.

20. "Pistons' Final Spurt Too Much for Gears in 60–49 Loop Contest; McDermott Has Big Night," *Fort Wayne News-Sentinel*, 2/5/45, p. 13.

21. "Pistons Lose as McDermott Sets Record," *Fort Wayne News-Sentinel*, 2/9/45, p. 11.

22. "Pistons Sign Sadowski to Aid in Playoffs, Meet," *Fort Wayne News-Sentinel*, 3/3/45, p. 10.

23. "Gears Beat Sheboygan in Playoff Game," *Chicago Tribune*, 3/6/45, p. 18; "Redskins Beat Gears to Even Playoff Series," *Chicago Tribune*, 3/7/45, p. 24; "Redskins Beat Gears, 57–27, in Play-off Final," *Chicago Tribune*, 3/9/45, p. 27.

24. B. Tenny, "Pistons Shoot Well to Hand Cleveland Quintet 78–50 Trimming," *Fort Wayne News-Sentinel*, 3/7/45, p. 11.

25. B. Tenny, "Pistons Enter Final Series Against Sheboygan," *Fort Wayne News-Sentinel*, 3/9/45, p. 11.

26. B. Tenny, "Pistons Hope to Get Even With Sheboygan Tonight," *Fort Wayne News-Sentinel*, 3/12/45, p. 11; B. Tenny, "Sheboygan Five Backs Pistons to Wall," *Fort Wayne News-Sentinel*, 3/13/45, p. 8.

27. B. Tenny, "Pistons Seek to Pull Even with Sheboygan Redskins Tonight," *Fort Wayne News-Sentinel*, 3/15/45, p. 25; B. Tenny, "Pistons, Redskins to Play Deciding Clash Sunday,"

Fort Wayne News-Sentinel, 3/17/45, p. 11; B. Tenny, "Pistons Beat Sheboygan, 59–49 to Retain Their Loop Crown," *Fort Wayne News-Sentinel*, 3/19/45, p. 9.

28. "Gears Beat Hartford in Pro Tourney," *Chicago Tribune*, 3/20/45, p. 20.

29. McNeill was actually Bruce Hale, playing under an assumed name to preserve his AAU amateur standing, notes Dick Triptow in his book (page 18), a claim confirmed by Hale's widow.

30. "Dow Chemicals, Pittsburgh Win in Pro Tourney," *Chicago Tribune*, 3/21/45, p. 26; B. Tenny, "Piston Cagers Start Defense of Professional Title Tonight," *Fort Wayne News-Sentinel*, 3/21/45, p. 22.

31. "Gears Defeat Globetrotter Five, 53 to 49," *Chicago Tribune*, 3/22/45, p. 30; B. Tenny, "Pistons Face Rens Friday in Semi-Finals of Pro Cage Meet," *Fort Wayne News-Sentinel* 3/22/45, p. 15.

32. M. Shevlin, "Zollners and Acme Five Gain Tourney Finals," *Chicago Tribune*, 3/24/45, p. 20; B. Tenny, "Pistons Meet Dayton Tonight in Finals of Pro Cage Meet," *Fort Wayne News-Sentinel*, 3/24/45, p. 18.

33. B. Tenny, "Pistons Are First Repeaters in World's Hardwood Tournament," *Fort Wayne News-Sentinel*, 3/26/45, p. 11.

34. "Pistons Gain Sweep in 59–47 Win Over National Loop Stars," *Fort Wayne News-Sentinel*, 3/28/45, p. 23.

Chapter 9

1. D. M. Fisher, "Lester Harrison and the Rochester Royals, 1945–1957," in S. A. Reiss, ed., *Sports and the American Jew* (Syracuse, NY: Syracuse University Press, 1998), p. 209.

2. Levane interview, 5/18/04.

3. See S. Rosenberg, *The Jewish Community in Rochester, 1843–1925* (New York: American Jewish Historical Society, 1954).

4. Fisher, p. 210.

5. P. Pinckney, "Graham Impresses Squad in Cage Drill," *Rochester Democrat and Chronicle*, 11/7/45, p. 22.

6. Telephone interview with Al Cervi, 5/20/04.

7. "George Glamack Signs with Royals," *Rochester Democrat and Chronicle*, 11/13/45, p. 19.

8. Levane interview, 5/18/04

9. "Al Cervi Returns; Royals Obtain Mahnken, Nagretti," *Rochester Democrat and Chronicle*, 11/18/45, p. C3.

10. "Chicago Gears Lose, 53 to 49, in League Opener," *Chicago Tribune*, 11/23/45, p. 31.

11. "Royals Make National League Bow at Arena Tonight," *Rochester Democrat and Chronicle*, 11/24/45, p. 14.

12. Fisher, p. 228.

13. See M. Nelson, *The Originals* for more developed discussion of this.

14. Levane interview, 5/18/04.

15. P. Pinckney, "Royals Win Debut in National Wheel," *Rochester Democrat and Chronicle*, 11/25/45, p. C1.

16. R. Triptow, *The Dynasty That Never Was*, p. 42.

17. "Cleveland Conquers Indianapolis, 51 to 44," *Rochester Democrat and Chronicle*, 11/26/45, p. 24.

18. This is discussed in more depth in T. Gould, *Pioneers of the Hardwood*, pp. 123–146.

19. Arnie Risen, telephone interview, 5/25/04.

20. "Risen Scholastically Ineligible," *Chicago Tribune*, 1/3/46, p. 17.

21. "Gears Score First League Victory, 47–38," *Chicago Tribune*, 11/26/45, p. 27.

22. "Chicago Gains Upset Over Oshkosh," *Rochester Democrat and Chronicle*, 11/26/45, p. 24.

23. "Sheboygan Scuttles Youngstown, 45–39," *Rochester Democrat and Chronicle*, 11/27/45, p. 23.

24. "Oshkosh Nips 'Skins, 33–30," *Rochester Democrat and Chronicle*, 11/30/45, p. 25.

25. Fisher, p. 228. Actually Holzman thought the opponent was Sheboygan as he noted in his quoted autobiography, but that was clearly not correct.

26. "'Skins Lose to Oshkosh," *Rochester Democrat and Chronicle*, 12/2/45, p. C1

27. "College Stars Lose, 63 to 55," *Chicago Tribune*, 12/1/45, p. 17. In his *The Zollner Piston Story*, p. 139, Rodger Nelson claimed that there were 23,912 people in attendance.

28. P. Pinckney, "Royals Nip Fort Wayne, 56–54," *Rochester Democrat and Chronicle*, 12/3/45, p. 23.

29. P. Pinckney, "Royals Defeat Youngstown," *Rochester Democrat and Chronicle*, 12/4/45, p. 21; P. Pinckney, "Royals Bag 5th Straight League Win, 61–49," *Rochester Democrat and Chronicle*, 12/9/45, p. C1.

30. "Stars, 'Skins Bag Verdicts in Double Bill," *Rochester Democrat and Chronicle*, 12/6/45, p. 31.

31. "Zollners Gain 60–51 Victory Over Chicago," *Rochester Democrat and Chronicle*, 12/8/45, p. 16.

32. "Fort Wayne Takes 70–52 Game," *Rochester Democrat and Chronicle*, 12/10/45, p. 27; "McDermott Notches 25 in 71–52 Ft. Wayne

Win," *Rochester Democrat and Chronicle*, 12/11/45, p. 20.

33. "Royals Rout Cleveland for 6th Win, 65–45," *Rochester Democrat and Chronicle*, 12/10/45, p. 27; "Oshkosh Spanks Indianapolis," *Rochester Democrat and Chronicle*, 12/10/45, p. 27.

34. Levane interview, 5/18/04

35. "Davies Joins Royals Quint," *Rochester Democrat and Chronicle*, 12/12/45, p. 20.

36. "Carpenter and Glamack Lead," *Fort Wayne News-Sentinel*, 12/13/45, p. 31.

37. One exception was the 49–48 loss to Dow on December 5 where Huck Hartman and Urgel "Slim" Wintermute led the Dows with 12 and 10 points.

38. "Shut 1292 Steel Plants," *Chicago Tribune*, 1/21/46, p. 1.

39. "Nation's Strike Situation at a Glance," *Fort Wayne News-Sentinel*, 1/4/46, p. 10.

40. "Sheboygan Assumes Division Lead in Win," *Rochester Democrat and Chronicle*, 12/17/45, p. 27.

41. G. Beahorn, "Royals Capture 7th, 72–55," *Rochester Democrat and Chronicle*, 12/16/45, p. Cl.

42. "Royals Sign Garfinkel," *Rochester Democrat and Chronicle*, 12/21/45, p. 24.

43. P. Pinckney, "Zollner Spurt Snaps Royals' String, 63–59," *Rochester Democrat and Chronicle*, 12/30/45, p. D1.

44. R. Triptow, *The Dynasty That Never Was*, p. 43.

45. "American Gears Beaten, 63 to 32, at Rochester," *Chicago Tribune*, 1/13/46, pt. 2, p. 4; "American Gear Five Loses 2d in Row, 71 to 43," *Chicago Tribune*, 1/14/46, p. 24.

46. G. Beahon, "Royals Spurt to Top Bears, 58–50," *Rochester Democrat and Chronicle*, 1/15/46, p. 18.

47. "Pistons Down Royal Cagers," *Fort Wayne News-Sentinel*, 1/17/46, p. 13; "Pistons Beat Wright Field," *Fort Wayne News-Sentinel*, 1/18/46, p. 11.

48. G. Beahon, "Cagers' Corner," *Rochester Democrat and Chronicle*, 1/16/46, p. 18.

49. B. Tenny, "Pistons Rally to Defeat Royals Here, Split Series," *Fort Wayne News-Sentinel*, 1/21/46, p. 24.

50. "Bears Upset Pistons in 60–57 Clash," *Fort Wayne News-Sentinel*, 2/1/46, p. 24.

51. "Royals Outlast Pistons, 58–55, to Reduce Margin," *Fort Wayne News-Sentinel*, 2/18/46, p. 9

52. B. Tenny, "Royals to Be Successor to Pistons?" *Fort Wayne News-Sentinel*, 2/20/46, p. 11.

53. B. Tenny, "Sports Calendar," *Fort Wayne News-Sentinel*, 12/21/46, p. 14.

54. G. Beahon, "Cagers' Corner," *Rochester Democrat and Chronicle*, 2/5/46, p. 18.

55. "Royals Whip Rens, 54 to 40," *Rochester Democrat and Chronicle*, 2/23/46, p. 20.

56. "Royals Spank Monarch Five at Cleveland," *Rochester Democrat and Chronicle*, 2/25/46, p. 21.

57. "Pistons Release Three to Cut Down to Workable Size," *Fort Wayne News-Sentinel*, 3/1/46, p. 13.

58. "Pistons Regular Season Champs Again, Look Better in Beating Sheboygan Quint, 53–49," *Fort Wayne News-Sentinel*, 3/4/46, p. 8.

59. Telephone interview with Al Cervi, 5/20/04.

60. "Davies Named Sports Coach at Seton Hall," *Rochester Democrat and Chronicle*, 1/18/46, p. 22.

61. B. Tenny, "Can Pistons Take Two-Tilt Series Lead? Learn Answer Tonight," *Fort Wayne News-Sentinel*, 3/13/46, p. 11.

62. "Royals Out of Tourney, Harrison Announces," *Rochester Democrat and Chronicle*, 3/14/46, p. 18.

63. E. Cushing, "Sports Eye View," *Rochester Democrat and Chronicle*, 3/25/46, p. 20.

64. "Pistons Eye Pro Tourney as Their Comeback Chase," *Fort Wayne News-Sentinel*, 3/18/46, p. 7.

65. E. Cushing, "Royals Humble Sheboygan in Opener," *Rochester Democrat and Chronicle*, 3/20/46, p. 20; E. Cushing, "Royals Win by 61 to 54," *Rochester Democrat and Chronicle*, 3/22/46, p. 28; E. Cushing, "Royals Rip 'Skins for League Title," *Rochester Democrat and Chronicle*, 3/24/46, p. Cl.

66. R. Triptow, *The Dynasty That Never Was*, p. 48.

67. "Mikan Scores 20 Points; Gears Triumph, 59 to 48," *Chicago Tribune*, 3/21/46, p. 31.

68. G.L. Mikan, and J. Oberle, *Unstoppable: The Story of George Mikan* (Indianapolis: Masters Press, 1997), p. 68.

69. "Stanczak and Wintermute Get Spotlight as Pro Meet Opens," *Fort Wayne News-Sentinel*, 3/26/46, p. 10; J. Segreti, "Gears Advance to Pro-Tourney Quarter-Finals," *Chicago Tribune*, 3/26/46, p. 24.

70. "Oshkosh, Rens, Baltimore Win in Pro Tourney," *Chicago Tribune*, 3/27/46, p. 29.

71. "Zollners and Gears Win in Pro Tourney," *Chicago Tribune*, 3/30/46, p. 20.

72. "Fort Wayne and Oshkosh Fives Gain Pro Final," *Chicago Tribune*, 4/4/46, p. 30.

73. "Stars Ride Out Big Lead to Beat Pistons," *Oshkosh Daily Northwestern*, 4/1/46, p. 11.

74. Oshkosh All Stars ad, *Oshkosh Daily Northwestern*, 4/6/46, p. 11.

75. Edwards was certainly the league leader in nicknames— Lefty, Cowboy, Li'l Abner, Moose and Horse, being the most common.

76. W. Smith, "Oshkosh Wins in Pro Meet Finals" *Chicago Tribune*, 4/6/46, p. 20; "Stars Win First Game of Tourney Playoff," *Oshkosh Daily Northwestern*, 4/6/46, p. 11.

77. J. Segreti, "Fort Wayne Evens Series; Wins 56–47," *Chicago Tribune*, 4/7/46, pt. 2, p. 2.

78. J. Segreti, "Zollners Keep Crown; Defeat Oshkosh, 73–57," *Chicago Tribune*, 4/9/46, p. 24.

Chapter 10

1. This bulletin, dated May 29, 1946, can be found in the Gene Englund Collection in the Archives of the Oshkosh Museum, Oshkosh, WI.

2. D. Ramsey, *The Nats* (Utica, NY: North Country Books, 1996), pp. 2–3.

3. "National League Roundup," *Anderson Daily Bulletin*, 11/1/46, p. 15.

4. "Packers Attend Jaycee Dinner," *Anderson Daily Bulletin*, 11/6/46, p. 12; "Major League Basketball Comes to Anderson on Monday," *Anderson Daily Bulletin*, 11/7/46, p. 17; "Packers Make Initial Appearance of Season v. Detroit," *Anderson Daily Bulletin*, 11/11/46, p. 10.

5. National Basketball League Official Bulletin, May, 29, 1946.

6. "Pistons, Midland Clash at New Haven," *Fort Wayne News-Sentinel*, 10/26/46, p. 10.

7. "Toledo Jeeps Take Opener," *Fort Wayne News-Sentinel*, 11/8/46, p. 58.

8. "Sheboygan Quintet Flies to Coast Games," *Chicago Tribune*, 11/4/46, p. 33.

9. "Twelve of Nazi Chiefs to Be Hanged," *Anderson Daily Bulletin*, 10/1/46, p. 1.

10. "Gears Lose to Oshkosh, 66–61, in Pro Opener," Chicago Tribune, 11/10/46, pt. 2, p. 3.

11. "17,205 Fans See Stags Win in Overtime," *Chicago Tribune*, 11/12/46, p. 25.

12. J. Enright, "Pro Tourney and All-Star Game," *1947 World Professional Tourney Program*, p. 23.

13. Ibid.

14. "All Stars Win Over Zollner Five," *Chicago Tribune*, 11/30/46, p. 17; B. Tenny, "Pistons Lose to All-Stars; Meet Detroit Gems Here Saturday," *Fort Wayne News-Sentinel*, 11/30/46, p. 11.

15. "Gears Deal 1st Defeat, 65 to 64, to Rochester," *Chicago Tribune*, 12/1/46, pt. 2, p. 2.

16. "Buffalo Pro Cagers Consider Move to Moline," *Moline Daily Dispatch*, 12/18/46, p. 30; "Offer Civic Plan to Bring Pro Cagers Here," *Moline Daily Dispatch*, 12/19/46, p. 29; "Pick

Blackhawks for Pro Team Name," *Moline Daily Dispatch*, 1/1/47, p. 22; "Blackhawks Drop Tough Battle to Fort Wayne," *Moline Daily Dispatch*, 1/4/47, p. 10; Blackhawks Win, 48–43," *Moline Daily Dispatch*, 1/13/47, p. 12.

17. Stan Von Nieda, telephone interview, 3/17/05.

18. M. Shevlin, "Mikan Retires After Gears Lose, 44 to 41," *Chicago Tribune*, 12/12/46, p. 59.

19. "Davey Banks Now Involved in Gear Tiff," *Fort Wayne News-Sentinel*, 12/14/46, p. 10.

20. R. Triptow, *The Dynasty that Never Was*, p. 71; J. Marcus, *A Biographical Directory of Professional Basketball Coaches* (Lanham, MD: Scarecrow Press, 2003), p. 127.

21. Mikan, G., and J. Oberle, *Unstoppabl: The Story of George Mikan*, p. 74.

22. M. Shevlin, "Mikan Scores 22 as Gears Win, 62 to 60," *Chicago Tribune*, 2/1/47, p. 16.

23. "Bulletin," *Fort Wayne News-Sentinel*, 12/21/46, p. 10.

24. B. Tenny, "Surviving Pistons Trim Redskins, 69–57," *Fort Wayne News-Sentinel*, 12/23/46, p. 11.

25. "Bob McDermott Signs as Player-Coach of Gear Five, *Chicago Tribune*, 1/3/47, p. 22; "Bob McDermott Given Outright Release," *Fort Wayne News-Sentinel*, 1/1/47, p. 27; "Mac To Lead Gears Against Indianapolis," *Fort Wayne News-Sentinel*, 1/3/47, p. 24.

26. R. Thomas, *They Cleared the Lane* (Lincoln: University of Nebraska Press, 2002), p. 14.

27. Cervi interview, 5/20/04.

28. Risen interview, 5/25/04.

29. P. Pinckney, "Zollners Outrough Royals, 72–67," *Rochester Democrat and Chronicle*, 2/9/47, p. 21.

30. "11,000 See Royals Win, 50–47," *Rochester Democrat and Chronicle*, 2/12/47, p. 21.

31. "Pistons Outlast Royals in Grueling Tilt," *Fort Wayne News-Sentinel*, 2/13/47, p. 30.

32. J. Cristgau, *Tricksters in the Madhouse: Lakers vs. Globetrotters, 1948* (Lincoln: University of Nebraska Press, 2004).

33. Ibid.

34. Cervi interview, 5/20/04.

35. Von Nieda interview.

36. "NBL All Star Teams," *Fort Wayne News-Sentinel*, 3/26/47, p. 24.

37. "Pistons Move Two Games Ahead in Set with Jeeps," *Fort Wayne News-Sentinel*, 3/21/47, p. 39.

38. "Pistons Lose at Toledo; Try Again Tonight to Avoid Decisive Battle of Set Wednesday," *Fort Wayne News-Sentinel*, 3/25/47, p. 25.

39. "Pistons, Jeeps Tangle Here Tonight in Series' Decisive Tilt," *Fort Wayne News-Sentinel*, 3/26/47, p. 24.

40. "Though Underdogs, Pistons Hope to Keep Going v. Royals," *Fort Wayne News-Sentinel*, 3/27/47, p. 40.

41. "Oshkosh Tips 'Skins, 53–45, Evens Series," *Rochester Democrat and Chronicle*, 3/22/47, p. 9.

42. "Gears Win First Play-Off Series Contest, 74 to 72," *Chicago Tribune*, 3/19/47, p. 29.

43. R. Triptow, *The Dynasty That Never Was*, p. 84.

44. "Gears Deal 2D Loss in Row to Kautskys, 69–61," *Chicago Tribune*, 3/21/47, p. 29.

45. "Kautskys and Risen Defeat Gears, 68–67," *Chicago Tribune*, 3/24/47, p. 30.

46. "Kautskys Beat Gears, 55 to 54, to Even Series," *Chicago Tribune*, 3/26/47, p. 33.

47. Triptow, p. 85.

48. Ibid.

49. "Ban Manager But Gear Five Wins, 60 to 54," *Chicago Tribune*, 3/28/47, p. 31; "Gears Go Into Finals With 61–60 Victory," *Chicago Tribune*, 3/30/47, pt. 2, p. 2. "Free Throw With 14 Seconds Left Gives Gears Win, 61–60," *Oshkosh Daily Northwestern*, 3/31/47, p. 13.

50. "Closing Rush of Rens Beat All Stars, 65–60," *Oshkosh Daily Northwestern*, 4/4/47, p. 13.

51. "Pistons Give New Men Plenty of Chance to Play; Rens Win," *Fort Wayne News-Sentinel*, 4/5/47, p. 15.

52. Al Cervi, telephone interview with Murry Nelson and Dick Triptow, May 20, 2004.

53. E. Cushing, "Sports Eye View," *Rochester Democrat and Chronicle*, 3/30/47, p.D1.

54. E. Cushing, "Vengeful Royals Wreck Fort Wayne, 76 to 47," *Rochester Democrat and Chronicle*, 4/2/47, p. 26.

55. B. Tenny, "Royals Shoot at .394, Plaster Pistons, 76–47," *Fort Wayne News-Sentinel*, 4/2/47, p. 28.

56. "Gears Beaten in Opener, 71–65," *Chicago Tribune*, 4/4/47, p. 27; "Stags Upset Capitols 2d in Row, 69–53," *Chicago Tribune*, 4/4/47, p. 27; "Davies Sparks Rochester Win," *Rochester Democrat and Chronicle*, 4/4/47, p. 29.

57. E. Cushing, "Sports Eye View," *Rochester Democrat and Chronicle*, 4/5/47, p. 20.

58. "George Mikan's 27 Points Help Gears Win, 67–63," *Chicago Tribune*, 4/6/47, pt. 2, p. 2; "Gears Stop Royals, 67–63, to Even Cage Series," *Rochester Democrat and Chronicle*, 4/7/47, p. 8.

59. E. Prell, "Redskin Five Advances in Pro Tourney," *Chicago Tribune*, 4/7/47, p. 31.

60. "Gears Shift into High in Play-off," *Chicago Tribune*, 4/8/47, p. 23; G. Beahon, "Gears Turn Back Royals, 78 to 70," *Rochester Democrat and Chronicle*, 4/8/47, p. 23.

61. "National League Withdraws from Basketball Group," *Rochester Democrat and Chronicle*, 4/9/47, p. 24; "NBL Quitting Court Group; War Looming," *Fort Wayne News-Sentinel*, 4/9/47, p. 26.

62. "Gears Blast Royals, 79–68, Win Series," *Rochester Democrat and Chronicle*, 4/10/47, p. 31; M. Shevlin, "Gears Defeat Royals, 79–68, Capture Title," *Chicago Tribune*, 4/10/47, p. 31.

63. W. Smith, "Indianapolis, Toledo in Pro Final Tonight," *Chicago Tribune*, 4/10/47, p. 32.

64. W. Smith, "Kautskys beat Toledo, 62–47, in Pro Final" *Chicago Tribune*, 4/11/47, p. 27.

65. "Joe Fulks Nearing New Pro Net Scoring Mark," *Fort Wayne News-Sentinel*, 4/1/47, p. 10.

66. Triptow, p. 89.

67. Cervi interview.

68. "Royals Nip Gears," *Rochester Democrat and Chronicle*, 4/12/47, p. 21; "Gears Shade Royals, 75–74," *Rochester Democrat and Chronicle*, 4/13/47, p. D1; J. Lippe, "Gears Again Topple Royals," *Rochester Democrat and Chronicle*, 4/14/47, p. 23.

69. Andrew "Fuzzy" Levane, telephone interview with Murry Nelson and Dick Triptow, May 19, 2004.

Chapter 11

1. November 18 memo from Ward Lambert to members of the Executive Committee of NBL, Inc., Gene Englund Collection, Oshkosh Museum.

2. "Pro Cage Loop Hits 'Jumpers,'" *Minneapolis Star*, 10/13/47, p. 20.

3. Triptow's book, *The Dynasty That Never Was*, provides the only in-depth examination of the PBLA. Glenn Dickey provides less than a page in his *History of Professional Basketball Since 1896* (New York: Stein and Day, 1982), and Robert Peterson has two paragraphs in his *Cages to Jump Shots*. George Mikan has two pages of discussion of the league from his perspective in his *Unstoppable: The Story of George Mikan*. Michael Schumacher discusses it in *Mr. Basketball*, drawing mostly from Triptow.

4. M. Shevlin, "National League Polls Clubs on Gears' Return," *Chicago Tribune*, 11/14/47, p. 47.

5. "League Rejects Franchise Bid of Homeless Gears," *Chicago Tribune*, 11/17/47, p. 38; "NBL Refuses Team Request; 4 Barred," *Rochester Democrat and Chronicle*, 11/17/47, p. 23.

6. B. Carlson, "Matson Joins Local Pro Five," *Minneapolis Star*, 10/6/47, p. 22.

7. B. Carlson, "Mikan on Laker List as Rival Loop Folds," *Minneapolis Star*, 11/13/47, p. 39.

8. Mikan describes his view of these negotiations in Mikan, *Unstoppable*, pp. 83–85.

9. "Lakers Prove Practice Must Make Mikan 'Fit,'" *Minneapolis Star*, 11/21/47, p. 34; "Lakers Bow; Mikan Shines," *Rochester Democrat and Chronicle*, 11/21/47, p. 40.

10. G. Mikan, with J. Oberle, *Unstoppable*, p. 87.

11. "Toledo, Zollners Win Thrillers," *Rochester Democrat and Chronicle*, 11/9/47, p. 6-D.

12. B. Tenny, "Pistons Score 69 Points! That's 13 Too Few, They Learn," *Fort Wayne News-Sentinel*, 11/21/47, p. 22.

13. B. Tenny, "Pistons' First Dive into Lake(rs) Fails; They Try Again Tonight," *Fort Wayne News-Sentinel*, 12/4/47, p. 49; B. Tenny, "Fans Wonder if Piston Slump Temporary or Permanent," *Fort Wayne News-Sentinel*, 12/5/47, p. 47.

14. B. Tenny, "If Teams Have to Win at Home, Fate of Pistons May Be Sorry One," *Fort Wayne News-Sentinel*, 12/11/47, p. 50.

15. "Pistons in Win; Home Sunday," *Fort Wayne News-Sentinel*, 12/13/47, p. 10.

16. "Kautskys Release Herman Schaefer," *Rochester Democrat and Chronicle*, 11/12/47, p. 25; B. Carlson, "Lakers Sign Up Schaefer; Smith May Not Make Trip," *Minneapolis Star*, 11/25/47, p. 21.

17. Stan Von Nieda, telephone interview, 3/17/2005.

18. "Mikan Tallies 24 in Lakers' Win," *Rochester Democrat and Chronicle*, 12/5/47, p. 39.

19. B. Carlson, "Laker Defense Tops," *Minneapolis Star*, 12/10/47, p. 47.

20. G. Beahon, "Royal Rally Nips Zollners in Overtime Thriller, 65–62, Bags 11th Arena Victory," *Rochester Democrat and Chronicle*, 12/21/47, p. C1; G. Beahon, "Toledo Pummels Royals, 74 to 65," *Rochester Democrat and Chronicle*, 1/11/48, p.C1.

21. B. Carlson, "Losing Lakers Next to Worst Offensively," *Minneapolis Star*, 12/18/47, p. 39.

22. Von Nieda interview.

23. "Whitey Von Nieda" in Neil D. Isaacs *Vintage NBA: The Pioneer Era (1946–1956)* (Indianapolis: Masters Press, 1996), p. 52.

24. Von Nieda interview.

25. B. Carlson, "Pollard Cold, Lakers Colder," *Minneapolis Star*, 1/3/48, p. 10.

26. "Pistons Hoping to Bounce Back as Underdogs Tonight," *Fort Wayne News-Sentinel*, 1/13/48, p. 12.

27. B. Tenny, "Pistons Come up With Perfect Game, Whip Royals, 70–56," *Fort Wayne News-Sentinel*, 1/15/48, p. 20.

28. B. Tenny, "Pistons Outlast Jeeps, 54–49, in Listless Game, *Fort Wayne News-Sentinel*, 1/19/48, p. 20.

29. "Pistons Lose Ground in Dropping 79–69 Decision to Tri-Cities; Home Thursday," *Fort Wayne News-Sentinel*, 1/21/48, p. 25.

30. N. Isaacs, *Vintage NBA*, p. 51.

31. B. Carlson, "Three Cage Marks Down, 4 To Go for Mikan," *Minneapolis Star*, 1/19/48, p. 19.

32. B. Carlson, "Lakers Face Extra Tough Rochester," *Minneapolis Star*, 1/22/48, p. 35.

33. B. Carlson, "Carlson Hurt, Lakers Sizzle," *Minneapolis Star*, 1/23/48, p. 25.

34. G. Mikan, with J. Oberle, *Unstoppable*, p. 88.

35. E. Cushing, "It's True, Folks: Royals 53, Minneapolis 50," *Rochester Democrat and Chronicle*, 1/29/48, p. 20.

36. "NBL Coaches Think 3 Seasons Needed to Bring Experience," *Fort Wayne News-Sentinel*, 1/31/48, p. 10.

37. N. Isaacs, *Vintage NBA*, p. 52.

38. R. Triptow, *The Dynasty That Never Was*, p. 230.

39. *Fort Wayne News-Sentinel*, 2/11/48, p. 25.

40. O. Fraley, "Netters of Today Better than Oldsters—Lapchick," *Fort Wayne News-Sentinel*, 2/10/48, p. 12. It should be noted that Lapchick eventually tired of this attitude on the part of players and returned to the coaching ranks at St. John's in 1957.

41. "Czech Reds Imprison 7 Opposition Leaders in Total Power Drive," *Rochester Democrat and Chronicle*, 2/24/48, p. 1.

42. B. Carlson, "Lakers 'Loaf' To New Mark," *Minneapolis Star*, 2/1/48, p. 22.

43. B. Carlson, "Lakers Ask Ousting of 'Piggy' Lambert," *Minneapolis Star*, 2/5/48, p. 33.

44. "Lambert to Quit at End of Season," *Minneapolis Star*, 2/14/48, p. 10.

45. This number, 93, was listed in pre-game publicity and printed in the *Minneapolis Star* of February 18. Later Globetrotter claims were that the Lakers' victory was their 103rd straight win.

46. Mikan, p. 90.

47. Ibid., p. 91.

48. "Last Second Win By Globetrotters Gives 17,823 'Biggest' Thrill," *Chicago Defender*, 2/28/48, p. 11.

49. J. Christgau, *Tricksters in the Madhouse*, 2004.

50. Despite having lost in the playoffs in 1947 to the Chicago Gears, the Royals, as regular season champions, were declared the NBL champs, the league discounting the playoff results for that one and only year. It was something that still had former players Al Cervi, Dick Triptow, Fuzzy Levane and Arnie Risen scratching their heads over fifty years later.

51. "Royals Clout Kautskys, 61 to 46," *Rochester Democrat and Chronicle*, 3/8/48, p. 20.

52. As of mid–March of 1948, the Meat Workers were set to strike, 194,000 coal miners had walked off the job over pension issues and there were threats of strikes at steel and glass factories.

53. "Ready to Accept Presidency, Says McArthur; Truman to Run if Named, He Advises Party," *Rochester Democrat and Chronicle*, 3/9/48, p. 1.

54. "Mikan Gets Auto; Lakers Hike Streak," *Minneapolis Star*, 3/1/48, p. 25.

55. "Mikan Bags Record 42," *Rochester Democrat and Chronicle*, 3/14/48, p.D-6.

56. G. Beahon, "Royals Take Game Lead Over Anderson as Cervi Sets Torrid Pace, 57–50," *Rochester Democrat and Chronicle*, 3/14/48, p. D-1.

57. B. Tenny, "Pistons Hope to Pull Even with Royals Tonight," *Fort Wayne News-Sentinel*, 3/24/48, p. 16; G. Beahon, "Royals Humble Zollners," *Rochester Democrat and Chronicle*, 3/24/48, p. 26.

58. G. Beahon, "Royals Sink Ft. Wayne for 2–1 Lead," *Rochester Democrat and Chronicle*, 3/26/48, p. 35; B. Tenny, "Pistons Drop 64–47 Decision to Royals in Third Playoff Game," *Fort Wayne News-Sentinel*, 3/26/48, p. 31.

59. B. Tenny, "Pistons Sidelined By Royals' Balance, Contemplate Tourney," *Fort Wayne News-Sentinel*, 3/29/48, p. 12.

60. "Englund's 2d-Half Spurt Whips Lakers for Stars," *Rochester Democrat and Chronicle*, 3/27/48, p. 31; "Minneapolis Annexes Oshkosh Series, 3–1," *Rochester Democrat and Chronicle*, 3/28/48, p. B-5.

61. "Lakers Win, 83–59; Two Hawks Injured," *Rochester Democrat and Chronicle*, 4/1/48, p. 24; B. Carlson, "'Spot' Jaros Sparks Lakers," *Minneapolis Star*, 4/1/48, p. 33.

62. G. Beahon, "Royals Subdue Anderson 71–66, to Capture Lead in Series; Davies Sparkles," *Rochester Democrat and Chronicle*, 3/31/48, p. 22.

63. "Todorovich Top NBL Rookie," *Rochester Democrat and Chronicle*, 4/2/48, p. 34.

64. G. Beahon, "Royals Pummel Packers, 74–58," *Rochester Democrat and Chronicle*, 4/4/48, p. D-1.

65. G. Beahon, "Royals Open at Minneapolis Apr. 13 In Final Playoffs; Risen May Play," *Rochester Democrat and Chronicle*, 4/5/48, p. 20.

66. E. Cushing, "Sports Eye View," *Rochester Democrat and Chronicle*, 4/5/48, p. 20.

67. Ibid.

68. "NBL Studies Entry Bids of 7 Cities," *Rochester Democrat and Chronicle*, 4/9/48, p. 32.

69. B. Carlson, "Lambert Out: Roan Possible as NBL Boss," *Minneapolis Star*, 4/6/48, p. 22.

70. B. Carlson, "Rumors Fly as Lakers Open Play" *Minneapolis Star*, 4/8/48, p. 33; C. Johnson, "Charlie Johnson's Lowdown on Sports," *Minneapolis Star*, 4/8/48, p. 33.

71. "NBL, BAA Heads Talk Merger Possibilities," *Fort Wayne News-Sentinel*, 4/8/48, p. 18.

72. "Lakers Miss Last Chance to Score 100," *Minneapolis Star*, 4/9/48, p. 32; B. Tenny, "Mac's Hawks Oust Pistons by 57–50,"*Fort Wayne News-Sentinel*, 4/9/48, p. 33.

73. "First World Title for City in Laker Grasp," *Minneapolis Star*, 4/10/48, p. 10.

74. M. Kurlansky, "Royals Clip All-Stars in Exhibition, 72–61," *Rochester Democrat and Chronicle*, 4/11/48, p. D-1; G. Beahon, "Royals Win 74–64, Injured Risen Seen Lost for Title Series," *Rochester Democrat and Chronicle*, 4/12/48, p. 21.

75. B. Carlson, "Lakers 'World Champions' Now," *Minneapolis Star*, 4/12/48, p. 23; "Lakers Win Tourney, 75–71," *Rochester Democrat and Chronicle*, 4/12/48, p. 21.

76. B. Carlson, "Lakers Trump Voids Rochester Cage Aces," *Minneapolis Star*, 4/14/48, p. 45. "Lakers Defeat Royals 'Shock Troops.' 80–72," *Rochester Democrat and Chronicle*, 4/14/48, p. 22.

77. G. Beahon, "Crippled Royals Again Bow to Late Laker Drive, 82–67," *Rochester Democrat and Chronicle*, 4/15/48, p. 24; B. Carlson, "Lakers Near NBL Crown," *Minneapolis Star*, 4/15/48, p. 37.

78. G. Beahon, "One for Our Side: Royals 74, Minneapolis 60," *Rochester Democrat and Chronicle*, 4/17/48, p. 8; "Rookie Foils Laker Hopes," *Minneapolis Star*, 4/17/48, p. 10.

79. "Lakers beat Royals for Title," *Rochester Democrat and Chronicle*, 4/18/48, p. D-1; B. Carlson, "Mikan May Coach Lakers," *Minneapolis Star*, 4/14/48, p. 23.

80. "NBL Threatens All Out War Against BAA," *Chicago Tribune*, 5/12/48, pt. 3, p. 1.

81. R. Nelson, *The Zollner Piston Story*, p. 158.

82. R. Peterson, *Cages to Jump Shots*, p. 164.

Chapter 12

1. *Official National Basketball League Pro Magazine, 1949 Edition* (West Liberty, Iowa: Liberty Publishing, 1949), p. 32.

2. For a fuller discussion of Denver and the AAU see A. Grundman, *The Golden Age of Amateur Basketball* (Lincoln: University of Nebraska Press, 2004).

3. Dolph Schayes, telephone interview, 2/1/05.

4. Schayes interview.

5. Von Nieda interview, 3/17/05.

6. *Official National Basketball League Pro Magazine*, p. 15.

7. See T. Gould, p. 159, for fuller details on this.

8. *Official National Basketball League Pro Magazine*, p. 12.

9. Schayes interview.

10. *Oshkosh Daily Northwestern*, 12/18/48, p. 13.

11. S. Rayl, "The New York Renaissance Professional Black Basketball Team, 1923–1950."

12. "Rens to Represent Dayton in National Court League," *Philadelphia Inquirer*, 12/18/48, p. 19.

13. B. Garlikov, "Dayton Finally Lands Franchise in National Pro Cage Loop," *Dayton Daily News*, 12/18/48, p. 8.

14. "Rens Join Pro Group," *Chicago Defender*, 12/25/48, p. 15.

15. F. Young, "Fay Says," *Chicago Defender*, 4/2/49, p. 14.

16. D. Ramsey, *The Nats*, p. 4.

17. Al Cervi, telephone interview, May 20, 2004.

18. "Moore Raps B.A.A. Curb on Salaries," *Chicago Tribune*, 11/5/48, pt. 3, p. 3.

19. "Podoloff Asking Talks with Duffey," *Oshkosh Daily Northwestern*, 10/29/48, p. 13.

20. "Good Luck All Stars," full page advertisement in *Oshkosh Daily Northwestern*, 10/29/48, p. 5.

21. C. Jordan, "Physical Ability No Handicap in Udall's Bright Success Story," *Denver Post*, 11/2/48, p. 25.

22. The *Chicago Tribune* reported 4,000 in its November 4 edition (pt. 4, p. 1) while the *Denver Post* reported 5,600 in its November 4 edition, p. 26.

23. "Hawks Beat Hawks," *Denver Post*, 11/17/48, p. 35.

24. "7536 See Waterloo Nip Tri-Cities, 61–59," *Denver Post*, 11/29/48, p. 25.

25. "Darling Gives Up as Coach After All Stars Lose," *Oshkosh Daily Northwestern*, 12/1/48, p. 20.

26. "Nats 53, Sheboygan 45," *Oshkosh Daily Northwestern*, 11/15/48, p. 12.

27. "Hammond Wins, 71–65,"*Denver Post*, 11/29/48, p. 25.

28. "Lakers Rap Stars, 60 to 42," *Denver Post*, 11/27/48, p. 9.

29. B. Garlikov, "Dayton Starts Cage 'Renaissance' Against Anderson Today," *Dayton Daily News*, 12/19/48, Sports, p. 3.

30. B. Garlikov, "Only 397 See Dayton Debut in Cage Loop," *Dayton Daily News*, 12/20/48, p. 23.

31. "Confident Nugs Ready for Oshkosh Tonight," *Denver Post*, 11/15/48, p. 24.

32. "Nugs Drop 8th in Row," *Denver Post*, 11/16/48, p. 27.

33. C. Jordan, "Nuggets Celebrate First Pro Cage Win," *Denver Post*, 11/25/48, p. 39.

34. "Syracuse Loses By Nod," *Denver Post*, 12/20/48, p. 20.

35. Nugs Overcome Nats' Fists, Tears to Win Fourth Straight, 60–54," *Denver Post*, 12/22/48, p. 30.

36. D. Ramsey, *The Nats*, p. 6.

37. C. Jordan, "Fist-Throwing Syracuse Cager Suspended for Season by NBL," *Denver Post*, 12/22/48, p. 37; J. Carberry, "The Second Guess," *Denver Post*, 12/22/48, p. 37.

38. C. Jordan, "Only One Fight Marks Nat Win As Nuggets Fail to Halt Schayes," *Denver Post*, 12/23/48, p. 12.

39. "Rens Win First," *Denver Post*, 12/23/48, p. 12; "Waterloo Wins, 50–45," *Denver Post*, 12/23/48, p. 12.

40. "First Defeat at Home," *Denver Post*, 12/27/48, p. 16.

41. "Bob Carpenter Resigns Post as Manager of Bucs," *Oshkosh Daily Northwestern*, 1/5/49, p. 15.

42. "Oshkosh Stars Request Waiver on Eddie Dancker," *Oshkosh Daily Northwestern*, 1/6/49, p. 21.

43. "Stars Lose Tilt at Charity Line, To Meet Bucs Here," *Oshkosh Daily Northwestern*, 1/7/49, p. 11.

44. "Jerry Rizzo Joins N.Y. State League," *Denver Post*, 1/3/49, p. 17.

45. "Syracuse Wins," *Denver Post*, 1/28/49, p. 27.

46. "Syracuse Triumphs," *Denver Post*, 1/31/49, p. 17.

47. "Syracuse Victor," *Denver Post*, 1/18/49, p. 26.

48. J. Carberry, "The Second Guess," *Denver Post*, 2/2/49, p. 28.

49. "2 Indiana Clubs Said Returning to National Pro Loop," *Dayton Daily News*, 1/25/49, p. 20.

50. J. Carberry, "The Second Guess," *Denver Post*, 2/11/49, p. 28.

51. J. Carberry, "The Second Guess," *Denver Post*, 2/18/49, p. 29.

52. "Rumors Persist Oshkosh May Lose All Stars," *Oshkosh Daily Northwestern*, 2/26/49, p. 9.

53. "BAA Denies NBL Claim that Help Wanted Sign is Up," *Oshkosh Daily Northwestern*, 3/2/49, p. 15.

54. "Darling Replies to Podoloff," *Oshkosh Daily Northwestern*, 3/3/49, p. 24.

55. "Release Eddie Riska from All Stars Squad," *Oshkosh Daily Northwestern*, 2/10/49, p. 25.

56. "Nuggets Sell Hoot Gibson to Tri-Cities," *Denver Post*, 2/11/49, p. 29.

57. R. Meyer, *The First Mr. Basketball: The Legend of Bobby McDermott*, p. 29.

58. "Easy Ed to Join NBL," *Oshkosh Daily Northwestern*, 2/23/49, p. 14.

59. "All Stars Corral Share of Honors in Year's NBL Selections," *Oshkosh Daily Northwestern*, 3/25/49, p. 12.

60. "Tri-Cities, Oshkosh to Clash for Western Playoff Championship," *Oshkosh Daily Northwestern*, 4/4/49, p. 15.

61. "Oshkosh Nips Hawks in Playoff Bow, 68–66," *Oshkosh Daily Northwestern*, 4/7/49, p. 46.

62. "Oshkosh Whips Tri-Cities Again," *Denver Post*, 4/10/49, p. 2E.

63. "Oshkosh Wins Western Division Championship," *Oshkosh Daily Northwestern*, 4/13/49, p. 24; "All Stars Cop Western NBL Playoff Title," *Denver Post*, 4/13/49, p. 34.

64. "Packers Trim Nats in First Playoff Test," *Denver Post*, 4/9/49, p. 11.

65. "N.B.L. Eastern Division Teams Resume Playoff," *Denver Post*, 4/11/49, p. 20.

66. "Stars to Try Tonight to Nail Western Flag," *Oshkosh Daily Northwestern*, 4/12/49, p. 17; "Stars to Meet Packers in Championship Playoffs," *Oshkosh Daily Northwestern*, 4/14/49, p. 26; "Packers Win, Face Oshkosh for '49 Title," *Denver Post*, 4/13/49, p. 34.

67. "All Stars Face Herculean Task in NBL Title Series," *Oshkosh Daily Northwestern*, 4/18/49, p. 13.

68. G. Mikan, and J. Oberle, *Unstoppable: The Story of George Mikan*.

69. "Anderson Takes Crown in NBL with Third Win Over Stars in Playoff," *Oshkosh Daily Northwestern*, 4/19/49, p. 15.

70. Quoted in T. Gould, *Pioneers of the Hardwood*, p. 162.

71. "3 Pro Basketball Players Sue Indianapolis Jets for Back Wages," *Chicago Tribune*, 5/21/49, pt. 2, p. 2.

72. "Indy Jets in Receivership," *Oshkosh Daily Northwestern*, 4/8/49, p. 11; R. Peterson, *From Cages To Jump Shots*, p. 167.

73. Quoted in T. Gould, p. 163.

74. R. Peterson, *Cages to Jump Shots*, p. 167.

75. T. Gould, p. 163.

76. "Pro Basketball Rivals May Merge Today," *Chicago Tribune*, 8/3/49, pt. 3, p. 2.

77. N. Miller, "Podoloff Plans to Keep Rivalries," *Philadelphia Inquirer*, 8/5/49, p. 31; "BAA and NBL Merge, Form 18-Team League," *Philadelphia Inquirer*, 8/4/49, p. 28; "Pro Basketball Leagues Merge," *Chicago Tribune*, 8/4/49, pt. 3, p. 1.

78. "Pro Court Teams Toss For Players," *Philadelphia Inquirer*, 8/12/49, p. 29.

79. L. Koppett, (1968) *24 Seconds to Shoot*, pp. 40–42.

80. *National Basketball Association, 1949–50 Record Book* (Minneapolis: Athletic Publications, 1949), p. 4.

Chapter 13

1. R. Peterson, p. 145.

Bibliography

Books/Periodicals

Christgau, John. *Tricksters in the Madhouse: Lakers vs. Globetrotters, 1948*. Lincoln: University of Nebraska Press, 2004.

Dickey, Glenn. *The History of Professional Basketball Since 1896*. New York: Stein and Day, 1982.

Gould, Todd. *Pioneers of the Hardwood*. Bloomington: Indiana University Press, 1998.

Grundman, Adolph H. *The Golden Age of Amateur Basketball*. Lincoln: University of Nebraska Press, 2004.

Guttmann, Allen. *Sports Spectators*. New York: Columbia University Press, 1986.

Isaacs, Neil D. *Vintage NBA: The Pioneer Era (1946–1956)*. Indianapolis: Masters Press, 1996.

Koppett, Leonard. *24 Seconds to Shoot: The Birth and Improbable Rise of the NBA*. New York: Macmillan, 1968.

Levine, Peter. *Ellis Island to Ebbets Field: Sport and the American Jewish Experience*. New York: Oxford University Press, 1992.

Lynd, Robert S., and Helen M. Lynd. *Middletown: A Study in Contemporary American Culture*. New York: Harcourt Brace, 1929.

_____. *Middletown in Transition*. New York: Harcourt Brace, 1937.

Marcus, Jeff. *A Biographical Directory of Professional Basketball Coaches*. Lanham, MD: Scarecrow Press, 2003.

Meyer, R. *The First Mr. Basketball: The Legend of Bobby McDermott*. Roxboro, MA: self-published, 2000.

Mikan, George, and Joseph Oberle. *Unstoppable: The Story of George Mikan*. Indianapolis: Masters Press, 1997.

National Basketball Association Record Book. Minneapolis, MN: Athletic Publications, 1949.

National Professional Basketball League. *Official National Pro Basketball League Magazine*. West Liberty, IA: NPBL, 1949.

Neft, David, Roland Johnson, Richard Cohen, and Jordan Deutsch. *The Sports Encyclopedia: Pro Basketball*. New York: Grosset and Dunlap, 1975.

Nelson, Murry. *The Originals: The New York Celtics Invent Modern Basketball*. Bowling Green, OH: Bowling Green State University Popular Press, 1999.

Nelson, Rodger. *The Zollner Piston Story*. Fort Wayne, IN: Allen County Public Library Foundation, 1995.

Oshkosh All Stars. *Souvenir Program, 1937–1938*. Oshkosh, WI: Oshkosh All Stars, 1937.

Peterson, Robert W. *Cages to Jump Shots: Pro Basketball's Early Years*. Lincoln: University of Nebraska Press, 2002.

Ramsey, David. *The Nats*. Utica, NY: North Country Books, 1996.

The Reach Official Basketball Guide. Philadelphia: A.J. Reach, 1922–1927.

Rumlow, Wayne O. *The Oshkosh All Stars and the NBL*. Self-published, 1979.

Schleppi, John. *Chicago's Showcase of Basketball: The World Professional Tournament of Professional Basketball and the College All-Star Game*. Haworth, NJ: St. Johann Press, 2008.

Schumacher, Michael. *Mr. Basketball: George Mikan, the Minneapolis Lakers and the Birth of the NBA*. New York: Bloomsbury, 2007.

Shouler, Ken, Bob Ryan, Sam Smith, Leonard Koppett, and Bob Bellotti. *Total Basketball: The Ultimate Basketball Encyclopedia.* Wilmington, DE: Sport Classic Press, 2003.

Smith, Seymour, Jack Rimer, and Richard Triptow. *A Tribute to Armed Forces Basketball.* Lake Bluff, IL: self-published, 2003.

Strasser, Myles. "All Stars Enter Wacky, Shaky World." *Oshkosh All Stars.* Oshkosh, WI: Oshkosh Daily Northwestern, 1979.

_____. "Lonnie Darling: Dream Chaser." *Oshkosh All Stars,* Oshkosh, WI: Oshkosh Daily Northwestern, 1979.

Thomas, Ron. *They Cleared the Lane.* Lincoln: University of Nebraska Press, 2002.

Triptow, Richard. *The Dynasty That Never Was.* Lake Bluff, IL: self-published, 1997.

Wooden, John R., with Jack Tobin. *They Call Me Coach.* New York: Bantam Books, 1973.

Newspaper Articles

"Akron Firestones Sweep Kautsky Quintet in National League Contest." *Indianapolis Star,* 2/21/39, p. 13.

"Al Cervi Returns; Royals Obtain Mahnken, Nagretti." *Rochester Democrat and Chronicle,* 11/18/45, p. C-3.

"All Factory Basketball Tourney Huge Success." *Firestone Non-Skid,* vol. 20, no. 6, 4/1/35, p. 1.

"All Stars Advance to Semifinals in Tourney." *Oshkosh Daily Northwestern,* 3/18/41, p. 13.

"All Stars Atone for Sunday's Loss with 56–41 Win." *Oshkosh Daily Northwestern,* 3/7/39, p. 13.

"All Stars Avenge Loss by Beating Rens by 47 to 35." *Oshkosh Daily Northwestern,* 12/3/41, p. 14.

"All Stars Battle Whiting Tonight in Final Contest." *Oshkosh Daily Northwestern,* 3/26/38, p. 13.

"All Stars Beat Celtics: Play at Bay Tonight." *Oshkosh Daily Northwestern,* 12/23/37, p. 13.

"All Stars Beat Chicago Duffy Florals Twice." *Oshkosh Daily Northwestern,* 1/17/38, p. 12.

"All Stars Beat Globe Trotters by 44–30 Score." *Oshkosh Daily Northwestern,* 11/18/38, p. 19.

"All Stars Beat Kautskys." *Oshkosh Daily Northwestern,* 1/15/41, p. 13.

"All Stars Beaten by Warren, 38–37, in Overtime Game." *Oshkosh Daily Northwestern,* 12/5/38, p. 13.

"All Stars Cop Western NBL Playoff Title." *Denver Post,* 4/13/49, p. 34.

"All Stars Corral Share of Honors in Year's NBL Selections." *Oshkosh Daily Northwestern,* 3/25/49, p. 12.

"All Stars Defeat Chicago Bruins by 61 to 43." *Oshkosh Daily Northwestern,* 2/2/42, p. 12.

"All Stars Defeat Dayton in Initial National Loop Tilt." *Oshkosh Daily Northwestern,* 1/3/38, p. 13.

"All Stars Defeat Famed New York Rens Again." *Oshkosh Daily Northwestern,* 3/11/38, p. 18.

"All Stars Defeat Firestones by 30 to 28." *Oshkosh Daily Northwestern,* 3/5/41, p. 13.

"All Stars Defeat Goodyear, to Play Rens Here." *Oshkosh Daily Northwestern,* 3/4/38, p. 17.

"All Stars Defeat Indianapolis Two Straight." *Oshkosh Daily Northwestern,* 3/2/42, p. 12.

"All Stars Defeat Redskins in Overtime Game." *Oshkosh Daily Northwestern,* 1/2/43, p. 11.

"All Stars Defeat Sheboygan, Lose to Whiting" *Oshkosh Daily Northwestern,* 2/7/38, p. 13.

"All Stars Defeat Whiting, Badger Collegians." *Oshkosh Daily Northwestern,* 3/28/38, p. 12.

"All Stars Down Detroit, Premeet Favorites." *Oshkosh Daily Northwestern,* 3/15/43, p. 11.

"All Stars Drop League Game to Whiting Five." *Oshkosh Daily Northwestern,* 1/11/38, p. 12.

"All Stars Eliminate Firestones, 47 to 41." *Oshkosh Daily Northwestern,* 3/7/41, p. 17.

"All Stars Face Herculean Task in NBL Title Series." *Oshkosh Daily Northwestern,* 4/18/49, p. 13.

"All Stars Have "Off" Night and Lose by 42 to 30." *Oshkosh Northwestern,* 11/25/38, p. 19.

"All Stars Increase League Lead to Two Games." *Oshkosh Daily Northwestern,* 1/4/43, p. 11.

"All Stars Join National Basketball League." *Oshkosh Daily Northwestern,* 12/8/37, p. 15.

"All Stars Lift Lid in Basketball in Turkey Day Test." *Oshkosh Daily Northwestern,* 11/24/37, p. 13.

"All Stars Lose Opener." *Oshkosh Daily Northwestern,* 3/1/38, p. 12.

"All Stars Lose the Crown." *Oshkosh Daily Northwestern,* 3/5/38, p. 13.

"All Stars Lose Thriller to Akron, Beat Hammond." *Oshkosh Daily Northwestern,* 1/16/-39, p. 11.

"All Stars Lose to Celtics at Bay by 44–39

Score." *Oshkosh Daily Northwestern*, 12/24/37, p. 17.

"All Stars Need Win Tonight to Clinch Crown." *Oshkosh Daily Northwestern*, 3/12/41, p. 13.

"All Stars Open with Game Saturday" *Oshkosh Daily Northwestern*, 11/6/42, p. 13.

"All Stars 'Pour it on' Kankakee Gallaghers." *Oshkosh Daily Northwestern*, 1/5/38, p. 13.

"All Stars Prove Packers' Master in the Cage Sport." *Oshkosh Daily Northwestern*, 2/13/39, p. 13.

"All Stars Repeat as National Loop Champs." *Oshkosh Daily Northwestern*, 3/7/42, p. 13.

"All Stars Return After Win Over Goodyears, 42–35." *Oshkosh Daily Northwestern*, 12/22/41, p. 21.

"All Stars Seek Second World's Title Tonight." *Oshkosh Daily Northwestern*, 3/17/43, p. 13.

"All Stars Skyrocket Back Into First Place." *Oshkosh Daily Northwestern.* 12/24/38, p. 17.

"All Stars Snow Under Fort Wayne by 72 to 47." *Oshkosh Daily Northwestern*, 2/16/42, p. 11.

"All Stars Split Even in Two League Games." *Oshkosh Daily Northwestern*, 12/7/42, p. 13.

"All Stars Split Two-Game Series with Rens." *Oshkosh Daily Northwestern*, 12/19/38, p. 17.

"All Stars Take Lead in National Cage League." *Oshkosh Daily Northwestern*, 1/31/38, p. 12.

"All Stars Trounce Akron Firestones, 37–19" *Oshkosh Daily Northwestern*, 11/23/38, p. 13.

"All Stars Win at Madison." *Oshkosh Daily Northwestern*, 12/12/38, p. 13.

"All Stars Win Ninth Straight Loop Victory." *Oshkosh Daily Northwestern*, 1/7/42, p. 13.

"All Stars Win Opener." *Oshkosh Daily Northwestern*, 3/12/40, p. 19

All Stars Win Opening National League Game." *Oshkosh Daily Northwestern*, 11/28/40, p. 19.

"All Stars Win Over Zollner Five." *Chicago Tribune*, 11/30/46, p. 17.

"All Stars Win Second Game by 60–46." *Oshkosh Daily Northwestern*, 3/13/40, p. 13.

"All Stars Win the Opener in Playoff Series." *Oshkosh Daily Northwestern*, 3/8/40, p. 15.

"All Stars Win Two...." *Oshkosh Daily Northwestern*, 1/10/38, p. 12.

"All Stars, Zollners Play for Title Tonight." *Oshkosh Daily Northwestern*, 3/6/42, p. 12.

"All Wisconsin Pro Finals Will Open Tonight." *Oshkosh Daily Northwestern*, 3/10/41, p. 14.

"American Gear Five Loses 2d in Row, 71 to 43." *Chicago Tribune*, 1/14/46, p. 24.

"American Gears Beaten, 63 to 32, at Rochester." *Chicago Tribune*, 1/13/46, pt. 2, p. 4.

"American Gears Five Defeats Pittsburgh, 62–60." *Chicago Tribune*, 2/1/45, p. 21.

"Anderson Takes Crown in NBL with Third Win Over Stars in Playoff." *Oshkosh Daily Northwestern*, 4/19/49, p. 15.

"BAA and NBL Merge, Form 18-Team League." *Philadelphia Inquirer*, 8/4/49, p. 28

"BAA Denies NBL Claim That Help Wanted Sign Is Up." *Oshkosh Daily Northwestern*, 3/2/49, p. 15.

"Ban Manager But Gear Five Wins, 60 to 54." *Chicago Tribune*, 3/28/47, p. 31.

Barry, H. "Bruins' Closing Rush Wins Over Oshkosh." *Chicago Tribune*, 1/23/41, p. 17.

Bartlett, Charles. "Bruin Quintet Wins, 28 to 19, Over Oshkosh." *Chicago Tribune*, 12/7/39, p. 28.

_____."Bruins Battle Akron; Bid for Pro League Lead." *Chicago Tribune*, 2/7/40, p. 25.

_____. "Bruins Beat Firestones by a Novak, 31–29." *Chicago Tribune*, 12/21/39, p. 29.

_____. "Bruins Lead All the Way, Defeat Akron." *Chicago Tribune*, 1/4/40, p. 20.

_____. "Bruins Seek to Handle Oshkosh Tomorrow Night." *Chicago Tribune*, 1/30/40, p. 19.

_____. "Bruins to Start Pro Basketball Season Tonight." *Chicago Tribune*, 12/6/39, p. 36.

_____. "Bruins Trounce Akron, 44–36 in Opening Game." *Chicago Tribune*, 12/19/40, p. 27.

_____. "Bruins Victors 50 to 34: Stay in Pro Title Race." *Chicago Tribune*, 3/2/40, pt. 2, p. 2.

_____. "Bruins Wallop Oshkosh 38–33, Take First Place." *Chicago Tribune*, 2/1/40, p. 30.

_____. "Bruins Whip Eagles, 34–24; Kautz Stars." *Chicago Tribune*, 12/14/39, p. 35.

_____. "Crippled Royals Again Bow to Late Laker Drive, 82–67." *Rochester Democrat and Chronicle*, 4/15/48, p. 24.

_____. "Firestone Five Triumphs Over Bruins, 39–33." *Chicago Tribune*, 2/8/40, p. 25.

_____. "Oshkosh Whips Bruins, 42 to 29 for 5th in Row." *Chicago Tribune*, 12/18/41, p. 33.

_____. "Sheboygan Five Rallies to Beat Bruins, 20 to 19." *Chicago Tribune*, 1/8/40, p. 19.

_____. "Zollners Beat Bruins, 47–38; 500 at Game." *Chicago Tribune*, 12/26/41, p. 18.

Beahon, G. "Cagers' Corner." *Rochester Democrat and Chronicle*, 1/16/46, p. 18, 2/5/46, p. 18.

_____. "Gears Turn Back Royals, 78 to 70." *Rochester Democrat and Chronicle*, 4/8/47, p. 23.

_____. "One for Our Side: Royals 74, Minneapolis 60." *Rochester Democrat and Chronicle*, 4/17/48, p. 8.

_____. "Royal Rally Nips Zollners in Overtime Thriller, 65–62, Bags 11th Arena Victory." *Rochester Democrat and Chronicle*, 12/21/47, p. C-1.

_____. "Royals Capture 7th, 72–55." *Rochester Democrat and Chronicle*, 12/16/45, p. C-1.

_____. "Royals Humble Zollners." *Rochester Democrat and Chronicle*, 3/24/48, p. 26.

_____. "Royals Open at Minneapolis Apr.13 in Final Playoffs; Risen May Play." *Rochester Democrat and Chronicle*, 4/5/48, p. 20.

_____. "Royals Pummel Packers, 74–58." *Rochester Democrat and Chronicle*, 4/4/48, p. D-1.

_____. "Royals Sink Ft. Wayne for 2–1 Lead." *Rochester Democrat and Chronicle*, 3/26/48, p. 35.

_____. "Royals Spurt to Top Bears, 58–50." *Rochester Democrat and Chronicle*, 1/15/46, p. 18.

_____. "Royals Subdue Anderson 71–66, to Capture Lead in Series; Davies Sparkles." *Rochester Democrat and Chronicle*, 3/31/48, p. 22.

_____. "Royals Take Game Lead Over Anderson as Cervi Sets Torrid Pace, 57–50." *Rochester Democrat and Chronicle*, 3/14/48, p. D-1.

_____. "Royals Win 74–64, Injured Risen Seen Lost for Title Series." *Rochester Democrat and Chronicle*, 4/12/48, p. 21.

_____. "Toledo Pummels Royals, 74 to 65." *Rochester Democrat and Chronicle*, 1/11/48, p. C-1.

"Bears, Bell's Sniping Too Much for Piston Cagers Beaten Out by World's Champs." *Fort Wayne News-Sentinel*, 12/7/43, p. 11.

"Bears Nose Pistons in 51–49 Clash." *Fort Wayne News-Sentinel*, 12/10/43, p. 30.

"Bears Upset Pistons in 60–57 Clash." *Fort Wayne News-Sentinel*, 2/1/46, p. 24.

"Birr Team Wins, Kautskys Beaten." *Indianapolis Star*, 1/29/40, p. 15.

"Blackhawks Drop Tough Battle to Fort Wayne." *Moline Daily Dispatch*, 1/4/47, p. 10.

"Blackhawks Win, 48–43." *Moline Daily Dispatch*, 1/13/47, p. 12.

"Bob Carpenter Resigns Post as Manager of Bucs." *Oshkosh Daily Northwestern*, 1/5/49, p. 15.

"Bob McDermott Given Outright Release." *Fort Wayne News-Sentinel*, 1/1/47, p. 27.

"Bob McDermott Signs as Player-Coach of Gear Five," *Chicago Tribune*, 1/3/47, p. 22.

"Bruin Defeats End at 7; Beat Toledo 53 to 31." *Oshkosh Daily Northwestern*, 1/15/42, p. 23.

"Bruins Call Off Home Opener — No Place to Play." *Chicago Tribune*, 12/9/41, p. 27.

"Bruins' Deadly Aim Triumphs in Rally, 27–20." *Chicago Tribune*, 12/20/40, p. 31.

"Bruins Lose to Fort Wayne in 2d Half, 48 to 46." *Chicago Tribune*, 12/2/41, p. 24.

"Bruins Put Out of Tourney By Toledo, 43 to 33." *Chicago Tribune*, 3/18/41, p. 20.

"Bruins Rally, Whip Fort Wayne Quintet, 51 to 47." *Chicago Tribune*, 1/22/42, p. 20.

"Bruins Stop Stars in Chicago Game by 34 to 32 Score." *Oshkosh Daily Northwestern*, 1/23/41, p. 19.

"Bruins Swamp Davenport Five in Tourney, Before 8500 at International "Amphitheatre Pro Tourney, 53–17." *Chicago Tribune*, 3/16/41, pt. 2, p. 3.

"Bruins Trounce Eagles, 36–28, as Kautz Stars." *Chicago Tribune*, 1/18/40, p. 23.

"Bruins Whip Sheboygan in Noisy Battle." *Chicago Tribune*, 2/22/40, p. 27.

"Bruins Win Game with Fast Finish." *Oshkosh Daily Northwestern*, 12/5/41, p. 19.

"Bruins Win in Overtime; Rens Lose to Harlem." *Chicago Tribune*, 3/19/40, p. 25.

"Bruins Win 3rd in Row; Defeat Ciesars, 27–18." *Chicago Tribune*, 2/27/41, p. 19.

"Buffalo Pro Cagers Consider Move to Moline." *Moline Daily Dispatch*, 12/18/46, p. 30.

"Bulletin." *Fort Wayne News-Sentinel*, 12/21/46, p. 10.

Butler, E. "Firestone Scores 40–34 Win Over Chicago Team." *Akron Beacon Journal*, 12/30/36, p. 17.

_____. "Goodyear Comes from Far Back to Beat Firestone, Capture Series." *Akron Beacon Journal*, 2/26/38, p. 15.

_____. "Nonskids Battle Deans in Wednesday Headliner." *Akron Beacon Journal*, 3/3/36, p. 22.

_____. "Skids Top Chicago 46–27; Gain National League Playoffs." *Akron Beacon Journal*, 3/1/41, p. 10.

_____. "Wingfoots' Second-Half Offensive Defeats Celtics, 38–36." *Akron Beacon Journal*, 12/5/41, p. 42.

_____. "Wings Beat Chicagoans." *Akron Beacon Journal*, 1/5/37, p. 17.

Carberry, J. "The Second Guess, *Denver Post*,

12/22/48, p. 37, 2/2/49, p. 28, 2/11/49, p. 28, 2/18/49, p. 29.

Carlson, B. "Carlson Hurt, Lakers Sizzle." *Minneapolis Star*, 1/23/48, p. 25.

_____. "Laker Defense Tops." *Minneapolis Star*, 12/10/47, p. 47.

_____. "Lakers Ask Ousting of "Piggy" Lambert." *Minneapolis Star*, 2/5/48, p. 33.

_____. "Lakers Face Extra Tough Rochester." *Minneapolis Star*, 1/22/48, p. 35.

_____. "Lakers 'Loaf' to New Mark." *Minneapolis Star*, 2/1/48, p. 22.

_____. "Lakers Near NBL Crown." *Minneapolis Star*, 4/15/48, p. 37.

_____. "Lakers Sign Up Schaefer; Smith May Not Make Trip." *Minneapolis Star*, 11/25/47, p. 21.

_____. "Lakers Trump Voids Rochester Cage Aces." *Minneapolis Star*, 4/14/48, p. 45.

_____. "Lakers 'World Champions' Now." *Minneapolis Star*, 4/12/48, p. 23.

_____. "Lambert Out: Roan Possible as NBL Boss." *Minneapolis Star*, 4/6/48, p. 22.

_____. "Losing Lakers Next to Worst Offensively." *Minneapolis Star*, 12/18/47, p. 39.

_____. "Matson Joins Local Pro Five." *Minneapolis Star*, 10/6/47, p. 22.

_____. "Mikan May Coach Lakers." *Minneapolis Star*, 4/14/48, p. 23.

_____. "Mikan on Laker List as Rival Loop Folds." *Minneapolis Star*, 11/13/47, p. 39.

_____. "Pollard Cold, Lakers Colder." *Minneapolis Star*, 1/3/48, p. 10.

_____. "Rumors Fly as Lakers Open Play" *Minneapolis Star*, 4/8/48, p. 33.

_____. "'Spot' Jaros Sparks Lakers." *Minneapolis Star*, 4/1/48, p. 33.

_____. "Three Cage Marks Down, 4 to Go for Mikan." *Minneapolis Star*, 1/19/48, p. 19.

"Carpenter and Glamack Lead." *Fort Wayne News-Sentinel*, 12/13/45, p. 31.

"Celtics Rap Rens by 36–33 Margin." *Indianapolis Star*. 2/28/39, p. 12.

"Celts Bow to Stars, Zollners Here Saturday." *Oshkosh Daily Northwestern*, 2/13/42, p. 15.

"Chanute Over Rens in Cicero, 39–37, in OT." *Chicago Tribune*, 2/14/42, p. 24.

"Chase Lose to Sheboygan, 46–45." *Cleveland Plain Dealer*, 2/7/44, p. 12.

"Chicago Bruins Beaten, 38 to 31, by Indianapolis." *Chicago Tribune*, 12/22/41, p. 25.

"Chicago Bruins Record 44–36 League Win Over Nonskid Foe." *Akron Beacon Journal*, 12/19/40, p. 40.

"Chicago Buys Connie Berry." *Fort Wayne News-Sentinel*, 12/29/44, p. 11.

"Chicago Five Bows to Oshkosh by 44 to 33 Score." *Oshkosh Daily Northwestern*, 12/28/42, p. 13.

"Chicago Five Wins Conference Crown." *Indianapolis Star*, 3/23/36, p. 13.

"Chicago Five Wins Title in Midwest." *Akron Beacon Journal*, 3/24/36, p. 26.

"Chicago Gains Upset Over Oshkosh." *Rochester Democrat and Chronicle*, 11/26/45, p. 24.

"Chicago Gears Lose, 53 to 49, in League Opener." *Chicago Tribune*, 11/23/45, p. 31.

"Chicago Is New Member of National Basketball League." *Oshkosh Daily Northwestern*, 6/5/39, p. 14.

"Chuckovitz Sets Scoring Mark, but 'Skins Beat Toledo." *Oshkosh Daily Northwestern*, 2/13/42, p. 15.

"Cleveland Conquers Indianapolis, 51 to 44." *Rochester Democrat and Chronicle*, 11/26/45, p. 24.

"Clifton 'Lefty' Byers Appointed Goodyear Basketball Team Coach." *The Wingfoot Clan*, vol. 25, no. 45, 12/16/36, p. 6.

"Closing Rush of Rens Beat All Stars, 65–60." *Oshkosh Daily Northwestern*, 4/4/47, p. 13.

"College Stars Lose, 63 to 55." *Chicago Tribune*, 12/1/45, p. 17.

"College Stars Rally to Beat Oshkosh, 61–55." *Chicago Tribune*, 11/28/42, p. 19.

"Conference Rules Add Zest to Game." *The Wingfoot Clan*, vol. 25, no.46, 12/23/36, p. 7.

"Confident Nugs Ready for Oshkosh Tonight." *Denver Post*, 11/15/48, p. 24.

Cushing, E. "It's True, Folks: Royals 53, Minneapolis 50." *Rochester Democrat and Chronicle*, 1/29/48, p. 20.

_____. "Royals Humble Sheboygan in Opener." *Rochester Democrat and Chronicle*, 3/20/46, p. 20.

_____. "Royals Rip 'Skins for League Title." *Rochester Democrat and Chronicle*, 3/24/46, p. C-1.

_____. "Royals Win by 61 to54." *Rochester Democrat and Chronicle*, 3/22/46, p. 28.

_____. "Sports Eye View." *Rochester Democrat and Chronicle*, 3/25/46, p. 20, 3/30/47, p. D-1, 4/5/47, p. 20, 4/5/48, p. 20.

_____. "Vengeful Royals Wreck Fort Wayne, 76 to 47." *Rochester Democrat and Chronicle*, 4/2/47, p. 26.

"Czech Reds Imprison 7 Opposition Leaders in Total Power Drive." *Rochester Democrat and Chronicle*, 2/24/48, p. 1.

"Darling Gives Up as Coach After All Stars Lose." *Oshkosh Daily Northwestern*, 12/1/48, p. 20.

"Darling Replies to Podoloff." *Oshkosh Daily Northwestern*, 3/3/49, p. 24.

"Davies Joins Royals Quint." *Rochester Democrat and Chronicle,* 12/12/45, p. 20.

"Davies Named Sports Coach at Seton Hall." *Rochester Democrat and Chronicle,* 1/18/46, p. 22.

"Davies Sparks Rochester Win." *Rochester Democrat and Chronicle,* 4/4/47, p. 29.

"Detroit and Rens Win Pro Contests." *Indianapolis Star,* 1/25/40, p. 16.

"Detroit Beats Army Quint in Pro Meet." *Chicago Tribune,* 3/9/42, pt. 2, p. 2.

"Detroit Eagles Add Garfinkel from Pro Tourney." *Chicago Tribune,* 3/3/42, p. 22.

"Detroit Eagles Back in National Basketball Loop." *Oshkosh Daily Northwestern,* 11/7/40, p. 19.

"Detroit Eagles Beat Hammond Quint, 61 to 52." *Chicago Tribune,* 1/24/41, p. 20.

"Detroit Eagles Win World's Pro Cage Tourney." *Oshkosh Daily Northwestern,* 3/20/41, p. 25.

"Detroit Knocks Bruins From Title Race, 56–53." *Chicago Tribune,* 3/6/40, p. 26.

"Detroit Plays Oshkosh for Pro Title Tonight." *Chicago Tribune,* 3/11/42, p. 25.

"Detroit Pros Sign Three Irish Stars for Tourney." *Chicago Tribune,* 3/13/43, p. 18.

"Detroit Upsets Globetrotters in Meet, 37–36." *Chicago Tribune,* 3/17/41, p. 20.

"Dow Chemicals, Pittsburgh Win in Pro Tourney." *Chicago Tribune,* 3/21/45, p. 26.

"Eagles Defeat Bruins, 45 to 43, on Free Throws." *Chicago Tribune,* 1/18/41, p. 16.

"Easy Ed to Join NBL." *Oshkosh Daily Northwestern,* 2/23/49, p. 14.

"Edwards Added to Kautsky Quintet." *Indianapolis Star,* 1/31/37, p. 23.

"Edwards Leads Stars to Victory Over the Bruins." *Oshkosh Daily Northwestern,* 12/15/41, p. 13.

"11,000 See Royals Win, 50–47." *Rochester Democrat and Chronicle,* 2/12/47, p. 21.

Elliott, Bob. "Firestone Beats Oshkosh 42–37...." *Akron Beacon Journal,* 1/13/38, p. 20.

_____. "Nonskids Beat Phillips Outfit...." *Akron Beacon Journal,* 1/27/38, p. 21.

_____. "Wings Win 42–40 Tilt." *Akron Beacon Journal,* 1/14/38, p. 29.

"Englund's 2d Half Spurt Whips Lakers for Stars." *Rochester Democrat and Chronicle,* 3/27/48, p. 31.

"Enzo Jels Defeat Oshkosh All Stars in a Hectic Battle." *Oshkosh Daily Northwestern,* 1/20/38, p. 15.

"Fans Already Ordering Wing-Firestone Tickets." *Akron Beacon Journal,* 1/21/37, p. 21.

"Firestone Battles Oshkosh Tonight." *Akron Beacon Journal,* 3/14/40, p. 36.

"Firestone Defeats Detroit, 46–35 to Win Playoffs." *Akron Beacon Journal,* 12/24/27, p. 12.

"Fort Wayne Tops Skids." *Akron Beacon Journal,* 12/16/36, p. 23.

Fraley, O. "Netters of Today Better Than Oldsters-Lapchick." *Fort Wayne News-Sentinel,* 2/10/48, p. 12.

"Free Throw With 14 Seconds Left Gives Gears Win, 61–60." *Oshkosh Daily Northwestern,* 3/31/47, p. 13.

Garlikov, B. "Dayton Finally Lands Franchise in National Pro Cage Loop." *Dayton Daily News,* 12/18/48, p. 8.

_____. "Dayton Starts Cage 'Renaissance' Against Anderson Today." *Dayton Daily News,* 12/19/48, Sports, p. 3.

_____. "Only 397 See Dayton Debut in Cage Loop." *Dayton Daily News,* 12/20/48, p. 23.

"Gears Beat Hartford in Pro Tourney." *Chicago Tribune,* 3/20/45, p. 20.

"Gears Beat Sheboygan in Playoff Game." *Chicago Tribune,* 3/6/45, p. 18.

"Gears Beaten in Opener, 71–65." *Chicago Tribune,* 4/4/47, p. 27.

"Gears Blast Royals, 79–68, Win Series." *Rochester Democrat and Chronicle,* 4/10/47, p. 31.

"Gears Deal 1st Defeat, 65 to 64, to Rochester." *Chicago Tribune,* 12/1/46, pt. 2, p. 2.

"Gears Deal 2d Loss in Row to Kautskys, 69–61." *Chicago Tribune,* 3/21/47, p. 29.

"Gears Defeat Cleveland Pro Quintet, 59–50." *Chicago Tribune,* 1/25/45, p. 21.

"Gears Defeat Globetrotter Five, 53 to 49." *Chicago Tribune,* 3/22/45, p. 30.

"Gears Defeat Oshkosh Pro Five, 52 to 46." *Chicago Tribune,* 12/21/44, p. 19.

"Gears Defeat Oshkosh, 52–50 in Last Minute." *Chicago Tribune,* 1/14/45, pt. 2, p. 2.

"Gears Go Into Finals With 61–60 Victory." *Chicago Tribune,* 3/30/47, pt. 2, p. 2.

"Gears Lose to Oshkosh, 66–61, in Pro Opener." *Chicago Tribune,* 11/10/46, pt. 2, p. 3.

"Gears Lose to Redskins Again, 52–48." *Chicago Tribune,* 1/12/45, p. 22.

"Gears Quintet Lose, 66 to 40, to Cleveland." *Chicago Tribune,* 2/2/45, pt. 2, p. 2.

"Gears Score First League Victory, 47–38." *Chicago Tribune,* 11/26/45, p. 27.

"Gears Shade Royals, 75–74." *Rochester Democrat and Chronicle,* 4/13/47, p. D-1.

"Gears Shift into High in Play-off." *Chicago Tribune,* 4/8/47, p. 23.

"Gears Stop Royals, 67–63, to Even Cage Series." *Rochester Democrat and Chronicle,* 4/7/47, p. 8.

"Gears Win First Play-Off Series Contest, 74 to 72." *Chicago Tribune,* 3/19/47, p. 29.

"George Glamack Signs with Royals." *Rochester Democrat and Chronicle.* 11/13/45, p. 19.

"George Mikan's 27 Points Help Gears Win, 67–63." *Chicago Tribune,* 4/6/47, pt. 2, p. 2.

"Globetrotters and Bruins Win: Reach Finals." *Chicago Tribune,* 3/20/40, p. 31.

"Good Luck All Stars." Full-page advertisement in *Oshkosh Daily Northwestern,* 10/29/48, p. 5.

"Goodyear Becomes Midwest Member." *Akron Beacon Journal,* 12/4/36, p. 49.

"Goodyear Defeats Hammond 33–30 in Cage League Opener." *Akron Beacon Journal,* 11/26/38, p. 11.

"Goodyear Defeats Oshkosh, 29–28...." *Akron Beacon Journal,* 3/1/38, 21.

"Goodyear Defeats Oshkosh, 35–27, Retain National Cage Honors." *Akron Beacon Journal,* 3/5/38, p. 14.

"Goodyear Halts Firestone Streak with 40–37 Win." *Akron Beacon Journal.* 2/16/39, p. 35.

"Goodyear Opposes Oshkosh Thursday." *Akron Beacon Journal.* 3/1/39, p. 18.

"Goodyear Plays Two Strong Clubs This Week." *The Wingfoot Clan,* vol. 25, no. 44, 12/9/36, p. 4.

"Goodyear-Renaissance Contest Ends in Fisticuffs in Four Minutes." *Akron Beacon Journal,* 2/10/38, p. 23.

"Goodyear Seeking Opening Cage Foe." *Akron Beacon Journal,* 11/21/36, p. 17.

"Goodyear Takes Honors as Champs of the Midwest." *Akron Beacon Journal.* 3/2/37, p. 28.

"Goodyear Wins, 31–27, Over Firestone Team." *Akron Beacon Journal,* 1/20/37, p. 19.

"Goodyears Beat All Stars in League Opener." *Oshkosh Daily Northwestern,* 11/24/39, p. 17.

"Goodyears Defeat Kautskys by 54–44." *Oshkosh Daily Northwestern,* 1/12/42, p. 12.

"Hammond Five Ends Oshkosh Streak, 43–32." *Chicago Tribune,* 1/13/41, p. 14.

"Hammond Sells Vaughn to Bruins...." *Oshkosh Daily Northwestern,* 2/21/41, p. 14.

"Hammond Wins, 71–65."*Denver Post,* 11/29/48, p. 25.

"Hapac and Kautz Lead Bruins to a 49–33 Triumph." *Chicago Tribune,* 2/25/41, p. 21.

"Hapac Stars as Bruins Win, 42–41, Over Goodyears." *Chicago Tribune,* 2/6/41, pp. 8, 19.

"Harlems Beat Bruins to Win Basket Title." *Chicago Tribune.* 3/21/40, p. 29.

"Hawks Beat Hawks." *Denver Post,* 11/17/48, p. 35.

"Indianapolis Falls Before Oshkosh by 56–44." *Oshkosh Daily Northwestern,* 1/5/42, p. 13.

"Indianapolis Five Wins Game, Takes Second in League." *Indianapolis Star.* 12/13/38, p. 15.

"It's Really True! Oshkosh Stars Trim Zollners by 49 to 45." *Oshkosh Daily Northwestern,* 12/11/44, p. 11.

"Jerry Rizzo Joins N.Y. State League." *Denver Post,* 1/3/49, p. 17.

"Joe Fulks Nearing New Pro Net Scoring Mark." *Fort Wayne News-Sentinel,* 4/1/47, p. 10.

Johnson, C. "Charlie Johnson's Lowdown on Sports." *Minneapolis Star,* 4/8/48, p. 33.

Jordan, C. "Fist-Throwing Syracuse Cager Suspended for Season by NBL." *Denver Post,* 12/22/48, p. 37.

_____. "Nuggets Celebrate First Pro Cage Win." *Denver Post,* 11/25/48, p. 39.

_____. "Only One Fight Marks Nat Win As Nuggets Fail to Halt Schayes." *Denver Post,* 12/23/48, p. 12.

_____. "Physical Ability No Handicap in Udall's Bright Success Story." *Denver Post,* 11/2/48, p. 25.

"Jump is Doomed Says Cage Official." *Akron Beacon Journal,* 1/25/37. p. 15.

"Kautsky Beaten in Opener, 44–40." *Indianapolis Star,* 11/30/39, p. 16.

"Kautsky Netmen Drop Pro Contest." *Indianapolis Star,* 12/21/39, p. 17.

"Kautsky Release Herman Schaefer." *Rochester Democrat and Chronicle,* 11/12/47, p. 25.

"Kautsky Team Victor, 50–32." *Indianapolis Star,* 3/21/36, p. 16.

"Kautskys and Risen Defeat Gears, 68–67." *Chicago Tribune,* 3/24/47, p. 30.

"Kautskys Beat Gears, 55 to 54, to Even Series." *Chicago Tribune,* 3/26/47, p. 33.

"Kautskys Deal Bruins Another Defeat, 37 to 33." *Chicago Tribune,* 1/1/42, p. 35.

"Kautskys Defeat All Stars, 43–36, at Indianapolis." *Oshkosh Daily Northwestern,* 1/19/42, p. 12.

"Kautskys Defeat U.S. Tires, 36–32." *Indianapolis Star,* 2/3/36, p. 12.

"Kautskys Here for Cage Tilt Dec.27." *Firestone Non-Skid,* vol. 20, no. 23, 12/24/35, p. 8.

"Kautskys Lead in Standings." *Indianapolis Star,* 3/2/36, p14.

"Kautskys Repulse Akron Five, 31–24." *Indianapolis Star*, 2/10/36, p. 12.

"Kautskys to Face Giant Cage Team." *Indianapolis Star*, 12/24/39, p. 18.

"Kautskys Top Wings." *Indianapolis Star*, 11/29/38, p. 20.

"Kautskys Triumph in Ragged Battle." *Indianapolis Star*, 3/2/36, p. 19.

"Kautskys Wallop Pro League Rival...." *Indianapolis Star*, 1/3/39, p. 13.

"Kautskys' Win from Sheboygan." *Indianapolis Star*, 12/14/39, p. 21.

Kurlansky, M. "Royals Clip All Stars in Exhibition, 72–61." *Rochester Democrat and Chronicle*, 4/11/48, p. D-1.

"Lakers Beat Royals for Title." *Rochester Democrat and Chronicle*, 4/18/48, p. D-1.

"Lakers Bow; Mikan Shines." *Rochester Democrat and Chronicle*, 11/21/47, p. 40.

"Lakers Defeat Royals 'Shock Troops,' 80–72." *Rochester Democrat and Chronicle*, 4/14/48, p. 22.

"Lakers Miss Last Chance to Score 100." *Minneapolis Star*, 4/9/48, p. 32.

"Lakers Prove Practice Must Make Mikan 'Fit.'" *Minneapolis Star*, 11/21/47, p. 34.

"Lakers Rap Stars, 60 to 42." *Denver Post*, 11/27/48, p. 9.

"Lakers Win, 83–59; Two Hawks Injured." *Rochester Democrat and Chronicle*, 4/1/48, p. 24.

"Lakers Win Tourney, 75–71." *Rochester Democrat and Chronicle*, 4/12/48, p. 21.

"Lambert to Quit at End of Season." *Minneapolis Star*, 2/14/48, p. 10.

"Last Second Win By Globetrotters Gives 17,823 'Biggest' Thrill." *Chicago Defender*, 2/28/48, p. 11.

"Leading Scores" *Indianapolis Star*, 12/18/38, p. 27.

"League Rejects Franchise Bid of Homeless Gears." *Chicago Tribune*, 11/17/47, p. 38.

Lippe, J. "Gears Again Topple Royals." *Rochester Democrat and Chronicle*, 4/14/47, p. 23.

"Local Pro Fives Drop Encounters." *Indianapolis Star*, 2/15/40, p. 16.

"Local Pro Team Shades Oshkosh." *Indianapolis Star*, 1/18/40, p. 17.

"Local Teams Lose to Negro Quintets." *Indianapolis Star*, 1/21/37, p. 15.

"Mac to Lead Gears Against Indianapolis." *Fort Wayne News-Sentinel*, 1/3/47, p. 24.

"Major League Basketball Comes to Anderson on Monday." *Anderson Daily Bulletin*, 11/7/46, p. 17.

"McDermott Notches 25 in 71–52 Ft. Wayne Win." *Rochester Democrat and Chronicle*, 12/11/45, p. 20.

"Mikan Bags Record 42." *Rochester Democrat and Chronicle*, 3/14/48, p. D-6.

"Mikan Gets Auto; Lakers Hike Streak." *Minneapolis Star*, 3/1/48, p. 25.

"Mikan Scores 20 Points; Gears Triumph, 59 to 48." *Chicago Tribune*, 3/21/46, p. 31.

"Mikan Tallies 24 in Lakers' Win." *Rochester Democrat and Chronicle*, 12/5/47, p. 39.

Miller, N. "Podoloff Plans to Keep Rivalries." *Philadelphia Inquirer*, 8/5/49, p. 31.

"Moore Raps B.A.A. Curb on Salaries." *Chicago Tribune*, 11/5/48, pt. 3, p. 3.

"Move Chicago-Akron Game Up to Tonight." *Oshkosh Daily Northwestern*, 2/3/42, p. 13.

"National AAU Tourney Opens Today." *Chicago Tribune*, 3/17/40, pt. 2, p. 2.

"National Basketball Championship at Stake at Goodyear Tonight." *Akron Beacon Journal*, 3/4/38, p. 28.

National Basketball League Official Bulletin, May, 29, 1946.

"National League Roundup." *Anderson Daily Bulletin*, 11/1/46, p. 15.

"National League Withdraws from Basketball Group." *Rochester Democrat and Chronicle*, 4/9/47, p. 24.

"Nation's Strike Situation at a Glance" *Fort Wayne News-Sentinel*, 1/4/46, p. 10.

"Nats 53, Sheboygan 45." *Oshkosh Daily Northwestern*, 11/15/48, p. 12.

"NBL All Star Teams." *Fort Wayne News-Sentinel*, 3/26/47, p. 24.

"NBL, BAA Heads Talk Merger Possibilities." *Fort Wayne News-Sentinel*, 4/8/48, p. 18.

"NBL Coaches Think 3 Seasons Needed to Bring Experience." *Fort Wayne News-Sentinel*, 1/31/48, p. 10.

"NBL Eastern Division Teams Resume Playoff." *Denver Post*, 4/11/49, p. 20.

"NBL Quitting Court Group; War Looming." *Fort Wayne News-Sentinel*, 4/9/47, p. 26.

"NBL Refuses Team Request; 4 Barred." *Rochester Democrat and Chronicle*, 11/17/47, p. 23.

"NBL Studies Entry Bids of 7 Cities" *Rochester Democrat and Chronicle*, 4/9/48, p. 32.

"NBL Threatens All Out War Against BAA." *Chicago Tribune*, 5/12/48, pt. 3, p. 1.

"New York Jewels Hand Skids Second Straight Loss." *Akron Beacon Journal*, 12/2/40, p. 18.

"90 Seconds Left, Goodyears Beat Bruins, 41 to 38." *Chicago Tribune*, 2/16/41, pt. 2, p. 3.

"Nonskid Cagemen Face Windsor in League Tilt Here Wednesday." *Akron Beacon Journal*, 1/28/36, p. 22.

"Nonskid Five Topples Rens." *Akron Beacon Journal.* 3/6/39, p. 17.

"Nonskids Beaten by Celtics." *Akron Beacon Journal*, 2/1/41, p. 10.

"Nonskids Beaten By Rens." *Akron Beacon Journal.* 3/14/39, p. 27.

"Nonskids Even City Series." *Akron Beacon Journal*, 1/8/41, p. 16.

"Nonskids in 41–28 Romp." *Akron Beacon Journal*, 1/20/38, p. 24.

"Nonskids Play Eight Contests on Eastern Basketball Junket." *Akron Beacon Journal*, 12/29/38, p. 22.

"Nonskids Prepare for Playoff Series." *Akron Beacon Journal*, 3/5/36, p. 26.

"Nonskids Score Double Win, Wingfoots Beaten." *Akron Beacon Journal*, 11/28/40, p. 30.

"Nonskids to Play Pittsburgh YMHA." *Akron Beacon Journal*, 1/30/36, p. 18.

"Nonskids Triumph at Oshkosh, 46–44." *Akron Beacon Journal.* 1/15/39, p. C-12.

"Nuggets Sell Hoot Gibson to Tri-Cities." *Denver Post*, 2/11/49, p. 29.

"Nugs Drop 8th in Row." *Denver Post*, 11/16/48, p. 27.

"Nugs Overcome Nats' Fists, Tears to Win Fourth Straight, 60–54. *Denver Post*, 12/22/48, p. 30.

"Offer Civic Plan to Bring Pro Cagers Here." *Moline Daily Dispatch*, 12/19/46, p. 29.

"On the Sidelines with the Sports Editor." *Oshkosh Daily Northwestern*, 12/20/38, p. 15.

"Oram's Return Raises Bruins Playoff Hopes." *Chicago Tribune.* 2/20/40, p. 21.

Oshkosh All Stars Ad. *Oshkosh Daily Northwestern*, 4/6/46, p. 11.

"Oshkosh All Stars Are on Their Way to the Top." *Oshkosh Daily Northwestern*, 12/18/39, p. 17.

"Oshkosh All Stars Beat Globe Trotters Twice." *Oshkosh Daily Northwestern*, 11/25/40, p. 12.

"Oshkosh All Stars Take Fifth Straight From Redskins 49–36 in Game Marred by Fisticuffs." *Oshkosh Daily Northwestern*, 2/24/39, p. 15.

"Oshkosh Beats Nonskids, 49–37, Evens Playoff Series." *Akron Beacon Journal*, 3/18/39, p. 11.

"Oshkosh Beats Toledo, 40 to 37 in Pro Tourney." *Chicago Tribune*, 3/19/41, p. 27.

"Oshkosh Cagers Lose College All Star Game." *Oshkosh Daily Northwestern*, 11/29/41, p. 13.

"Oshkosh Conquers Firestone Combine." *Akron Beacon Journal*, 3/5/39, p. C-1.

"Oshkosh Five Beaten 37–36 by Hammond." *Chicago Tribune*, 2/5/40, p. 22.

"Oshkosh Five Defeated by Studebakers." *Chicago Defender*, 12/12/42, p. 21.

"Oshkosh Five Top Pittsburgh Rivals, 55 to 50." *Chicago Tribune*, 12/31/44, pt. 2, p. 3.

"Oshkosh Is Champion of National Cage League." *Oshkosh Daily Northwestern*, 3/12/41, p. 20.

"Oshkosh Nips Hawks in Playoff Bow, 68–66." *Oshkosh Daily Northwestern*, 4/7/49, p. 46.

"Oshkosh Nips 'Skins, 33–30." *Rochester Democrat and Chronicle*, 11/30/45, p. 25.

"Oshkosh Noses Out Goodyear in Last Minute." *Oshkosh Daily Northwestern*, 1/6/41, p. 13.

"Oshkosh Plays in Series Semifinal Tonight." *Oshkosh Daily Northwestern*, 3/27/39, p. 15.

"Oshkosh Pro Five to Play All-Star Cage Aggregation." *Oshkosh Daily Northwestern*, 2/4/42, p. 11.

"Oshkosh, Rens, Baltimore Win in Pro Tourney." *Chicago Tribune*, 3/27/46, p. 29.

"Oshkosh Spanks Indianapolis." *Rochester Democrat and Chronicle*, 12/10/45, p. 27.

"Oshkosh Stars Defeat Chicago Quintet, 47 to 29." *Chicago Tribune*, 12/3/44, pt. 2, p. 2.

"Oshkosh Stars Request Waiver on Eddie Dancker." *Oshkosh Daily Northwestern*, 1/6/49, p. 21.

"Oshkosh Tips 'Skins, 53–45, Evens Series." *Rochester Democrat and Chronicle*, 3/22/47, p. 9.

"Oshkosh Tops Nonskid Quint in 45–43 Fray." *Akron Beacon Journal*, 1/19/41, p. C-1.

"Oshkosh Tops Wingfoots 43–30: Eagles Edge Nonskids, 34–33." *Akron Beacon Journal*, 12/14/40, p. 10.

"Oshkosh Whips Bruins, 53 to 43; Edwards Stars." *Chicago Tribune.* 1/21/40, pt. 2, p. 2.

"Oshkosh Whips Tri-Cities Again." *Denver Post*, 4/10/49, p. 2E.

"Oshkosh Win String Snapped By Akron." *Oshkosh Daily Northwestern*, 1/19/42, p. 12.

"Oshkosh Wins Western Division Championship." *Oshkosh Daily Northwestern*, 4/13/49, p. 24.

"Oshkosh's Late Rally Drops Wings, 35–33, in League Fray." *Akron Beacon Journal*, 1/5/41, p. C-1.

"Packers Attend Jaycee Dinner." *Anderson Daily Bulletin*, 11/6/46, p. 12.

"Packers Make Initial Appearance of Season v. Detroit." *Anderson Daily Bulletin*, 11/11/46, p. 10.

Bibliography

"Packers Trim Nats in First Playoff Test." *Denver Post*, 4/9/49, p. 11.

"Packers Win, Face Oshkosh for '49 Title." *Denver Post*, 4/13/49, p. 34.

"Patrons Still Attend Sporting Event." *Oshkosh Daily Northwestern*, 1/9/43, p. 10.

Patton, W. Blaine. "Kautsky All Americans Fail in Bid for Western Division Pinnacle." *Oshkosh Daily Northwestern*, 2/13/39, p. 12.

_____. "Local Pro Quintet Wins First League Tilt from Akron Goodyears." *Indianapolis Star*, 11/29/38, p. 13.

_____, "Ren's Brilliant Attack Humbles Kautsky Quintet by 47 to 33 Margin." *Indianapolis Star*, 1/10/39, p. 13.

"Pelkington to Face Wingfoots." *Akron Beacon Journal*, 11/30/41, p. 4-C.

Peterson, R. "Indy Jets in Receivership." *Oshkosh Daily Northwestern*, 4/8/49, p. 11.

"Pick Blackhawks for Pro Team Name." *Moline Daily Dispatch*, 1/1/47, p. 22.

Pinckney, Paul. "Graham Impresses Squad in Cage Drill." *Rochester Democrat and Chronicle*, 11/7/45, p. 22.

_____. "Royals Bag 5th Straight League Win, 61–49." *Rochester Democrat and Chronicle*, 12/9/45, p. C-1.

_____. "Royals Defeat Youngstown." *Rochester Democrat and Chronicle*, 12/4/45, p. 21.

_____. "Royals Nip Fort Wayne, 56–54." *Rochester Democrat and Chronicle*, 12/3/45, p. 23.

_____. "Royals Win Debut in National Wheel." *Rochester Democrat and Chronicle*, 11/25/45, p. C-1.

_____. "Zollner Spurt Snaps Royals' String, 63–59." *Rochester Democrat and Chronicle*, 12/30/45, p. D-1.

_____. "Zollners Outrough Royals, 72–67." *Rochester Democrat and Chronicle*, 2/9/47, p. 21.

"Piston Cagers Start Defense of Professional Title Tonight." *Fort Wayne News-Sentinel*, 3/21/45, p. 22

"Pistons Beat Cleveland Twice, Lengthen Their lead in League." *Fort Wayne News-Sentinel*, 12/27/43, p. 9.

"Pistons Beat Sheboygan: Face Three Road Clashes." *Fort Wayne News-Sentinel*

"Pistons Beat Wright Field." *Fort Wayne News-Sentinel*, 1/18/46, p. 11.

"Pistons Down Royal Cagers." *Fort Wayne News-Sentinel*, 1/17/46, p. 13.

"Pistons Eye Pro Tourney as Their Comeback Chase." *Fort Wayne News-Sentinel*, 3/18/46, p. 7.

"Pistons' Final Spurt Too Much for Gears in 60–49 Loop Contest; McDermott Has Big Night." *Fort Wayne News-Sentinel*, 2/5/45, p. 13.

"Pistons Gain Sweep in 59–47 Win Over National Loop Stars." *Fort Wayne News-Sentinel*, 3/28/45, p. 23.

"Pistons Give New Men Plenty of Chance to Play; Rens Win." *Fort Wayne News-Sentinel*, 4/5/47, p. 15.

"Pistons Hoping to Bounce Back as Underdogs Tonight." *Fort Wayne News-Sentinel*, 1/13/48, p. 12.

"Pistons in Win; Home Sunday." *Fort Wayne News-Sentinel*, 12/13/47, p. 10.

"Pistons, Jeeps Tangle Here Tonight in Series' Decisive Tilt." *Fort Wayne News-Sentinel*, 3/26/47, p. 24.

"Pistons Keep Going By Downing Cleveland in 50–42 Clash; Mel Riebe Outscores McDermott." *Fort Wayne News-Sentinel*, 1/24/45, p. 11.

"Pistons' Late Spurt Defeats Sheboygan, 55–44, in Loop Tilt." *Fort Wayne News-Sentinel*, 12/3/43, p. 26.

"Pistons Lose as McDermott Sets Record." *Fort Wayne News-Sentinel*, 2/9/45, p. 11.

"Pistons Lose at Toledo; Try Again Tonight to Avoid Decisive Battle of Set Wednesday." *Fort Wayne News-Sentinel*, 3/25/47, p. 25.

"Pistons Lose Ground in Dropping 79–69 Decision to Tri-Cities; Home Thursday." *Fort Wayne News-Sentinel*, 1/21/48, p. 25.

"Pistons Lose to Bears, Try Again Tonight." *Fort Wayne News-Sentinel*, 11/9/43, p. 27.

"Pistons Lose to Oshkosh, Then Take Overtime Clash." *Fort Wayne News-Sentinel*, 12/11/44, p. 11.

"Pistons Make Pittsburgh 55–41 Victim; Eye Heavy Schedule Starting on Saturday Night." *Fort Wayne News-Sentinel* 1/25/45, p. 15.

"Pistons, Midland Clash at New Haven." *Fort Wayne News-Sentinel*, 10/26/46, p. 10.

"Pistons Move Two Games Ahead in Set with Jeeps." *Fort Wayne News-Sentinel*, 3/21/47, p. 39.

"Pistons Need Only One Win to Clinch League Championship." *Fort Wayne News-Sentinel*, 2/14/44, p. 9.

"Pistons, Oshkosh to Renew Hostilities at North Side Gym Tonight." *Fort Wayne News-Sentinel*, 2/8/44, p. 9.

"Pistons Outlast Chicago to Turn in Victory by 59–49; Spurt in Last Quarter Takes Clash." *Fort Wayne News-Sentinel*, 1/17/45, p. 11.

"Pistons Outlast Royals in Grueling Tilt." *Fort Wayne News-Sentinel*, 2/13/47, p. 30.

"Pistons Regular Season Champs Again, Look Better in Beating Sheboygan Quint, 53–49." *Fort Wayne News-Sentinel*, 3/4/46, p. 8.

"Pistons Release Three to Cut Down to Workable Size." *Fort Wayne News-Sentinel*, 3/1/46, p. 13.

"Pistons Sign Sadowski to Aid in Playoffs, Meet." *Fort Wayne News-Sentinel*, 3/3/45, p. 10.

"Pistons Split on Trip East: Open at Home Tuesday Night." *Fort Wayne News-Sentinel*, 11/29/43, p. 9.

"Pistons Take Bears; Fight is Aftermath." *Fort Wayne News-Sentinel*, 2/26/44, p. 10.

"Pistons Trim Raiders, 63–53: Chicago Next Home Foe." *Fort Wayne News-Sentinel*, 1/31/45, p. 11.

"Pistons Trounce Cleveland, 64–37, in Opener." *Fort Wayne News-Sentinel*, 3/6/44, p. 15.

"Pistons Try to Stop Riebe, Cleveland Seeks to Halt Zollners." *Fort Wayne News-Sentinel*, 1/18/44, p. 20.

"Pistons Two Up, Hope to End Series Tuesday." *Fort Wayne News-Sentinel*, 3/13/44, p. 9.

"Pistons Win, Face Rens in Semi Finals of Tourney." *Fort Wayne News-Sentinel*, 3/23/44, p. 14.

"Podoloff Asking Talks with Duffey." *Oshkosh Daily Northwestern*, 10/29/48, p. 13.

"Postpone Midwest Tournament Series." *Akron Beacon Journal*, 3/7/36, p. 15.

"Preliminary on Bruin Card Wins Fans' Attention." *Chicago Tribune*, 1/21/41, p. 18.

Prell, E. "Redskin Five Advances in Pro Tourney." *Chicago Tribune*, 4/7/47, p. 31.

Price, Bernie, photograph caption. *Chicago Defender*, 12/19/42, p. 19.

"Pro Basketball Leagues Merge." *Chicago Tribune*, 8/4/49, pt. 3, p. 1.

"Pro Basketball Rivals May Merge Today." *Chicago Tribune*, 8/3/49, pt. 3, p. 2.

"Pro Basketball Title Tourney Opens Today." *Chicago Tribune*. 3/26/39, pt. 2, p. 3.

"Pro Cage Loop Hits 'Jumpers.' *Minneapolis Star*, 10/13/47, p. 20.

"Pro Cage Loop Will Retain Center Jump." *Oshkosh Daily Northwestern*, 12/13/37, p. 14.

"Pro Court Teams Toss For Players." *Philadelphia Inquirer*, 8/12/49, p. 29.

"Pro Finals Will Be at Stadium." *Oshkosh Daily Northwestern*, 2/23/43, p. 11.

"Quaker City Team Defeats Kautskys." *Indianapolis Star*, 2/4/37, p. 15.

"Ready to Accept Presidency, Says McArthur; Truman to Run if Named, He Advises Party." *Rochester Democrat and Chronicle*, 3/9/48, p. 1.

"Red Hot Oshkosh Team Whips Chicago in Thriller, 47 to 39." *Oshkosh Daily Northwestern*, 12/4/45, p. 11.

"Redskins Beat Gears, 57–27, in Play-off Final" *Chicago Tribune*, 3/9/45, p. 27.

"Redskins Beat Gears to Even Playoff Series." *Chicago Tribune*, 3/7/45, p. 24.

"Redskins Beat Oshkosh Stars by 42–36 Margin." *Chicago Tribune*, 2/16/40, p. 33.

"Redskins Defeat All Stars in Two Straight." *Oshkosh Daily Northwestern*, 2/22/03, p. 11.

"Redskins Even Series." *Oshkosh Daily Northwestern*, 3/9/40, p. 13.

"Redskins Lose Tilt in Chicago, 40 to 36." *Oshkosh Daily Northwestern*, 2/19/42, p. 19.

"Redskins Win Season's Opener by 46 to34 Score." *Oshkosh Daily Northwestern*, 11/19/42, p. 11.

"Release Eddie Riska from All Stars Squad." *Oshkosh Daily Northwestern*, 2/10/49, p. 25.

"Renaissance Conquer Tires; Fistic Outbreak Mars Game." *Indianapolis Star*, 3/4/37, p. 21.

"Renaissance, Duffy Florals Play Tonight." *Chicago Tribune*. 12/17/39, pt. 2, p. 2.

"Renaissance Five Shades Kautskys." *Indianapolis Star*, 1/17/36, p. 36.

"Rens Beat Stars in Final Contest of Series." *Oshkosh Daily Northwestern*, 3/14/38, p. 15.

"Rens, Bruins Win Openers in Pro Meet." *Chicago Tribune*, 3/18/40, p. 25.

"Rens Gain Second Win Over Nonskids." *Akron Beacon Journal*, 2/22/38, p. 21.

"Rens Join Pro Group." *Chicago Defender*, 12/25/48, p. 15.

"Rens Take Final Game of Series from All Stars." *Oshkosh Daily Northwestern*, 12/4/41, p. 23.

"Rens to Represent Dayton in National Court League." *Philadelphia Inquirer*, 12/18/48, p. 19.

"Rens Top Nonskids in 28–26 Clash." *Akron Beacon Journal*, 3/7/39, p. 26.

"Rens Win First." *Denver Post*, 12/23/48, p. 12.

"Reserves Carry Wings to 43–28 Win Over Buffalo." *Akron Beacon Journal*, 1/4/39, p. 15.

"Risen Scholastically Ineligible." *Chicago Tribune*, 1/3/46, p. 17.

"Rookie Foils Laker Hopes." *Minneapolis Star*, 4/17/48, p. 10.

"Royals Clout Kautskys, 61 to 46." *Rochester Democrat and Chronicle*, 3/8/48, p. 20.

"Royals Make National League Bow at Arena

Tonight." *Rochester Democrat and Chronicle*, 11/24/45, p. 14.

"Royals Nip Gears." *Rochester Democrat and Chronicle*, 4/12/47, p. 21.

"Royals Out of Tourney, Harrison Announces." *Rochester Democrat and Chronicle*, 3/14/46, p. 18.

"Royals Outlast Pistons, 58–55, to Reduce Margin." *Fort Wayne News-Sentinel*, 2/18/46, p. 9.

"Royals Rout Cleveland for 6th Win, 65–45." *Rochester Democrat and Chronicle*, 12/10/45, p. 27.

"Royals Sign Garfinkel." *Rochester Democrat and Chronicle*, 12/21/45, p. 24.

"Royals Spank Monarch Five at Cleveland." *Rochester Democrat and Chronicle*, 2/25/46, p. 21.

"Royals Whip Rens, 54 to 40." *Rochester Democrat and Chronicle*, 2/23/46, p. 20.

"Rumors Persist Oshkosh May Lose All Stars." *Oshkosh Daily Northwestern*, 2/26/49, p. 9.

Schlemmer, James. "Even Sheeks Laughs." *Akron Beacon Journal*, 2/1/37, p. 21.

_____. "Fans Shout Business." *Akron Beacon Journal*, 1/30/37, p. 25.

_____. "Fighting Nonskids Defeat Oshkosh, 35–32, Keep Series Alive." *Akron Beacon Journal*, 3/15/40, p. 41.

_____. "Firestone Beats Goodyear, 43–41, in Series Opener." *Akron Beacon Journal*, 1/19/39, p. 25.

_____. "Firestone in Danger." *Akron Beacon Journal*, 1/12/37, p. 27.

_____. " Firestone Romps." *Akron Beacon Journal*, 2/25/40, p. C-1.

_____. "Goodyear Has Easy Time Topping Nonskids, 40–24." *Akron Beacon Journal*, 2/22/37, p. 17.

_____."Hot Industrial Series Seen as Firestone Wins." *Akron Beacon Journal*, 1/17/38, p. 17.

_____. "Jim Schlemmer" column. *Akron Beacon Journal*, 11/5/41, p. 23, 12/19/41, p. 42.

_____. "A New Forgotten Man." *Akron Beacon Journal*, 2/10/37, p. 20.

_____. "Nonskids Battle Oshkosh Tonight at Kent for National Toga." *Akron Beacon Journal*, 3/16/40, p. 11.

_____. "Nonskids Nip Wings in Overtime." *Akron Beacon Journal*, 2/23/41.p. C-1.

_____. "Nonskids Spank Dayton in Midwest Conference." *Akron Beacon Journal*, 12/5/35, p. 27

_____. "Nonskids Take Eastern Title in Midwest Loop." *Akron Beacon Journal*, 3/2/36, p. 15.

_____. "Nonskids Toy With Oshkosh in Winning First, 50–38." *Akron Beacon Journal*, 3/15/39, p. 21.

_____. "On Basketball." *Akron Beacon Journal*, 1/25/38, p. 22.

_____. "Oshkosh Beats Skids, 38–36, to Tie Playoff Series." *Akron Beacon Journal*, 3/16/39, p. 40.

_____. "Oshkosh's Rally Trips Nonskids, 37–32." *Akron Beacon Journal*, 12/17/40, p. 30.

_____. "Ozburn Gets 25 as Skids Blast Detroit, 48–35." *Akron Beacon Journal*, 3/7/40, p. 26.

_____. "Wingfoots, Skids Groom Stronger Cage Outfits." *Akron Beacon Journal*, 11/14/35, p. 24.

_____. "Wings' Season Short." *Akron Beacon Journal*. 2/26/37, p. 37.

Segreti, J. "Fort Wayne Evens Series; Wins 56–47." *Chicago Tribune*, 4/7/46, pt. 2, p. 2.

_____. "Gears Advance to Pro-Tourney Quarter-Finals." *Chicago Tribune*, 3/26/46, p. 24.

_____. "Zollners Keep Crown; Defeat Oshkosh, 73–57." *Chicago Tribune*, 4/9/46, p. 24.

"Set New Scoring Record in National Basketball Loop." *Oshkosh Daily Northwestern*, 2/9/38, p. 13.

"7536 See Waterloo Nip Tri-Cities, 61–59." *Denver Post*, 11/29/48, p. 25.

"17,205 Fans See Stags Win in Overtime." *Chicago Tribune*, 11/12/46, p. 25.

"Sheboygan Assumes Division Lead in Win." *Rochester Democrat and Chronicle*, 12/17/45, p. 27.

Sheboygan Beats Zollners in Playoff Battle." *Oshkosh Daily Tribune*, 3/2/43, p. 11.

"Sheboygan Loses to Fort Wayne by a 50 to 35 Score." *Oshkosh Daily Northwestern*, 12/18/41, p. 25.

"Sheboygan Loses to Hoosier Quint in Overtime Game." *Oshkosh Daily Northwestern*, 1/30/42, p. 14.

"Sheboygan Quintet Flies to Coast Games." *Chicago Tribune*, 11/4/46, p. 33.

"Sheboygan Scuttles Youngstown, 45–39." *Rochester Democrat and Chronicle*, 11/27/45, p. 23.

"Sheboygan Wins National Loop Championship." *Oshkosh Daily Northwestern*, 3/10/43, p. 13.

"Sheboygan's Playoff Chances Grow Dimmer." *Oshkosh Daily Northwestern*, 2/16/42, p. 11.

Shevlin, M. "Gears Defeat Royals, 79–68, Capture Title." *Chicago Tribune*, 4/10/47, p. 31.

_____. "Mikan Retires After Gears Lose, 44 to 41." *Chicago Tribune*, 12/12/46, p. 59.

_____. "Mikan Scores 22 as Gears Win, 62 to 60." *Chicago Tribune*, 2/1/47, p. 16.

_____. "National League Polls Clubs on Gears' Return." *Chicago Tribune*, 11/14/47, p. 47.

_____. "Zollners and Acme Five Gain Tourney Finals." *Chicago Tribune*, 3/24/45, p. 20.

"Shut 1292 Steel Plants." *Chicago Tribune*, 1/21/46, p. 1.

"Skids Bow at Oshkosh in Overtime." *Akron Beacon Journal*, 3/7/41, p. 36.

"Skids Take Double Loss." *Akron Beacon Journal*, 1/28/37, p. 25.

"Skids Trump on Detroit, Win, 41–35." *Akron Beacon Journal*, 12/5/40, p. 35.

"Skins Beat Stars; Hoosiers Win 78–62, to Play Here Tonight." *Oshkosh Daily Northwestern*, 1/9/43, p. 11.

"'Skins Lose to Oshkosh." *Rochester Democrat and Chronicle*, 12/2/45. p. C.1

Smith, W. "All Stars Beat Pros 44 to 42 in Overtime." *Chicago Tribune*, 11/30/40, p. 29.

_____. "Indianapolis, Toledo in Pro Final Tonight." *Chicago Tribune*, 4/10/47, p. 32.

_____. "Kautskys Beat Toledo, 62–47, in Pro Final" *Chicago Tribune*, 4/11/47, p. 27.

_____. "Oshkosh Beats Detroit, 43–41, for Pro Title." *Chicago Tribune*, 3/12/42, p. 21.

_____. "Oshkosh Wins in Pro Meet Finals" *Chicago Tribune*, 4/6/46, p. 20.

_____. "Washington Beats Oshkosh for Pro Title." *Chicago Tribune*, 3/18/43, p. 27.

"Stags Upset Capitols 2d in Row, 69–53." *Chicago Tribune*, 4/4/47, p. 27

"Stanczak and Wintermute Get Spotlight as Pro Meet Opens." *Fort Wayne News-Sentinel*, 3/26/46, p. 10.

"Standings." *Akron Beacon Journal*, 2/3/37, p. 20.

"Stars Beat Firestones, Clinch Western Title." *Oshkosh Daily Northwestern*, 3/6/39, p. 13.

"Stars Beat Redskins in Opening Game, 53 to 38." *Oshkosh Daily Northwestern*, 3/11/41, p. 13.

"Stars Beat Redskins in Tourney in Memphis." *Oshkosh Daily Northwestern*, 2/6/43, p. 11.

"Stars Beat Redskins, Play Here On Thursday." *Oshkosh Daily Northwestern*, 2/22/39, p. 11.

"Stars Beat Rens by 43–24 Score; to Play at Fondy." *Oshkosh Daily Northwestern*, 1/16/41, p. 19.

"Stars Beat Rens in First Battle of Series, 52–42." *Oshkosh Daily Northwestern*, 12/1/41, p. 13.

"Stars Beat Whiting, Play Goodyears Tonight." *Oshkosh Daily Northwestern*, 2/28/38, p. 12.

"Stars Begin Quest for Loop Championship." *Oshkosh Daily Northwestern*, 2/20/43, p. 11.

"Stars Defeat Defending Champs, 37–32." *Oshkosh Daily Northwestern*, 12/17/40, p. 15.

"Stars Edge Sheboygan: Will Meet Bruins Here." *Oshkosh Daily Northwestern*, 12/12/41, p. 21.

"Stars Keep League Record Clear of Defeat." *Oshkosh Daily Northwestern*, 1/12/42, p. 12.

"Stars Keep Slate Clean, Win No. 10 from Toledo Five." *Oshkosh Daily Northwestern*, 1/8/42, p. 17.

"Stars Lose 52–50: Triptow's Sensational Field Goal Is Clincher." *Oshkosh Daily Northwestern*, 1/15/45, p. 9.

"Stars Lose Game by 43–30 Score to Fort Wayne." *Oshkosh Daily Northwestern*, 2/3/42, p. 13.

"Stars Lose Opener, Must Win at Home Tonight or Else...." *Oshkosh Daily Northwestern*, 3/5/42, p. 19.

"Stars Lose Tilt at Charity Line, to Meet Bucs Here." *Oshkosh Daily Northwestern*, 1/7/49, p. 11.

"Stars Lose to Rochester, but Defeat Sphas." *Oshkosh Daily Northwestern*, 1/26/42, p. 14.

"Stars Meet Detroit Tonight for Championship." *Oshkosh Daily Northwestern*, 3/19/41, p. 13.

"Stars Meet Globetrotters in Semi Finals." *Oshkosh Daily Northwestern*, 3/10/42, p. 13.

"Stars, Rens Begin Four Game Series." *Oshkosh Daily Northwestern*, 11/29/41, p. 13.

"Stars Ride Out Big Lead to Beat Pistons." *Oshkosh Daily Northwestern*, 4/1/46, p. 11.

"Stars Take Victory." *Oshkosh Daily Northwestern*, 12/14/40, p. 13.

"Stars Win First Game of Tourney Playoff." *Oshkosh Daily Northwestern*, 4/6/46, p. 11.

"Stars Win Opening Round in Tournament." *Oshkosh Daily Northwestern*, 3/17/41, p. 12.

"Stars [sic] Winning Streak Ends." *Oshkosh Daily Northwestern*, 1/13/41, p. 12.

"Stars, 'Skins Bag Verdicts in Double Bill." *Rochester Democrat and Chronicle*, 12/6/45, p. 31.

"Stars to Face Strong Foe Here." *Oshkosh Daily Northwestern*, 11/10/42, p. 13.

"Stars to Meet Packers in Championship Playoffs." *Oshkosh Daily Northwestern*, 4/14/49, p. 26.

"Stars to Try Tonight to Nail Western Flag." *Oshkosh Daily Northwestern*, 4/12/49, p. 17.

"Stars Win by 55–34 Score in Season's Opener." *Oshkosh Daily Northwestern*, 11/9/42, p. 11.

"Stars, Zollners Split Two Games." *Oshkosh Daily Northwestern*, 11/16/42, p. 13.

"Studebakers Over Oshkosh in 73–60 Game." *Chicago Tribune*, 2/1/43, p. 20.

"Syracuse Loses By Nod." *Denver Post*, 12/20/48, p. 20.

"Syracuse Triumphs." *Denver Post*, 1/31/49, p. 17.

"Syracuse Victor." *Denver Post*, 1/18/49, p. 26.

"Syracuse Wins." *Denver Post*, 1/28/49, p. 27.

"Takes More Than Broken Neck to Stop Goodyear's Ebaugh." *Akron Beacon Journal*, 12/18/41, p. 43.

Tenny, B. "Can Pistons Take Two-Tilt Series Lead? Learn Answer Tonight." *Fort Wayne News Sentinel*, 3/13/46, p. 11.

_____."Fans Wonder if Piston Slump Temporary or Permanent" *Fort Wayne News-Sentinel*, 12/5/47, p. 47.

_____. "If Teams Have to Win at Home, Fate of Pistons May Be Sorry One." *Fort Wayne News-Sentinel,* 12/11/47, p. 50.

_____. "Mac's Hawks Oust Pistons by 57–50." *Fort Wayne News-Sentinel*, 4/9/48, p. 33.

_____. "Pistons Are First Repeaters in World's Hardwood Tournament." *Fort Wayne News-Sentinel*, 3/26/45, p. 11.

_____. "Pistons Beat Sheboygan, 59–49 to Retain Their Loop Crown." *Fort Wayne News-Sentinel*, 3/19/45, p. 9.

_____. "Pistons Come Up with Perfect Game, Whip Royals, 70–56." *Fort Wayne News-Sentinel*, 1/15/48, p. 20.

_____. "Pistons Drop 64–47 Decision to Royals in Third Playoff Game." *Fort Wayne News-Sentinel*, 3/26/48, p. 31.

_____. "Pistons Enter Final Series Against Sheboygan." *Fort Wayne New-Sentinel*, 3/9/45, p. 11.

_____. "Pistons Face Rens Friday in Semi-Finals of Pro Cage Meet." *Fort Wayne News-Sentinel*, 3/22/45, p. 15.

_____. "Pistons' First Dive into Lak(ers) Fails; They Try Again Tonight." *Fort Wayne News-Sentinel*, 12/4/47, p. 49.

_____. "Pistons Hope to Get Even With Sheboygan Tonight." *Fort Wayne News-Sentinel*, 3/12/45, p. 11.

_____."Pistons Hope to Pull Even with Royals Tonight." *Fort Wayne News-Sentinel*, 3/24/48, p. 16.

_____. "Pistons Lose to All-Stars; Meet Detroit Gems Here Saturday." *Fort Wayne News-Sentinel*, 11/30/46, p. 11

_____. "Pistons Meet Dayton Tonight in Finals of Pro Cage Meet." *Fort Wayne News-Sentinel*, 3/24/45, p. 18.

_____. "Pistons Outlast Jeeps, 54–49, in Listless Game, *Fort Wayne News-Sentinel*, 1/19/48, p. 20.

_____. "Pistons Prove Greatness with 44–38 Victory Over All-Stars." *Fort Wayne News-Sentinel*, 12/2/44, p. 12.

_____. "Pistons Rally to Defeat Royals Here, Split Series." *Fort Wayne News-Sentinel*, 1/21/46, p. 7.

_____. "Pistons Rule Professional Basketball Realm for 1944." *Fort Wayne News-Sentinel*, 3/27/44, p. 9.

_____. "Pistons Score 69 Points! That's 13 Too Few, They Learn." *Fort Wayne News-Sentinel*, 11/21/47, p. 22.

_____. "Pistons Seek to Pull Even with Sheboygan Redskins Tonight." *Fort Wayne News-Sentinel*, 3/15/45, p. 25.

_____. "Pistons, Redskins to Play Deciding Clash Sunday." *Fort Wayne News-Sentinel*, 3/17/45, p. 11.

_____. "Royals Shoot at .394, Plaster Pistons, 76–47." *Fort Wayne News-Sentinel*, 4/2/47, p. 28.

_____. "Pistons Shoot Well to Hand Cleveland Quintet 78–50 Trimming." *Fort Wayne New-Sentinel*, 3/7/45, p. 10.

_____. "Pistons Sidelined by Royals' Balance, Contemplate Tourney." *Fort Wayne News-Sentinel*, 3/29/48, p. 12.

_____. "Royals to Be Successor to Pistons?" *Fort Wayne News-Sentinel*, 2/20/46, p. 11.

_____. "Sheboygan Five Backs Pistons to Wall." *Fort Wayne News-Sentinel*, 3/13/45, p. 8.

_____. "Sheboygan Humbles Pistons by 41–29: Cleveland Here Sunday." *Fort Wayne News-Sentinel*, 1/26/44, p. 10.

_____. "Sports Calendar." *Fort Wayne News-Sentinel*, 12/21/46, p. 14.

_____. "Surviving Pistons Trim Redskins, 69–57" *Fort Wayne News-Sentinel*, 12/23/46, p. 11.

"Though Underdogs, Pistons Hope to Keep Going v. Royals." *Fort Wayne News-Sentinel*, 3/27/47, p. 40.

"3 Pro Basketball Players Sue Indianapolis Jets for Back Wages." *Chicago Tribune*, 5/21/49, pt. 2, p. 2.

"Todorovich Top NBL Rookie." *Rochester Democrat and Chronicle*, 4/2/48, p. 34.

"Toledo Jeeps Take Opener." *Fort Wayne News-Sentinel*, 11/8/46, p. 58.

"Toledo Out of Pro Loop." *Toledo Blade*, 12/23/42, p. 29.

"Toledo, Zollners Win Thrillers." *Rochester Democrat and Chronicle*, 11/9/47, p. 6-D.

"Tri-Cities, Oshkosh to Clash for Western Playoff Championship." *Oshkosh Daily Northwestern,* 4/4/49, p. 15.

"Twelve of Nazi Chiefs to Be Hanged." *Anderson Daily Bulletin,* 10/1/46, p. 1.

"23,825 See College Stars Defeat Pros." *Cleveland Plain Dealer,* 12/4/43, p. 16.

"2 Indiana Clubs Said Returning to National Pro Loop." *Dayton Daily News,* 1/25/49, p. 20.

"U.S. Tire Cagemen Strengthen Lineup for Opening Game." *Indianapolis Star,* 11/28/36, p. 14.

"Washington's Big Rally Tops Wings, 33–31, at Philadelphia." *Akron Beacon Journal,* 12/15/40, p. C-1.

"Waterloo Wins, 50–45." *Denver Post,* 12/23/48, p. 12.

"Wingfoots Defeat Skids in First Playoff Game." *Akron Beacon Journal,* 2/25/38, p. 27.

"Wingfoots Start Over." *Akron Beacon Journal,* 12/12/36, p. 16.

"Wings Beat League Foe by 46 to 30." *Akron Beacon Journal,* 12/7/41, p. C-1.

"Wings Beaten by Indianapolis as Chuck Bloedorn is Injured." *Akron Beacon Journal.* 2/17/39, p. 33.

"Wings Cagers Are Beaten." *Akron Beacon Journal,* 11/28/41, p. 43.

"Wings Crush Hammond by 54–38 Margin." *Akron Beacon Journal,* 12/2/40, p. 18.

"Wings Play Final Game." *Akron Beacon Journal,* 2/25/37, p. 27.

Young, Fay. "Fay Says." *Chicago Defender,* 4/2/49, p. 14.

Zirin, A. "Riebe Tallies 30 as Chase Bag First Pro Victory, 56–51." *Cleveland Plain Dealer,* 12/23/43, p. 14.

"Zollner Pistons' Home, League Road Schedules Are Completed." *Fort Wayne News-Sentinel,* 10/27/43, p. 19.

"Zollners and Gears Win in Pro Tourney." *Chicago Tribune,* 3/30/46, p. 20.

"Zollners Beat Studebakers in Playoff Final." *Chicago Tribune,* 2/24/43, p. 20.

"Zollners Gain 60–51 Victory Over Chicago." *Rochester Democrat and Chronicle,* 12/8/45, p. 16.

Interviews and Personal Correspondence

Bennett, Carl. Telephone interview. 10/27/03.
_____. Personal correspondence. 11/20/04.

Cervi, Al. Telephone interview. 5/20/04.

Dietrich, Phil. Telephone interview. 2/18/02.

Harrison, Lester. Telephone interview. 10/4/94.

Isaacs, John. Telephone interview. 5/18/02, 11/15/02.

_____. Interview at State College, Pennsylvania. March 2004.

Levane, Andrew "Fuzzy." Telephone interview. 5/19/04.

Luksta, Robert. Telephone interview. 7/24/03.

Prasse, Erv. Telephone interview. 7/10/03.

Risen, Arnie. Telephone interview. 5/25/04.

Schayes, Dolph. Telephone interview. 2/1/05.

Szukala, Stan. Telephone interview. 3/19/03.

Towery, Carlisle "Blackie." Telephone interview. 10/16/03.

Triptow, Dick. Interviews. 1999–2006.

Von Nieda, Stan "Whitey." Telephone interview. 3/17/05.

Wooden, John. Personal correspondence. 9/29/01, 11/18/01.

Zummach, Frank. Telephone interview. 7/15/08.

Chapters/Journal Articles/ Dissertations

Bourdieu, P. "Sport and Social Class." *Social Science Information* 17.6 (1978): 819–840.

Carlton, Frank. "Labor in the Twentieth Century." In *The History of the State of Ohio* 6, Carl Wittke, editor. Columbus: Ohio State Archaeological and Historical Society, 1943. pp. 94–119.

Enright, James, "Pro Tourney and All-Star Game." In *World Professional Tourney Program* (1947): 23.

Fisher, D.M. "Lester Harrison and the Rochester Royals, 1945–1957." In *Sports and the American Jew,* S.A. Reiss, editor. Syracuse: Syracuse University Press, 1998. p. 209.

Funke, M. "The Chicago Studebakers; How the UAW Helped Integrate Pro Basketball and Reunite Four Players Who Made History." *Solidarity* 35, no. 7 (July 1992): 16–19.

Genovese, E. "The Politics of Class Struggle in the History of Society: An Appraisal of the Work of Eric Hobsbawm." In *The Power of the Past-Essays for Eric Hobsbawm,* P. Thane, G. Crossick and R. Floyd, editors. Cambridge: Cambridge University Press, 1984. pp. 13–36.

Harris, D. *From Class Struggles to the Politics of Pleasure — The Effects of Gramscianism on Cultural Studies*. London: Routledge, 1992. pp.154–158.

Rayl, S. "The New York Renaissance Professional Black Basketball Team, 1923–50." Unpublished doctoral dissertation, Pennsylvania State University, 1996.

Wilkes, C. "Bourdieu's Class." In R. Harker, C. Mahar and C. Wilkes, *An Introduction to the Work of Pierre Bourdieu*. London: Macmillan Press, 1990. p. 118.

Archival Sources

Gene Englund Collection, Oshkosh Museum.

Financial Statements of Oshkosh All Stars, Oshkosh Public Museum, Oshkosh, WI.

James A. Naismith Basketball Hall of Fame Archives, Springfield, MA.

Sheboygan Redskins Archives, Sheboygan County Research Center, Sheboygan Falls, WI.

Oshkosh Public Library, Oshkosh, WI.

University of Akron Archives, Akron, OH.

Index